FAMILY, VICTIMS AND CULTURE: YOUTH JUSTICE IN NEW ZEALAND

by
GABRIELLE M. MAXWELL
and
ALLISON MORRIS

1993

WIPF & STOCK · Eugene, Oregon

Wipf and Stock Publishers
199 W 8th Ave, Suite 3
Eugene, OR 97401

Family, Victims and Culture
Youth Justice in New Zealand
By Maxwell, Gabrielle M. and Morris, Allison
Copyright©1993 by Maxwell, Gabrielle M.
ISBN 13: 978-1-60899-906-4
Publication date 8/6/2010
Previously published by Social Policy Agency, 1993

Whakahokia te mana

o te iwi ki te iwi

o te hapu ki te hapu

o te tangata ki te tangata

me tona raukotahi

To bestow the mana

of iwi with iwi,

of hapu with hapu,

of whanau with whanau and

of the person with the person

in whom generations of

the past are present

Waho Tibble

FOREWORD

The Children Young Persons and Their Families Act 1989 has revolutionised the way youth justice proceedings are managed in New Zealand. The Act established the new Youth Court to replace the former Children and Young Persons court and created a new forum, the Family Group Conference, which is aimed at providing a real alternative to court proceedings as a means of dealing with young people who have offended, by involving families in deciding what would be most appropriate response to their young people's offending.

This report represents the first major research study into the way the new youth justice system has been functioning. It involved a large-scale survey of the various components of the youth justice system, from the decisions of front-line police officers when apprehending young people for offending through to the outcomes of proceedings in Family Group Conferences and the Youth Court. During the course of the study a wealth of data was collected on how the new system is functioning and the report provides an excellent account of the ways in which the new system is succeeding and the ways in which it has yet to come up to the mark.

Just how well is the new system functioning? In a number of respects the findings are very encouraging indeed. Far fewer young people now appear before the court and are convicted than before the act came into effect. And fewer youngsters are being sentenced to prison, corrective training or residence in Department of Social Welfare custody. Yet, despite this, young people are being held to account for their offending to a greater extent than in the past – by being required either to make an apology or to pay reparation or to carry out work in the community. The families of young offenders are very much involved in the process of taking decisions about responses to the offending of their young people. Almost all Family Group Conferences end in agreement about the most appropriate outcome and their recommendations are generally followed by the Youth Court.

Nevertheless, the report also shows that there is still some distance to go before the Act can be regarded as meeting the expectations held for it when it was introduced. In particular, the report signals a need for the police to examine their practice when arresting young people and to ensure that their rights to due process are protected. The Department of Social Welfare needs to ensure that the outcome of cases do not focus on the offending to the exclusion of consideration of other needs for assistance which families might have and must also endeavour to ensure that an adequate range of local programmes exists to which young people and their families can be referred for assistance. There were clearly difficulties in meeting the needs of victims through the Family Group Conference where the focus was generally on the young offender and his or her family. And there is also concern that youth justice professionals have tended to resist involving families fully in the decision-making process. The Youth Court evidently found difficulty in making its proceedings accessible and understandable to young people and families, especially those of Maori and Pacific Island background. Overall, while the new system showed ample potential to function in ways that are appropriate for people of the many different cultures of New Zealand, such flexibility occurred too infrequently during the course of the study.

The report was commissioned by the Department of Social Welfare from the Institute of Criminology at Victoria University of Wellington. I would like to take this opportunity to congratulate the Institute, and in particular the authors of the report, Dr Gabrielle Maxwell and Dr Allison Morris, on the publication, which will be of very great importance in mapping out the future development of our youth justice system. I am pleased too that such a significant report represents the first research publication from the Department's new Social Policy Agency. The Agency, together with the New Zealand Children and Young Persons Service, now faces the challenge of building on the successes detailed in the report and improving practice in those other areas where the results have been less encouraging. It is my firm belief that by ensuring that the youth justice system functions in the way anticipated in the legislation, we will be giving young offenders and their families the best chance they will have have to reclaim control over their lives and to break the pernicious cycle of recidivist offending.

Jenny Shipley
Minister of Social Welfare

ACKNOWLEDGEMENTS

This project has been undertaken by the Institute of Criminology at Victoria University of Wellington. Dr Warren Young has been the Director of the project and it has been funded by the Department of Social Welfare. The authors, Dr Allison Morris, a lecturer at the Institute of Criminology, University of Cambridge and Dr Gabrielle Maxwell, research fellow at the Institute of Criminology at Victoria University of Wellington, have been the principal investigators and involved in all aspects of the project.

A team of researchers helped us to collect the data: Maire Leadbeater and Gary MacFarlane-Nathan in Auckland; Jennifer Bradshaw, Roy Couch and Paul Dodge in Masterton; Willis Katene, Talosaga Manu, Teresea Olsen and Jeremy Robertson in the greater Wellington area; and Rowena Morgan and Nicky Walsh in Christchurch. Jeremy Robertson and Paul Dodge helped in collating and checking the data. Most of the team assisted at times in the preparation of the manuscript and we are particularly appreciative of the contributions from Teresea Olsen, Nicky Walsh, Gary Macfarlane-Nathan, Jeremy Robertson and Warren Young. Stephen Haslett of the Institute of Statistics and Operational Research at Victoria University advised on statistical matters and helped with the logistic regressions. David Scott and Jeremy Robertson read the proofs. Johanna Moeller corrected and formatted the final manuscript.

The Maori advisory committee included: Tamati Cairns, Terepowai Higgins, Harry Walker, Donna Hall, John Rabarts, Claire Metakingi, Mereana Potaka, Meri Stewart and other members of Te Ropu Awhina Ki Porirua. As well as meeting at the start and end of the project, at various times individual members of the committee have been very supportive. In particular Donna Hall assisted in recruiting a researcher and Tamati Cairns and Terepowai Higgins assisted with the development of methodology and checking the glossary.

Members of the Departments involved with the Act were very cooperative and without their help the project would not have been possible. In the Department of Social Welfare, the staff in the research and evaluation units (now part of the Social Policy Agency) and the Child and Family Unit (now either in the policy unit of the Social Policy Agency or in the Children and Young Person's Service) were all involved at some point – it seems unfair to single out particular individuals but we particularly appreciated the support of Ross Mackay, Anne Donnell, Marlene Levine, Michael Harvey, Marg Gilling, John Angus, Ann Caton, Faith Denny and Brenda Hegarty. In the various offices we worked closely with the Youth Justice Co-ordinators, social workers and staff of social services including the assistant directors and clerical staff. For the most part they were truly welcoming. Although the project was intrusive and time-consuming for them as well as involving them in having their own practice scrutinised, they generally responded warmly and positively, actively seeking feedback which could enable them to improve their service. Thanks also to Jenny Smith, Linda Allan and Catherine Callaghan for helping with the publication.

Inspector Des Drummond was our chief advisor at Police Headquarters. He supplied us with all the information we asked for and kept us informed of anything else that was important to us. He also eased the task of contacting the various police stations with which we worked where most of the staff, particularly district commanders, senior community officers and youth aid staff, especially the latter, helped us and answered our many questions. In addition we would like to thank the front-line staff, detectives and prosecutors whom we interviewed.

At the Youth Court, our task was eased by the welcome and support we received from Judge Brown, the Principal Youth Court Judge, and other members of his team. The court registrars, clerks of the court and other court staff were very helpful as we pursued minor queries. We were privileged to be welcomed in the Youth Court as a useful part of the team rather than treated as unwelcome investigators.

We need also to thank the many youth advocates and social workers attached to private agencies who helped us at various times. We are very grateful to the members of the public who were victimised by the offences that we were involved with and who responded by sharing their experiences and views with us.

Finally, we owe a great debt to the people without whom the project would have been doomed, the children, young people and their families who shared with us very private matters and who looked to us to voice their concerns. We hope we have done this and that, as a result, the processes of youth justice will be able to be improved from the perspective of both the clients and the wider public.

CONTENTS

SUMMARY OF FINDINGS — xvi

Chapter 1
**THE CHILDREN YOUNG PERSONS AND THEIR FAMILIES ACT:
A NEW PARADIGM FOR RESPONDING TO YOUNG OFFENDERS**

The Objectives and Principles Underlying Youth Justice in New Zealand	1
A Description of the Youth Justice System in New Zealand	8

Chapter 2
RESEARCH DESIGN, METHODOLOGY AND SAMPLE

Introduction	13
Aims of the Research	13
Research Methods	14
The Data	18

Chapter 3
THE POLICE DECISION TO ARREST

Introduction	25
National Statistical Data on Arrest Cases	25
The Research Sample	27
Conclusions	43

Chapter 4
FRONT-LINE POLICE INTERVIEWING AND ARREST PROCEDURES

Introduction	45
Rights of Young People on Arrest and Questioning	47
Conclusions	55

Chapter 5
YOUTH AID DECISIONS

Introduction	56
The Outcome of Youth Aid Decisions	57
Conclusions	66

Chapter 6
FAMILY GROUP CONFERENCES: PROCESS AND PRACTICE

Introduction	68
The Process of Referral for an FGC	68
Arranging the FGC	71
The FGC Process	86
FGC Outcomes	92
What Happens after the FGC	102
Cultural Issues	103
Conclusions	107

Chapter 7
PARTICIPANTS' VIEWS OF FGCS

Introduction	109
Parents' and Young People's Views of the Process of Decision-making at FGCs	109

Parents' and Young People's Views on 'Who Decided'	111
Parents' and Young People's Satisfaction with Outcomes	115
Families' Views on Meeting Victims	117
Victims' Satisfaction with the FGC Process	111
Victims' Satisfaction with Outcomes	120
Professionals' Views of the FGC Process and Outcomes	122
Families' and Victims' Satisfaction with FGC Follow Up	123
Cultural Issues	125
Conclusions	127

Chapter 8
THE YOUTH COURT

Introduction	131
National Statistics on the Youth Court	133
Data from the Research Study	136
Conclusions	162

Chapter 9
MEETING OBJECTIVES: A REVIEW OF CRITICAL ISSUES RELATING TO THE PRACTICE OF YOUTH JUSTICE

Introduction	165
Models of Juvenile Justice	165
Meeting Objectives	173
Inherent Contradictions	188
Conclusions	190

REFERENCES	192
GLOSSARY OF MAORI WORDS	197

Appendix 1
OBJECTIVESAND PRINCIPLES OF THE CHILDREN, YOUNG PERSONS AND THEIR FAMILIES ACT 1989   198

Appendix 2
ADDITIONAL DETAILS OF METHODOLOGY   201

Appendix 3
A STATISTICAL OVERVIEW OF JUVENILE OFFENDING BEFORE AND SINCE THE INTRODUCTION OF THE ACT   207

Appendix 4
TECHNICAL APPENDIX   218

LIST OF TABLES

Table 2.1	Distinct Police Cases in Each Area During the Sample Period, each Area Compared with Total Population Aged 10-16 and Showing Detected Offence Rate Per 10,000 Population Aged 10-16	22
Table 2.2	Ethnicity of Sample Coming to Police Attention, Being Referred for FGC and Appearing in the Youth Court Compared to Population Figures; Percentages	22
Table 2.3	Numbers of Maori in the Police Sample in each Area Compared with Expected Numbers Based on Population of each Area	23
Table 2.4	Percentages of Parents, Young People and Victims Interviewed in each Area and Percentage of Cases where at least one FGC was Attended	23
Table 3.1	Police Arrest Rates for Juvenile Offenders in Selected Areas; 1990	26
Table 3.2	Sample Arrest Numbers and Percentages by Area Compared with Annual Totals for 1990	28
Table 3.3	Seriousness of all Offences (N=669) and of Arrest Cases (N=68) only by Area; Showing Percentage Rated Medium, Medium/Maximum, or Maximum Seriousness and Percentage Arrested for each Area	29
Table 3.4	Reasons for Arrest of Young Person; Distinct Arrest Cases for which Reasons were Given; Numbers and Percentages; N=57	30
Table 3.5	Offence Characteristics for Police Arrests; Distinct Cases; Numbers and Percentages; N=38	34
Table 3.6	Offenders' Characteristics for Police Arrests; Distinct Cases; Numbers and Percentages; N=38	34
Table 3.7	Comparison of Arrest with Non-arrest Cases on Information Available at Time of Arrest; Distinct Police Cases Aged 14-16; Percentages; N=462.	36
Table 3.8	Comparison of Arrest with Non-Arrest Cases on Information Not Necessarily Available at Time of Arrest; Distinct Police Cases Aged 14-16; Percentages; N=462	37
Table 3.9	Offence and Offender Characteristics by Seriousness of Offending; Percentages	40
Table 3.10	Seriousness of Offence by Arrest versus Non-arrest; Distinct Police Cases; Aged 14-16 Years; Percentages Sum to 100 for each Row	41
Table 3.11	Ethnicity and Other Factors; Distinct Police Cases; Percentages within each Ethnic Group.	42
Table 4.1	How Released; Distinct Arrest Cases; N=55	52
Table 4.2	Complaints about Police Handling of Arrested Young People; N=14	54
Table 5.1	Outcomes of Non-arrest Cases Dealt with by the Police; National Statistics from 1.11.89 to 30.4.90 Compared with Data from the Research Sample; Percentages	57
Table 5.2	Comparison of Youth Aid Decisions by Area; Distinct Youth Aid Cases; Percentages; N=602	58
Table 5.3	Nature of Warning; Distinct Cases in one Area; N=78	59
Table 5.4	Informal Sanctions; Distinct Cases all Areas; N=72	60

Table 5.5	Characteristics of the Offence and the Offender Seen by Youth Aid Officers to Increase the Likelihood of a Decision to Refer for an FGC; Data from Interviews on Cases Referred to an FGC in three areas; Percentages; N=128	60
Table 5.6	Comparison of 'Police Diversion' vs FGC Cases; Distinct Cases; Percentages	63
Table 6.1	Source of Referrals Showing National Figures for 1990, Total Sample Figures and Areas within the Sample; Percentages	68
Table 6.2	Number of FGCs and Sex and Ethnicity of Juveniles Referred for FGCs in 1990 in Selected DSW Offices; Percentages	69
Table 6.3	Number of FGCs and Sex and Ethnicity of Juveniles; Percentages of Referrals for an FGC in the Sample	69
Table 6.4	Time Taken to Convene FGCs Showing Court and Non-Court Referrals Separately and Giving Cumulative Percentages; N=189	72
Table 6.5	Total Number of People Attending FGCs Showing Area Differences in Range and Means; N=203	75
Table 6.6	Summary of Who Was Present at the FGC; Percentages; N=203	75
Table 6.7	Whanau Involvement in FGCs by Area and Ethnicity; Percentages	77
Table 6.8	Presence at FGC of Siblings and Family Support by Ethnicity; Numbers and Percentages of Cases in each Ethnic Group	79
Table 6.9	Presence of Social Workers by Area; Percentages	83
Table 6.10	Number of FGCs and Proportion Facilitated by YJCs for 1990 in Selected DSW Offices	87
Table 6.11	Number of FGCs and Proportion Facilitated by YJCs During the Sample Period of Three Months	87
Table 6.12	Numbers of FGC Meetings Needed to Resolve Matters by Area; Percentages	89
Table 6.13	Withdrawal of Professionals; Percentage of Cases where this Did Not Occur, by Area; N=177	92
Table 6.14	Main Results for Those Involved in the Youth Justice Family Group Conferences 1990; N=5851	93
Table 6.15	FGC Outcomes of FGCs by Area; Percentages; N=295	93
Table 6.16	Outcomes Recommended by FGCs Showing Numbers and Percentages	95
Table 6.17	Severity of FGC Outcomes by Sex, Ethnicity and Age Ranked from 0=Least Severe to 9=Most Severe; Percentages; N=199	96
Table 6.18	Severity of FGC Outcome by Area; Percentages; N=199	99
Table 6.19	FGCs Reconvened within Approximately 3-4 Months of the Original FGC by Area; Percentages; N=203	103
Table 7.1	Involvement in FGC Decisions Reported by Parents and Young People; Percentages	110
Table 7.2	Who Decided the Outcome: Views of Parents, Young People and the Researcher; Percentages	112
Table 7.3	Parents and Young People's Satisfaction with FGC Outcomes; Percentages	115
Table 7.4	Satisfaction with FGC Outcomes and Severity of Penalties for Young People and Parents; Percentages Expressing Satisfaction	116

Table 7.5	Victim Satisfaction with FGC Outcome as a Function of Attendance at the FGC; Percentages Sum in Rows; N=141	120
Table 8.1	Number of Informations Laid in Selected Youth Courts; National Data Comparing Pre- and Post-Act periods	133
Table 8.2	Youth Court Orders, National Data for November 1989 to December 1990, on the Five Highest Tariffs; N=357*	135
Table 8.3	Description of the Court Sample; Distinct Cases; Percentages; N=70	138
Table 8.4	Bail Conditions; Percentages; N=34	141
Table 8.5	Times to Decide and Finalise Youth Court Cases where there has been No Denial; N=59 Cases	142
Table 8.6	Number of Times Called and Times Appeared; Percentages for Not-Denied Cases; N=59	142
Table 8.7	Decisions of the Court; N=66	156
Table 8.8	Comparison of FGC Recommendations and Court Decisions; N=63	156
Table 8.9	Maori-Pakeha Differences in Offender and Offence Characteristics and Outcomes; Distinct Court Cases; Percentages of each Ethnic Group	160
Table A2.1	Categories Used for Rating the Seriousness of Offences	202
Table A3.1	Comparison of All Detected Offenders with Detected Juvenile Offenders by Type of Offence; Percentages for Year from 10/88 to 9/89	212
Table A3.2	Comparison of Girls and Boys by Type of Offence; Percentages for Year from 10/88 to 9/89	213
Table A3.3	Comparison of Detected Juvenile Offenders Aged 10-13 with those Aged 14-16 by Type of Offence; Percentages for Year from 10/88 to 9/89	213
Table A3.4	Comparison of Ethnicity of Detected Male Juvenile Offenders by Type of Offence; Percentages for Year from 10/88 to 9/89	214
Table A3.5	A Selection of Indices Showing the Percentage of Juvenile Involvement in Cleared Offending Comparing 10/88 to 9/89 with 1990	214
Table A3.6	Percentage of Cleared Juvenile Offending by Type of Offence Comparing 10/88 to 9/89 with 1990	215
Table A3.7	Percentage of Cleared Juvenile Offenders Committing Offences of Dishonesty Comparing 10/88 to 9/89 with 1990	215
Table A3.8	For each Type of Offence, Percentage of Cleared Offenders who are Juveniles Comparing 10/88 to 9/89 with 1990	216
Table A4.1	Detailed Data for Table 3.7: Comparison of Arrest with Non-arrest Cases on Information Available at Time of Arrest; Based on an Analysis of 462 Distinct Police Cases Aged 14-16, Numbers and Percentages	218
Table A4.2	Detailed Data for Table 3.8: Comparison of Arrest with Non-Arrest Cases on Information Not Necessarily Available at Time of Arrest; Based on an Analysis of 462 Distinct Police Cases Aged 14-16; Numbers and Percentages	219
Table A4.3	Detailed Data for Table 3.9: Offence and Offender Characteristics by Seriousness of Offending; Percentages of Total Number in each Seriousness Category Sum to 100% in each Column	220
Table A4.4	Detailed Data for Table 5.6: Comparison of `Police Diversion' (N=415) vs FGC Cases (N=187); Distinct Cases	221

Table A4.5	FGC Outcomes; Number of Cases Showing Severity of Outcome for Comparison with Tables 6.16 and 6.17	222
Table A4.6	Youth Court Cases Showing Numbers for Maori and Pakeha on a Variety of Variables Corresponding to Table 8.9	223
Table A4.7	Predicting the Arrest Decision; Results of Stepwise Regression; N=363 Cases	225
Table A4.8	Predicting the Arrest Decision; Results of Logistic Regression; N=347 Cases	225
Table A4.9	Predicting the Youth Aid Decision to Refer for an FGC; Results of Stepwise Regression; N=449 Cases	226
Table A4.10	Predicting the Youth Aid Decision; to Refer for an FGC Results of Logistic Regression; N=417 Cases	226
Table A4.11	Predicting the Severity of the Decision at the FGC; Results of Stepwise Regression; N=168 Cases	227
Table A4.12	Predicting the Severity of the Decision of the FGC; Results of Logistic Regression; N=165 Cases	227
Table A4.13	Predicting the Severity of the Youth Court Decision; Results of Stepwise Regression; N=62 Cases	227
Table A4.14	Predicting the Severity of Youth Court Decision; Results of Logistic Regression both with and without Severity of FGC; N=57 Cases	228

LIST OF FIGURES

Figure 1.1	Flow Chart Indicating Pathways through the System	9
Figure 2.1	Sketch Diagram Indicating the ways in which Cases Entered the Sample and Entered into each of the Databases	20
Figure 3.1	Reasons for Arrest of Juveniles; 1990	26
Figure 3.2	Type of Offences for Arrest Cases: Total Juveniles; 1990	27
Figure 8.1	Youth Court or Children and Young Persons Court 1980-1990; Distinct Cases Involving Young Offenders	134
Figure 8.2	Sketch Plan of Two Contrasting Youth Court Rooms	150
Figure A3.1	Offence Rates for Cleared Offences Attributed to (a) Total Offenders per 10,000 Total Population and (b) Juvenile Offenders per 10,000 Juvenile Population; 1978-1990	208
Figure A3.2	Cleared Offences Attributed to Young Offenders Showing Ages, 1978-90; Numbers Aged 0-9, 10-13 and 14-16	210
Figure A3.3	Rates per 10,000 Population for Cleared Offences Attributed to Male and Female Offenders Aged 14-16 Years	210
Figure A3.4	Ethnicity of Detected Juvenile Offenders 1978-90; Bargraph Showing Proportion of Total Offenders in each of the Three Main Ethnic Groups; 1978 to 1990	211

LIST OF BOXES

Box 3.1	Factors Associated with Seriousness of Offence	41
Box 3.2	Factors Associated with Maori Offending	43
Box 3.3	Factors Associated with the Decision to Arrest	43
Box 5.1	Characteristics Associated with Chances of 'Police Diversion' as Opposed to being Referred for an FGC	66
Box 8.1	A Chronology of Q's Court Appearances and Remands	143
Box 9.1	The Goals of Youth Justice in New Zealand	173

Restorative Justice Classics Series Foreword

The phrase "restorative justice" was unknown before the 1970s. Forty years later restorative justice is a vast international movement: nearly a million pages on the Internet refer to it; Google Scholar lists 16,600 books and essays on restorative justice; many states around the world have written it into law; and more important, hundreds of thousands of people and communities have had their fear and shame transformed by encounters with and efforts of those practicing restorative justice.

Along the way, while having intentions to repair harm, restorative justice initiatives have also added to harm. The growth of this mass movement is not without missteps and failures, some very painful. If this movement is to be advanced wisely into the future, its advocates need to remember both fruitful attempts and painful ones.

The Restorative Justice Classics Series is an attempt to help create foundations and share memories for those interested in restorative justice. In a movement that grows and changes so incredibly fast and in so many diverse places, this book series creates space for cultivating restorative justice memory. Amidst the frenzy of work, growth, and missteps, this book series represents a commitment to bring back into print those restorative justice books and articles that could be considered classic. The label "classic" is used here loosely to refer to books that have shaped the restorative justice movement and whose writing continues to be worth remembering, worth sharing, and worth reconsidering amidst the changing scene. In most cases there is still a need for the content and thus a continuing demand for the books.

Books are chosen in this series because they will be of special ongoing value to practitioners and scholars of restorative justice. Wipf and Stock Publishers, at the instigation of Series Editor Ted Lewis, has set up the series in such a way that the books will stay in print and remain available. Anyone wanting to understand the origins, history, diverse practices, and spirit of restorative justice will find the series particularly helpful.

Jarem Sawatsky, Series Consultant
Canadian Mennonite University
Winnipeg, Manitoba
April 2009

To see a complete listing of books in this series, go to www.wipfandstock.com and click on "Advanced Search" to locate the Restorative Justice Classics Series in the series box. Recommendations for further reprints in this series can be directed to Ted Lewis, Series Editor, at tedlewis@wipfandstock.com or can be made by calling 541-344-1528.

PREFACE TO THE 2010 EDITION

It is now twenty years since we began the research that is reported here. Since then, restorative justice has become a major influence in criminal justice systems around the world. But, at the time of this research, restorative justice was not a phrase that we had heard and it does not appear in this volume. However, the thinking underlying restorative justice was already reflected in traditional cultural practices for conflict resolution in New Zealand and these in turn were endorsed in the legislation introducing the new youth justice system in New Zealand in 1989. Thus the underpinnings though not the language provided a theoretical framework for us to interpret our data.

By the time *Family, Victims and Culture* was first published, we had come to see the "Family Group Conference" as the first practical example of restorative justice in any modern Western justice system. It emphasizes the participation of all who are affected by the offending; it focuses on accountability to the victim of that offending by acknowledging the wrong that was done and by attempting to repair the harm; and it seeks ways of reintegrating the young offender into society.

Today families, victims and culture are still at the heart of responses to young people who offend in New Zealand. That ethic is now part of police actions, part of the practice of the Youth Court and part of the support services for families and children as much as it a part of the family group conference itself.

Responses to victims are now better managed than they were in the early years described in this book, although many still choose not to participate in the conferences and that is their right. Other aspects of the system that were not working as well as they might be are still proving problematic. Support services for families and children have developed but still fail to reach the standard envisaged in the original legislation or achieved in other Western countries. Cultural recognition, however, has certainly increased and Maori have become important service providers in their own communities. Most recently the adoption of "Whanau Ora"—a plan to devolve service provision to communities—will allow the delivery of services in ways consistent with the cultural values. This program could be the beginning of another new and ground breaking change to conventional justice practices in New Zealand.

Meanwhile, both the theory and practice of restorative justice has grown: justice systems have been enriched and many new practice options have developed. We had the privilege of being part of the beginning of the restorative revolution, but we recognize just how much it has grown and has been enriched by the contributions of people from all parts of the world.

Arohanui
(With love)
Gabrielle Maxwell and Allison Morris
June 2010, New Zealand

SUMMARY OF FINDINGS

Introduction

The Children, Young Persons and Their Families Act 1989 sets out new principles and procedures governing the intervention of the State into the lives of children, young people and their families. This report describes the youth justice provisions, records how they operate in practice and assesses their impact on young people and their families. The research recorded what happened to 692 cases where young people became involved with the Police or the Ministry of Transport in five different districts of the country. Mostly, the young people (nearly 500) were warned by the police who sometimes also arranged an informal sanction with their family. The remaining young people (just over 200) had a Family Group Conference (FGG) to discuss what should be done and 70 also went to the Youth Court.

When an FGC was held, usually the parents and the young person attended along with the police or MOT officer and the Youth Justice Co-ordinator. In about two out of three cases, a social worker also attended and so did other relatives, whanau or friends of the family and the young person. Victims, however, attended in less than half the cases.

Most FGCs were held in Department of Social Welfare (DSW) offices but some were held in the family's own home or on the marae and this increased the family's satisfaction with the FGC. Families did not always want other relatives or whanau involved but, when the wider family attended, the results were often very positive – particularly when the offences were more serious or when the offending had continued over a period of time.

The research looked at whether the Act was meeting its objectives, at difficulties with practice and at conflicts in the goals of the Act.

Meeting Objectives

The Goals of Youth Justice in New Zealand:

- **diversion** – keeping young people out of courts and preventing the case of labels that make it difficult for young people to put early offending behind them
- **accountability** – emphasising the importance of young people paying no appropriate penalty for their crime and making good the wrong they have done to others.
- **enhancing wellbeing and strengthening families** – making available services that will assist young people and their families
- **due process** – emphasing the protection of young people's rights
- **family participation** – involving families and young people in making decisions for themselves and taking charge of their lives
- **victim involvement** – involving victims in the decisions about what will happen
- **consensus decision-making** – reaching agreement among all those involved in the FGC on the outcome
- **cultural appropriateness** – providing for different ways of resolving matters and obtaining help depending on the culture of the young person and his or her family.

The Act has been successful in meeting many of its objectives.

Diversion

Now, far fewer young people appear in court and receive convictions compared with what used to happen before the Act was introduced in 1989: prior to the Act, there were 10,000 to 13,000 court cases each year – in 1990 there were 2,587. In 1988, 262 cases involving young people resulted in a sentence of imprisonment or corrective training – in 1990 there were only 112. Furthermore, the number of young people now sentenced to residence in a DSW home has halved since the Act came into effect. This national pattern is reflected in our research where only 50% of the young people who went to court received court orders and only 18% went to a DSW residence or prison.

Accountability

On the other hand, FGCs often resulted in moderately severe penalties and thus made more young people accountable for their actions than previously. Almost all FGCs (94%) decided on some form of penalty for the young person. Usually this involved an apology, payment for damages or some type of work for someone in the community. Sometimes arrangements were made for a the young person or the family to receive assistance through a social service programme. In a few cases, it was decided that the young person should go to live with another member of the family.

The most serious cases also appeared in the Youth Court. But about half of the time, the Judge accepted the recommendations of the FGC and did not make a court order. For only a small number of cases was an order made for supervision, supervision with activity, supervision with residence or transfer to an adult court (eg the District or High Court) so that a prison or corrective training sentence could be considered.

Enhancing Wellbeing and Strengthening Families

FGCs often made arrangements to meet the needs of young people and to strengthen families by funding places on programmes providing services such as job training, alcohol counselling, defensive driving and so on. But appropriate programme to meet the specific needs of young people were not always available. In addition, families often wanted more support than they received: for example, in areas such as parenting advice.

Due Process

Important sections of the Act concern the protection of young people's rights. We found that these provisions were not always followed. The police did not always use the proper procedures in cautioning young people before questioning them and parents were not always notified as soon as their child was taken to the police station. Statements were sometimes taken before an adult was present. Only 59% of court-ordered FGCs were attended by the youth advocate (the young person's lawyer). There was sometimes pressure to admit to offences, especially because a denial would mean a court hearing and long delays.

Family Participation

Parents participated fully in the FGCs for the most part. About two thirds felt very much involved. On the other hand, only a third of young people felt involved and they often said little in the FGC. This must be a cause for concern. The Act says that both families and young people should be fully involved in any decisions which affect young people.

Victim Involvement

Only 41% of victims attended the FGC. Many could not attend because they were not told of the FGC or were told too late to arrange to come. When they did come, some felt very pleased with what happened: about half said they were satisfied and a third went away feeling better. However, about a third said they felt worse – some did not feel the young person was really sorry, some were dissatisfied that they did not get any repayment for damage, some felt the family was making excuses for what had happened and some were scared that the young person would seek revenge on them. Victims of serious offences found it particularly difficult attending FGCs where they felt outnumbered and unsupported, especially when the FGC took place in the family's home or on a marae. Nevertheless, despite these problems victims are now more involved in the youth justice process than ever before.

Consensus Decision-making
Almost all FGCs (95%) ended in an agreement about the decision. At times, however, we were concerned about the extent to which family agreements were 'coerced' by the professionals. Nevertheless, families and young people reported high levels of satisfaction with the decisions – 85% and 84% respectively. Equally high was the satisfaction of professionals; 91% of the police and 86% of YJCs expressed satisfaction with the outcome of the FGC. On the other hand, as we have already reported, victims' satisfaction was much lower and this casts doubt on the extent to which many of the decisions were truly the result of a consensus.

Cultural Appropriateness
The Act says that the procedures used in the youth justice system should be culturally appropriate and that services should be provided to families and young people that are culturally sensitive. This goal can not be fully realised until the iwi and cultural authorities, referred to in the Act, are recognised and funded. Sometimes Maori were able to make the arrangements for the FGC and have it run according to their own kaupapa – this generally worked very well and often resulted in finding new solutions for families who had been having difficulties with their young people. At other times, the procedures seemed to be quite foreign to some families – especially to Pacific Island families whose first language was not English. Families need to be enabled to make arrangements that are comfortable and affective for them, especially when the offences are serious. But at the same time, thought needs to be given to the situation of victims from a different culture to that of the family.

Other Practice Difficulties

During our study there were still a lot of difficulties in getting the right people together in the right place to make decisions as soon as possible. Delays often occurred at the Youth Court. Sometimes young people and families did not have enough time to get the advice of their youth advocate before the hearing. Knowing what to expect and what they should do was a problem for many – both at the FGC and in the Youth Court. Sometimes there was inadequate follow-up to see that tasks were done, that help was provided or that victims were informed about the outcome.

Conflicts in the Act's Objectives

There are conflicts and tensions between the various aims of the system for example, meeting victims' needs at the same time as the needs of families and young people; or emphasising the young person's accountability and helping young people and families. Decision-making is also inevitably individualised when families vary so much in their views of what punishment will be best – and different victims also have different views. Some of these conflicts can be resolved, for instance, by setting priorities among objectives or by changing practice standards, but others can not be so readily resolved.

Conclusion

The new system of youth justice in New Zealand follows many overseas trends, but it also has unique features. There is more diversion than in the past – fewer young people are appearing in court and going into residences or prisons. There is also more accountability than in the past with more young people apologising to the victims of their offences, making reparation and accepting tasks as punishments. There is more real family involvement than before; 85% of families and young people were satisfied with the outcomes. Different cultural practices and the needs of victims are often being recognised even though there is room for improvements in both of these areas. Further, there are five areas of practice of considerable concern to us: the tendency for professionals to take over and thereby distort and undermine the FGC process; the vulnerability of families to this through a lack of information on both the process and the possibilities; inadequate protection of the rights of young people at all stages of the proceedings; the failure to ensure that victims are invited, given adequate notice of meetings and informed about what might happen; and the lack of resources and support services to meet the needs of both families and young people which can undermine the FGC decisions.

Chapter 1

THE CHILDREN YOUNG PERSONS AND THEIR FAMILIES ACT: A NEW PARADIGM FOR RESPONDING TO YOUNG OFFENDERS

The Objectives and Principles Underlying Youth Justice in New Zealand

The Children, Young Persons and Their Families Act 1989 is probably unprecedented in the English speaking world in setting out in statutory form not only its objectives but also a comprehensive set of general principles which govern both State intervention in the lives of children and young people and the management of the youth justice system. Furthermore there is no doubt that some of these objectives and principles are unique. The objectives[1] aim to:

- promote the well-being of children, young people and their families and family groups by providing services which are appropriate to cultural needs, accessible and provided by persons and organisations sensitive to cultural perspectives and aspirations

- assist families and kinship groups in caring for their children and young people

- assist children and young people and their families when the relationship between them is disrupted

- assist children and young people in order to prevent harm, ill-treatment, abuse, neglect and deprivation

- provide protection for children and young people

- ensure that young offenders are held accountable for their actions

- deal with children and young people who commit offences in a way that acknowledges their needs and enhances their development

- promote cooperation between organisations providing services for children, young people, families and family groups.

A series of general principles emphasise the need to:

- involve family, whanau, hapu and iwi[2] in decisions

- strengthen and maintain child/family relationships

- consider both the welfare of the child and family stability

- consider the wishes of the child or young person

- obtain the support of the child and the family for outcomes

- work in a time frame appropriate to the age of the child or young person.

Specific principles governing the Youth Justice sections of the Act emphasise that:

- criminal proceedings should not be used if there is an alternative means of dealing with the matter

---

[1] The exact wording of the objectives and principles is set out in Appendix 1.

[2] The nearest literal translation of these Maori words is extended family, clan and tribe. But the words carry additional meaning relating to the way Maori society functions and the role these basic kinship units play in social organisation.

- criminal proceedings must not be used for welfare purposes
- measures to deal with offending should strengthen the family, whanau, hapu, iwi and family group and foster their ability to deal with offending by their children and young people
- young people should be kept in the community
- age is a mitigating factor
- sanctions should be the least restrictive possible and should promote the development of the child in the family
- due regard should be given to the interests of the victim
- the child or young person is entitled to special protection during any investigations or proceedings.

To some extent these objectives and principles reflect current trends (and tensions) in juvenile and criminal justice practice: disillusionment with aspects of a welfare approach, the separation of welfare and justice issues, the endorsement of certain principles of 'just deserts' (that is, proportionality, determinacy and equity of outcomes), an emphasis on accountability and responsibility, the protection of children's and young people's rights, a preference for diversion from formal procedures, deinstitutionalisation and community based penalties, a shift in resources from state agencies to the voluntary and private sector, and the use of least restrictive alternatives. More generally, the New Zealand system attempts to move some way towards a justice approach without abandoning the desire to achieve positive outcomes for young people who offend.

However, the new system also reflects certain innovatory strategies: the rights and needs of indigenous people have been taken into account; families are central to all the decision-making processes involving their children; young people themselves have a say in how their offending should be responded to; victims are given a role in negotiations over possible penalties for juvenile offenders; and the model of decision-making advocated is by group consensus. These strategies are achieved partly through changes in police and court processes and practice but mainly through a new decision making forum, the Family Group Conference (FGC), which enables mediation between victims and offenders, negotiation about the appropriate penalty between the enforcement agency and the family, and the involvement of the family and the young person in decision making at a venue and using a procedure of their own choice and in accordance with their culture. Before describing in more detail how the Act's objectives are translated into a practical reality, we will first elaborate on these various innovatory strategies.

Integration of Indigenous and Western Approaches

Marshall (1985;46-7) identifies features of strategies for dispute settlement in small scale societies which differentiate them from criminal justice arrangements in modern urbanised and industrialised societies. First, the emphasis is on consensus and involves the whole community rather than a single individual making the decision for the parties; second, the desired outcome is reconciliation and a settlement acceptable to all parties rather than the isolation and punishment of the offender; third, the concern is not to apportion blame but to examine the wider reasons for the wrong (an implicit assumption is that there is often wrong on both sides); and fourth, there is less concern with whether or not there has actually been a breach of the law and more concern with the restoration of harmony. A key factor in these distinctions seems to be the existence of prior relationships between the parties.

These features were all apparent in the methods of dispute resolution which existed in New Zealand prior to colonisation. The early settlers believed that the indigenous Maori people, who had arrived in New Zealand from the Pacific Polynesian Islands before the European colonisation of 150 years ago, had no 'law' because they saw no written legal rules, police, prisons or the like; instead they described what they saw as 'primitive and barbaric customs' (Jackson, 1991). But it is clear that Maori did not live in a lawless society. There were rules by which they lived and which covered all aspects of Maori life.

Tikanga o nga hara, for example, translates broadly into the law of wrongdoing in which there were clear concepts of right and wrong. The law, however, was based on notions that responsibility was collective rather than individual and that redress was due not just to any victim but also to the victim's family. Understanding why an individual had offended was also linked to this notion of collective responsibility. The reasons were felt to lie not in the individual but in a lack of balance in the offender's social and family environment. The causes of this imbalance, therefore, had to be addressed in a collective way and, in particular, the imbalance between the offender and the victim's family had to be restored through mediation.

Maori had also created runanga o nga tura which translates broadly into a council of law or court. These were headed by tohunga o nga ture, experts in law, but also contained kaumatua or kuia (elders), a representative from the offender's family and a representative from the victim's family. This group sorted out the wrongdoing and restored the balance. For example, they might have ordered the transfer of the offender's goods to the victim or work by the offender for the victim.

Colonialism, however, all but destroyed indigenous systems of justice in all parts of the British Empire and New Zealand was no exception (Jackson, 1988; Pratt, 1991). The culture and values of the Maori were marginalised and Maori processes and institutions largely displaced by those of European orgin. Dismantling these and the subsequent enforced assimilation to 'the British way of life' was what Pratt (1991) ironically calls the 'gift of civilisation'. To be 'one people' required one set of laws and since the colonisers had the power (first through weapons and later through increased numbers), it was their law which dominated. Indeed, removing Maori law was a powerful mechanism for destabilising the foundations of Maori society.

The new legislation, on the other hand, stresses the provision of services which are **culturally sensitive** and a process which is **culturally appropriate**. Hence it seeks to re-introduce elements of indigenous responses to dealing with offenders. This is partly a reflection of the resurgence of Maori culture and values over the last 15 years but it is also a recognition of the fact that the New Zealand population is made up of a number of different ethnic groups[3]. Numerically, the most significant are Pakeha[4]: more than 80% of the juvenile population. Maori make up around 12% of the juvenile population and Pacific Island Polynesians, who have immigrated more recently make up 4%[5]. It is estimated that by the year 2020, 1 in 4 of the population will be of Polynesian descent including both New Zealand Maori and Pacific Island Polynesian (Interdepartmental Committee on Population Policy Guidelines, 1990).

Although Maori and Pacific Island Polynesian make up together only a small part of the New Zealand population, they are over-represented in various indices of social and economic deprivation: higher infant mortality rates, lower life expectancy rates, higher unemployment rates and lower incomes than the dominant (Pakeha) group (Ministerial Advisory Committee on a Maori Perspective for the Department of Social Welfare, 1986). Maori are also over-represented in the population of known offenders, including juvenile offenders (Maxwell and Morris, 1991). Thus, according to current police statistics (1988), 37% of known offenders are described as Maori; amongst the known juvenile offender population, 43% are described as Maori[6]. The new procedures recognise the over-representation of Maori among juvenile offenders and respond to it by attempting to incorporate traditional, extended family decision-making methods for the resolution of conflict.

---

[3] We recognise that ethnicity and culture are not necessarily identical, but this research has, in practice, been unable to distinguish them.

[4] Pakeha refers to anyone of European origin.

[5] These figures are estimates obtained for 1990 from the Department of Statistics. More recent census figures suggest these are underestimates.

[6] There are problems with the identification of ethnicity, particularly for Maori. The police usually include as Maori all those who appear to be Maori or have a Maori name while population data based on the census describe as Maori persons of half or more Maori blood or those who identify as Maori. The police categories, therefore, are likely to include a larger number than would be identified as Maori in the usual population statistics. Even statistics on New Zealanders of Maori descent are unlikely to be as inclusive as police identifications, as the former depend on self-identification as Maori. On the other hand, it could also be argued that police identification could fail to acknowledge Maori with a European name and appearance.

The role of whanau is important in both Maori (and Pacifc Island Polynesian) child-rearing and decision-making. It is not unusual, for example, for Maori children to live from time to time with different relatives within their whanau. This occurs in part because the child is considered not simply the child of the birth parents but also of the whanau, hapu and iwi. Bringing up children, therefore, and hence dealing with their delinquencies, is a communal responsibility. Moreover, in pre-colonial times most decisions, whatever their nature, were customarily made by the whanau, hapu or iwi depending on the importance and nature of the decision. Hence the involvement of whanau, hapu and iwi is explicitly recognised within the new legislative framework in both discussions and decisions about appropriate solutions to juvenile offending.

The re-assertion of traditional Maori cultural values is of symbolic as well as of practical importance. As a result of colonisation, decisions affecting Maori people in such areas as social welfare and criminal justice have been made for Maori and with little consultation with Maori. Thus traditional Maori structures have been weakened. The 1989 Act seeks, therefore, to empower Maoridom. It seeks to involve Maori directly in decisions about their young people and thus to acknowledge their identity as tangata whenua (the people of the land). Such an emphasis has implications for other cultural groups in New Zealand and has the potential for the validation of a variety of cultural practices.

However, it would be a mistake to describe the new system as the rejection of a Western criminal justice system in favour of the adoption of an indigenous method of resolution (and certainly the advocates of a Maori indigenous model would reject such a depiction). A distinction must be drawn between a system which attempts to re-establish the indigenous model of pre-European times and a system of justice which is culturally appropriate. The new New Zealand system is an attempt to establish the latter, not to replicate the former. As such, it seeks to incorporate many of the features apparent in whanau decision-making processes and seen in meetings on marae today, but it also contains elements quite alien to indigenous models (for example, the presence of representatives of the State) and other principles which, to our mind, are equally important: the empowerment of families, offenders and victims. Although families and victims had recognised roles in the resolution of disputes in traditional Maori society, their part in the new system is not necessarily identical with traditional roles. We will discuss in later chapters the extent to which whanau have become involved in youth justice processes and the ways in which these various principles interact. We will also raise questions about whether or not it could ever be possible for a Western criminal justice system to be married successfully with an indigenous model, especially given the context of a modern and mixed society.

Empowerment of the Family

A recurrent theme in conventional criminological literature is that deficiencies in the family lie at the root of juvenile crime (see Rutter and Giller, 1983 for a review) and so traditionally the State has acted to usurp the rights of families in situations of alleged abuse and neglect and the responsibilities of families whose children have committed offences. The exception is when the State has recognised family responsibility in a negative sense by holding the family accountable for their children's misdemeanours (as, for example, in the provision in England to fine parents whose children commit offences). Indeed, despite rhetoric about the importance of families, families have been undermined by the ways in which juvenile justice systems have tended to operate: by exclusion.

The idea of a **partnership** between the State and families in resolving issues which affect their children is a novel one. Thus, in contrast with most systems of juvenile justice, it is intended in the new system that responsibility be given to families, whanau, hapu, iwi and family groups to respond to their child's offending. The underlying intention is to empower families to deal with offending themselves and to restrict the power of professionals, in particular the power of social service professionals. Thus, except for minor and inconsequential offending which is usually dealt with by the police by means of a warning, families are given the opportunity to formulate a plan. The plan must be considered by the judge should the case be referred to court, but it is more commonly accepted by both the police and the victim(s) so that a court appearance is avoided. The family, therefore, is a key agency in diverting young people from formal proceedings and we comment in subsequent chapters on the way in which this has worked in practice.

Empowerment of Offenders

To speak of the empowerment of offenders in conventional criminal justice systems is a contradiction in terms. Offenders do not participate much in court procedures, a situation well depicted in Carlen's (1976) description of them as 'dummy players'. The 'game' takes place all around them for the benefit of 'repeat players' (Galanter, 1974) such as judges, prosecutors, defence counsel and the like, while they watch passively and uninvolved. They take on the status of objects or 'dependants' and participate little (Ericson and Baranek, 1982). O'Connor and Sweetapple (1988), for example, describe as follows the position of young people in the Australian Courts:

> *For children the structure and mechanisms of the court routinely strip them of their ability to participate in the court process. ... In many cases ... legal representation simply reinforces the child's disadvantaged and dependent position and at the same time allows the court to proceed under the fiction that the child's wishes and interests are represented ... they are powerless to impinge on their fate. (p 98)*

One method of meeting these concerns, they suggest, is through the introduction of mediation schemes:

> *The necessity of reconciliation is especially important for juveniles because their crimes are primarily committed in their local community. Crime is prevented, not by threat and intimidation, but by the fabric of social connectedness to the people. (pp 128-130)*

Mediation schemes also address a further concern which arises from practice in traditional criminal justice systems: the absence of any direct contact between the victim and the offender. Many consequences come from this. To quote O'Connor and Sweetapple again:

> *The young people charged with these crimes rarely see the personal distress and inconvenience caused ... their attention is not effectively directed at the consequences of their behaviour for others ... so the victim rarely sees the offender and the offender rarely sees the victim. Both remain ignorant of the other, of the other's potential suffering. The child does not encounter the hurt of the victim, nor have to grapple with making recompense in a meaningful way. The victim never sees the offender ... never has the comfort of knowing the offender ... – far from being a violent thug – is most likely a somewhat pathetic young person from their own neighbourhood. (pp 117-118)*

To understand the consequences of their actions from the perspective of the victim, to accept responsibility for them and to actively make a commitment to some reparation requires that young people feel a part of (rather than apart from) the proceedings.

Mediation was a growth industry in the USA in the 1970s-80s and has expanded to other countries since (Wright and Galaway, 1989; Marshall and Merry, 1990). The intention is not to make decisions for people, but to help them make their own decisions. As a practice, it has been used in a range of situations: for example, industrial disputes and arguments between landlord and tenants. More recently, it has been extended to include resolution between victims and offenders through the introduction of reparation schemes and restitution or compensation. In England, for example, in some circumstances, offenders who are cautioned are asked to make reparation and there are a number of mediation schemes in which offenders and their victims meet together to discuss such issues as reparation or where a group of offenders and a group of victims discuss more general issues of offending behaviour (see Marshall and Walpole, 1985; Davis et al, 1987 and Marshall and Merry, 1990, for more information).

The basic premises of mediation are that in order to restore balance offenders must accept **responsibility** for their actions and make amends. In theory, both offenders and victims are **empowered**: offenders by taking responsibility for their actions and victims by regaining control of their lives. It is these premises which underlie the new system of youth justice in New Zealand.

At a general level, Rock, in the Foreword to Marshall (1985:vii), identifies various advantages in mediation. Chief amongst these are:

- a reduction in the number of people appearing before the court and sentenced to custody
- the replacement of what is seen to be an inefficient adversarial system which increases alienation and division
- the fostering of 'peaceableness'
- the provision of quick, cheap and accessible justice.

More specifically for offenders, the advantages are:

- participation throughout the process
- receiving information
- an awareness of the consequences of the harm caused
- receiving an 'appropriate' sentence.

That is not to say that there are no potential disadvantages for offenders. If mediation is an alternative to prosecution, it is important to ensure that all offenders have a similar chance of involvement in such alternatives and are not subject to discrimination or unpredictable decision-making. Nor should they experience any pressure to accept mediation. Some commentators have argued that offenders should have legal advice at this stage so that they are fully aware of the choices open to them and of the consequences of these choices. A simple admission of guilt before proceeding, particularly where the offender is a juvenile, may not provide adequate protection. Similarly, acquiescence in a decision to make amends without advice as to the consequences of failure to adhere to that decision or of the penalties likely to be imposed by a court may be an insufficient safeguard against agreement to 'severe' sanctions. Moreover, 'failure' after mediation may lead later to greater intervention by courts because of the offender's supposed unwillingness to 'co-operate'. We comment in subsequent chapters on the extent to which the practice of youth justice in New Zealand meets these concerns.

Empowerment of Victims

Traditionally, the criminal justice system has given only a minimal role to victims. Indeed, in part, one of its functions has been to protect offenders from the vengeance of victims. However, increasingly, criminal justice systems are giving more weight to the needs and wishes of victims. There are a number of reasons for this shift in emphasis: in particular, acceptance of the failure of criminal justice systems to reform and/or deter offenders and, consequently, the need to substitute alternative justifications for intervention; and the emergence of pressure groups from a range of political backgrounds (from the women's movement to 'law and order' proponents) which have begun to highlight victims' concerns.

Thus, in most jurisdictions in recent years, there have been a number of significant changes in the provision of services for victims. In New Zealand the Victim of Offences Act 1987 recognised the legitimacy of concerns for victims and provided for taking 'victim impact statements' which could be used in evidence in court proceedings. There has also been an increase in the number of agencies providing support services, improvements in court procedures and the introduction of reparation as a sentence. In a review of these developments, Hutton and Young (1989) comment that, at that time, there had been little concerted effort to set up, and no indication of official support for, reconciliation meetings between victims and offenders or to provide a forum in which victims could participate in the sentencing process or, at least, have their views taken into account. The new youth justice system introduces both of these provisions.

It should be noted here, however, that giving victims a greater voice and role fits too with many indigenous systems of justice. There, as we outlined in brief earlier, the victim is central rather than peripheral to the proceedings and the objective is not simply to punish the offender but to restore community balance. Traditionally, for example, Maori were concerned not only with atonement for the offence and restitution to the victim, but also with the individual offender's potential for reintegration within the whanau, hapu and iwi.

The main argument used in favour of increasing victims' representations about how offenders should be dealt with (through the presence of victims or their representatives at hearings, consultation with victims about appropriate outcomes, the introduction of victim impact statements and the like) is that they possess the information required to reach a 'just' outcome. To do otherwise, it is argued, retains an imbalance in favour of offenders; for those making decisions about offenders can be influenced by information about the offender's situation, for example, the impact of a particular outcome on them or their families.

There are other arguments in favour of victim involvement. Koehler (1988), for example, argues that, by providing victims with information and facilitating their participation in the process, the system will increase victim satisfaction, enhance the prospects of reconciliation and 'peace-making' and provide a more effective means of restitution and reparation. It is this participation which empowers.

Counter-arguments are that the involvement of victims introduces subjectivity and emotion into what should be an objective and rational task, that outcomes will inevitably, therefore, become more punitive, and that disparities in outcomes will increase depending on the whims or idiosyncrasies of victims. Rock (1985) also draws our attention to some potential pitfalls for victims – in particular, the time consumed by meeting with minor offenders for minimal return and the pain caused by meeting with serious offenders. We comment on these issues in subsequent chapters.

Group Consensus Decision-making

The particular adaptation of whanau decision-making chosen in the new procedure not only involves face to face contact between the juvenile offender (and his or her family and whanau) and the victim(s) (or their representatives), but has been modified by introducing representatives from the police and social welfare services and providing for legal representation in the more serious cases.

However, the model of decision-making promoted is quite different both from traditional courtroom decision-making practices and from traditional diversionary procedures. The conventional approach can be characterised as both 'linear' and 'professional'. A 'linear' approach is when one person or group of people (for example, a judge or magistrate) makes the decision for others (for example, the young person and the family). A 'professional' approach assumes that the decision-maker has certain qualities or training which ensure that the decision is 'right' (for that young person and family) and hence that it is appropriate for the decisions to be (en)forced on the offender.

In contrast, the Children, Young Persons and Their Families Act 1989 involves a group approach to decision-making which allows all the participants in a particular forum to contribute to the process and to work towards the determination of an outcome. A 'facilitator' is provided whose role is that of a mediator who negotiates between parties with potentially different views, for example, between the family and the victim or between the family and the police. The aim is to move away from the adversarial and confrontational procedures apparent in courtrooms towards outcomes shaped by the families themselves and agreed to by all the participants, including the victims. Again, we discuss the extent to which this has been achieved in subsequent chapters.

Like most systems of juvenile justice, the New Zealand system has multiple goals and some of these are in conflict: for example, involving families in decisions may conflict with the requirement to consider the wishes of the child or young person and giving due regard to the interests of the victim may conflict with the emphasis on the enhancement of the development of children and young people. We explore in subsequent chapters how and to what extent these conflicts are resolved in practice.

A Description of the Youth Justice System in New Zealand

The age of criminal responsibility in New Zealand is 10, although published police statistics present data on offending below that age. However, children under the age of 14 cannot be prosecuted except for the offences of murder and manslaughter. In other cases where such children's offending causes concern, they may be dealt with by warning, police diversion or a Family Group Conference (FGC). Alternatively they may be referred to the Department of Social Welfare (DSW) as in need of care and protection and, if necessary, matters can be dealt with in the Family Court. This replaces the former system by which such children could only come to court by way of a complaint brought against their parents after, at least in theory, a referral to what was known as a Children's Board. This was an informal meeting between the parent, child, a representative of the police, DSW and Department of Maori Affairs and various appointed representatives of the community at which it was discussed whether or not complaint proceedings should be brought or whether or not a warning or some other informal action would suffice. The emphasis was on dealing with such children without recourse to court and on providing appropriate support to the families. The Children's Boards, however, were not generally effective in achieving these goals. These goals are now primarily to be met through either the care and protection or the youth justice procedures of the new Act.

A young person who commits offences beyond the age of 16 is dealt with in the same manner as an adult, that is, in the District Court or, if the offence is serious, in the High Court. The very serious offences of murder and manslaughter by any juvenile aged 10 years or over are automatically transferred by the Youth Court to be dealt with in the High Court. The Youth Court can transfer other cases involving serious offences (for example, arson and aggravated robbery) to the High Court. There is also provision in other cases for the Youth Court to transfer matters to the District Court depending on the seriousness of the case and the previous offending history of the young person. Such cases are rare and the vast majority of juvenile offending by young people is now dealt with under the procedures described below.

These reflect marked changes from the previous system. Then, as now, juveniles aged 14 to 16 arrested by the police were referred to court. However, the police were required to consult with a social worker from the DSW before there could be a prosecution in the Children and Young Persons Court of a young person who had not been arrested. The primary intention of this requirement to consult was to explore whether or not the matter could be resolved informally and so reduce the number of young people processed in the court. The procedure was ineffective, however, since the decision whether or not to prosecute had almost invariably already been made by the police. Indeed, arresting young people was used in some areas as a way of avoiding the consultation process and of ensuring that the case was dealt with in court. The consultation process, therefore, did not act as a filter to prosecution; rather, at least in some areas, consultation and prosecution, were seen as alternatives.

Figure 1.1 provides a diagrammatic description of the possible pathways through the new system. These are explained further in the following text.

Police

The intention underlying the 1989 Act is to encourage the police to adopt low key responses to juvenile offending except where the nature and circumstances of the offending mean that stronger measures are required to protect the safety of the public. Thus juvenile offenders cannot be arrested unless certain tightly drawn conditions are met[7]. The most important are that the arrest is necessary to ensure the juvenile's appearance in court, to prevent the commission of further offences, or to prevent the loss or destruction of evidence or interference with witnesses.

Also, as in most jurisdictions now, it is expected that minor and first offenders will be diverted from prosecution by means of an immediate (street) warning. Where further action is thought necessary,

---

[7] See section 214 of the Children Young Persons and Their Families Act 1989. These conditions are detailed in Chapter 4.

Figure 1.1
Flow Chart Indicating Pathways Through the System

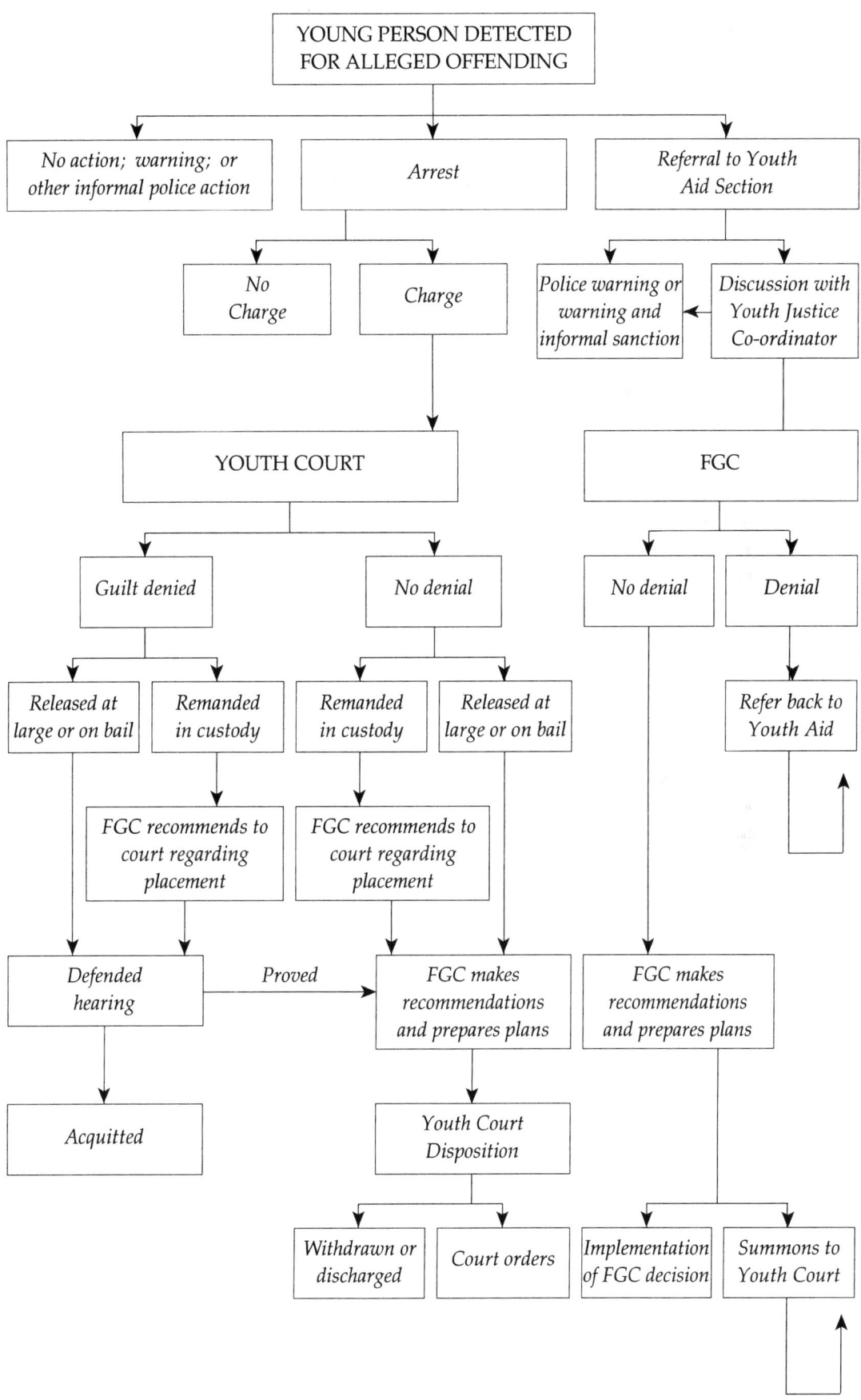

the police can refer juveniles to the police Youth Aid section (a specialist unit dealing only with juveniles) for follow-up – for example, a warning in the presence of the parents. The Youth Aid section may also require an apology to the victim and give the child or young person an additional sanction (for example, some work in the community).

Youth Justice Co-ordinator

Where Youth Aid sections feel that action beyond that which they normally arrange themselves is required, they must now refer the juvenile to the Youth Justice Co-ordinator (YJC). It is his or her responsibility to negotiate with the police to divert juveniles themselves rather than arrange an FCC unless the offence is moderately serious or because of previous offending. The YJC also receives court referrals and referrals from other enforcement agencies, for example, the Ministry of Transport (MOT), which at the time of the study still retained responsibility for dealing with traffic offences. The YJC plays a similar negotiating role with these other enforcement agencies.

The Youth Justice Co-ordinators come from a range of backgrounds – for example, social services, probation, and the prison system. Many are Maori. They are appointed by and are officers within the DSW.

The Family Group Conference

The Family Group Conference lies at the heart of the new procedures: both as another means of avoiding prosecution and also as a means of determining how young people who commit offences should be dealt with. It is mandatory for an FGC to be held to consider the case whenever criminal proceedings are contemplated (non-arrest cases) or brought (arrest cases).

Where a young person is not arrested but is referred to the police Youth Aid section, an FGC must be held before a prosecution can be brought. The FGC has responsibility for formulating a plan for the juvenile or making such recommendations as it sees fit (including prosecution). The range of possibilities here cover ways of repaying the victim and the community, penalties for misbehaviour and plans designed to reduce the chances of reoffending. The exact details are limited only by the imagination of the parties. Common options include an apology, reparation, work for the victim or the community, donations to charity, restrictions on liberty such as a curfew or grounding and programmes of counselling or training.

Similarly, where a young person is arrested and brought before the court for alleged offending (other than murder, manslaughter or a traffic offence not punishable by imprisonment), the court must adjourn the matter to enable an FGC to be held if there has not been a denial or if there has been a finding of guilt. The FGC then has the responsibility again for formulating a plan for the juvenile or making such recommendations as it sees fit. The court in dealing with the case must have regard to this plan or these recommendations.

The FGC is made up of the young person, his or her advocate if one has been arranged, members of the family, whanau or family group and whoever they invite, the victim(s) or their representative, the police, the YJC and a DSW social worker in cases where the DSW has had a statutory role in relationship to the custody, guardianship or supervision of the young person. In line with the 1992 report of the Ministerial Review team, the Government has agreed to amend the legislation to add victims' supporters. The family and those it invites are entitled to deliberate in private during the FGC and can ask for the meeting to be adjourned to enable discussions to continue elsewhere. FGCs can take place wherever the family wish, for example, in the Department of Social Welfare, in the family's home or on marae (meeting houses).

The jurisdiction of the FGC is limited to the disposition of cases where the young person has not denied the alleged offences or has already been found guilty.[8] The intended focus of the FGC is the young person's offending and matters related directly to the circumstances of that offending. The Act clearly states that criminal proceedings should not be used to intervene in the life of the young

---

[8] See section 259 of the Children Young Persons and Their Families Act 1989.

person on welfare grounds and this objective has been interpreted to imply that FGCs themselves should primarily focus on issues of accountability rather than welfare. Welfare issues should only be addressed as voluntary additions to offence-based sanctions or separately in care and protection proceedings. In the latter case, the YJC should refer the case to the Care and Protection Co-ordinator.

The YJC has the following role in relation to the FGC:

- to convene the FGC within the time limits set down by the Act
- to consult with the family or whanau about the FGC arrangements including the date, time, place, participants and the procedures to be adopted
- to notify all those entitled to attend and to ascertain the views of those unable to attend
- to ensure that everyone present is adequately informed about what happened and to determine whether or not the young person denies the information in the summary of facts
- to ensure that information on the impact of the offence on any victims is given to the FGC
- to provide families, whanau, hapu, iwi and family groups with the information they need in order to arrive at decisions
- to ensure that the family is given the opportunity to deliberate privately
- to seek agreement to the decisions and, if necessary, adjourn the conference or negotiate between the family and enforcement agency
- to record the decisions of the FGC and to provide a copy to the participants and others who are entitled to be informed
- to facilitate access to any resources that the family may need to carry out the decisions.

The plans and decisions are binding when they have been agreed to by all those present at an FGC, and, where it is relevant, accepted by the court. An FGC can be reconvened to review decisions at a later date. This can be arranged by the YJC on his or her initiative or at the request of two members of the FGC. This provision can be used when a young person fails to complete the tasks on which the FGC has agreed. At this stage, a new plan is formulated. At any stage, plans can include a recommendation for prosecution in court.

In order to ensure that the process works swiftly, the legislation has set time limits within which FGCs must be held. Where a young person is in custody, an FGC must be convened within 7 days to consider placement; where the court requests an FGC to be held, it must be convened within 14 days; and where the YJC receives notification of an intended prosecution of a young person who has not been arrested or a child aged 10 to 13 is alleged to be in need of care and protection by reason of offending, the FGC must be convened within 21 days of that notification. In response to the report of the Ministerial Review team, the Department has defined convene as referring to 'the action of setting the date, time and place of conference and notifying those entitled to attend'. However, at the time of the research it was generally accepted that 'convened' was equivalent to 'held'. These time frames stem from an awareness that young people already work within much shorter time frames than adults and that responses to offending tend to have more 'meaning' when applied relatively quickly.

Youth Court

A court process is reserved for a minority of young offenders. The Youth Court has been created as a branch of the District Court to deal with youth justice cases only. It replaces the Children and Young Persons Court which dealt with care and protection as well as control and youth justice cases. Its establishment underlines the importance of the principle that the offending of young people should be premised on criminal justice not welfare principles; that is, on notions of accountability and responsibility for actions, due process, legal representation, requiring judges to give reasons for certain decisions, and imposing sanctions which are proportionate to the gravity of the offence.

The Youth Court is closed to the public to preserve the confidentiality of its proceedings. It is supposed to operate an appointments' system in an attempt both to prevent young people from associating with each other at court and to reduce the amount of time families are kept waiting. The court always appoints a youth advocate (a barrister or solicitor) to represent the young person where the young person does not already have a legal representative. The court may also appoint a lay advocate to support the young person in any proceedings in the Youth Court. Lay advocates are individuals of standing within the young person's culture and it is their responsibility to ensure that the court is aware of cultural matters that are relevant to the proceedings.

Where cases are referred to the Youth Court, the possible outcomes are as follows in order of severity: transfer to the District Court; supervision with residence; supervision with activity; community work; supervision; fine, reparation, restitution, or forfeiture; to come up if called upon within 12 months (a type of conditional discharge); admonition; discharge from proceedings; and police withdrawal of the information. In addition, it is possible to order the disqualification of a driver involved in a traffic offence.

Transfer to the District Court can take place at two different stages of the process. First, it can occur at the charge stage if the juvenile is at least 15 years of age; and either the offence is purely indictable or the offence is punishable by imprisonment for a term exceeding three months and the young person elects trial by jury under section 66 of the Summary Proceedings Act. Secondly, it can occur at the disposition stage when the nature or circumstances of the offence are such that if the young person was an adult he or she would be sentenced to custody and the court is satisfied that any order of a non-custodial nature would be inadequate. A supervision with residence order may last for up to 9 months and is made up of 3 months in the custody of the Department of Social Welfare (reduced to 2 months if the young person does not abscond or commit further offences during the custodial placement) and up to 6 months' supervision following the period of residence. Supervision with activity involves up to 3 months' structured supervised activity and may be followed by up to 3 months' supervision. Community work is for a minimum of 20 and a maximum of 200 hours and has to be completed within 12 months. Supervision is limited to a maximum of 6 months.

Thus court orders are for a determinate period of time and plans must be prepared for the court detailing how the order is to be implemented, including the nature of any programme to be provided and the person or agency who is primarily responsible for the supervision. Orders other than supervision with residence can be administered by any person or organisation so nominated. This enables cultural or tribal authorities to work directly with young people who offend. Resources are available to support such arrangements (although it cannot yet be said that a full and adequate range of community programmes has been developed). The person or organisation nominated is also required to report to the Youth Court at the expiry of the order on the effectiveness of the order, the young person's response to it and any other matter considered relevant.

The intention of the legislation is to enable families to influence outcomes. Thus the Youth Court cannot make a disposition unless an FGC has been held and it must take into account the plan and recommendations put forward by the FGC.

Chapter 2

RESEARCH DESIGN, METHODOLOGY AND SAMPLE

Introduction

In 1984 and 1985, the Institute of Criminology, with funding from the New Zealand Family Trust, undertook research into the operation of the Children and Young Persons Act 1974, which was intended to provide baseline data for an evaluation of the legislative changes being discussed at the time. The research focused upon police decision-making, consultations between police and social workers, the operation of Children's Boards, the perceptions which juveniles and their families had of the court process, and the role and impact of legal representation. The results of that research were presented in a report by Morris and Young (1987).

The research confirmed many of the criticisms which had been levelled at the juvenile justice system during the 1980s: that it had failed to implement an effective diversion strategy; that it had resulted in an undue reliance upon formal court action; and that it had failed to involve family groups and offenders in a meaningful way in the process. It thus showed that, in these respects, the Act had failed to achieve its objectives.

The present study was designed to describe the decision-making procedures which have been implemented under the new legislation, to consider how these differ from the practices identified in the earlier research and to determine the extent to which the new statutory principles are reflected in current practice.

An analysis of the flowchart in Chapter 1 (Figure 1.1) shows that there are four major decision points which determine the way in which juvenile offenders are handled by the system. The first is the decision by front-line police officers either to take no action or give a warning, to arrest, or to refer to police Youth Aid section. The second is the decision by Youth Aid officers, either alone or after discussion with the Youth Justice Co-ordinator, to take informal action such as issuing a police warning or to refer the young person to the YJC for a Family Group Conference which can draw up a more detailed management plan or recommend prosecution. The third is the decision of the Family Group Conference, either after the case has been referred to the YJC by the Youth Aid officer or after an arrest case has appeared in the Youth Court. The final decision-point is in the Youth Court. This study explores each of these decision-making stages in detail, to determine the extent to which practice is conforming with the principles laid down in the Children, Young Persons and Their Families Act 1989.

Aims of the Research

The research, therefore, provides an overview of practice under the new legislation, focusing primarily on the key processes involved in the making of decisions about children and young people who offend. It examines also whether or not the process meets the expectations and needs of relevant parties and involves family groups and victims in decision-making.

The more precise aims of the research are as follows:

1) To identify the criteria used by front-line police officers in determining what action to take against children and young people who come to their notice for offending – that is, whether to give a warning, to take other informal action, to arrest, or to refer to the Youth Aid section.

2) To assess the extent to which these decisions accord with the presumptions and criteria laid down in section 209 of the Act, which specifies the conditions under which warning should be considered as an alternative to prosecution, and section 214, which specifies the grounds for arrest.

3) To describe the procedures used by Youth Aid section, Youth Justice Co-ordinators, Family Group Conferences and Youth Courts.

4) To determine the extent to which these procedures enable effective participation in decision-making by family groups and victims, and more generally to evaluate whether or not such procedures conform with the principles laid down in the new legislation.

5) To describe the plans or recommendations made by Family Group Conferences, to record whether or not they are accepted by the Youth Court, and to determine how and to what extent they are implemented as intended.

6) To determine the extent to which the decision-making of the police, Family Group Conferences and Youth Courts meets the expectations and needs of victims, family groups and young offenders.

Research Methods

Study Areas

We focused upon five geographical areas for detailed study – four metropolitan areas and one provincial area. These are: Henderson (Auckland West Police District excluding New Lynn), Kapiti-Mana (corresponding to Kapiti-Mana Police District which includes Porirua City and the coast up to Paraparaumu), Christchurch City (corresponding to the Christchurch Central Police Youth Aid District), Lower Hutt and Masterton (both from the Hutt Police District; Lower Hutt includes Wainuiomata but excludes Upper Hutt). These areas appeared to be suitable for the following reasons:

- Lower Hutt and Kapiti-Mana were covered by our previous research (Morris and Young, 1987), and thus the results were likely to be comparable
- they provided a good geographical spread
- they each had a different type of ethnic mix
- they were areas in which we had reliable research assistants available to us or where we could provide day to day supervision, thus ensuring the collection of good quality data.

Only one provincial area was included in the above. In addition we were informed that practice differences occurred throughout the Auckland metropolitan area. We therefore augmented the scope of the main study with an overview of the range of practice in provincial and rural areas, as well as the Central and South Auckland urban areas, by interviewing Youth Aid officers, front-line police, Youth Justice Co-ordinators, social workers and court staff in ten additional areas throughout the North Island. In the following account of the results, statistical comparisons between the study areas are based on data from the five Social Welfare or Police Districts most comparable in geographic boundary to the areas covered in the study. National figures are also routinely presented in these analyses. In addition, we have sometimes also included data on Auckland Central and Wellington, as these are the two other largest urban areas not included in our sample.

The Sample

During the research period, we selected all the cases involving children or young people that came to attention in one of the following ways:

- appeared on police charge sheets
- were referred to Youth Aid by front-line police officers
- were referred by MOT to DSW for an FGC
- appeared in the Youth Court on charges or informations laid by MOT
- appeared in the Youth Court by way of transfer from the District Court.

The data were collected over a three month period from 1 September to 30 November 1990, except in Henderson where various delays resulted in data collection from the second week of November to the second week of February 1991.

Data Collection

We have collected and analysed data relating to each of the major decision stages identified above:

1) Decisions by Front-line Police Officers to Arrest or Refer

In respect of arrest cases, details of the name and age of the offender, the nature of the alleged offence and the name of the arresting officer were collected from the Charge Book. The reports of arresting officers under section 214, outlining the reasons why the child or young person was arrested without warrant, were also examined. Where these reports required clarification, arresting officers were contacted and interviewed. The general views of these officers about the Act were also recorded.

In respect of cases referred to Youth Aid section, basic social and demographic data about the juveniles and the circumstances (including the nature of their offending) which brought them to police notice were obtained from the Police Juvenile Report Form – Form 333.

2) Decision-making by Youth Aid Officers and Youth Justice Co-ordinators

The main data source here was again the 333 forms, since these contain details of the Youth Aid officer's assessment of the juvenile and his or her family (where a home visit has been conducted), the preferred course of action and the reasons for this. In some cases, when the incident was relatively minor, data were recorded on Form 101. Both forms record name, address, age, gender, and ethnicity as well as the details of the incident. Where the reasons for the decision or the expected outcome required clarification, the Youth Aid officer in charge of the case was interviewed. In some cases which were referred for an FGC, the police officer who originally referred the case to Youth Aid was also interviewed.

The degree and nature of any contacts between Youth Aid officers and the Youth Justice Co-ordinator about cases in the sample were recorded and a researcher attended any regular formal meetings held between the two. Issues examined include the roles played by police officers and the Youth Justice Co-ordinator; the extent to which they respectively contributed information about cases being discussed; their respective input into the decisions reached; and the extent to which, and the way in which, victims' views were sought and taken into account.

3) Family Group Conferences

For the most part, Family Group Conferences proceeded in three stages: first, all participants met to receive information about the case and to discuss it; the juvenile and family group were then left alone to decide on how best they would like to deal with the offending behaviour; and finally all participants reconvened to reach decisions and to make recommendations and plans. Where cases in the sample proceeded to a Family Group Conference, subject to the consent of the family and the young person[9], we observed the first and third stages of the Conference, focusing in particular upon the procedures adopted, the information provided about the case by various participants, the extent to which possible or desirable outcomes were suggested by the police or social workers, and the extent to which the plan or recommendation of the family group was subsequently endorsed or modified in discussion with the police and other participants at the third stage.

We also observed and recorded the following information about each case:

- the time taken to arrange the conference

---

[9] In some cases, the Youth Justice Co-ordinator or the social worker sought such consent when arranging the Family Group Conference. In all cases we introduced ourselves to the young person and the family prior to the conference and asked permission to observe the FGC.

- the venue of the conference
- the identity of each participant at the conference (for example, family member, victim, enforcement officer etc)
- the plan or recommendation made by the family group (for example, what sanctions or controls were proposed, whether reparation or an apology to the victim was required, what support for or supervision of the juvenile or family was envisaged, whether or not there were to be changes in arrangements for care etc)
- the ethnic identity of the family, the Youth Justice Co-ordinator and other participants
- who was present in the room during the second stage when the family decided upon a plan or recommendation
- the length of each stage of the conference
- in relation to the referral sample, whether the plan or recommendation was agreed to by the enforcement officer and, if not, what action was taken
- in relation to the arrest sample, whether the plan or recommendation was agreed to by the Youth Court and, if not, what decision was reached.

4) Youth Court Hearings
Where cases in the sample proceeded to the Youth Court, the proceedings of that court were observed. As in the previous research (Morris and Young, 1987), we recorded the interaction between different agencies in the courtroom, the participation of juveniles and other family members and the extent to which the operation of the Youth Court accorded with the new statutory principles.

5) Perceptions of Juveniles, Family Groups and Victims
Where cases in the sample proceeded to a Family Group Conference or to the Youth Court, we attempted to interview juveniles, their parents or other relevant family group members and victims.

Where the case proceeded to the Youth Court, the interviews were conducted at the conclusion of the court proceedings; but otherwise they were held after the Family Group Conference. These interviews were semi-structured, so that interviewers were left free to explore issues in the order in which they were raised by respondents. However, since a different interviewer was employed in each district, there was a defined checklist of questions and issues which were to be covered at some point in every interview.

Previous 'consumer studies' both in New Zealand and overseas (Morris and Young, 1987; Morris and Giller, 1977; Parker et al, 1981) have demonstrated that there is frequently a gap between the expectations and experiences of consumers and the working practices of 'professionals' in the system; and it is important to measure whether or not the new legislative framework has managed to avoid this. Thus the interviews focused upon perceptions of, and satisfaction with, both the process and the outcome of Family Group Conferences and Youth Court proceedings in order to determine whether or not the system made sense to its constituents.

Alternative Cultural Perspectives

We recognise that much social research in the past has had a limited cultural perspective. We wished to ensure that our data collection methods accurately and sensitively reflected the experiences and feelings of people from a variety of cultural backgrounds. We therefore attempted to adapt the research strategies to take account of different cultural perspectives.

For this purpose, the data collection methods outlined were modified in some respects. We consulted people from the Maori community about appropriate ways of eliciting the views and experiences of Maori. Their advice was that the goals of the research should be discussed with Maori people, the research interviews with Maori should be conducted by Maori interviewers, the proposed questions should be reviewed from a Maori perspective and the results should be interpreted by Maori people.

In practice we had three meetings with a group of Maori advisers including people from the Department of Social Welfare, a community group, Victoria University of Wellington and Maori Congress. Two of the advisory group went over the questionnaires with us to see whether or not there could be problems for Maori in the questions. They also devised three additional questions to explore cultural issues. A Maori researcher was appointed in each research area. These researchers attended FGCs involving Maori families and interviewed those involved afterwards[10]. At the conclusion of the research, three of the Maori researchers came together to comment on preliminary drafts of the results, to discuss their experiences and to meet with the community members of the advisory group. The comments of these researchers have been incorporated in appropriate places throughout the report. Specific issues relating to the interpretation of Maori material have been discussed extensively with them and their comments have often been included in the text. However the responsibility for any misinterpretation of cultural issues must remain with the principal investigators.

The Maori researchers raised a number of concerns about the research process which have implications for understanding the findings. The same questions were, for the most part, used for both Maori and Pakeha and, as a consequence, it would be easy to interpret the answers in the same way, especially when the responses of the two groups were similar. But Maori carry with them the fact that they are a minority culture within a dominant one and that, although Aotearoa is the homeland for Maori, they still do not control their own destiny. This means that a question such as: Who really made the decisions in the FGC? may have contained different elements for Maori compared to Pakeha. Maori live in a world where members of their race do not construct most of the societal structures which surround them. Their expectations of involvement in decision-making processes within the state system may be very different from those of Pakeha and, thus, their experience of involvement may be interpreted against a different baseline. The Maori researchers felt that other questions may also have been perceived differently by Maori participants and that apparent similarity in the responses of Maori and Pakeha should not necessarily be taken to imply a similarity in views.

Similar issues can be raised with respect to the questions chosen to explore directly the effects of cultural differences, in particular the question: Did being Maori make a difference? The fact that Maori often did not feel that being Maori made a difference cannot be taken to imply that their ethnicity was unimportant; indeed it is likely to have been important for all those involved at all stages of the proceedings, whether for good or ill. Being able to be consciously aware of the impact of one's ethnicity is certainly not a critical test of the importance of ethnicity. Maori families could only judge from their own experience and had no comparative base from which to judge how Pakeha might have felt or been treated in similar circumstances. Thus the replies to these questions may tell us more about awareness of the impact of being Maori than about what being Maori really meant. With hindsight, we would have chosen to ask very different questions to explore this issue.

Pacific Island young people also made up a substantial group in our sample. It was not possible to employ and train researchers from all the ethnic groups included in the study but, in Lower Hutt and Kapiti-Mana, a Samoan researcher attended Family Group Conferences and interviewed Pacific Island families and her comments on what she observed have also informed our discussion.

---

[10] In some cases, Pakeha researchers interviewed the Pakeha victims of Maori offenders and both Maori and Pakeha researchers stood in for one another in case of illness or unavoidable clashes.

The Data

Completeness of the Sample

Although we attempted to obtain a record for every case of contact between the police and a juvenile over the period of the study, the data may be incomplete.

In some cases the contact between a police officer and a young person was minimal and consequently not recorded. For example, an officer may have seen a young person behaving in a suspicious manner but not followed through with a report because of the time that would have been involved and because the outcome would still have been a warning which they themselves could deliver verbally at the time.

A second source of under-reporting may have been staffing shortages which could have led to delays in cases being processed and sent on to Youth Aid or in being reported to us by the Youth Aid officer. We discussed with station commanders and staff the possibility of such problems and in all areas staff indicated their desire to ensure complete coverage so that their work would be accurately represented by the research.

Thus, overall, we are reasonably confident that the vast majority of the offences known to the police which were attributed to a juvenile and which were not trivial in nature were included in the sample.

Analysis of Data

In this study we focused on decisions at four different points: decisions taken by police who may arrest, by Youth Aid officers who may refer for an FGC, by the participants who attend Family Group Conferences, and by the Youth Court which disposes of matters brought to its attention. At each of these decision points the number of cases in the sample was different. Police make their arrest decision each time that they apprehend a young person. Youth Aid made their decision only for those cases referred to them. The Family Group Conference occurred only for a sample of the cases that passed through Youth Aid as well as those who had been arrested and charged in the Youth Court. And, finally, only a small proportion of the original sample ever appeared in the Youth Court. To complicate matters further, the same individual could come into the sample on more than one occasion. However, although the same young person may, for example, have been arrested twice, he or she may only have appeared as a single case in the Youth Court sample and, similarly, a young person who was referred to Youth Aid twice may only have appeared once in the FGC sample and so on.

Thus at each decision point we have based our discussion on a different number of *distinct cases*. A *distinct case* was always defined by the fact that a single resolution was made about the outcome, even though the proceedings may have dealt with a number of different offences and a number of different occasions on which the young person came to attention.

A total of 692 distinct cases came to the attention of the police or were referred by MOT for an FGC or a Youth Court hearing in the five sample areas over the period of the study. From these cases a number of different databases were derived which enabled us to examine the various decisions on which the research focuses.

- **The police decision to arrest:** At the first decision point the database comprised a total of 671 distinct cases which came to police attention during the study. A *distinct case* here represents each occasion on which a young person was apprehended by a police officer. Thus it was possible for the same young person to be apprehended several times in the course of the study and comprise several distinct cases. On the other hand, one *distinct case* could involve multiple offences as the young person might have owned up to or been detected in several offences at the one time. Of these 671 distinct police cases, 69 resulted in an arrest and a subsequent charge in the Youth Court, 5 were arrested but referred to Youth Aid without a charge, and the remaining 597 were referred to Youth Aid without an arrest.

- **The Youth Aid officer's decision to refer to an FGC:** At the second decision point, the distinct cases were a subset of the first sample where the young person was not arrested and charged but was referred to the Youth Aid officer. A total of 602 distinct Youth Aid cases were referred to a Youth Aid officer who then made a decision about warning, diversion or referral for an FGC, sometimes after consultation with the Youth Justice Co-ordinator. Of these 602 distinct Youth Aid cases, 187 cases were referred for an FGC.

- **The decisions at the FGC**: At the third decision point, the FGC, the 211 distinct FGC cases derived from three different referral sources: Youth Aid, Ministry of Transport (MOT) and the Youth Court.

  The number of police-referred cases was 126 which was rather less than the 187 cases actually referred for an FGC by the Youth Aid officer. There were a number of reasons for this. The YJC sometimes decided against an FGC and referred the matter back to Youth Aid. More commonly, several different offences, which brought particular young offenders into the police sample on more than one occasion were brought together after the Youth Aid decision-making stage and dealt with at a single FGC.

  Sometimes an FGC was adjourned and several meetings were held, but these were regarded as making up a single *distinct case* because the earlier meetings did not result in a resolution of matters. Similarly, both MOT and the Youth Court sometimes referred several matters to a single FGC or a series of FGC meetings.

  For 203 of these 211 distinct cases, the FGC was held, although in three cases the FGC did not lead to a conclusion because all matters were denied. Subsequently the police reviewed these cases and, in all three, laid charges in the Youth Court which led to defended hearings. Of the eight cases where no FGC was held, five were not arranged by DSW before the conclusion of this study and three went straight to the Youth Court without an FGC because an FGC had been held recently and the Youth Court considered that the family had already considered the options. These included two cases where the family had made specific recommendations that the matter should be referred directly to the Youth Court in the event of reoffending.

- **The decisions of the Youth Court**: At the fourth decision point, a total of 70 distinct cases, coming from the police and/or the MOT, appeared before the Youth Court. Of these 70 distinct Youth Court cases, 55 had at some stage involved a police arrest, nine came by way of a police summons after an FGC and five came from an MOT arrest or summons. One case came as a referral from the District Court when it was recognised that one of the offences with which the defendant had been charged had been committed while he was still a juvenile.

  A *distinct case* at the Youth Court sometimes incorporated a number of distinct cases from earlier decision points:

  - as we have already noted, a single individual may have been subject to multiple arrests before his or her case was resolved
  - Youth Court cases sometimes brought together cases involving arrests or summons by both the police and MOT
  - in some cases, because the young person was already appearing in court, subsequent offences referred to the Youth Aid officer were laid by way of summons in the court and dealt with along with the other matters.

  Furthermore a case which was not initially laid in the Youth Court could later appear for the following reasons:

  - when an FGC agreed that a court order was the best way of dealing with offending, the case would be laid by summons in the Youth Court
  - when the FGC was unable to agree, the case was also likely to be laid in the Youth Court by way of summons
  - when the offence was denied at an FGC and the charge had not already been laid in the Youth Court, it was subsequently likely to be laid by way of summons.

The sketch diagram in Figure 2.1 summarises the ways in which cases entered each of the databases used in the study.

Figure 2.1
Sketch Diagram Indicating the ways in which Cases Entered the Sample and Entered into each of the Databases

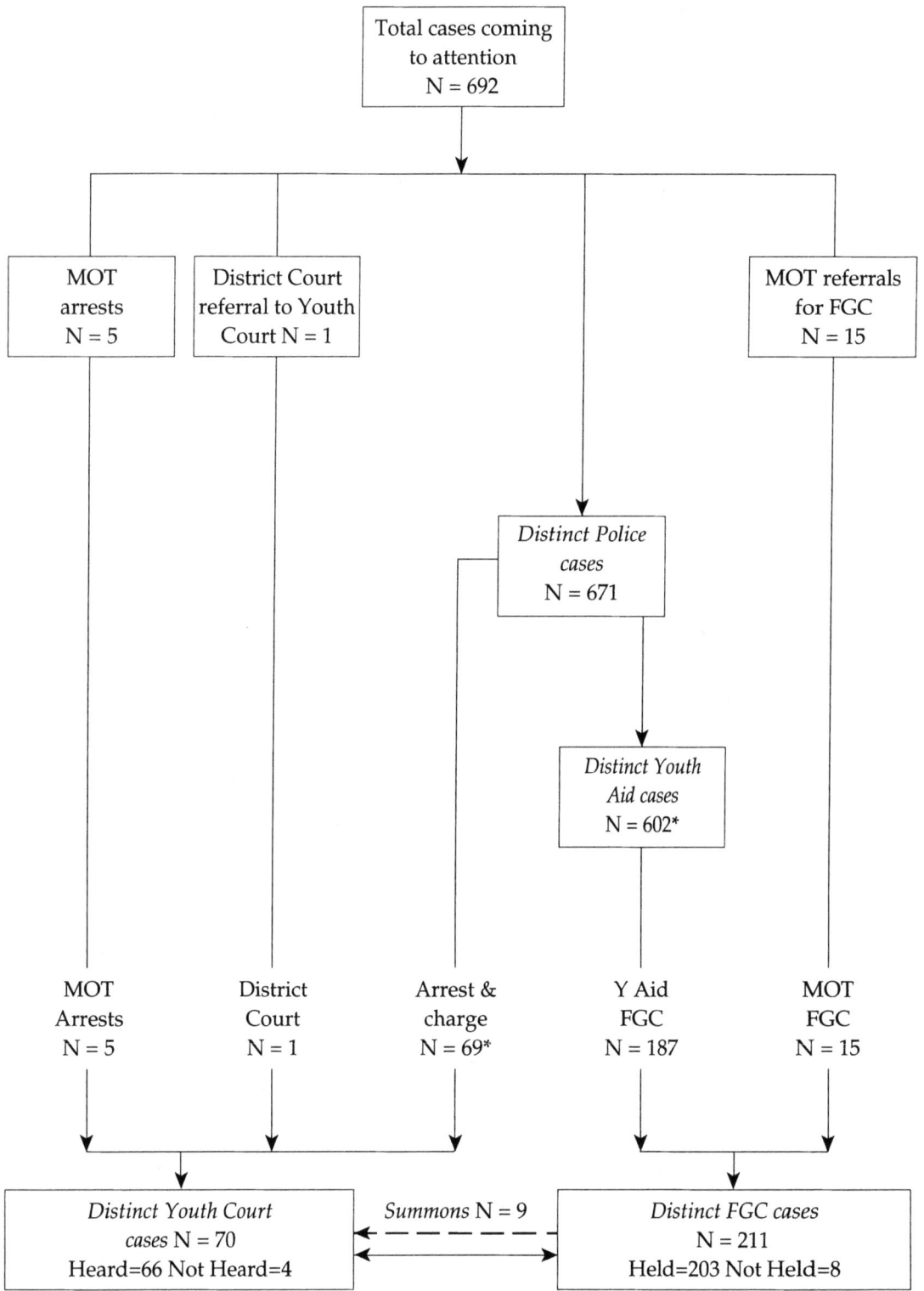

* One arrest case and two FGC cases were transferred to another district before the Court hearing or the FGC was finalised. These therefore do not appear in the Youth Court or FGC samples.

It is important to recognise that MOT cases do not form part of the databases that were used to examine police decisions but that these cases came into both the FGC and the Youth Court databases. Moreover, the Youth Court cases were derived both from all the police and MOT arrest cases and also from cases referred by way of a summons. In some cases, a summons was issued after the FGC had been held, so that some cases which were originally shown as Youth Aid referrals for an FGC later became Youth Court cases by way of a summons. Matters are further complicated by the fact that sometimes, as described above, different distinct cases at one level were brought together as a single distinct case at another level and that some cases were referred by both police and MOT.

The reader may wish to have more detail on how cases entered and left each of the separate databases. Rather than provide this detail here where it is inevitably abstracted from a discussion of the details of the decision-making processes, we have chosen to present the information in the subsequent chapters where the meaning of the ways in which matters were handled can be clarified.

Police Arrest and Charge Cases

Of the 692 total cases coming to attention from all sources, 74 entered the sample initially via a police arrest. Of these cases, five did not involve a subsequent charge in court but were referred on to Youth Aid. Of these five cases, Youth Aid referred two for an FGC, warned two and diverted one (ie arranged a sanction with the family). An additional five arrests which resulted in charges were made by MOT. Overall, 11% of the total police cases coming to attention (74 cases) involved an arrest and a subsequent charge in the Youth Court, although, because of multiple arrests of the same individual, these make up only 60 of the *distinct Youth Court cases*. Thus ten offenders were arrested on more than one occasion during the study; eight were arrested twice, one was arrested three times and one five times.

Statistical Methods

The main analysis of the data was done using the StatView statistical package. Tests of statistical significance of the differences between the percentages in different groups have been based throughout on the use of a chi-squared test. Allowances have been made for unusual distributions by aggregating similar categories when the expected values were less than 10, by deleting infrequently used categories or by using the correction for continuity available in StatView. Comparisons of differences between the means of groups have used a t test. The step-wise regression procedure in StatView or the 'logistic' procedure in SAS has been used, as appropriate, in the regression analyses. Simple correlations use the product moment formula. Statistical significance has been, unless otherwise stated, set at the 1% level.

Throughout the report, the procedure normally followed has been to report differences between groups or areas only when they are statistically significant. A technical appendix (Appendix 4) presents additional tables of raw numbers that would enable statements about statistically significant differences to be checked (except where providing numbers would allow particular areas to be identified) and which sets out the detailed results of the regression analyses.

Percentages have normally been rounded to a whole number. In some instances, rounding has resulted in the percentages adding to 99 or 101 rather than 100.

Area Differences

A total of 692 distinct cases entered the sample either as a case dealt with by the police (671 cases), as a referral from the District Court (one case) or as a referral for an FGC or to Court by the MOT (20 cases). Table 2.1 below sets out the number of police cases in each area and compares these figures with the total population aged 10 to 16 years in each of the sample areas. The variation between areas in the rate (based on the juvenile population of each area) of young offenders coming to notice is not statistically significant. In fact, the offence rate per 10,000 juvenile population is remarkably similar in all five areas.

Table 2.1

Distinct Police Cases in Each Area During The Sample Period Showing Percentage in Each Area Compared With Total Population Aged 10-16 and Showing Detected Offence Rate Per 10,000 Population Aged 10-16

Area	Number in sample	Rate per 10,000 population aged 10-16	% sample by area	% population by area
Henderson	161	140	24	24
Kapiti-Mana	156	134	23	25
Lower Hutt	184	153	27	25
Masterton	97	153	14	13
Christchurch	73	115	11	13
Total	671	140	100	100

The table shows that over the three month period of the study there was an offence rate among the juveniles of 140 per 10,000. Extrapolating to a whole year would give a figure of 560 which is somewhat higher than the national rate for 1988 of 387 per 10,000. The discrepancy could reflect our focus on urban areas. Another possibility is that we are recording more of the minor offences than would normally get on to the police computer system.

Ethnicity

Maori and Pacific Islanders are over-represented in known crime data. The pattern reported nationally (which is discussed in greater detail in Appendix 3) was almost exactly replicated in the sample of young people coming to police attention. In 1988, 43% of young offenders were Maori and 43% of our sample were Maori. Table 2.2 shows that Maori made up 15% of the juvenile population in our sample areas but the proportion in the police sample was nearly three times that figure. The proportion of Pacific Island young people in the police sample was about double what would be expected on the basis of population figures. The over-representation of Maori juveniles is more marked in the FGC sample than in the general police sample and is higher again in the Youth Court sample. However, the proportion of Pacific Island young people in the police and FGC samples was similar and the proportion dropped slightly in the Youth Court sample.

Table 2.2

Ethnicity of Sample Coming to Police Attention, Being Referred For FGC and Appearing in the Youth Court Compared to Population Figures; Percentages[11]

Ethnicity	Population in Sample areas %	Distinct Police Cases %	FGC Referrals %	Youth Court appearances %
Pakeha	74	40	40	39
Maori	15	43	45	50
Pacific Island	8	16	15	11
Other	3	1	0	0

In terms of area, the proportion of Maori young people coming to police attention was, as Table 2.3 shows, higher than would be expected in the Lower Hutt, Masterton and Christchurch areas, whereas a relatively smaller proportion of Maori young people came to police attention in Kapiti-Mana. These differences are much greater than would be expected by chance[12], but we can offer

---

[11] Throughout, unless otherwise stated, the percentages in the tables sum to 100 in columns.

[12] Chi-squared =20, df=4, p<.001.

no definite explanation for them. One possible explanation suggested by our Maori team was that the strength of the community and the relative number of tangata whenua (local Maori people) and tauahire (Maori from outside the local area) may be a factor. The distribution of Pacific Island young people coming to attention was, however, much as would be expected from the size of Pacific Island population in each area (although the numbers are small).

The differences in the number of Maori appearing in different areas and the increase in their representation in the youth justice system as the gravity of the consequences increases raise questions about whether or not Maori offending patterns are different from other groups, whether or not Maori are treated differently from other ethnic groups by those making decisions, and whether or not Maori respond differently to their experiences of the youth justice system because of cultural differences. These issues will be developed in subsequent chapters.

Table 2.3
Numbers of Maori in The Police Sample in Each Area Compared With Expected Numbers Based on Population of Each Area[13]

Area	Actual Numbers From Police	Expected Numbers Based on Population
Henderson	68	73
Kapiti-Mana	58	86
Lower Hutt	91	74
Masterton	46	37
Christchurch	24	16

Attending FGCs and Interviewing Families, Young People and Victims

It was rare for families to refuse permission for the researchers to attend their FGC. We attended at least one FGC for 80% of cases. The most common reason for non-attendance was that the social worker omitted to notify the researcher of the time of the FGC. Over half of the families whose FGC was not attended by a researcher were nevertheless willing to be interviewed when contacted independently by a researcher. Other reasons for non-attendance at FGCs by the researchers were illness and, in three cases, a mis-match of iwi descent between the family and the researcher. Table 2.4 sets out attendance at the FGC by area and shows the proportion of different participants who were interviewed by the researchers.

Table 2.4
Percentages of Parents, Young People and Victims Interviewed in each Area and Percentage of Cases where at least one FGC was Attended

Area	A	B	C	D	E	Total	
Person Interviewed	%	%	%	%	%	N	%
Parents	79	87	80	87	84	176	84
Young People	72	74	72	72	88	157	75
Victims	81	82	74	88	65	149	81
FGCs attended	79	76	88	74	90	162	80

---

[13] This calculation of expected numbers assumes the total number of Maori in our sample was distributed according to the distribution of the Maori population across the five areas: ie 6% of the Maori in the sample could be expected to have come from Christchurch, 30% from Kapiti-Mana, 26% from Lower Hutt, 13% from Masterton and 25% from Henderson.

Overall, the response rate to requests for an interview was relatively high: 84% of parents and 75% of young people involved in the FGC process agreed to be interviewed (see Table 2.4). The proportion of young people who were interviewed tended to be lower compared to parents because young people had sometimes moved to another area or were in custody in another area. The proportion agreeing to be interviewed was slightly higher for Pakeha (87%) and Pacific Island parents (94%) than for Maori parents (79%) and slightly higher for Pakeha young people (79%) than for Pacific Island (71%) and Maori young people (71%).

There were some differences in response rates between the areas ranging from 87% to 79% for interviews with parents, from 88% to 72% for interviews with young people and from 90% to 74% for attendance at FGCs. Of course, we have no way of knowing how representative the experience of those who agreed to be interviewed was. They could, for example, have been those most or least satisfied with the youth justice process. Nevertheless, the response rates are sufficiently high to give reasonable cause for confidence in the representativeness of the data. Interviews were carried out by interviewers of the same ethnicity as the respondents wherever this was possible.

We were able to make contact with and interview a victim (sometimes more than one) in 81% of the cases which involved a victim (see Table 2.4). This figure ranged from 88% to 65% across the five areas. The main reason for this variation was that in some areas there was insufficient information on the files from which to try to determine the whereabouts of the victim. Where the offence was committed outside the local area, for example, full details about the victim might not have been forwarded to the local police or to the Youth Aid section. Of course, some of the victims approached declined to be interviewed. YJCs and Youth Aid officers were interviewed in connection with almost all cases.

Where the researchers were unable to attend the FGC and where the family did not agree to be interviewed, we were nevertheless able to obtain information from police and DSW files.

Chapter 3
THE POLICE DECISION TO ARREST

Introduction

The new legislation emphasises the avoidance of criminal proceedings and sets out the procedures to be used. It aims to reduce the number of young people who go through an arrest procedure by setting down criteria for arrest. It tries to minimise the extent to which young people are placed in custody pending a hearing, again by setting out criteria. It emphasises due process and formally delineates the rights of young people, when they are questioned or arrested. The police use of a variety of diversionary processes has been legitimated and the standard police instructions on obtaining evidential statements have been codified in law. This and the following chapter examine the extent to which current practice reflects the legislative intentions.

As described in Chapter 1, the response to an incident is decided on two main levels. First the investigating officer, sometimes in consultation with his or her supervising officer, will make a decision whether or not to arrest and charge the young person. Alternatively the investigating officer may decide that there are insufficient grounds for arrest, or, in some cases where the arrest has already been made, that there are insufficient grounds to charge the young person. In these cases, the file, together with any recommendation from the investigating officer, will normally be passed to the Youth Aid section for a decision. It is these two decision points, the decision to arrest and the decision by Youth Aid, that are the focus of this part of the study. This chapter deals with the arrest decision and Youth Aid decisions are dealt with in Chapter 5.

As well as these decisions that determine the future handling of the case, the investigating officer will be responsible for the immediate practical steps including questioning the young person, taking any statement that could be later used in evidence, contacting parents or arranging for detention of the young person in custody. These matters are discussed in Chapter 4.

Before presenting the information from the sample studied in the research, this chapter examines national statistical information on how decisions have been made since the Act came into force and compares the data for 1990 with data collected before the Act. Information is presented on the number of young people arrested, area differences in arrest rates, the reasons given for the arrest, the characteristics of those arrested, and the types of offences for which they were arrested. Wherever possible comparisons are made between periods before and after the Act.

National Statistical Data On Arrest Cases [14]

Numbers of Arrests

Statistics on the method of disposal of cases involving juveniles are compiled separately for arrests and for all other processes. Arrest cases tend to involve the more serious offences and will usually involve a court appearance, while other cases can be handled by diversion from the start and most do not result in court appearances.

We have been able to examine arrest data on juveniles for the calendar year 1990. During this time, 1,510 juveniles were arrested. This represents only 5% of all detected juvenile offenders. Such a percentage is in sharp contrast with the figure quoted by Morgan in an internal police report that 29% of juveniles were arrested in a sample taken from 1984 records. Morgan's data are consistent with that of Morris and Young (1987) who commented that, in 1984, arrests of juveniles were common and comprised at least a third of a sample taken from police records in selected districts.

---

[14] These data come from information compiled at Police Headquarters based on the returns made by arresting officers to the Police Commissioner. These are commonly referred to as *YOUTH.

Area Differences

The number arrested varies in different police areas and this variation is not accounted for by differences in the number of offenders being detected. For instance, Table 3.1 shows that arrest rates in the Auckland, Kapiti-Mana and Christchurch districts can be estimated at about 4-5% compared to figures of over 7% for Wellington and the Hutt districts. These figures can be compared with the national average which, as stated above, is just under 5%.

Table 3.1
Police Arrest Rates For Juvenile Offenders in Selected Areas; 1990

District/Station	Number of Arrests	Number of Offences Cleared	%
Auckland Central	103	2,308	5
Christchurch	67	1,597	4
Auckland West	37	809	5
Hutt*	121	1,644	7
Kapiti-Mana	38	954	4
Wellington	66	926	7
New Zealand	1,510	32,819	5

Source: Unpublished police statistics.
* Masterton is included in these figures.

Reasons For Arrests

The grounds for the arrest of a juvenile offender are more limited than for an adult and are set out in section 214 of the Children, Young Persons and Their Families Act 1989. These grounds are: to ensure the appearance of the young person at the Youth Court, to prevent the commission of other offences, to prevent the loss or destruction of evidence or interference with witnesses, when it is required in the public interest and when the offence is purely indictable. It is clearly the intention of the Act that arrest followed by a charge in the Youth Court should be used very sparingly so that the opportunity is given to settle matters through an FGC rather than involving young people and their families in court proceedings.

The 1990 national data show that two main reasons were given by the police for arresting juveniles: to prevent further offending (53%) and to ensure the juvenile's appearance at court (31%). The next most common reason cited was 'to prevent interference with witness or evidence' (7%). Figure 3.1 sets out this information graphically.

Figure 3.1
Reasons for Arrest of Juveniles; Percentages; 1990

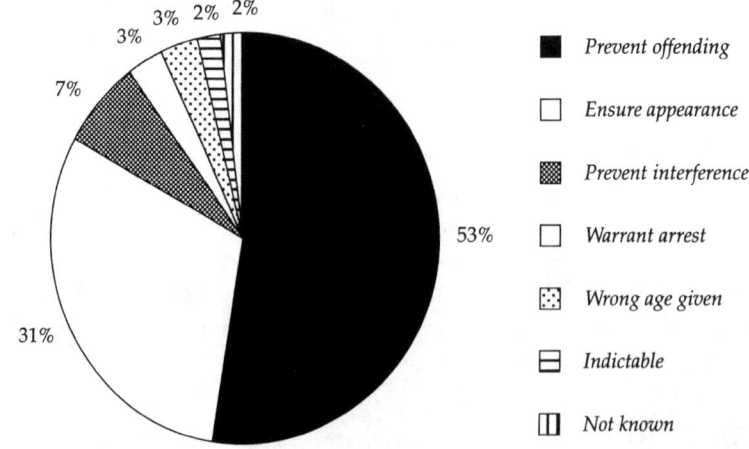

Source: Unpublished police statistics.

Characteristics Of Those Arrested And Types Of Offences Committed

A further analysis of data on the arrested juveniles in the first full year after the Act shows that these offenders were more likely to be male, older and to have committed more serious offences (such as offences against the person) than those dealt with by the police in other ways. Eighty three per cent of those arrested were male. More than half (56%) were 16 years old; only 1% were under 14.

The offences most commonly committed by those arrested were burglary (28%) and car conversion (20%). Less than 1% were alleged to have committed sex offences; 4% were alleged to have committed robberies; and 12% were alleged to have committed assaults or to have assaulted the police. These results are depicted in Figure 3.2. Boys and girls were generally arrested for similar types of offences though the boys were more likely to be arrested for burglary, robbery or assault and the girls were more likely to be arrested for drug offences.

Figure 3.2
Type of Offences for Arrest Cases: Total Juveniles; 1990

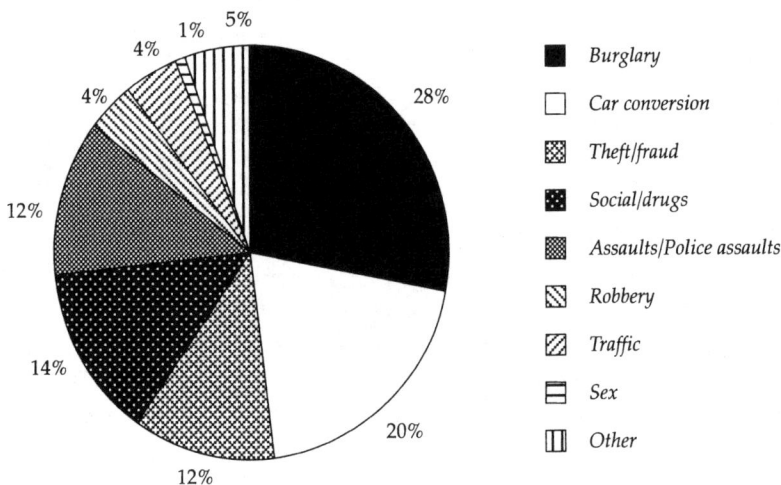

Source: Unpublished police statistics

The Research Sample

Number of Arrests

A total of 75 police cases which involved an arrest came into our sample and this represents 11% of the police cases coming to notice. However only 69 cases involved both an arrest **and** a charge. In another five cases an arrest was made but no charge was laid and matters were referred to Youth Aid section. Another case was originally referred to the Youth Court as a result of a District Court summons and the offender was later arrested on a warrant when he failed to appear. This case has not been included among the arrest cases in the sample as the decision to arrest was not taken at the time he was apprehended.

Thus, the total number arrested **and** charged represented 10% of the police cases and this is twice the national figure for 1990 of 5%. The discrepancy can be accounted for in a number of ways. The first three possibilities relate to the consequences of our sampling strategy while the second two raise issues about the completeness of the data collection.

First, it is possible that the districts we sampled are different from the national pattern. The 1990 statistics given in Table 3.1 above show that this is the case. Three of the four police districts involved in our study had higher percentages of arrests than the national average and an estimate based on data shown in Table 3.1 suggests that the official police statistics for our areas for the whole of 1990 would have shown an arrest rate of 5.2% rather than the 4.6% national average.

But the problem extends beyond that of the selection of the areas for the study as is shown by the data in Table 3.2 below, which sets out the actual number of arrests over our sample period in each area and compares the arrest rate with the annual figures quoted in Table 3.1.

Table 3.2
Sample Arrest Numbers and Percentages by Area Compared With Annual Totals For 1990

	Sample Number	Sample %	Total 1990 %
Henderson	9	6	5
Kapiti-Mana	12	8	4
Lower Hutt*	25	14	
Masterton*	9	9	
Hutt District			7
Christchurch	14	19	4
Total	69	10.3	4.6

* Both Lower Hutt and Masterton police stations are in the Hutt police district.

Table 3.2 clearly indicates a considerable discrepancy between the annual data for our areas and our own sample data, particularly in Christchurch, Lower Hutt and Kapiti-Mana where we have recorded considerably higher arrest rates.

A second reason for the discrepancy lies in the extent to which our sample areas did not coincide exactly with the police districts. The Hutt district data combine data from 3 stations – Masterton, Upper Hutt and Lower Hutt. It is generally believed by the police that arrest rates are lower in Upper Hutt which is not part of our sample, so that the figures for Lower Hutt and Masterton could be expected to exceed the 1990 total for the Hutt district. In the Auckland West District, we excluded the New Lynn station which generally had a lower arrest rate than Henderson. In Christchurch, the Youth Aid area differed from the Christchurch police district and this may have resulted in a discrepancy between our sample, which was based on the central city area, and the district figures quoted in Table 3.1.

Third, there may have been an increase over time in the proportion of juveniles being arrested. The figure of 4.6% is for the calendar year of 1990, whereas an analysis carried out by Youth Aid staff at Police Headquarters shows that arrests for the year from 1 July 1990 to 30 June 1991 was 7.7%.

Fourth, there are problems with the completeness of the police arrest data. Our data came from a weekly search of the Charge Book in the police station in each study area which was unlikely to produce false positives, ie counting cases that do not exist. Police data depend on each police station reporting all arrests to Headquarters and this could have resulted in false negatives, ie overlooking cases that do exist. Over the period of the study, only half of the arrests which came into our sample were recorded in Police Headquarters[15]. Thus Police Headquarters data, almost certainly, seriously underestimate the arrest rate.

Fifth, it is possible that our sample underestimates the number of cases being dealt with by the use of police diversionary processes because of our method of data collection. Our data were collected either from the Charge Book or from Youth Aid officers. In theory, all juvenile offence files, other than arrests, should be referred to Youth Aid. However, it is possible that some minor matters were cleared and entered on the computer directly by the officer in charge of the case without being referred to Youth Aid. It is also possible that in some instances the Youth Aid officer overlooked passing cases on to us. While we would have picked up any FGC or court cases from DSW or the Youth Court, we had no way of checking the completeness of the sample of cases dealt with by the police in diversionary ways.

---

[15] Data were kindly supplied by Youth Aid section at Police Headquarters.

Thus, in summary, our sample shows a considerably higher arrest rate than the national 1990 figure based on police statistics. This is due in part to the fact that arrest rates in the districts chosen for study are higher than the national average, in part to the fact that the areas we studied and the districts on which 1990 data are available do not exactly coincide, in part to the fact that arrest rates probably rose in the latter part of 1990, in part to an underestimate of arrests in the police statistics and possibly in part to an omission from our sample of some of the less serious cases which were handled by warnings.

Area Differences

The area differences in the arrest rates shown in Table 3.2 are considerable and this finding of district variation is substantiated by the national figures for 1990 quoted in Table 3.1. In the study the percentage of arrests ranged from a low of 6% in Henderson to highs of 14% in Lower Hutt and 19% in Christchurch.

One possible reason for the variation in arrest percentages across areas is the nature of the offences. It is possible that more serious offending is likely to occur in urban as opposed to rural areas, for instance, and thus arrest rates could be expected to be lower in a rural area such as Masterton. One way of examining seriousness of offences is to compare offences against property and good order with offences against persons on the grounds that the latter are generally viewed more severely and result in heavier penalties. But this is a very crude measure as it does not take into account the fact that burning down a school, for instance, is a much more serious offence than giving someone a black eye in a fight. Another strategy for rating seriousness has been to use average length of custodial sentence as a criterion (Spier, Luketina & Kettles, 1991) but that also has problems in a study like ours, as the gravity of the actual offence can vary enormously even though the charge is the same; for example, a burglary could involve many thousand dollars worth of property or simply some sweets and soft drinks. Thus we developed a five-point scale on which all the actual offences in the sample were rated. Details of the rating procedure are described in Appendix 2. Using these ratings of seriousness, it is possible to examine the extent to which the variations in arrest rate across areas can be explained by differences in the relative seriousness of offending in different parts of the country.

Table 3.3 sets out the percentage of cases in the total sample and the percentage of arrest cases which were rated medium or higher in seriousness for each area. It also shows the arrest percentage for each area.

Table 3.3[16]

Seriousness of All Offences (N=669) and of Arrest Cases (N=68) Only by Area; Showing Percentage Rated Medium, Medium/Maximum, or Maximum Seriousness and Percentage Arrested For Each Area

Serious %	Henderson	Kapiti-Mana	Lower Hutt	Masterton	Christchurch
All cases	45	30	52	31	33
Arrest only	89	91	64	56	62
Arrest %	6	8	14	9	19

The data in Table 3.3 show that two areas, Lower Hutt and Henderson, have a higher proportion of relatively serious cases. However, while Lower Hutt also has a high percentage of arrests of young people, Henderson has the lowest percentage of young people arrested. The figures on the seriousness of arrest cases show a very wide fluctuation across the five areas. In Kapiti-Mana and Henderson, about 90% of the arrest cases involved relatively serious offending. But in the other

---

[16] Note, there are some missing data which means that Ns quoted in the tables are sometimes less than the number in the sample.

three areas, Christchurch, Lower Hutt and Masterton, only about 60% of the arrest cases involved relatively serious offending. Thus it is clear that the gravity of offences which lead to arrests differs widely from one area to another.

The Reasons For Arrest

The fact that there are considerable differences in the rate of arrests across districts and that these differences do not correspond to differences in the relative seriousness of offences suggests that policies may not be operating uniformly. Furthermore, it may be possible that, rather than using arrest simply to minimise the chances of reoffending and escaping, in some districts some police may be using arrest as a method of ensuring that more serious offences get to court and the more serious offenders experience more rigorous scrutiny (as found by Morris and Young, 1987). Also, the use of arrest 'to prevent reoffending' is a matter which calls for a judgement by the arresting officer. Thus a close examination of the reasons given for an arrest is important.

The data on the reasons for arrest come principally from interviews with the arresting officer. However, the information we have here is limited. No interviews were conducted in Masterton due to limitations on the researcher's time (nine cases), the arresting officer was not always available in the other areas (eight cases), the arrest was made outside the sample areas in nine cases and not all questions were always answered. In all cases of missing data, we attempted to supplement the responses with information from the police files and from the *YOUTH return made to Police Headquarters. For these reasons, the data in this section should be treated as illustrating the type of factors that are important in the arrest decision rather than the absolute importance of particular reasons.

Table 3.4 presents the reasons given for the arrest of young people. The reason most commonly cited for an arrest under section 214 of the Children, Young Persons and Their Families Act 1989 was to prevent reoffending. This was given as a reason in 61% of the sample cases. To ensure appearance was given as a reason in a third of cases. Other reasons were less common. These figures are reasonably similar to those given above for the national statistics for 1990, especially when we take into account that the number in our sample is relatively small, that the national data include some don't knows which were excluded from the study percentages, that the national data include only one reason while multiple reasons could be recorded in our results, and that arrests by warrant were excluded from our sample.

Table 3.4
Reasons for Arrest of Young Person; Distinct Arrest Cases For Which Reasons Were Given; Numbers and Percentages; N=57[17]

Reason	N	%
Prevent Reoffending	35	61
Ensure Appearance	18	32
Purely Indictable	8	14
Protect Evidence	6	11
Wrong Age	4	7
Protect a Witness	1	2

The interviews with the arresting officers helped to explain how the arrest actually occurred and the factors that were actually considered. But first it is worth noting the context in which the arrest decision usually occurs. Most arrests arise in the course of apprehending an offender at or near the scene of the crime. Nearly 80% of the arrest cases in our sample can be categorised in this way. Some of the comments of arresting officers which explain matters further are given below. While some

---

[17] Multiple reasons were given in 13 cases.

quotes indicate that arrest appeared to be clearly justified, others illustrate a liberal interpretation of 'prevention of reoffending' and the importance to officers of ensuring court appearances in some of the cases. We have organised the comments under headings for each of the main grounds for arrest:

To prevent reoffending and ensure appearance

> *It was the same thing two weeks running. He was found on the street preparing to commit a burglary, with other known burglars. He is wanted in Auckland on other offences.*

> *It was a serious assault on a taxi driver. He was placed in DSW custody to ensure appearance and to stop reoffending.*

> *The offence was an attempted burglary. He admitted to 20+ other offences. His lawyer agreed at court to keep him in DSW custody 'because of the nature and extent of offending'. The court put him in his foster mothers' custody but he decamped. Then he was given into DSW care again but he escaped from the social worker. When he was apprehended again, he was put in (a residence) but he escaped that night. Further offences were committed. If I didn't arrest him he would have broken into somewhere else. It was the number of offences rather than just the offence.*

> *He was interviewed at DSW in the presence of a social worker. I didn't arrest then as he would have had to have been kept in the police cells because it was a purely indictable matter and only the court can give bail. I made the arrest on the next day and then we went to court. It was a serious offence and he was already on bail for a similar offence. The arrest was a means of getting the matter before the court.*

> *I made the arrest because the young person had no fixed abode.*

> *He was not living at home so I arrested him.*

To prevent the loss or destruction of evidence

> *This arrest was because of a refusal to accompany an officer after a breath test.*

> *I made the arrest because property was still outstanding and may be disposed of.*

> *I made the arrest before they could concoct a story.*

Purely indictable

> *This is a serious matter and it is indictable (sexual violation). He abused a position of trust. I wanted to get him away from the victim's sight. She is a neighbour and he has hassled her before.*

> *It is a very serious matter (rape) and was traumatic, especially for one victim. He is a risk to other women. I think reoffending is likely because of the serious nature of the offence and he admits to an earlier attempted rape as well.*

> *I thought the offence was purely indictable (sexual violation) but if I arrested him straight away it would have meant a night in the cells so I sent him home and arranged to see him next day. Then I decided on the arrest charge because it was a serious matter and he was already on bail for a similar offence.*

The only other category of note in the official record was 'insufficient information because the offender gave a wrong age' (or refused to give this information and/or was assumed to be over 16). This led to eight arrests, but only four of these cases led to a subsequent charge and court appearance. Comments from the arresting officers give further insight into how these situations arose:

> *He told me he was 17 and so he was arrested. He later said that he had given the wrong age because he wanted to be processed quickly.*

> *Originally he gave his age as 19 – otherwise he may not have been arrested. He gave three different names.*

I believed she was over 17 years – those others who were also involved in the offence and who claimed to be under 17 were not arrested. The parents were notified when it was found she was a young person. She wanted to be with her mates, I suppose. She gave false names. I told her she wouldn't be released until she could establish her identity, then someone recognised her. She was held for three to four hours but was not interviewed. I released her into her mother's custody.

Information From Interviews With The Arresting Officer

When we interviewed the officers they sometimes gave other reasons for arrest, including the fact that the young person was wanted regarding other offences on a warrant or that they had not completed previous FGC tasks:

I feel on this occasion we should make an attempt to have all of these matters referred back to the court, as I believe T requires a short, sharp stay in [a residence]. (This officer made no reference to any arrest criteria.) The reason for the arrest was that he was not carrying out the community work recommended from the previous FGC; so there is no point in having another FGC – he won't carry out recommendations. Whatever they come up with, we want [supervision with residence]. He was arrested so that matters can go before court.

He was coming up for an FGC at the time of this offence.

Sometimes the reasons were a mixture of the grounds set down in the Act and other reactions:

This was a theft of wine valued at $25. He is an 'out and out thief and burglar'. He was arrested after consultation with Youth Aid who suggested arrest because of other recent offences.

She was arrested because she refused to tell the police her name or address. Her mother has an anti-police attitude.

There was a warrant for uncompleted FGC tasks prior to this one. He absconded from [a residence] and was then arrested for a minor theft.

The victim had placed great store on his bike [which had been stolen by the young person]. [The young person] was arrested for care & protection reasons. He was 'not under proper control'. His mother seemed not to care where he was, what he was doing. There was also no guarantee they would see he got to court. His mother did not know what day it was and so we wanted the grandparents consulted. But they were in the pub and when they arrived at the police station finally they were drunk.

It was a matter of form so that DSW and the police can keep the young person in custody until court. He is currently at [a residence]. The police want a corrective training sentence as he has not done the tasks from his previous FGCs.

When he was located, the evidence was clear. He gave false names ... and was held for some time before his statement was taken. This may have been due to the false names or to the time of day [it was early morning].

Sometimes the inability to find someone to take care of the young person was cited but not all these cases resulted in a charge and a court appearance:

The parents were unable or unwilling to collect the young person until morning. (not charged)

I went to his mother's place – she didn't want anything to do with him. I would have left him with the mother if she had been willing to have him – there is no father – she can't handle him. I wouldn't have left him as the mother had no control and the young person was intoxicated. I thought there might be reoffending as the building was insecure. (charged)

I had a problem finding relatives as the first lot didn't want anything to do with him. There was no-one to bail him to so we kept him overnight. In the morning he went to court and then to [a residence]. (charged)

> *She was swearing at the police who were trying to deal with a domestic incident. I had to break up the situation, the harassment was interfering with them dealing with the original fight. It was decided to unarrest her when we realised her age. I tried to contact her family but no one was home and she wouldn't give any information to the police. In the end we released her to her sister's boyfriend's care. It was decided to unarrest her because we wanted to keep it out of court. (not charged)*

> *He was kept in the cells overnight as his mother would not pick him up until he was sober. He was not really questioned. (charged)*

It is possible that in some cases the young person was initially arrested because of a misapprehension but when the misapprehension was realised, it did not necessarily result in release:

> *We responded to a report of broken letter boxes (1.30 am). The suspects had run into the bush area nearby and would not come out when called. We sent in dogs and they got some bites. We didn't know they were young people. (charged)*

> *This was his second arrest for drug dealing. (In this case, the information given by the arresting officer was inconsistent with the file. There was no indication of any previous arrest, nor was there any drug-related offence noted on the Youth Aid files. Furthermore, the only evidence was the possession of 3 bullets of cannabis and a pipe; there was no evidence or subsequent charge of drug dealing despite initial suspicions.)*

The view that police attitudes to arrest sometimes reflect resentment about the procedures they were required to follow or disagreement with the principles embodied in the Act is also substantiated by some of their more general comments. Some clearly felt that to arrest juveniles was too much trouble:

> *Carrying out the actual paper work procedure can be a factor in deciding to arrest.*

> *Officers are merely disinterested (sic) due to having too little power under the Act. The attitude sometimes is 'why bother'.*

Others clearly felt that arrest should be the first stage in a general process of crime control through the use of custody:

> *I think we should be able to arrest juveniles and they should be locked up, rather than let out onto the street to commit further crimes.*

> *I feel a curfew should be established in 'dangerous areas' for young people; similar to USA areas. For example there should be no young people in Auckland city after 7 at night. They should be arrested on sight if seen.*

A related attitude comes through some of the earlier quotes, including the first one in this section (see page 32), and that is that arrest gives police more control over both the process and outcome. Arrest ensures that the matter is dealt with by a charge and a court appearance. The arrest is viewed as the necessary first stage of ensuring a custodial result and in this respect there is some similarity with the study we carried out on juvenile justice in 1984 (Morris and Young, 1987).

Although not all arresting officers were able to be interviewed, it is informative to present a statistical analysis of the information obtained from those interviews which we were able to carry out.

Offence Characteristics

Table 3.5 presents information on the offence characteristics that led to the decision to arrest. For 71% of the officers replying, the seriousness of the offending was a factor in deciding to arrest. Next most frequently mentioned was the need to protect the public from offending or from the offender, followed by the impact of the offence on the victim and the particular circumstances of the offence (which might refer to time of day, attempting to run away and so on). In 13% of the cases, the need for reparation, the fact that the offender was intoxicated due to alcohol or drugs or that an adult co-offender was present were given as reasons. It is difficult to reconcile all these reasons with the grounds for arrest spelt out in the Act.

Table 3.5
Offence Characteristics for Police Arrests; Distinct Cases; Numbers and Percentages; N=38[18]

	N	%
Offence seriousness	27	71
Public protection	22	58
Impact on victim	16	42
Circumstances of offence	10	26
Reparation	5	13
Alcohol or drugs	5	13
Adult co-offender	5	13
Other	8	21

Offenders' Characteristics

Table 3.6 presents information on the offenders' characteristics. A history of prior offending was mentioned by about three quarters of the arresting officers interviewed. The two other factors most commonly noted were a poor attitude on the part of the offender and poor family background or support.

Table 3.6
Offenders' Characteristics for Police Arrests; Distinct Cases; Numbers and Percentages; N=38[18]

	N	%
Previous history of offending	29	76
Poor attitude	15	39
Family support/background poor	15	39
Poor potential	11	29
No fixed abode	1	3
Other	7	18

Some quotes provide extra information:

> *It was his attitude – yes – he was very difficult. It was the deciding factor, if he had agreed he had done it, then he would have not been arrested.*

> *He lives with [a named] gang.*

> *We interviewed him for an hour before we got the truth. G is going to be a real problem to the police in the future. Although he is only 14 years of age, he is already showing the traits of an experienced criminal. We are concerned about his father, a recovering alcoholic, with little control of kids.*

While the likelihood of reoffending may indeed be related to previous offence history, family background and attitude, it is unlikely that a general assessment by the officer of the offender on these criteria was what was intended under section 214 of the Act. Although the Act is not explicit about how the probability of reoffending should be assessed, a reasonable interpretation would seem to be based on the need to prevent further offending in the immediate 24 hours following the incident rather than on a general psycho-social assessment of the young person. Nevertheless, the arresting officer's judgement that the young people showed poor potential or came from poor family circumstances was, in many cases, a factor in deciding that the court should become involved – perhaps as a punishment or as a deterrent or simply because this was the strongest option available.

---

[18] Replies have only been used for those cases where there was an interview in which the arresting officer answered all questions and this represents 55% of the arrest cases.

Other Information from Interviews with the Arresting Officer

Arresting officers in most cases consulted with their Senior Sergeant. This was often done to clarify the arrest procedure for young people, as front-line officers typically had little experience with these types of cases. Data from non-arrest cases indicate that in some cases the Senior Sergeant advised that there were not sufficient grounds for arrest.

In a few cases, a Youth Aid officer or a member of DSW staff was contacted for advice, and in at least three cases their advice was to arrest the juvenile:

> *He was arrested after consultation with Youth Aid who suggested arrest because of other recent offences.*
>
> *The second time a DSW worker was contacted as the relatives were not located. She recommended arresting and charging him.*
>
> *He was caught running from the shops with some jeans. The Youth Aid officer recommended arrest and dealt with him from then on.*

Characteristics of Those Arrested

As well as the data on arrests supplied by the front-line officers, it is possible to examine data from the whole police sample in order to compare the arrest and the non-arrest cases. The information we have been able to record can be divided into two categories: information normally available to the officer at the time the decision was made and information not necessarily available at the time of the arrest decision or which is itself a consequence of the decision to arrest and charge.

Information Available at the Time of the Decision to Arrest

Information available at the time of the arrest decision includes the sex and ethnicity of the offender, whether or not there were co-offenders, the time the offence was committed and the type of offence. In addition, officers will usually have an impression of the offender's age, which is likely to be reasonably accurate, and will take into account their own view of the seriousness of the offence (this latter will not necessarily be exactly in keeping with our rating of seriousness but is likely to be reasonably similar).

Table 3.7 shows that all these factors, except the presence of co-offenders, were significantly related to the decision to arrest. Boys were more likely than girls to be arrested. The older the offender and the later the time at which the offence was committed, the more likely there was to be an arrest. These findings are consistent with the national statistics which show that boys and older offenders were more likely to be arrested. The findings also point to a factor not available in the national data: the likelihood of an arrest was related to the time of day.

Figure 3.2 presents national statistics on the type of offences committed by young people and showed a similar pattern to the data for our sample. Most of the discrepancies between national figures and our results can be accounted for by the relatively small number of arrests in our sample and the fact that we have only recorded the most serious offence while the national data include all offences. The largest discrepancy is that we record relatively few drug and anti-social offences (4% compared with 14% nationally for boys), but even this could be attributable to chance, especially as arrests on these matters often involved groups arrested at the same time.

When we compared arrest and non-arrest cases on type of offence, we found that offences against the person (ie assault, robbery and sexual offences) were more likely to lead to an arrest than property offences and offences against good order.[19] The one exception to that was that burglary was also more likely to lead to an arrest than other property offences and offences against order. In addition, our ratings of seriousness of offences allowed a more detailed analysis of the impact of the seriousness of the offence on the arrest decision. Maximum seriousness offences made up 15%

---

[19] 28% of those who committed offences against the person were arrested and 23% of those who committed burglaries compared with 11% of all young offenders in the sample (see Appendix 4).

of the arrest sample compared to only one percent of the non arrest sample. The arrest sample also had more offences that were of medium seriousness compared to the non arrest sample. Ten percent of arrest cases were, surprisingly, classified as minimum seriousness, a finding which we explore more fully later.

Table 3.7
Comparison of Arrest* With Non-arrest Cases on Information Available at Time of Arrest Decision; Distinct Police Cases Aged 14-16; Percentages; N=462

	Arrest (N=69)[20] %	Non-arrest (N=393) %
Sex		
Boys	88	78
Girls	12	22
Ethnicity		
Maori	62	38
Pakeha	28	45
Pacific Island Polynesian	10	17
Age		
14	9	30
15	36	35
16	55	35
Seriousness		
Minimum	10	51
Medium/Minimum	21	11
Medium	51	36
Medium/Maximum	3	2
Maximum	15	1
Time of offence		
Daytime (ie before 6pm)	42	68
Evening (ie 6pm–11pm)	18	14
Night (ie 11pm–6am)	40	18
Co-offenders		
None	46	39
With one other	32	34
With 2 or more others	22	27
Type of Offence		
Assaults/robbery/sex	22	10
Burglary	29	17
Car conversion	16	13
Theft/fraud etc.	16	41
Social/drugs	4	5
Other including traffic	12	14

* Includes only those arrest cases where there was a subsequent charge in the Youth Court.

---

[20] The Ns in this and the following two tables represent the maximum number of cases. Some information is missing on some variables so that actual Ns are sometimes slightly smaller. Full details are included in the technical appendix. (Appendix 4)

Finally, there was a clear finding that Maori were more likely to be arrested than Pakeha. There was no significant difference in the percentage of Pacific Island Polynesians arrested compared to Pakeha but the sample size was small. Later we present a more detailed analysis to determine whether the prevalence of Maori in the arrest figures can be accounted for by the nature of the offences they commit or whether other explanations must be sought.

Information Not Necessarily Available at the Time of Arrest Decision

A comparison between arrested and non-arrested young people with respect to information not necessarily available to the police at the time of the arrest decision is presented in Table 3.8.

Table 3.8
Comparison of Arrest* With Non-Arrest Cases on Information Not Necessarily Available At Time of Arrest Decision; Distinct Police Cases Aged 14-16; Percentages; N=462

	Arrest (N=69) %	Non-arrest (N=393) %
Previous offending history		
Yes	90	52
No	10	48
Number of Offences		
1	57	83
2	31	9
3	6	2
4	3	2
5 or more	4	4
Live with family		
Yes	75	92
No	25	8
Unemployed		
Yes	52	12
No	48	88

* Includes only those arrest cases where there was a subsequent charge in the Youth Court.

Young people who were arrested proved to be more likely to have had a previous offending history according to the Youth Aid files. This history will sometimes have been known to the arresting officer (and as the above quotes show was clearly an influential factor in the decision to arrest in some cases) but would not necessarily have been known at the time of the arrest decision (although admittedly the young person who was arrested five times in our sample period was widely known to all the local police). The explanation of the effect lies to some extent in the fact that those with a previous known history of offending were more likely to have some of the other known characteristics associated with a higher likelihood of arrest; such as being older, being Maori and having committed more serious offences.

Those arrested usually had more offences attributed to them. However, this does not necessarily indicate that they were involved in more incidents. For instance, in one case of vandalism, three adjacent letter boxes were destroyed in a short space of time on a single evening. These offences led to three separate charges in the Youth Court of wilful damage. In other cases, officers entered more than one charge for the same incident. For example, in a case of aggravated robbery, there was also a charge of injuring with intent and in the case of a young person suspected of drug dealing who was arrested for possession of cannabis and a pipe, three separate charges were laid in regard to this single incident. Thus we attempted to make a decision about the number of incidents involved in each case and then compared the arrest and non-arrest cases on the number of incidents.

The result showed that there was no longer any significant difference between the two groups in the number of incidents. This confirms our impression that the number of offences recorded probably reflects the seriousness with which the police view the offence and the offender rather than directly influencing the decision to arrest.

Finally there are a group of social factors associated with arrest cases that are similar to those reported in overseas studies (eg Gale *et al*, 1990): namely that those arrested were more likely to be unemployed and to be living away from their families. These factors are also associated with offenders who committed more serious offences, older offenders and offenders with a previous offending history. All these factors comprise a linked set which has often been described in the criminological literature and which has other correlates including ethnicity, poverty, lack of education, a history of frequent changes of care and a history of abuse or neglect.

Predicting the Decision to Arrest

It is possible to assess the relative importance of the factors associated with the decision to arrest or to refer the young person to Youth Aid by using a technique known as multiple regression. The technique tries out each individual factor in turn as a predictor and then sorts out those which, in order, and uninfluenced by the other factors, are the best predictors of the decision to arrest. Finding that there is a statistical connection between various factors and the decision to arrest does not prove a causal connection but, providing the factors chosen are ones than might reasonably be supposed to play a part in the decisions, the statistical analysis can be helpful in making an estimate on how important the particular factors actually are. But arriving at firm conclusions about what explains an arrest depends on more than the statistical evidence: statistical connections can occur acccidentally, or their importance can be overestimated because a more important factor has been overlooked or was not measured.

It would have been useful if a regression analysis to predict the decision to arrest could have been made using the grounds set down in the Act such as likelihood of reoffending or likelihood of absconding, but objective measures of these factors were not available. Moreover, we have already seen from the interviews with front-line police officers that their judgements about the need to arrest were affected by offence characteristics and offender characteristics. It seems likely, therefore, that it is the offence and offender characteristics which are known to the police officer that determine his or her judgement about the likelihood of reoffending or absconding. Thus we chose variables on which we had data, which were routinely available to the officer at the time the arrest decision was made (although we recognise that information on previous offending history was available and influential in some cases) and were either mentioned by the police officers themselves or seemed potenially relevant to factors mentioned by them.

For the regression analysis we selected only those finalised police cases where the arrest had been followed by a charge being laid in the Youth Court and where the offender was either Maori or Pakeha (as we could only use two categories and these were the two largest groups). The results showed that, of the factors we were able to measure, the seriousness of the offence was the most important, followed by the time of the offence, the age of the offender and the ethnicity of the offender. The sex of the offender was not a significant predictor independent of the other factors. Thus the regression analysis showed that relatively serious offences, committed at night by older offenders and by Maori offenders were most likely to result in an arrest.

Overall, however, these measurable factors do not provide a strong prediction of the decision to arrest. Together, they gave a multiple correlation of 0.45[21] and accounted for 20% of the variance. This means that only in a relatively small proportion of cases would it have been possible to predict

---

[21] A correlation describes the amount of association between two factors. A correlation of 1.00 indicates complete agreement between two factors while a correlation of 0 indicates no association whatsoever. In this case the multiple correlation of 0.45 is only a moderate correlation and accounts for 20% of the variance. This means that it would be possible to predict police officers' decisions accurately in only about 20% of the cases from knowing the seriousness of the offence, whether or not it occurred at night and the age and ethnicity of the offender.

accurately the decision to arrest from information on seriousness, time of offence, age and ethnicity alone. Thus it is clear from the statistical analysis, as indeed we already know from the interviews, that other factors were likely to be substantially influencing the decision of the police officer.

Putting together information from all sources, including the regression analysis, a picture of what determines an arrest begins to emerge. From the interviews with officers, it seems clear that judgements about the likelihood of reoffending and the likelihood of absconding were important and that these judgements were being made on the basis of the behaviour of the offender and the impression created by the offender at the time of the decision to arrest. Both the regression analysis and the comments suggest that the seriousness of the offence and its circumstances, such as time of day, played a part. The fact that age and ethnicity emerged in the regression suggests that these characteristics of the offender may have affected the impression they created. In some cases, previous knowledge of the offender and his or her family background are undoubtedly likely to have been a factor. Moreover, just as the evidence showed that police practice varied across areas, it is equally possible that variability may have occurred within a district. In particular it is possible that sections on shift together under a single sergeant, who supervised decisions, may have developed different standards. The effect of area on the arrest decision was tested by using another statistical procedure, logistic regression, which showed that area differences were indeed important, although they were not as important as, and did not cancel out, the other variables we have already mentioned.

The fact that Maori were more likely to be arrested and that this effect operated in addition to any effect from other measurable factors known to the officer at the time of arrest, such as seriousness, age and time of offence, is an important finding with serious implications for the impartiality of front-line police officers. Thus we explored the matter further by examining the other factors associated with being Maori. A discussion of the correlates of ethnicity is contained below. In addition, because seriousness of offence was such an important predictor of both Youth Aid and arresting officers' decisions, we also explored how this related to other factors.

Seriousness of Offending

Minimum seriousness offences accounted for 49% of the offences in the sample. Another 11% were classified as minimum/medium in seriousness. Medium seriousness offences made up 36% of the cases. Another 2% were on the borderline between medium and maximum seriousness. Only 2% of offences fell into the maximum seriousness category.

A number of factors were associated with seriousness: in particular, previous offending history, time of the offence, area in which the offender lived, sex of the offender, ethnicity of the offender, whether or not the offender was unemployed and whether or not the offender was living at home. Table 3.9 sets out the data on these factors and we discuss below each of these factors in turn.

The more serious offences were more likely to have been committed by someone with a previous offending history, but it is important to note that a third of the minimum seriousness offences were committed by those already known to Youth Aid and that one in six of the most serious offences were committed by those with no known offence history.

The time that the offence was committed was important in distinguishing minor from more serious offences; 84% of the least serious offences were committed during the day. However, over half of the medium and maximum seriousness offences were committed during the day and only about one in four of these offences was committed after 11pm at night.

The seriousness of offences varied by area, as we have already discussed. Greater numbers of offences were rated as medium in seriousness or above in Lower Hutt and Henderson and fewer in Masterton and Christchurch (see Table 3.3).

Employment was also important. Those who were at school accounted for most of the least serious offences. Those who were unemployed were more likely to commit the relatively more serious offences, rated as minimum/medium or above, and being unemployed was, of course, related to age. The figures in the table show a general trend in relation to age but further analysis of the data provided more information. Those under the age of 12 did not commit any of the offences rated as medium/maximum or maximum in seriousness and most of the most serious offences were committed by those aged 16. There was also an association between the seriousness of the offence and where young people were living; those living with their family were less likely to commit the most serious offences compared to those living away from their family. However, it is important to note that those living away from their family were also likely to be older and to have a previous offence history.

Table 3.9
Offence and Offender Characteristics by Seriousness of Offending; Percentages

	Minimum (N=327) %	*Min/med* (N=73) %	*Medium or above* (N=268) %
Sex			
Boys	70	90	90
Girls	30	10	10
Ethnicity (excluding other)			
Pakeha	48	51	28
Maori	37	40	51
Pacific Island	15	10	21
Age			
5 to 13	36	22	26
14	21	18	16
15	24	26	23
16	18	34	34
Time of offence			
Evening or later (after 6 pm)	16	39	40
Daytime (6 am to 6 pm)	84	61	60
Previous History			
Yes	35	64	70
No	65	36	30
Where Living			
With non-family	4	11	13
With family	96	89	87
Employment			
At school	92	74	76
Employed	3	5	5
Unemployed	5	21	19

As usual, most of the more serious offences were committed by boys rather than girls. The data in Table 3.9 show that more of the offences rated medium and above in seriousness were committed by Maori youth. However, further inspection showed that this result did not hold for offences of medium/maximum or maximum seriousness; these offences were equally likely to have been committed by offenders from the three main ethnic groups in the sample. Indeed, ethnicity was the least important of the predictors so far discussed as being associated with seriousness. The pattern was for Maori offenders to be more likely to be involved in offences of medium seriousness and for Pakeha offenders to be more likely to be involved in offences of minimum seriousness. The pattern for Pacific Island offenders was similar to that for Maori offenders.

A number of consequences flow from the relative seriousness of the offence. As already discussed, more serious offences were likely to be dealt with by arrest and Youth Court proceedings. Also, as already discussed, the number of charges arising out of a single incident was likely to be greater for cases appearing in the Youth Court than when the matter was less serious and handled outside the court. Table 3.10 shows that 83% of the most serious offences were dealt with by arrest and charge in the Youth Court, compared to 20% of the medium seriousness offences and only 3% of the minimum seriousness offences. In all but one case where an offence of minimum seriousness led to an arrest, the offender had also been charged with more serious matters at another time during the study[22].

Table 3.10
Seriousness of Offence by Arrest Versus Non-arrest; Distinct Police Cases; Aged 14-16 Years; Percentages Sum to 100 for Each Row

Seriousness	Arrest %	Non-arrest %	Total N
Minimum	3	97	206
Min/Med	25	75	57
Medium	20	80	176
Med/Max	20	80	10
Maximum	83	17	12

A summary of the factors that predict the seriousness of the offence and how seriousness affects police decisions is presented in Box 3.1.

Box 3.1
Factors Associated with Seriousness of Offence

Predictors
- Having a previous offence history
- Later time of offence
- North Island urban areas rather than South Island or rural North Island
- Boys rather than girls
- Being unemployed rather than at school
- Being older
- Being Maori for medium rather than minimum seriousness offences

Consequences
- Arrest rather than diversion

---

[22] There was one case where an arrest was made and charges were laid in Youth Court on the basis of a single minimum seriousness offence. The offender (aged 15) was arrested on a Sunday afternoon when, having removed a petrol cap from a car, he acted as a lookout for associates who tried to steal the petrol. The FGC recommended that the offender make an apology and give a $20 petrol voucher to the owner of the vehicle and on this basis the charge was withdrawn in Court after 4 appearances over a period of 6 weeks.

Ethnicity of Offenders

In order to explore the reasons for the difference noted in arrest rates for Maori and Pakeha, differences between Maori and Pakeha on other characteristics were examined and comparisons were also made with Pacific Island offenders.

Most of the variables that have been measured are unrelated to ethnicity (see Table 3.11). Offenders from Maori, Pakeha and Pacific Island backgrounds were similar in whether or not they lived with their family, in whether they offended alone or with others, in their age and gender and in the time at which they committed the offence. The fact that Maori offending more often fell in the medium rather than the minimum seriousness category has been described in the previous section. Of other variables examined, the only ones showing differences by ethnicity were previous history of offending and employment status. More of the Maori young people were unemployed and more of the Pakeha young people were at school, with Pacific Islanders in the middle in this regard. By comparison with Pakeha young offenders, more of the Maori were already known to Youth Aid, with Pacific Islanders again intermediate in this regard.

Table 3.11
Ethnicity and Other Factors; Distinct Police Cases; Percentages Within Each Ethnic Group

	Maori (N=286) %	Pakeha (N=271) %	Pacific Island (N=109) %	Total (N=671) N
Previous History				
Yes	66	42	48	53
No	34	58	52	47
Employment				
School	77	89	86	84
Employed	4	4	4	4
Unemployed	19	6	10	13
Arrested				
Yes	15	7	6	10
No	85	93	94	90

Table 3.11 also shows the proportion arrested in each ethnic group and this clearly demonstrates that young Maori were more likely to be arrested than young people from the two other major ethnic groups in our sample. While the overall arrest rate was 10%, 15% of Maori were arrested compared to only 7% of Pakeha and a slightly lower proportion of Pacific Islanders. It is also apparent, from the earlier analyses which attempted to predict the arrest decision, that young Maori were more likely to be arrested when the other circumstances which we have been able to measure at the time of the decision to arrest appeared to be similar. It is possible that other unmeasured factors, such as the attitude of the offender as perceived by the police officer or knowledge of the offender's prior history, were also relevant and might explain these differences. It is also possible that negative attitudes and expectations about one another have built up over time between the police and young Maori offenders and that these attitudes can sometimes lead to an over-reaction on both sides and, consequently, to more arrests of young Maori. The factors more likely to be associated with Maori than Pakeha offending are summarised in Box 3.2.

Box 3.2
Factors Associated with Maori Offending

> *Predictors*
> - Having a previous history of offending
> - Committing medium rather than minimum seriousness offences
> - Being unemployed rather than at school
>
> *Consequences*
> - Arrest

Conclusions

Arrest decisions were recorded by police officers under the various grounds set down in the Act. However, determining these grounds is a matter for judgment. Police officers reported to us on a variety of factors that affected their judgment and analysis of the data indicated the importance of other factors as well. Box 3.3 provides a summary of all the various factors that were associated with the decision to arrest; both the factors which have been able to be measured and compared using statistical techniques and the factors that became apparent from interviews with arresting officers. It shows that the decision to arrest was more likely to be taken when the offence was relatively serious, committed by a Maori rather than a Pakeha, committed by an older rather than a younger person and committed in the evening or in the early hours of the morning. Furthermore, those arrested were more likely to have had a previous offence history, to be unemployed and to be living away from home. These results are consistent with the results of interviews with the police which indicated that the decision to arrest was based on the characteristics of the offence, particularly seriousness, public protection issues and circumstances, and the characteristics of the offenders, particularly their previous history of offending, their attitude and their family circumstances. The consequences of the decision to arrest were likely to include a decision by the police to charge with a larger number of offences and this was related, in part, to the fact that those arrested had committed more serious offences.

Box 3.3
Factors Associated with the Decision to Arrest

> *Arrested Offenders, Compared to Others, are Likely to Be:*
> - Committing more serious offences
> - Older rather than younger
> - Maori rather than Pakeha
> - Offending in the evening or night
> - Boys rather than girls
> - Previous offenders
> - Unemployed
> - Living away from family
> - Charged with more offences
>
> *Other Factors Affecting Arrest Decisions:*
> - Arrest practice varies by district
> - Different officers have different views that may affect practice
> - Attitude and behaviour of the offender at time of the decision to arrest
> - Assessment of family background and circumstances
> - Knowledge of previous history
> - Consultations with others
> - Reactions of the victim
> - Judgement of likely outcome if sent to court compared to FGC

Evidence presented earlier in this chapter on area differences has shown that the probability of being arrested, even taking into account the seriousness of the offence, differed widely from one police district to another. Thus local police practice is almost certainly a significant factor and so too are differences in the attitudes of individual police officers which emerged from the way they discussed arrest practice under the Act.

There also seems little doubt that equally as important in the arrest decision as the factors which were measured in the study was the judgement made by the police officer at the time of the decision based on his or her own impressions of the young person and knowledge, if any, of the young person's family circumstances and background. In making this judgement, arresting officers may have had the benefit of consultation with colleagues, some of whom may have already known the young person, and they may also have been influenced by their contact with the victim. Interview comments show that the officer's views on the probable outcome of an arrest compared to a referral to Youth Aid was sometimes a factor in the arrest decision which may, to some extent, have reflected the views of the particular officer on what was likely to happen in an FGC.

It is interesting to compare these findings with those reported by Morris and Young (1987) in the study which examined practice in 1984. Then it was the seriousness of the offence, knowledge of a previous offence, the juvenile's attitude and co-operativeness and family background which were most often mentioned as reasons for an arrest. They write:

> *These factors appeared to be associated with notions of culpability and indicators of 'troublesomeness', but were loosely connected with officers' perceptions of the likelihood of reoffending. (page 17)*

In 1984, arrest was being used to ensure that the young person appeared in the Children and Young Persons Court because a referral to Youth Aid was often seen as unlikely to lead to effective penalties. Area differences were marked and the rate was lower in Henderson than elsewhere in the research areas.

Current findings seem remarkably similar to those of the earlier study. Judgements of the likelihood of reoffending seemed still to be based on police perceptions of the 'troublesomeness' of the young person and were certainly not confined to the immediate period after apprehension. Likelihood of absconding was probably still judged on the basis of knowledge of family circumstances and the offender's previous history. Seriousness of the offence was still the most important criterion. Even the lower arrest rate in Henderson is replicated in the current study. The greater emphasis in the new Act on accountability through the FGC process appears not to have entirely changed police attitudes. Later we will return to this question after exploring the reality of accountability at the FGC.

Thus in terms of the objectives of the Act and the criteria for arrest in section 214, the results reported here are mixed. Arrest rates have definitely been reduced. But the criteria for arrest seem to have changed little since 1984 and so too have the attitudes of police to the effectiveness of diversionary processes and of Youth Aid procedures.

Chapter 4

FRONT-LINE POLICE INTERVIEWING AND ARREST PROCEDURES

Introduction

The Children, Young Persons and Their Families Act 1989 formally confirms the importance of protecting the rights of children and young people and for the first time puts certain rights into statutory form. There has been resistance by some front-line police officers to the sections of the Act that deal with these rights. Police have claimed that the requirements are cumbersome, that they make it more difficult to question young people and that they prevent them from carrying out other duties because of the time involved.

It has sometimes been claimed that a consequence of the increases in complexity of procedures has been that police officers are 'turning their backs' on juvenile offending. In order to explore this possibility, we examined police statistics on recorded juvenile offending both before and after the Act and compared the pattern with respect to age, ethnicity and gender of the offender, the types of offences being committed and the rates per 10,000 population under 17 years of age. Appendix 3 presents this analysis. The results show that the population rates for juvenile offending do show a slight downward trend but that this was first apparent in 1988, before the Act. In most other respects the pattern of juvenile offending appears to be remarkably similar for comparable periods before and after the Act. It is possible that, as serious adult offending has tended to rise over recent years, the lesser offences committed by juveniles have tended to be ignored. Nevertheless, the statistical evidence fails to confirm that there has been any major change in the policing of juvenile offending as a consequence of the Act.

That is not to deny that the police have sometimes found it difficult to comply with the provisions of the Act. A particularly contentious example was R v Irwin (Fisher J 2 Dec 1991 High Court Hamilton T 32/91) which made media headlines as the 'Slavich' case after the name of the victim. In this case, two young people stopped a car to ask for a lift, a gun was put to the head of the driver, two shots were fired, and the car was driven off with the body dragging behind. The car and the dead man were later found by the roadside. One offender was responsible for the shooting and driving the car off, while the other ran away after the first shot. The youngster who ran away was apprehended and taken to the police station where he was questioned in order to establish what had happened and to assist with apprehending the other offender who was still at large and armed. In the early stages, the police did not follow the procedures set down under the Act for informing the young person of his rights. When the matter came to trial, almost a year later, the boy pleaded not guilty to murder and the case was dismissed. The judge held that the statement made by the young person on the night he was taken in for questioning was not admissible and that there was insufficient other evidence for a conviction on the murder charge. Public opinion has varied from the view that a young murderer 'walked free' to the view that, since there was insufficient evidence to convict the young person, justice was done by the dismissal of the case. With respect to police actions on the night, views ranged from anger at the Act which supposedly impeded the work of a police officer to the view that, for whatever reasons, the police erred in not following proper procedures.[23]

Thus it is important to monitor practice both in terms of whether or not the procedures set down in the Act are being followed and in terms of whether or not the provisions are unnecessarily cumbersome. First we set out a number of accounts based on police information which illustrate what happens when young people are apprehended. Then we present more systematically some information based on the 69 cases where an arrest was made and a charge laid in the Youth Court.

---

[23] The latter view has been expressed by both the Auckland District Law Society (1991) and the Police Complaints Authority (1991).

We describe the requirements of the Act and present police descriptions of their practice in informing young people of their rights, in arranging for statements to be made in the presence of parents and, when it was considered to be necessary, in arranging for detention of young people in custody. Throughout, the accounts of the police are compared and contrasted with information from interviews with young people and their families. In addition, some information about police procedures in non-arrest cases is presented on the basis of material from interviews with young people and their parents. Finally we analyse the complaints that were brought to our attention during the course of the study.

Case Histories [24]

> *At 1.30 in the morning a farmer called the police to report the theft by two men of one of his sheep. The police patrol car was sent and the two were located just after having loaded a dead sheep into a car at 3.10 am. When the two offenders were questioned, T who was a juvenile gave a false name. They were both arrested and taken to the station where further questioning (3.57-4.35 am) established T's true identity and age. He had no kin locally except his sister with whom he was staying and the brother-in-law who was the co-offender. From 8.45 am to 9.00 am he was re-interviewed in the presence of a community volunteer. No statement was taken. He was then released on police bail to appear on the next Youth Court day.*

> *A police patrol located L at the back of some buildings at 2.00 in the afternoon. He was carrying bolt cutters. Police recognised his companion as 'a known burglar' and later established that L had been arrested for a similar offence 2 weeks earlier. He spontaneously admitted the offence. He was then taken to his aunt's home but as she wasn't there he was taken to the police station. His social worker was contacted who recommended arrest and remained during the subsequent interview and taking of a statement. He was formally arrested and charged with possession of burglary tools and preparing to commit a crime. He was then released on police bail into the custody of the social worker as no family had been found. The procedure took about two hours to complete.*

> *The police stopped a car at 3.35 am. The driver [P] ran away leaving his shoes and the passenger, an older person who later appeared in the District Court, was arrested. When the police visited the home of the older co-offender his mother suggested that P could have been involved. The police then went to P's house where P's mother identified his shoes and said her son came home about 3.30 am. P was interviewed at his home but denied stealing the car and refused to make a formal statement. The police went through all the steps on the checklist and read the notebook entry to the young person and his mother. The police said they believed P was the offender and they would arrange for an FGC. They did not make an arrest.*

Finally we present a detailed police account of four of the five separate occasions on which M was arrested in the course of our study:

> *M was arrested for a burglary. The police officer concerned described the situation as follows: "I thought he had property on him and was trying to get away. At 1800 hours I tried to contact his parents but there was no reply. I asked him to suggest someone else. M didn't want a lawyer or anyone. At 1930 hours I rang the duty social worker and she gave permission to keep him overnight. I invited her to the station but she declined saying: `it's not our job'. M was happy to make a statement but I wanted someone there so I went through the list of Maori wardens – but it was out of date and no-one was available. If we had interviewed and no-one was there, then it could be challenged in court. The station got busy about 2300 hours so the young person was left until morning. The Youth Justice Co-ordinator agreed to come in in the morning for an interview but, by then, M wouldn't talk. We held him in the ordinary cells overnight as the holding room was not suitable. We released him on S19A [constable summons] in the morning."*

---

[24] The case histories we present are all based on actual material from files and interviews but we have varied some of the details to prevent the identification of any individual or family.

M was arrested for wilful damage. The arresting officer said: "when I tried to contact his parents at 0130 hours, no-one was home so I tried to advise DSW. I arrested him as a persistent offender. Taking M home wouldn't have helped as his father has no control and I couldn't contact the social worker. When he was questioned at the scene, he denied the offence so I decided that speaking further would get nowhere. The kid was out of it – glue sniffing. Witnesses had seen him and he had glass fragments on his boots. We held him overnight as a precautionary measure to stop him committing further offences. If he had been taken home, he would have left and gone to the city centre and caused more damage or committed burglaries."

M was initially arrested for breach of bail. The police officer said: "there was enough evidence to say he had committed a burglary as well. He was kept overnight to appear in court the next day when we asked for a remand in custody because there were 15 active charges. The judge had previously already remanded him in DSW custody, but we found him on the street when he was supposed to be in [the residence]. He was not interviewed. He was invited to make a statement in the presence of an adult of his choice but he didn't want to talk. That was fine by me, I had enough evidence for a charge. The new Act hasn't done anything for him. His family background is a problem. He needs proper supervision. The father is anti-police and we always get a negative response from him."

M was arrested for unlawfully getting into a motor car. The arresting officer described the situation as follows: "I picked him up while I was investigating a burglary and found him on the street outside high on solvents. We took him to the station and when we checked on the computer, we found he was wanted for the theft of a car. He admitted this so he was arrested and we charged him. This was about 1700 hours. We took him home. He is already on a curfew from 1900 to 0700. Then another officer found him again, at the scene of the earlier burglary at 1910 hours and this time he had stolen property on him. He continually offends. We needed to get him off the street and so we put him in a cell overnight so that we knew where he was. His problem is he can't stop offending. There was no parent there when we questioned him – he wouldn't nominate one anyway. We went through all the other steps in the 388 [police checklist for use when apprehending and interviewing a juvenile]."

Rights of Young People on Arrest and Questioning

Requirements Of The Act

Sections 215 to 220 of the Act set out the rights of children and young people when being questioned, charged with an offence or arrested; sections 221 to 226 cover the admissibility of any statement to be used in evidence; sections 227 to 228 set out the entitlement to consult a barrister or solicitor; and sections 229 to 232 cover the notification of parents and other persons where the child or young person is being questioned or arrested.

Any juvenile being questioned regarding an offence is required to be informed of their rights including the right not to accompany the officer to the station unless arrested, the right not to make a statement, the right to consult a solicitor and the right to have a person of their own choice present when any statement is taken. When they are arrested, they must be informed of their rights again, unless the police have already done so in the past hour. A recent ruling in the High Court has confirmed that these sections require the enforcement officer to inform the young person of his or her rights before a request to accompany the police officer to the station[25]. Statements made as a result of questioning are only admissible if the correct procedures with respect to questioning, arrest and charge have been substantially followed, if the opportunity has been given to consult a barrister or solicitor and another adult and if the statement has been taken in the presence of the barrister or solicitor or an adult nominated by the young person. The officer questioning or arresting the young person is obliged to inform an adult nominated by the young person, usually

---

[25] R v Toko, Sinclair J, 9 April 1991, High Court Auckland T 1/91.

the parents, as soon as practicable of the fact that the young person is being questioned or arrested and that they are entitled to visit and consult privately with the child or young person.

Sources and Nature of Information Collected

Information was obtained directly from the arresting police officer in 44 of the 69 cases of arrest and charge. Some additional information was also available from the 388 checklist designed for use when a young person is arrested, from the charge sheet, or from the 333 sheet which records offence details. Officers were not asked in detail about all the steps that should have been followed but data were recorded on: who was notified and when; whether or not a statement was taken; whether or not the young person was cautioned; who was present at the interview; and the length of time the young person was at the police station. The data represent only a partial coverage of the steps required and cover a relatively small proportion of all the cases in which a young person was asked to accompany an officer back to the police station.

In addition, all those parents and young people interviewed, including those cases where the young person was not arrested, were asked: when they were notified about the offence; whether or not the young person was cautioned; and whether or not a parent or other person was present when the young person was questioned. These replies relied heavily on people's memory of distant events and, sometimes, events which had seemed relatively unimportant in the midst of an action-packed episode. Thus the data should be treated with caution. On the other hand, whenever a complaint was made about the way the police behaved, and these cases are discussed at the end of this section, people gave a clear and detailed account of what had happened.

Questioning and Taking a Statement

In most cases, the officer asked the young person a few questions when initially apprehending him or her. In some cases, the young person made a spontaneous admission. Usually the young person was then taken either, most commonly, to the police station or, sometimes, to his or her own home where the police officer asked additional questions. Following these questions, a formal written statement giving details of the young person's actions was taken in 31 (70%) of the arrest cases where an arresting officer was interviewed.

Section 221 sets out the procedures which should be followed whenever a child or young person is questioned about the possibility that they have committed an offence and whenever they have been arrested or are about to be charged or have been detained in custody. It states that no oral or written statement will be admissible in evidence in any proceedings against the child or young person unless the the child or young person has had explained to them in language and in a manner appropriate to their age and level of understanding the matters specified in section 215 (c) to (f), namely that:

- they are under no obligation to make a statement
- if they consent to making a statement, the consent can be withdrawn at any time
- the statement could be used in evidence
- they are entitled to consult and make the statement in the presence of a barrister or solicitor **and** any person nominated by the child or young person.

Where formal written statements were made by the young people in our sample, the police officers interviewed stated that they had given the caution required under section 221. A minority (16%) of young people disputed this: three said that they had not been informed of their rights during questioning and the taking of a statement and two others, although signing a statement which included an acknowledgment of the cautioning procedure, claimed that the caution was not put to them prior to their making the statement. Whatever the truth in these cases, it is clear that the procedure was not always fully followed. Of those cases in our sample that went to a defended hearing, one resulted in a dismissal of the charge because of inadequacies in police procedures and in another the young person's statement was ruled inadmissible because evidence from the interviewing officer showed that he had used the normal short caution for adults (ie 'you are not obliged to say anything but anything you say may be given in evidence'), rather than informing the young person of his full set of rights under section 215 (c) to (f).

Where formal written statements were not taken, it was far more common for young people not to be advised of their rights under section 215 (c) to (f) at all. Sometimes this was because the police did not ask any questions, on the basis either that there was already sufficient evidence or that the young person was uncooperative or intoxicated. In such cases, some police officers felt that it was unnecessary to inform the young people of their rights, apparently in the belief that section 221 is only relevant where the admissibility of the confession or other statements may be an issue:

> *S has not been interviewed. There is ample evidence without an interview. As you will appreciate an interview will involve advising of rights and would be pointless in the circumstances. I suggest prosecution is in order and that it be authorised if possible by the FGC.*

In other cases in our sample, police officers did ask young people questions without advising them of their rights, although it seems that they did not intend that the answers to these questions would be used in evidence. For example, three young people said that they had been questioned without a caution, but the police officers involved said that no statement had been taken, implying that since the answers were not wanted as evidence, cautioning was unnecessary.

In our view the failure to observe section 221 procedure in both these circumstances is clearly contrary to the Act. Furthermore, we would suggest that failure to comply with the specific provisions of the Act is mistaken as, without a caution, it is possible that young people may make a spontaneous admission to the arresting officer which implicates others or further implicates themselves. A standard procedure for providing young people with information on their rights under section 215(c) to (f) would also seem an appropriate protection against a possible change of mind about the need for a statement as was said to have occurred, for example, in the Slavich case.

Informing Someone of the Arrest

Information was available on who the police contacted to inform of the arrest in 47 cases, on how soon after the arrest this occurred in 42 cases and whether there were problems notifying parents in 43 cases. Information from parents on when they were notified was available in 30 cases.

Although approximately half the police officers interviewed reported that they had problems in contacting the parents, 81% indicated that contact occurred almost straight away or at least within an hour. Parents' replies generally confirmed that, where they were available, contact was made fairly quickly.

In most (83%) of the cases for which we have data from the police, the person contacted was a parent or relative. A friend was contacted in three cases, and another person known to the young person was contacted in four cases. In one case, according to the police, no-one was contacted.

In six cases, parents claimed that they, themselves, were never notified by the police and, as we will see later, a number of parents in the non-arrest cases made a similar claim. They said that the first information they received about their child's involvement in offending was from the Youth Court, the Youth Justice Co-ordinator or the social worker when the FGC was being arranged:

> *The Youth Justice Co-ordinator was the first contact we had and he told us of the Family Group Conference. We should have been informed by the police that found him. We could have bailed him out – we're not happy about that. (Father)*

In one of these cases, the police reported having contacted a parent, in two other cases the police said they had contacted a relative and, in the remaining cases, the police officer involved was not interviewed.

Although someone appears to have been notified about the offending in most cases, we suggest that it is important that those who have the primary responsibility for the young person should be personally notified by the police as soon as possible, although we recognise the difficulties that this can present, especially when the family has no telephone.

Thus, although the police commonly report difficulty in contacting parents and have asked for this provision to be removed, the data from the study suggest that in most cases they are very successful in finding someone in a relatively short time. Irritation with this requirement probably reflects the police officers' evaluation of its usefulness as, in most cases, the actual inconvenience amounts to making one or more phone calls and having to wait for the parent to arrive before proceeding with the interview. The crux of the matter is that many officers do not believe that this is an important or appropriate part of police work.

Who Was Present When a Statement Was Taken

The police officers we interviewed almost all complained about the requirement to find a parent on the grounds of time. In other respects they had varying views on the usefulness of having parents present during interviews and it is clear that the outcomes varied in different cases. The quotes below give an idea of the variety of opinions we elicited:

It can help or hinder; having a neutral person there gives us credibility.

It changes the relationship, you automatically become more of a prosecutor in the kid's eyes. The kid sees someone else as looking after his welfare.

Young people don't talk in front of their parents. They feel too ashamed even though they were co-operative beforehand.

Sometimes the parent obstructs the interview – they don't believe their child could do wrong.

It is very useful to have them there. Their presence protects the police.

The kids are more likely to tell the truth in front of their parents.

Both the difficulties reported by some police in contacting an adult and the fact that some police officers held negative opinions about the usefulness of having an adult present explain why there appeared to be so many instances in which parents or other adults were not present during questioning. Compliance with the provisions of the Act was greatest where a formal written statement was taken; in two thirds of these cases, the parents, a relative, or a friend of the young person was present. In four cases, another person sat in on the interview. In five cases, according to police reports, no independent adult was present. The reasons given for the absence of an independent adult related to difficulties in contacting the parents or ensuring their presence. Examples of cases when parents were reluctant to help are given below:

Detective J contacted me at work – I was heavily committed and unable to go immediately. He said they would call a community person. (Father)

The young person's mother would not come to the police station until 5 hours later and meanwhile he was kept in the cells. She said she felt it would do him good – it might shake up his ideas – he doesn't take any notice of us.

When there is difficulty in getting a parent to come, either a community person is contacted or as one officer put it:

We may interview without a parent, if we have taken reasonable steps to get them, and let the court decide on admissibility.

In practice, the courts do not take such a flexible view, having clearly held that such statements are not admissible as evidence[26].

In another case, an officer started an interview with no one present, only to stop and wait for an adult from the community when advised by a senior officer to do so:

---

[26] R v Irwin, Fisher J, 2 Dec 1991, High Court Hamilton T 32/91.

> *The interview was briefly begun without an adult – but discontinued after the Senior Inspector had consulted with Youth Aid and decided this was not OK. The young person did not want anyone called in. The father could not come and no-one on the list of JPs/community people was available immediately. Eventually the interview was done two hours later in the presence of a community person.*

When young people were asked who was present when they were questioned, there was agreement with the police about the presence of an independent adult, except in four cases. In one case the young person probably believed no independent adult was present because the adult contacted by the police was not known to him. In the three other cases the young person claimed to have been questioned with no independent adult present while the police indicated that no-one was present because *no statement had been taken.*

Some parents and young people indicated that although parents or other adults were present at a later stage, the young person was initially interviewed for some time on his or her own. The exact number of such cases can not be determined as no direct question was asked but the following quotes from parents and young people are illustrative:

> *I learnt about the offence at 6 in the morning when I was rung by the police. J had been there for about 4 hours. I wasn't there when he was questioned. It was just the kids on their own. They gave a statement and signed it. (Mother)*

> *We were taken to the police station. No, I wasn't cautioned. My mother was called and arrived halfway through when I was making my statement. (Young Person)*

> *I wasn't there at first when he was questioned and I'm really upset about it. The police called and asked for my permission but I declined. They went ahead anyway. (Mother)*

> *I was questioned by two constables on my own. I wasn't told my rights. There was no-one else there. I was very scared. (Young Person)*

> *I was not cautioned and no one was present when I was interviewed. I asked for a lawyer but they made up excuses. I was never offered an adult. I was taken to the police cells and kept overnight until court the next day. Then I was put into DSW custody and brought to (a residence). (Young Person)*

> *They took a statement while I was on my own. They put us in the cells and then called our parents. (Young Person)*

> *No one else was present and I was not cautioned. I felt the police were trying to demean me. (Young Person)*

The practical difficulties of contacting a suitable adult are undoubtedly real in some cases, but the data show that it was possible to obtain someone reasonably quickly in the vast majority of cases once the police decided that it was necessary to take a formal written statement. On the other hand, when it came to providing information on rights, the police often made a distinction between general questioning and the taking of a statement. This is not a distinction that young people and their parents were able to appreciate. Nor, as we have already noted, is it a distinction that is recognised in the law which requires that **all children and young people questioned, arrested or taken into custody should be informed of their rights** and that **any questioning should be in the presence of an adult.**

Custody

About half of those arrested were held for up to three hours after their arrest. Others were held for as long as seven hours, and about a quarter were held overnight. The reasons for the delays in release were varied. Some involved difficulty in contacting parents or arranging for an adult to collect them. At other times, the officers dealing with the case were called away to more urgent work or were delayed by dealing with other co-offenders. Sometimes there was difficulty establishing whether or not the juvenile could be released into a parent's or relative's care.

Normally, under section 234, young people who have been arrested are released: either on police bail if the young person can appear in court within seven days; or on a constable summons if a Youth Court hearing is not likely to occur within seven days; or to the custody of a parent; or to the custody of another approved person. The exceptions are described in sections 235 and 236. Section 235 provides that when the young person is likely to commit further offences or when custody is considered necessary to prevent the destruction of evidence or interference with witnesses the young person must be delivered to a social worker in the Department of Social Welfare within 24 hours. Section 236 allows for the detention in police custody until a court hearing of a young person who is likely to be violent or to abscond.

Table 4.1 sets out what happened to 55 of the arrested young people in our sample.

Table 4.1
How Released; Distinct Arrest Cases; N=55

Released	N	%
Police bail	15	27
S19A constable summons	11	20
Custody of parent or guardian	12	22
DSW care	11	20
Kept in police custody	6	11

Two thirds of the cases were dealt with by the release of the young person. In 11 cases, the young people were placed in DSW custody and in six cases they were held by the police. In most of the police custody cases, a young person was simply kept overnight in police custody because he or she was intoxicated. In cases where the police arranged for continued DSW custody, it was almost always because they were concerned about the probability of further offending. It is not, however, the responsibility of the police to decide on where the young person will be placed after being given into the custody of the DSW. The policy of the DSW is, in accordance with the principles of the Act, wherever possible, to try to keep the young person in the community. Thus the young people placed in DSW care are often released to their family or placed in a foster home rather than in the more secure care of an institution which is often the preferred alternative of the police. The quotes below illustrate police officers' reasons for placing children with DSW. They show that the availability of suitable family often determined whether or not the police thought that reoffending was likely to be avoided although in more serious cases, especially when there had been a history of offending, they usually wanted a more secure place than where the young person had been living previously:

> *The parents were spoken to but they didn't want their son back so we placed him with DSW.*
>
> *I went to the mother's place – she didn't want anything to do with him. I would have left him with his mother if she had been willing to have him but there is no father and she can't handle him. I wouldn't have left him as she had no control and the young person was intoxicated. I also thought he might reoffend as the building was insecure.*
>
> *This was a serious assault on a taxi driver. He was placed in DSW custody to ensure appearance and stop reoffending.*
>
> *It is the usual form for DSW and the police to keep someone like this [a repeat offender involved in multiple burglaries] in custody until court. He is currently at [a residence]. We want corrective training as he has not done the tasks from previous FGCs.*
>
> *At a previous court hearing the lawyer agreed to keeping him in DSW custody because of the nature and the extent of offending. The court put him into the custody of a foster mother but he decamped. He was put into DSW care again but escaped from the social worker. When he was apprehended again he was put in [a residence] but escaped that night and further offences were committed.*

There was a problem finding relatives as the first lot we contacted didn't want anything to do with him. He was kept in police custody overnight, went to court and then DSW placed him in [a residence].

Police Procedure in Non-Arrest Cases

In cases where no arrest was made there was usually little information from a police perspective. For 95 distinct police cases where there was no arrest but an FGC was held on the basis of a Youth Aid referral, some information was available on police procedures from the interviews with young people and their families.

The data show that, as in arrest cases, young people not subject to arrest were most likely to have been detected at the scene of the crime (70% of non-arrest cases compared to 80% of arrest cases). In nearly 60% of non-arrest cases, young people were taken to the station for questioning, nearly a quarter were questioned in their own home and most of the rest were questioned at the scene of the offence. In just over half the non-arrest cases, a family member or another adult was present, usually the parents but, according to the information from the interviews, no independent adult was present in approximately 40% of the non-arrest cases. Police were said to have contacted the parent or caregiver in three quarters of these cases but, in the remainder (N=25 cases), their first knowledge of the offence came from the young person or DSW. Only just over one third (35%) of the young people interviewed about this said they had been cautioned and almost half (46%) said they had not, while the remainder did not know.

It is possible, as with the arrests, that in some of these cases, another adult not known to the family was present while the young person was being questioned or that the presence of an adult was considered unnecessary because no statement was taken. It is also possible that the police contacted a family member other than the person we interviewed to inform them of the offence. And, with respect to the failure to caution, it is possible, as with arrests, that this was seen as unnecessary because no statement was taken or that it was overlooked by the young person in the confusion of the surrounding events. Nevertheless the data suggest that police practice in giving clear information about rights and contacting parents could be improved in non-arrest cases as well as in cases where an arrest was made. The following cases are examples of aspects of police practice which could be criticised:

Two boys from neighbouring homes were found in the bushes at the home of one of them. They admitted to having climbed into the local school and having interfered with another neighbour's car. The police took them to the station. The boys said that they were each questioned separately in the police car and later at the station but that the police had treated them fairly although they do not remember being cautioned. The parents were not contacted at the time the boys were picked up and were only informed of the incident some time later (approximately one and a half hours according to the father on whose property they were when found). The parents then went to the station and were present while a statement was taken.

H was caught in a shopping mall having been part of a group which broke in to a local cafe. He was questioned briefly at the scene and then taken to the station. He said he hated it because "the police took me around the side of the school and choked and kicked me." The mother was very concerned about the way her son had been treated and the fact that no adult was there when he had been questioned. She said: "they had made no contact with me to tell me what was happening. My son told me but then we heard nothing more and thought it had all been dropped until we were visited by DSW."

M and a co-offender had stolen a plant in a pot and dropped the pot from an overbridge onto a motorway. M said that when the police stopped them they claimed that he and his friend had also carried out a number of other offences committed that night. He said: "they talked to us for about 15 minutes and then took us to the police station. We thought we'd been arrested and we were told to get into the car and given no choices. At the police station they told us they wanted to put us in a cell but they weren't able to as we were too young. They put us in separate rooms and questioned us for quite a while. We were not told we could have an adult present and I wouldn't have said anything if I knew I had the choice. I would have wanted my parents present for the questioning. I was pretty drunk at the time. I felt pretty scared, I didn't know what my rights were and they took advantage of that."

On the other hand, parents do not necessarily share the concerns we have raised. For example:

M's mother (see above) said she was contacted by the police: "when the kids were picked up at about 2 am. We weren't present when they were questioned and they were put in separate rooms. The police were quite rough and rightly so. Various things had happened that night and the police assumed it was them. The police told us it was not serious – it was just that they were trying to give them (the boys) a bit of a scare. I think that's quite a good way to try and make it the last time."

Complaints

During the course of our interviews with young people and their families there were 30 cases where rough handling or verbal abuse by the police was mentioned and this represents 18% of the cases where a young person or parent was interviewed. In 14 of these cases specific complaints were made about the handling of the young person by the police during an arrest and this represents 25% of the arrest cases where the parent or young person was interviewed. A breakdown of these 14 specific complaints is presented in Table 4.2.

Table 4.2
Complaints About Police Handling of Arrested Young People; N=14

Complaint	N
Dogs	2
Physical abuse	8
Verbal abuse	1
Physical/Verbal abuse	2
Dog/Physical abuse	1

Most complaints concerned the physical handling of the young person. Sometimes the young person complained of being hit or pushed by arresting officers or being handcuffed unnecessarily. Other incidents involved the use of police dogs, where the police dog was not properly controlled by the handler with the result that the young person was bitten. In a few cases the young person received verbal threats. The quotes below present some examples and include one allegation against the MOT which indicates that the same issues can arise in the area of traffic policing:

They left the handcuffs on for ages (this young person was held in a cell for 2-3 hours with handcuffs on as the police had lost the key) and they were hurting my hands. A couple of boys [older co-offenders] were kicked about a bit but I was lucky. (Young person)

The constable was aggressive. He hit me when I was with my mate – on the head. Later also he threatened to put me in to the cells or beat me up again. (Young person)

Force was used by the MOT officers who said that it was necessary because the young person would not leave his car when he was told to do so. The young person admitted being angry and uncooperative but claimed that the way the officers pushed him about and abused him was "over-the-top". His reason for being unwilling to co-operate was that they were going to leave his dogs in his car, where they would be stolen. (In this case, the offender was proved correct as the dogs were stolen before he was released on bail and could return to get them.) (Researcher's notes on FGC)

The suspects had run into a bush area and would not come out when called. We sent in the dogs and they got some bites. (Police officer)

In one case the parent attributed the rough treatment received by a young person to the fact that he was a Maori:

Being Maori the police hassle you. The police gave [my son] a real hiding. When he came home, I'd never seen him look this bad. I took him to the doctor's the next day to get a medical certificate to verify the bruising and bashes to his head. This is why we don't want to write a letter of apology to the police but we are too scared to say any of this.

In a larger number of cases, the young people commented that the police had treated them well compared to earlier bad experiences:

They just asked me straight. They didn't push me.

It was not bad compared to other times I have been arrested.

The cops were pretty good to me because they had recovered most of the stolen gear they were looking for.

Some additional information on the circumstances of young people's apprehension comes from the interviews with young people who were not arrested but who had FGCs about non-arrest offences. In these cases, nearly half said that the police treated them okay or that they were treated fairly. In the remaining cases they used words like 'bad', 'scared', 'threatened', 'demeaning', 'worried', 'angry', 'unhappy' and 'unfair' to describe their feelings about what happened during their contact with the police. But often these negative feelings were related to being upset at getting caught and feeling bad about what they had done. On the other hand, in 16 cases the young people claimed they had been physically or verbally abused and in a further 12 they felt that they had been threatened, demeaned or unfairly treated. Thus over a quarter of the young people who were not arrested but went to an FGC were distressed by the way they had been treated by the police. These findings are similar to those reported in the previous study by Morris and Young (1987).

Conclusions

The information collected from police and families showed that when a young person was arrested or taken in for questioning there were problems on both sides. The police sometimes had difficulty in contacting and obtaining co-operation from families so that the young person could be rapidly questioned and released into the care of the family. On the other hand, some families appeared not to have been notified as soon as possible, if at all, that their son or daughter had been taken to the police station, especially when there was no arrest.

In terms of informing young people of their rights, there was some confusion. Police believed they were complying with the Act but their interpretation appeared to be inaccurate in some cases. It seems clear that young people were not always being informed fully of their rights before a statement was taken and were not usually being informed of their rights when they were arrested and no statement was taken. With respect to the taking of statements, it seemed apparent that questioning sometimes started before an adult of the young person's choice was present and that, in some cases, statements were being taken without any independent adult present at all.

Some young people reported being roughly handled. We did not check these claims with the officers concerned, as the officers had usually been interviewed before the parents or young people. Moreover, only a small minority of cases produced such complaints and in some of them the young people may have been intoxicated or difficult. However, in some cases involving dog bites or rough handling, the charge sheets confirmed the allegations. While we recognise that the evidence from the reports of young people and families is not conclusive, we do wish to record our concern that some police officers may be behaving with unnecessary force or responding with verbal abuse when arresting juveniles.

We note that when the procedures were well followed by the police, the families and young people responded with praise and respect for the police. We believe it is in the best interests of the police to improve performance in these matters. A professional approach to front-line policing increases the chances of a conviction if the matter is defended, it increases the public's respect for the police and it is likely to ensure the co-operation of young people and their families.

Chapter 5

YOUTH AID DECISIONS

Introduction

The New Zealand Police has a separate section, called Youth Aid, with a special role in relation to juveniles. Each station has at least one Youth Aid officer who is expected to work both preventively in conjunction with the local community and reactively in dealing with cases of juvenile offending. The preventive role is carried out by providing community education, liaising with schools and developing a relationship with young people and their families. In responding to young offenders, officers of the Youth Aid section, when they consider it warranted by the seriousness or repetition of offending, visit the homes of offenders, make contact with their families and offer advice. Increasingly in the period prior to the Act, Youth Aid officers arranged informally with the families of young offenders for some type of informal sanction rather than proceeding with prosecution. Now, 'police diversion' using either some type of warning or warning plus an informal sanction is recognised as a legitimate and preferred procedure for dealing with offences by juveniles which are seen by the police as not being sufficiently serious for referral to an FGC[27].

The Youth Aid officers are also supposed to be notified of all cases where a juvenile has been involved in offending. This information is seen as important not only in determining their immediate response but also in allowing them to build up information on each young person's offending history. They keep informal records of all cases involving contact between young people and the police and, although warnings and diversions are not part of the formal police record of a young person, these are noted in the Youth Aid files.

Since the Children, Young Persons and Their Families Act 1989, the role of the Youth Aid officers has been extended both by their new responsibility for referring cases for FGCs and attending FGCs and by the increased amount of diversion. In many areas, the Youth Aid officer (especially if the senior officer has the rank of sergeant) also acts as a prosecutor in the Youth Court. However, few additional resources have been made available and thus, in some areas, Youth Aid officers are stretched in simply coping with the work involved in arranging and attending FGCs. It is the view of most of the officers we spoke to that their ability to make home visits and to take part in preventive work in the community is now severely limited.

Our concern in this chapter is not, however, with the wider issues of the role of the Youth Aid section in policing in New Zealand but simply with the responsibility it has for deciding the outcome of all non-arrest cases involving young offenders. The options are relatively straightforward – the offender may be warned, with or without the addition of informal sanctions, or referred for an FGC. In this chapter we firstly present national statistics on the results of this decision and compare these with the results from the sample. We then describe how the decisions are taken, discuss the factors that influenced the decision and finally examine the extent to which the decisions can be predicted from the standard objective criteria on which we have data.

Sources of data

The primary source of data for these analyses is the same as that described in previous chapters which examined front-line police practice, ie police records of the offence. In addition, information was obtained from Youth Aid files and from detailed interviews with Youth Aid officers in three areas about the reasons for their decisions in each case. Youth Aid decision making differed across

---

[27] In fact, all the activities of Youth Aid including referral for an FGC could be seen as diversionary in that they avoid criminal proceedings in court. However, the use of the term, 'police diversion', has come to mean arrangements made by the police without the involvement of either an FGC or the court and we use it in this sense throughout the text. 'Police diversion' can involve either a warning only or a warning together with some activities arranged by the family which serve as an informal sanction. We refer to the former in the text as 'warning' and to the latter as 'warning plus informal sanction'.

areas. In three areas, the Youth Aid section reviewed each case and made an immediate decision on those considered suitable for a warning. Some cases were similarly immediately referred for an FGC, usually because they were already known to Youth Aid. Others were referred to one of the Youth Aid team for further investigation and this usually included most of those eventually dealt with by diversion or FGC. In another area Youth Aid officers were not directly involved in these decisions; instead the senior sergeant responsible for Youth Aid made a decision on the basis of the report of the offence and what he already knew about the young person and the family. Hence, in this area, Youth Aid officers rarely made home visits or additional enquiries and so were not interviewed about the reasons for the decision. A note was made, however, of the senior sergeant's reasons for his decisions and these are the same as the criteria considered most important in other areas. The Youth Aid data from the fifth area were mislaid. However, discussions with the Youth Aid officers in this area indicated that their approach was similar to that in other areas.

It is important to note, also, the differences between areas in how consultation occurred with the Youth Justice Co-ordinator. In four areas, most of the cases were accepted by the Youth Justice Co-ordinator but on occasion a case would be referred back after consultation between the two agencies. In one area, all decisions were made in consultation between Youth Aid and DSW staff, including decisions about whether or not the cases would be dealt with by 'police diversion'.

The Outcome of Youth Aid Decisions

National Statistical Data

Statistics on the decisions being taken in non-arrest cases are not routinely compiled. The only national data that are available since the Act come from two special analyses of police records. The first is an analysis by Police Headquarters of computer records of offences cleared between 1 November 1989 and 30 April 1990, ie a six-month period immediately after the Act came into force. The second is an analysis of special returns filed with Police National Headquarters during the four-month period from November 1989 to February 1990 inclusive by those police districts which had recorded at least 100 juvenile offenders over that period. These special returns allow a comparison of practice across the larger districts.

The national statistics for the six-month period 1 November 1989 to 30 April 1990 show that 6,845 offences involving juveniles were reported to the police (excluding those juveniles who were arrested). Of these, 36% were warned by the investigating officer, 30% were warned by Youth Aid and a further 13% were warned by Youth Aid and given an additional informal sanction. The remaining 21% were referred for a Family Group Conference. Thus, for non-arrest cases, 79% of juveniles brought to the notice of the police were dealt with by them. These results are compared in Table 5.1 with data from the research sample.

Table 5.1
Outcomes of Non-arrest Cases Dealt with by the Police; National Statistics from 1.11.89 to 30.4.90 Compared with Data from the Research Sample; Percentages

	National police statistics 1.11.89 to 30.4.90 (N=6,845) %	Research study data Sample from 5 areas late 1990 to early 1991 (N=602) %
Warnings	66	57
Warning + informal sanction	13	12
Family Group Conference referral	21	31

Source: Unpublished police statistics

Comparing National Data and Data from the Research Sample

A total of 602 distinct cases were referred to Youth Aid officers during the course of the study. Of these, the Youth Aid officers warned over half (our data did not make a distinction between street warning and formal warning by Youth Aid), warning plus an informal sanction was arranged for 12%, while almost a third were referred for an FGC (see Table 5.1 above). Overall, there is considerable similarity between our data and the outcomes reported nationally in the six-month period shortly after the introduction of the Act. However, our sample shows a rather greater use of FGCs and rather less use of warnings than in the national statistics, perhaps reflecting the relatively greater seriousness of the offending in our areas which covered some of the largest urban areas in the country.

Area Differences in Decisions

National data

Over the four-month period November 1989 to February 1990 inclusive, 20 police districts filed returns indicating that at least 100 juveniles came to their attention. Analysis of these showed considerable variation in practice. In New Brighton, for example, 93% of juveniles were warned either by uniformed branch police or by Youth Aid. Similarly, 73% were warned in Palmerston North. At the other end of the scale, only 43% were warned in Otara and 52% in Auckland Central. On average, 65% of juveniles were warned. Referrals to FGCs varied in a similar (but converse) way. That is, only 2% of juveniles were recorded as having FGCs in New Brighton and 7% in Palmerston North, compared with 41% in Otara and 42% in Auckland Central.

Research sample data

As for both the national data on Youth Aid decisions and the arrest data in Chapter 3, it is clear that there were marked differences in the way cases were being dealt with in the various areas within the research sample (see Table 5.2). In three areas between 40% and 50% of cases were referred for an FGC. At the other extreme, in two other areas (D and E in Table 5.2), only a quarter and 14% of the cases respectively were referred for an FGC, with much more frequent use being made of police warnings.

Table 5.2
Comparison of Youth Aid Decisions by Area[28]; Distinct Youth Aid Cases; Percentages; N=602

Area	A	B	C	D	E	Total	
	%	%	%	%	%	N	%
Warn	39	49	49	62	74	342	57
Warn + sanction	19	3	11	13	12	73	12
FGC	42	48	41	25	14	187	31

Reasons for the differences in the proportion of cases referred for an FGC can be suggested in at least three of our most divergent areas. Area B had the highest proportion of offences rated as medium or maximum seriousness. In area A, there was a close relationship between the police and DSW staff; in fact, they consulted over all the cases coming to police attention and made the decision about how to deal with the young person as a team. As a result, and because the relatively small numbers of offences allowed it, they sent a lot of the less serious cases for an FGC which, in other areas, would have been dealt with by the police on their own using warning or warning plus an

---

[28] Except where national statistics are used, areas have not been named in the tables and text in order to prevent the identification of particular staff. Alphabetic letters have been used inconsistently in tables so that, for example, area A referred to in one table may be area B in another.

informal sanction. Conversely, in area E the police took the view that they would rather handle matters themselves unless they were serious enough to warrant Youth Court attention. On the other hand, there is no immediately obvious reason for the relatively high rate of referrals for FGCs in area C.

'Police Diversion'

We were informed that most of the children or young people referred to Youth Aid after being involved in minor incidents would already have been warned by the police officer who apprehended them. In such cases, Youth Aid would normally decide to take no further action except to send the child or young person an official warning letter. A copy of the letter normally goes to the parents unless the officer believes their response to a minor incident would be excessive (foe example, the child or young person would get a severe thrashing). Thus, parents will almost always be routinely informed in writing of the incident involving their child.

However, during fieldwork it became apparent that there was often more contact between the Youth Aid officer and the family in these cases. To examine this issue, data were collected in one of the busiest areas on the nature of the cases involving only a warning and on whether or not a home visit had been involved.

Table 5.3
Nature of Warning; Distinct Cases in One Area; N=78

	N	%
Front-line police verbal & Youth Aid written	22	28
Youth Aid – verbal & written	39	50
Youth Aid – written only	17	22

As Table 5.3 indicates, in over a quarter of the cases involving warnings the action was, as expected, for a verbal warning by the front-line officer to be followed with a written warning. However, in half the warned cases the Youth Aid officer as well as the front-line police officer had some contact with the offender or his or her family, either over the phone, or on a home visit. Teachers were also contacted in some cases where the offending occurred at school or in school hours. In these cases, both front-line and Youth Aid officers may have issued a verbal warning which was followed up in writing. For the remaining 22% of the cases, the Youth Aid officer decided that a written warning would suffice although no verbal warning had been recorded by the front-line police officer.

When the Youth Aid officer follows up a case he or she may decide to arrange informal sanctions, even in cases where a street warning has already been given. The informal sanctions can be very similar to the range of options considered at an FGC. The nature of the informal sanctions arranged for our sample is described in Table 5.4. Apologies were the most common form of informal sanction (40%) followed closely by reparation (36%). Community work was used in over a quarter of cases involving informal sanctions, while other activities included counselling, changes in residence or sporting activities. Informal sanctions were often negotiated between Youth Aid and parents. Victims also sometimes had an input when the Youth Aid officer had had contact with the victim or was aware of the victim's views. In some cases, the Youth Aid officer found that the parents had already organised some form of sanction including the payment of reparation to the victim. In such cases, Youth Aid was simply endorsing the actions of the family.

Informal actions of parents such as groundings, curfews and loss of pocket money were also likely to have happened in many instances (they certainly were in many of the FGC cases), but these were not recorded as cases involving an informal sanction on the police forms.

Table 5.4
Informal Sanctions; Distinct Cases All Areas; N=72*

	N	%
Apology	29	40
Reparation	26	36
Community work	21	29
Counselling	7	10
Residence	3	4
Activities	1	1
Other	8	11

* Note: Percentages add to more than 100% as more than one sanction was possible.

Reasons for Youth Aid Decisions

When interviewed, Youth Aid officers reported that the main criteria on which they decided whether or not to arrange 'police diversion' were the seriousness of the offence and the young person's offending history. Minor and first time offenders with a good attitude and a positive response from the family were most likely to get a warning. These are the criteria which have been demonstrated to be the most important in previous research both in New Zealand and elsewhere (Morris and Young 1987; Farrington and Bennett, 1981; Landau, 1981; Laycock and Tarling, 1984; Mott, 1983). Table 5.5 shows in detail the factors mentioned by the 128 officers interviewed in three areas.

Table 5.5
Characteristics of the Offence and the Offender Seen by Youth Aid Officers to Increase the Likelihood of a Decision to Refer for an FGC; Data From Interviews on Cases Referred to an FGC in three areas; Percentages; N=128

	N	%
Having a previous offence history	87	68
Offence characteristics; especially more serious offences	86	67
Co-offenders already known to police	68	53
Older age group	14	11
Poor attitude and potential	73	57
Poor family support/background	91	71

The data from the interviews show that the nature of the offence, particularly its seriousness, but also the circumstances such as time of day, and the offender's previous offence history, were important in over two thirds of the cases. The nature of the co-offenders, particularly whether or not they were also known to the police, was seen as a factor for half and so, also, was the young person's attitude and potential, with those seen as having poor attitude or potential being more likely to warrant referral for an FGC. But the factor mentioned most often, in 71% of all cases, was the extent of family support and the nature of the family background, and an FGC referral was seen as having the potential to strengthen the family and enlist its support. The same main three factors were reported by police officers in both the other two areas as influencing their decisions. On the other hand, age, although an important factor in the decision to arrest, was rarely cited by the Youth Aid officers who made the decision about whether or not to refer the case for an FGC.

Much of the information on family circumstances comes from home, school and work visits and these were often seen as critical in making the decision. In the areas where Youth Aid officers were interviewed about the cases they had referred for an FGC, they reported visiting the home in 40% and the school or employer in 29% of the cases. For at least another 30% of the cases, the family and/

or the offender were already known to the Youth Aid officer. In total, therefore, the Youth Aid officer already knew or had visited the family or the young person in 80% of the cases referred for an FGC in these three areas. In one of the other areas, the senior Youth Aid officer said his section would always make contact with the family if the attending officer had not already done so. In the fifth area, the senior sergeant reported that almost all of the young people referred to an FGC or their families were known to him.

Consultation with the Youth Justice Co-ordinator or a social worker could also affect the decision although there were considerable differences in practice in different areas. All the cases in one area were discussed with DSW. In 63% of the cases in another area, there was some consultation with DSW. In contrast, while informal discussions occurred from time to time in two other areas, the decision to refer for an FGC during the time of the study was generally made solely by Youth Aid. Similarly in the fifth area there was rarely any consultation between police and DSW staff over referrals for an FGC. In the other ten areas we visited, we were told that the police and DSW did on occasions consult each other about whether or not an FGC was necessary, but only two areas reported actually meeting together.

Interviews with the victim were another potential influence upon the Youth Aid decisions; these were held in 23% of the cases where Youth Aid officers were interviewed. Information about the victim passed on to Youth Aid officers by their fellow police officers was seen as influential in another 61% of cases.

Fellow officers also passed on other information in some cases and this, too, could possibly influence the decision:

> *I had decided initially that this might not go to an FGC, but then I was told about other 'unreported offending', and so I decided that an FGC was necessary.*

The views of the reporting officer recorded in the file were also influential. Youth Aid officers reported that any recommendation made by the reporting officer was taken seriously in making the decision. Some examples of recommendations from the files are given below:

> *The above mentioned has been involved in three serious offences. Could you please arrange to have a FGC?*

> *Because of the serious nature of the incident and because a serious accident was avoided more by good luck and the prompt attendance of police patrols, either prosecution through the courts or at the very least a severe penalty through FGC is sought.*

> *F has been to notice previously, he is a prolific offender. It is my recommendation that we hold an FGC in relation to this youth. Property to a value in excess of $2,000 was taken and only a small amount was recovered.*

> *I have been struggling for almost six months to get this conniving, crafty little sod before the court, but am being stymied by the requirements of the CYP & F Act. I would insist on a period of corrective training as suitable retribution for his offences.*

The Youth Aid officers were also asked the reasons for their decision. Some of the quotations below put flesh and blood on the drier statistical tables. As indicated previously, the emphasis was almost always on the seriousness of the offence and previous offending history. Thus the issues are much more clear-cut and straightforward than in the case of the arrest decisions. However, in some cases the offender's attitude and family background and the judgement of the officer also played a part:

> *The young person has a long history of minor offending in the past. In August this year I spoke to him and his mother about stealing. The matter was left in her hands although the idea of an FGC was raised should he reoffend – ergo this.*

> *He is a regular offender with [XY]. He was FGCed earlier this year. He still hasn't learned his lesson.*

> *He is going to be a real problem to the police in the future. Although he is only 14 years of age, he is already showing the traits of an experienced criminal.*

This was a big theft. It was well thought out and his choice of friends is not good.

This is [the young person's] second recent offence. He is a liar.

Others comments were commonly added as supportive or confirmatory information and they often implied a concern over the young person's welfare: for example, 'mixing with bad company', 'runaway from home', 'drinks and smokes dope', 'has a lot of freedom', 'at risk', 'regularly truanting from school', 'well known to DSW' but such concerns seemed secondary to the importance of the offending. However, there is no doubt that 'welfare' issues were, on occasion, the primary reason for the referral, as is made clear by the following examples of notes recorded on the file by the Youth Aid officer after home visits:

This family is known and has other children involved in offending. Most community agencies have had contact with the family over many years to little avail. There are secondary care and protection concerns.

This matter was referred to an FGC due to the attitude of the mother to the daughter. There is a need for counselling – the daughter needs support and guidance.

The father is a very weak person who obviously has no control over his two sons. He was not aware that they had gone out that night.

R and his family are well known to me. Several years ago he was exhibiting the same behaviour – multiple offending, truancy and uncontrollable behaviour. His mother is a waste of time. She is on her seventh boyfriend in several weeks – she is seldom home.

In one area, the comments recorded at consultation meetings or mentioned in interviews with the police have a slightly different flavour. They suggest that the police regarded an FGC as a possible way of starting a dialogue with the family; the reason for the FGC was *to get family input or to get some family response*. A letter from a reporting constable to Youth Aid in this area indicated that reporting officers also advocated an FGC referral on the grounds of welfare:

An FGC may see fit to see to these matters. She needs a confidence building course and assistance with her driver's licence rather than taking the easy way out of going to prosecution.

Factors Associated with the Decision to Refer for an FGC

More detail on the differences between the cases referred for an FGC and those which resulted in a 'police diversion' came from the Youth Aid data base which was compiled from police file information. Youth Aid officers' views on the importance for their decision of offence characteristics and the offender's previous history were supported by the analysis of these data. Table 5.6 presents a comparison between cases referred for an FGC and 'police diversion' cases on the range of variables for which quantitative data were available.

The results presented in Table 5.6 clearly differentiated the 'police diversion' cases from those referred for an FGC. However, sex, ethnicity and age did not have such a marked effect as other factors on the probability of going to an FGC compared to 'police diversion'. But there were significant differences on these variables: girls were less likely than boys to be referred for an FGC, younger offenders were less likely to be referred for an FGC than older offenders and Maori were most likely and Pakeha least likely to be referred for an FGC. As we will see later, differences in decisions about boys and girls and older compared to younger offenders can be explained by the fact that boys and older offenders commit more serious offences and are more likely to have a previous offence history.

Table 5.6
Comparison of 'Police Diversion' vs FGC Cases[29]; Distinct Cases; Percentages

	'Police Diversion' (N=415) %	Family Group Conference (N=187) %
Sex		
Boys	76	88
Girls	24	12
Ethnicity		
Pakeha	47	31
Maori	35	52
Pacific Islander	17	17
Other	1	0
Age		
9 and under[30]	6	1
10-13	32	25
14-16	62	74
Seriousness of offence		
Minimum	70	16
Medium/minimum	9	11
Medium	20	66
Medium/maximum or maximum	1	7
Time of offence		
Daytime (before 6pm)	83	59
Evening (6-11pm)	8	19
Night (11pm-6am)	9	22
Co-offenders		
None	41	27
With one other	34	29
With 2 or more others	25	44
Type of offence		
Assaults/robbery/sexual	4	14
Dishonesty – Burglary	13	35
– Conversion	8	16
– Theft/fraud etc	53	26
Drugs/anti social	6	3
Property damage & abuse	15	3
Other incl traffic	1	3
Previous offending history		
Yes	31	83
No	69	17

---

[29] 187 distinct Youth Aid cases were recommended for an FGC but these made up only 127 of the distinct FGC cases as more than one offence was dealt with by many of the FGCs. It is important, also, to note that in these tables there are some missing responses. Thus, N in the table heading indicates the possible number of cases although the actual number of cases on which data were available is sometimes smaller.

[30] Arranging a youth justice FGC for a child under 10 is not consistent with the law and this case is accounted for by the fact that it was a joint offence involving two brothers and their friends.

Table 5.6 continued

	'Police Diversion' (N=415) %	Family Group Conference (N=187) %
Number of offences		
1	92	68
2	5	17
3	2	5
>3	1	10
Live with family		
Yes	96	86
No	4	14
Unemployed		
Yes	4	16
No	96	84

A previous offence history and relatively more medium as compared to less serious offences are also factors associated with being Maori and these differences can explain the relationship between Youth Aid decisions and ethnicity. In this instance interpretation is more problematic as, in view of the finding that Maori may be more likely to be arrested, one could also hypothesise that being Maori may generally make one more likely to be apprehended and hence gain a history of previous offending. However, this is not an issue that can be resolved by the data in this study and the simpler explanation would be to accept that the higher probability of an FGC referral for Maori results principally from the fact that Maori were more likely to have committed relatively more serious offences.

As noted by the Youth Aid officers, offence characteristics were important. The data show that offences against the person (including assaults, robbery and sexual offences), burglaries and car conversion were most likely to be dealt with by an FGC rather than by 'police diversion'. Theft, property damage and abuse, and drug or anti-social offences were most likely to result in 'police diversion', with relatively few going to an FGC.

However, type of offence was not as important as the related variable, seriousness. Those who had committed relatively serious offences (ie those classified as medium seriousness or above), those committing more than one offence, and those with a previous history of offending were much more likely to be referred to an FGC; approximately 60% of cases in these categories were referred for an FGC. The probability of going to an FGC rose to approximately 75% or more when the offence was in the medium/maximum or maximum seriousness categories, when there were multiple types of offences and when there were more than 3 offences. On the other hand, those with no previous offending history, those who committed offences in the daytime and those who had committed an offence rated as minimum on the seriousness scale, had 7 out of 8 chances or better of receiving 'police diversion'.

Youth Aid officers mentioned that they might refer a young person for an FGC because co-offenders were going to be dealt with by means of an FGC. Indeed the data in Table 5.6 bear this out. More FGC cases involved co-offenders (44%) than 'police diversion' cases (25%).

The attitude of the offender and his or her family background are more difficult aspects to assess objectively. Previous research (Gale *et al*, 1990) has shown that whether or not the offender is unemployed and whether or not the offender is living with his or her family are both factors associated with the outcome of police decision-making in South Australia. Living with one's family could in part indicate the potential presence of family support, while being unemployed may be taken by some police officers to indicate relative irresponsibility. Data on these two variables are also given in Table 5.6. Unemployment was significantly associated with the nature of Youth Aid decisions. Similarly, those who were warned were very unlikely to be living away from their families, whereas rather more of those who were referred for an FGC lived away from their families. Unfortunately our interviews with the police did not explore their views on these matters.

Predicting the Decision to Refer for an FGC

It is possible to assess the relative importance of the factors associated with the decisions to handle the matter within the police or to refer the young person for an FGC by using a multiple regression, as we did in Chapter 4 to predict the decision to arrest.[31] Thus we attempted to predict whether a case would be dealt with by a warning or referred for an FGC (excluding the more infrequently occurring cases that were dealt with by a warning and an informal sanction). The variables we used as predictors were those that have already been shown to be associated with the Youth Aid officer's decision: namely, previous history, seriousness of the offence, number of offences, age of the offender, sex, ethnicity, and whether or not the young person was employed, lived with his or her family and offended with others.

The results show that the two most important predictors were previous offence history and offence seriousness which coincides with both official policy and the results of the interviews with Youth Aid officers. Together these two factors gave a multiple correlation of 0.61. Two other factors made a slight additional contribution – whether or not the offender was unemployed and the time of the offence; together all four variables produced a multiple correlation of 0.63. None of the other factors showed any independent effect, although number of offences was almost as strongly linked as the time of offence and would have served equally effectively as a predictor. Thus although many variables were linked to the decision-making, they were also linked to the two most important predictors: seriousness of offence and previous offence history. It is important to note that ethnicity was **not** a predictor independently of the other factors, suggesting that ethnicity was not a factor affecting the referral decisions of Youth Aid officers.

Together, the two main predictor variables accounted for 38% of the variance, which is a moderately high figure under the circumstances for this type of analysis, and all four variables together accounted for 40% of the variance. Nevertheless, the figure of 40% indicates that other factors not included in the analysis were also influencing the Youth Aid decision. One obvious factor, the relevance of which has already been demonstrated, is the area in which the offender was dealt with. It was clear that there were different thresholds in different areas for what was a 'serious enough' offence to warrant an FGC. It may also be the case that in different areas different factors were seen as warranting an FGC referral. To check on this we therefore carried out a second type of regression[32] which enabled us to determine the extent to which area differences affected the decision. We did indeed find that area made a contribution although this contribution was not sufficiently large to change the general pattern which we have already described.

As well as seriousness of offence and previous offence history, there may be other important factors influencing Youth Aid decisions which we have not been able to measure adequately and these are likely to be associated with perceptions of the social and personal characteristics of the offenders and their families.

---

[31] To remind the reader, a stepwise multiple regression of the type used here tries out each individual factor in turn as a predictor and then sorts out those which, in order, and uninfluenced by other factors, are the best predictors.

[32] Because of the continual importance of area differences, we checked the results of the normal stepwise regressions by then running a logistic regression including four of the five areas as separate variables to check whether or not the general findings applied to all areas or only to some areas. However, we found that, although areas were important independent predictors explaining small amounts of variance, their effect was less than that of the other main factors discussed in the text. The numbers were not large enough to determine whether or not different patterns existed between areas, but the analyses confirmed the importance of previous offence history and seriousness of offence for all areas.

Conclusions

The Children, Young Persons and Their Families Act 1989 has changed the way cases referred to Youth Aid are dealt with. It has strengthened the ability of the police to use their own diversionary procedures by providing a legal basis for the process and it has added a new diversionary process in the opportunity to refer the young person to an FGC. The Act envisages that the FGC will also be used as an alternative for some of the cases which might previously have involved an arrest and a court hearing. Our results showed that 90% of young offenders from the sample were being referred to the Youth Aid section of the police. National figures showed that 1 in 5 Youth Aid cases were being referred for an FGC in 1990; in our sample the figure was closer to 1 in 3. Another approximately 1 in 8 cases were concluded by an arrangement with the family for an informal sanction as well as a warning, and a warning only was used to deal with the great majority of cases: two thirds nationally and 57% in our sample.

Thus the picture emerges of a much changed pattern in Youth Aid practice. Now, compared to the past, Youth Aid are much more actively engaged in ensuring that young offenders are made accountable in some manner for their offences and this is being done, usually in collaboration with the family, either through 'police diversion' or an FGC. The belief amongst front-line police officers that Morris and Young (1987) noted as prevalent in 1984, *that Youth Aid did nothing about young offenders*, would be hard to sustain in 1990.

A quantitative analysis of the factors influencing the decisions of Youth Aid officers about how best to deal with particular cases shows that two main variables stand out: the seriousness of the offence and the previous history of the offender. Box 5.1 summarises the main characteristics of the cases that resulted in 'police diversion':

Box 5.1
Characteristics Associated with Chances of 'Police Diversion' as Opposed to being Referred for an FGC

> *Very unlikely*
>
> - Maximum or medium/maximum offence seriousness
> - More than 3 offences
> - Multiple types of offences
>
> *Fairly unlikely*
>
> - A previous offence history
> - Medium or greater seriousness of offence
> - More than one offence
>
> *Very likely*
>
> - Minimum seriousness of offence
> - No previous offence history

The box shows that, along with the seriousness of the offence and previous offence history, the age of the offender and the number of offences are also associated with Youth Aid decisions. Other analyses showed that being a boy, being Maori, being unemployed, living away from one's family, committing an offence at night and having co-offenders were also associated with being more likely to be referred for an FGC, but most of these variables were correlated with, and therefore contributed little in addition to the effects of seriousness of the offence and previous offence history. Practice differed also between areas and this appeared to be related in part to the nature of the relationship between the police and DSW staff and in part to the levels of staff available to handle the workload.

Equally important as previous offence history and seriousness of the offence in the eyes of the Youth Aid officer is the family background and circumstances of the young person. For this reason, visiting the home can be seen as very important. It is worth noting that in one of our study areas home visits had been curtailed and that in at least one other area there was serious concern about the fact that home visits had declined in frequency due to the increased workload of Youth Aid sections since the Act.

Thus the Act has changed the nature of Youth Aid practice. Their active involvement with young offenders in the 1990s contrasts with the largely preventive role they have had in the past. Increased staffing levels would appear to be necessary if preventive policing is to continue to be an important aspect of Youth Aid work.

Chapter 6

FAMILY GROUP CONFERENCES: PROCESS AND PRACTICE

Introduction

The success of the philosophy underlying the Children, Young Persons and Their Families Act depends to a large extent on the success of Family Group Conferences. They lie at the heart of the new process. This chapter briefly describes the process of and reasons for referral to an FGC and the characteristics of those in the FGC sample. It then goes on to describe in more detail the organisation and practice of FGCs. This includes the setting up and composition of FGCs, procedures adopted at FGCs and the recommendations or outcomes reached by FGCs. We examine, also, certain cultural issues. Where possible we contrast the research data with the national picture.[33]

The following chapter deals more directly with the views of FGC participants and explores the extent to which young people and their parents and victims have been involved in both the process and determination of outcomes of FGCs. It also discusses participants' satisfaction with outcomes.

The Process of Referral for an FGC

As we have already noted in previous chapters, young people become the subject of an FGC after an arrest and subsequent referral for an FGC by the Youth Court or after a referral directly from an enforcement agency. In this study, 211 cases were accepted by the YJCs as referrals for an FGC and, in 203 of these cases, an FGC was held. In most (67%) of the cases in the FGC sample, referrals were made by the police Youth Aid officer, sometimes after discussion with the YJC to determine whether or not an FGC was necessary[34]. The next largest source of referrals was the Youth Court (25%) and a further 8% were referred by the MOT. Table 6.1 presents this information for each area and nationally.

Table 6.1
Source of Referrals Showing National Figures for 1990, Total Sample Figures and Areas within the Sample; Percentages

	National %	Sample Total* %	Henderson %	Masterton %	Kapiti-Mana %	Christchurch %	Lower Hutt %
Youth Aid	77	67	79	82	60	48	62
Court	16	25	14	13	36	26	33
MOT	6	8	7	5	4	26	5

* Some cases were referred from more than one source. Those which involved a referral both from Youth Aid and from the Youth Court after a charge by the police have been attributed to 'Youth Aid' as that was usually the first point of origin. However, joint referrals involving the MOT have been categorised as 'MOT' although this may result in overestimating direct MOT referrals and underestimating 'Court' referrals, as in several of these cases the charge would also have been laid in the Youth Court in the first instance.

It is clear from this that there are considerable area differences in the sources of referrals to FGCs. Court referrals conformed to the national average in Henderson and Masterton but in Kapiti-Mana

---

[33] National statistics come from Department of Social Welfare quarterly statistics for 1990. In 1990, there were in all 8,066 notifications from which 5,851 FGCs were held. Notifications include all those cases where police consulted with the YJC about offending including those cases where no subsequent referral was made.

[34] While there is a statutory requirement for police and the YJC to consult over referrals, this was by no means a universal practice.

and Lower Hutt they were considerably higher. In Christchurch, the major difference lies in the relatively large proportion of cases involving the MOT, a pattern which we are unable to explain.

Reasons for Referral for an FGC

We showed in the previous chapter that, overall, older offenders with histories of previous offending who had committed more serious offences tended to be referred for FGCs and that younger offenders with no previous offences who had committed minor offences tended to be warned. We also showed that police practice in making referrals differed between areas over and above the effect of the type of offence and the characteristics of the offender.

Characteristics of Those Referred for FGCs

The vast majority of those referred to FGCs were male and, as is clear from previous chapters, Maori were over-represented. The following table (Table 6.2) provides details of the numbers of FGCs held in 1990 in selected DSW offices and gives percentages for sex and ethnicity.

Table 6.2
Number of FGCs by Sex and Ethnicity of Juveniles Referred for FGCs in 1990 in Selected DSW Offices; Percentages

Area	N of FGCs	% Male	% Maori	% Pakeha
Auckland	336	88	42	29
Christchurch	99	89	31	55
Henderson	172	91	47	44
Lower Hutt	238	88	50	37
Masterton	136	84	50	46
Porirua	136	87	46	27
Wellington	150	82	33	31
New Zealand	5,851	86	53	36

Source: Unpublished Department of Social Welfare quarterly returns.

Table 6.3 provides similar information for the sample.

Table 6.3
Number of FGCs by Sex and Ethnicity of Juveniles; Percentages of Referrals for an FGC in the Sample

Area	N of FGCs	% Male	% Maori	% Pakeha
Christchurch	32	81	28	72
Henderson	43	77	42	33
Lower Hutt	72	93	63	21
Masterton	39	77	46	49
Kapiti-Mana	25	96	24	44
Total	211	85	45	39

Note: The basis for calculating percentages in each area varies slightly in this chapter. In the above table, percentages are based on the total sample of 211 cases referred for an FGC, whereas in later tables, percentages are based on the 203 cases where FGCs were actually held.

A comparison of sample data with national data shows considerable similarity in the characteristics of those referred for FGCs. Furthermore, the total numbers of referrals to FGCs during the sample period closely approximated the number that would be expected from the yearly totals, although there were fewer than expected on the basis of yearly totals in Kapiti-Mana and more in Lower Hutt and Masterton. Sex and ethnicity data also corresponded with what might have been expected from the national figures. The largest and only significant discrepancy was in the relatively small numbers of Maori offenders during the sample period in Kapiti-Mana, an occurrence which was not characteristic of the area in the periods immediately before or after the sample period and which we therefore attributed to chance. Nevertheless, we can conclude that the FGC sample is, on the whole, reasonably representative of offenders in 1990 in the areas we studied.

As is apparent from Table 6.3, there was some regional variation with respect to both the sex and ethnicity of those dealt with by FGCs. Girls, for example, made up only 4% of the FGC sample in Kapiti-Mana and 7% in Lower Hutt compared to nearly a quarter in Henderson and Masterton.

Further analysis of the data showed that the girls in the sample were less likely than the boys to have had previous offences (33% of girls compared with 19% of boys had no previous offences) or to have previously had an FGC (80% of girls compared with 64% of boys had not previously had an FGC). Girls were also more likely to have committed less serious offences (29% of the least serious offences were committed by girls compared with 8% of the most serious offences).

The ethnicity of young people in our sample varied from area to area. This is to be expected given the geographic distribution of different ethnic groups in New Zealand, but there have to be other explanations for this variation too. Maori, for example, made up 63% of the Lower Hutt sample and 46% of the Masterton sample but only 24% of the Kapiti-Mana sample, although the proportion of Maori population in the Kapiti-Mana area is greater than in the other two areas. Pacific Islanders, on the other hand, were represented in the sample in a similar manner to their relative representation in the general population. They made up 32% of the Kapiti-Mana sample (compared with 15% of all young people in the area) and 25% of the Henderson sample (11%) compared to 15% in Lower Hutt (7%) and 3% in Masterton (1%). There were no Pacific Islanders in the Christchurch sample.

An important issue to attempt to resolve is the extent to which this over-representation of particular ethnic groups can be explained by different patterns of offending across ethnic groups rather than the ethnicity of the offender. A much higher proportion of Pakeha than Maori and Pacific Island FGC young people had no previous record: 38% compared with 16% for each of the other groups. However, the proportions who had previously had an FGC were almost identical (34%, 34% and 37% respectively). Similarly, a greater proportion of the least serious offences (i.e., those rated minimum or minimum/medium) were committed by Pakeha than by Maori (58% and 37% respectively). However, a greater proportion of the most serious offences were also attributed to Pakeha (50% compared with 32% for Maori and 14% for Pacific Islanders in the maximum or medium/maximum seriousness categories). On balance, it seems likely that the greater representation of Maori among FGC referrals is explained by the fact that they were more likely to have a previous offence history and less likely to have committed less serious offences compared to Pakeha.

Most of the young people referred for FGCs were in the older 14-16 year age group. Overall, only 16% were under 14. However, again, there were clear area differences. Thus, this younger age group made up less than 5% of the samples in two areas but 30% in another area.

There was little difference in the proportion of young people of various ages committing offences rated differently in seriousness. The only significant difference was that those aged 16 were more likely to have committed offences rated as maximum or medium/maximum in seriousness. Similarly, there was little difference in the proportion of various age groups who had not offended previously; for example, the figure for those under 14 was identical to that for 16 year olds (26%).

There seems to be an anomaly here. Regardless of age, those referred for an FGC seemed to be similar with respect to both the relative seriousness of offences and previous offence history. However, very young offenders seem not to be being referred to FGCs in some areas. It seems probable that, in these areas, young offenders are being dealt with by 'police diversion' despite the type of offence they commit whereas, in other areas, age is not a factor in the decision whether or not to refer to an FGC. This may reflect differences in the interpretation of the legislation in different areas or simply different police practices.

Arranging the FGC

Setting-up

Once a referral for an FGC has been received by a YJC, the way in which the arrangements are made for the FGC varies by area. In addition to the research areas, we visited 10 other DSW districts to gauge the extent of regional variations and the extent to which those areas we were most familiar with demonstrated 'typical' practice. In most districts, setting up the FGC and inviting participants to it was done by a specialist youth justice social worker; this was also the case in three areas in our sample. In a few of the other areas, including one in our sample, preliminary arrangements were made by the YJC, with details being finalised by any one of the generic social workers in the Social Services section. A third pattern, as for the fifth area in our sample, was for the co-ordinator to be responsible for all the arrangements. Other variations were also noted where the tasks were split in different ways between the co-ordinator and the social worker; for example, the social worker contacted the family and the co-ordinator the victim. Our impression is that setting up the FGC was best carried out within the framework of a specialist youth justice team and when one individual made all the arrangements rather than when the responsibilities were shared between different individuals. Those offices where the responsibilities were shared were the same offices where cases were overlooked and those cases which resulted in the greatest confusion among the participants about what to expect were often the cases where several people had shared the responsibility for the initial contact with various participants.

There are a number of ways in which we can judge whether or not an FGC has been well set up: the FGC takes place within the statutory time frame, key individuals are present, the timing and venue of the FGC are suitable for the participants, adequate notice of the FGC is provided and the parties involved feel that they had adequate briefing in advance of the meeting. We will now consider each of these in turn.

Time Limits

Less than a half of the FGCs in our sample took place within the required time limit although two thirds were convened within a week of the due date[35]. There was some area variation here: just over a third of FGCs were held within the time limit in one area compared with almost two thirds in another. Since time limits differ for non-court referrals (21 days) and court referrals (14 days), we need to examine these two situations separately. Tables 6.4 (a) and (b) provide this information.

From the tables it is clear that slightly more of the court referrals than non-court referrals met the statutory time limits. It was also noticeable that there were marked regional variations. For example, 73% of non-court referred cases met the statutory time limits in one area and 71% in another, compared with only 25% and 28% in two other areas. Even at the 5 week point there was substantial regional variation with three areas still not having arranged FGCs for at least a quarter of the non-court referrals. A greater volume of work in these areas compared with others may be a partial explanation for this variation but neither differences in the volume of work nor in the number of staff allocated to youth justice work seems entirely to explain why some districts appear to have more problems than others in meeting the statutory time frames.

If we look only at court referred cases, the percentage of cases which met the statutory time frame was slightly higher but still surprisingly low: 53%. There were also marked regional variations here with only 22% and 25% of court referred cases meeting the time limit in two areas (although in both these areas the numbers were small) compared with 78% in another.

---

[35] At the time of this research, the word 'convened' was thought to be equivalent to 'held' and the discussion of time limits in this report has been based on this interpretation.

Table 6.4
Time Taken to Convene FGCs Showing Court and Non-Court Referrals Separately and Giving Cumulative Percentages; N=189[36]

a) Court Referred FGCs

Time	N	Cum%
14 days	33	53
3 weeks	13	74
4 weeks	5	82
5 weeks	5	90
6 weeks	1	
7 weeks	3	
8 weeks	1	
9 weeks	1	
21 weeks	1	
Total No.	63	
Median in weeks		2

Note: The statutory time limit is shown in bold. Cumulative percentages have not been presented after 5 weeks as the numbers become too small.

b) Non-Court Referred FGCs

Time	N	Cum%
21 days	56	45
4 weeks	26	66
5 weeks	10	74
6 weeks	14	85
7 weeks	5	
8 weeks	2	
9 weeks	7	
10	1	
11	1	
12	3	
13	1	
Total No.	126	
Median in weeks		4

Note: The statutory time limit is shown in bold. Cumulative percentages have not been presented after 6 weeks as the numbers become too small.

Large differences **within** areas are also apparent. In one area, for example, the proportion of cases meeting the statutory time limits was 78% for court referrals but only 28% for non-court referred cases. This might reflect the greater priority given to court-referred cases, perhaps because of the impact of the existence of an external monitor – the Youth Court judge. Such a suggestion is partly borne out by the data from another area where the Youth Court sat every four weeks rather than every two weeks. There, 71% of non-court referred FGCs were completed within the statutory time limit but only 22% of the court referrals met it. However, more than three quarters (77%) of the court referred cases had been dealt with within four weeks. Social workers were apparently working towards the court date rather than the statutory time frame.

There are a number of reasons why FGCs do not meet the statutory limits – families and victims who are not on the phone are difficult to contact, staff shortages, work-load pressures and the priorities given to youth justice work in generic social work departments. These complications

---

[36] Some dates were missing on some files and some FGCs were not actually held, hence the number of cases on which complete data are available is only 189.

made it difficult for the researchers to assess the impact of staffing levels on the completion of work within time frames, but staffing numbers did not seem to us to be the only explanation. Some social workers felt that statutory time limits did not in practice provide sufficient time for adequate briefing of the families and/or victims or for contacting whanau or the extended family, especially when they lived out of the area. However, the fact that some of the research areas seemed better able than others to meet these deadlines raises some doubts about the validity of these suggestions. Two of the areas had specialist youth justice social workers but were quite disparate in the proportion of cases meeting the time limits. The number of FGC cases dealt with in one of these areas over the research period was, however, considerably greater. In the two research areas with the most similar numbers of FGC cases, again the proportion of cases meeting the time limits was very different (59% and 35% respectively). There is no simple explanation for failure to meet time limits, but one possibility, inevitably untestable, is that the different individuals involved have different priorities and meeting time limits may not be one of them.

Time of Day for FGCs

Overall, 54% of FGC cases were held before 4pm on a weekday; only 24% were held at or after 6pm. This figure of 24% for FGCs held in the evenings can be compared with the figure of 16% cited by Paterson and Harvey (1991) for care and protection FGCs. Marshall and Merry (1990) report from their analysis of victim/offender mediation schemes in England that the majority of meetings were held after 4pm. In some of their areas, this was as high as 80%. We discuss later whether or not the timing of the FGC affected participants' attendance at FGCs. There were very few FGCs held at weekends during the sample period.

There were clear differences between the research areas in the proportion of FGCs held before 4pm. The range was from 67% to 39%. Arguably this is a time which suits neither victims nor families, since those in work would probably need to take time off and hence lose income and those still at school would lose school time. There were also area differences at the other end of the spectrum. The proportion of FGCs held at or after 6pm ranged from 17% to 43%.

The Venue of FGCs

The most common venue for FGCs in the research areas was DSW offices or facilities – for example, former family homes. Overall, these were the venue for 66% of the FGC cases, although there was some regional variation ranging from 88% to just under a half. The offender's home was the next most common venue. Overall, the FGC was held there in 25% of cases though again there was considerable area variation: from 34% to only 4%. A slightly higher proportion of Maori FGC cases were held in the young person's home: 34%. Marae (Maori meeting houses) were rarely used; only 5% of Maori FGCs (3% of the total FGC sample) were held on marae during the sample period. The pattern here is close to that reported for care and protection FGCs (Paterson and Harvey, 1991): 48% were held in DSW offices or facilities, 16% were held in the home of a family member and only 4% were held on marae.

The main reason for the prevalence of DSW offices as the FGC venue seems to have been, quite simply, that families were not offered any other option; that is, they often did not realise that the meeting could be held elsewhere and where they wished. The explicit intention of the new Act was that families would nominate, or at least be consulted about, both the timing and venue of the FGC[37]. This does not always happen.

Holding FGCs in DSW facilities is no doubt convenient for the YJCs and social workers involved, but it does not meet the spirit of the legislation. It was put to us that the rationale behind the use of DSW offices (or former family homes for that matter) was that they were 'neutral' territory. This is not so. They represent *social welfare* territory and as such carry symbolic significance. It could also be argued that DSW offices or facilities provide a 'good' environment: for example, usually they are central and they have facilities for making coffee and/or tea. But in our experience, they were often too large or too small for the size of the group; they were sterile, cold and intimidating;

---

[37] Section 250 instructs YJCs to consult with the family, whanau or family group about the date, time and place of the FGC.

they lacked privacy; and coffee or tea was not usually provided. As one parent put it: *I found the environment a bit intimidating.* The Maori researchers commented that for Maori families, the DSW environment lacked the features that would have linked them to their own culture. Nor could DSW facilities provide the sense of warmth and safety which families would have had on the marae or in their own homes. One young Maori participant commented: *we had it at home and that was better than anywhere else.*

It is difficult to imagine that the practice of holding FGCs on DSW premises is culturally appropriate for any ethnic group. Families in effect could be disempowered by the choice of venue. On DSW territory, the symbolic (and hence potentially the actual) power remains with the professionals and this may discourage the participation of families and young people in the process of deciding on the best outcome and may hinder families in the process of taking responsibility for their young people. Moving the venue to the home of the family is one way of transferring power to the family. But an even more powerful transfer was seen by our Maori researchers to occur when the venue was the marae. The following account of a marae FGC written by the Maori researcher involved[38] emphasises these differences:

> *After several unsuccessful attempts to resolve the problems being encountered by O, a family decision was made not only to hold the next FGC on the marae but also to ensure the presence of O's extended whanau. Forty members of O's whanau came to the FGC and each of them came ready to contribute constructive alternatives for O. The very fact that the FGC was held on the marae made some subtle differences in the way the FGC was run. The taking back of the power from the Youth Justice Co-ordinator and placing it in the rightful hands of the kaumatua (elder) was the single, most important process that was involved. It was not a physical taking back of the power, but this happened because it was held on the marae. The roles of other departmental people who were present quickly became advisory only. The whanau were truly empowered not only because they had received good, sound information and advice; but by the fact that they were on their own turangawaewae (place). The wairua (spirit) was right, they were where they should have been to make decisions about their own son and mokopuna (grandson). The korero (discussion) that followed not only left the young person in no doubt about how the whanau felt about what he had done and how he had to account for his actions, but at the same time left O with his dignity intact and knowing that his whanau loved him. O's mother was challenged and her lack of mothering skills were brought out and laid bare, but, as they were for O, the pieces were put back together again and all was made whole. The processes were right and our people were empowered quite simply because the kaupapa (process) was ours.*

In many overseas victim/offender mediation schemes, the majority of the meetings are held in the **victim's** place of residence or place of work (the latter is almost always so for institutional victims). This reflects a clear difference in emphasis between such overseas schemes, which seem to be designed primarily to serve victims' needs, and the Family Group Conference process in New Zealand where the primary emphasis is on the young person and his or her family and victims seem, in part, to be 'used' as a means of holding young offenders accountable for their offences (See Marshall and Merry, 1990 and Coates and Gehm, 1989 for more detail of experience overseas). We came across no examples of FGCs being held in the victim's place of residence or work in our research.

The Composition of FGCs

The average number of people attending the FGC cases in the sample was 9 (in different areas the range was from an average of 7 to an average of 10). The smallest number of people attending was 2 and the largest was 39. For almost two thirds of FGCs, the numbers fell between 5 and 10. Table 6.5 provides this information.

---

[38] This FGC was held for an offence that occurred after the end of the sample period and hence has not been included in the quantitative analyses of the venue and the number present at the FGC.

Table 6.5
Total Number of People Attending FGCs Showing Area Differences in Range and Means; N=203

	Total	A	B	C	D	E
Minimum	2	4	5	2	4	4
Maximum	39	39	19	18	30	17
Mean	9	10	9	7	8	8
% under 5	9	7	0	12	19	9
% 5-10	63	49	68	72	68	63
% 10 & over	28	44	32	16	13	28

Ethnicity made a difference; the largest Pakeha FGC included 18 people but several Maori FGCs exceeded this number, with the largest involving 39 people. On average there were 8 people at Pakeha FGCs, 9 at Maori FGCs and 10 at those involving Pacific Islanders.

A satisfactory FGC with respect to the composition of its participants should include at least the young person, a family member, a co-ordinator, a victim (if the victim wishes to attend), a representative of the enforcement agency, a youth advocate where the case has been referred by the Youth Court and a social worker representing DSW if he or she is entitled to be present. We discuss each of these participants in turn.

Table 6.6 shows in summary how often different participants were present at the FGC.

Table 6.6
Summary of Who Was Present at the FGC; Percentages; N=203

Person	%
Young person	96
Parent or carer	98
Whanau or extended family	39
Siblings	21
Family supporter	19
Victim or victim's representative*	46
Enforcement agency	94
Youth advocate*	59
Social worker	62

* Where applicable

Parents And Young People
In the main, the young person and his or her family attended the FGC. In our sample of cases, the young person did not attend the FGC which determined the outcome on only 8 (4%) occasions and the parents did not attend the outcome FGC on 13 (6%) occasions. However, in most of the cases where the parents were absent, a carer was present. In only 4 (2%) cases were there neither parents nor carers present.

Where the young person and/or his or her family did not attend the FGC it would usually be adjourned for them to attend (though in 5 such cases the FGC was never subsequently held – the referral was simply 'forgotten' about and nothing further happened). On a few occasions, the FGC did continue without the presence of either the young person or his or her parents and, more rarely, without both, though in such situations there would always be a carer or a member of the extended family or whanau present.

The main reason for non-attendance by parents and young people was a failure in communication by DSW, but it was also caused by such mundane factors as the breakdown of cars. More serious reasons for the non-attendence of parents were refusals to become further involved with DSW and a desire to wash their hands of their child. Both of these reasons, however, were very rare. As we said above, parents or carers were absent from only 4 FGCs which decided on an outcome.

Although it has been held that an FGC without the presence of a parent or the young person can satisfy the statutory requirements of the Children, Young Persons and Their Families Act 1989 provided they were notified of the FGC[39], the effectiveness of such FGCs in meeting the statutory objectives of the Act can be questioned. Such FGCs cannot be said to meet the objectives of holding young people accountable for their actions or of encouraging families to take responsibility for formulating responses to these actions. Such FGCs are also clearly at variance with the requirement that young people should be present in any court where sentence is being pronounced. One victim described his feelings when an FGC continued without the presence of the young person as follows:

> *A disgrace. There should be sufficient legal authority to force attendance. I was surprised we proceeded. It diminished the value of the thing.*

Another victim echoed this:

> *I was annoyed. The system is really mickey mouse. It was a total waste of time to continue.*

A Youth Aid officer at this FGC expressed much the same sentiments:

> *It was shocking as far as I was concerned. It shouldn't have gone ahead without him. He has to admit or deny the offences before we can proceed.*

And in another case a whanau member commented that it gave the FGC *a certain unreal dimension* when the young person was not present since it meant to his mind that the meeting could not get to grips with the issue. The YJC in this particular case said that it would have been *nicer* to have had the young person present!

When parents are absent, this can cause subsequent difficulties in implementing the FGC outcome. An example is presented in the following case history:

> *In T's case the boy was already subject to a supervision with residence requirement. Because of persistent absconding and further offending the Department was planning to request cancellation and a review of the order. He was currently appearing in the Youth Court on more than 20 offences and, on the cancellation of the supervision with residence order, would be subject to sentence on more than 90 further offences. The total sum involved was around $26,000. The father was not present at the outcome FGC [he had attended a previous one], but had visited T that afternoon and the youth reported to the FGC that he and his father had together worked out a plan proposing reparation, community work, apologies and attendance at an outward bound training programme and so this was prepared for presentation to the Youth Court. At the court hearing, however, the father indicated that he felt unable to control T and could not support the recommendation. In the event, the youth was transferred to the District Court and subsequently sentenced to corrective training and ordered to forfeit the money he had in a bank account and a car which he had bought with the proceeds of his crime.*

On a few occasions, victims commented on the absence of a parent. In one case, the victim contacted the researcher after the interview to elaborate on her concern:

> *I agree with the boy. His father should have been there. I would have discussed things with him [the father]. I believe in the parent's responsibility for the child's behaviour. Shouldn't there be some power to force parents to attend?*

Difficulties can also arise as to who constitutes 'the family' for the purposes of a valid FGC. In one case, the youth's father and sister were expected at the FGC but had not arrived 20 minutes after the appointed starting time and so the meeting began. (The researcher involved was subsequently told that the family's car had broken down en route to the FGC.) When the meeting reached the stage at which the 'professionals' usually withdrew, the boy was left with his social worker and current

---

[39] Police v Linda and Graham, Carruthers J, Youth Court Wellington, 11 July 1990.

caregiver who had known the boy only one week and who acted as 'the family' in making recommendations. The boy in his interview with us made it very clear that he was unhappy about this. He felt no part of the decision and it can hardly be said that his family were involved in the process.

Whanau or Family Group

The new Act encourages the involvement of whanau or family groups in responding to young people's offending. For Maori, this is viewed as culturally appropriate since the young person is the child not simply of the nuclear family but also of the extended family and hence whanau (and hapu and iwi) have both rights and responsibilities with respect to the development of the child. Whanau or family groups can also provide support and advice in dealing with young people's offending where parents wish for support and advice.

It is difficult to judge the adequacy of whanau or extended family involvement in FGCs. Whanau or extended family members were only involved in 39% (80) of the FGC cases. They were more frequently involved in cases involving reoffending (they were present for 42% of those where there had been previous offending compared with 30% of those where there had been no previous offending), in court-referred cases (whanau or extended family members attended 58% of court-referred FGCs as opposed to 34% of non-court referred FGC cases), and in the more serious cases (only 21% of the least serious offence cases but 77% of the most serious offences had whanau or members of the extended family present). These findings match the comments of YJCs who remarked that, while they often held an FGC for minor first offences with only the immediate family present, they felt it was very important to locate extended family when the offences were more serious and when the young person was involved in repeated offending. There was, in addition, a tendency for more extended family to be present in those cases where more than one FGC was held before a resolution was reached; the reason for an adjournment was often to enable more family to attend. Whanau were also considerably more likely to be involved in Maori cases than were the extended family in Pakeha cases and the involvement of aiga[40] in Pacific Island cases was intermediate. Thus 58% of Maori cases had whanau present; the comparable figures for Pakeha and Pacific Island cases were 20% and 37% respectively. When whanau were present, they numbered from 1 to 27, with 2 being the most common number and the average being 4. We present later some case histories of extensive whanau involvement.

The fact that the presence of whanau or family groups varied by area also raises the question whether or not their involvement was seen by the YJC as more crucial in some areas than others. Table 6.7 presents these data in full.

Table 6.7
Whanau Involvement in FGCs by Area and Ethnicity; Percentages

Area	Pakeha (N=80) %	Maori (N=91) %	Pacific Island (N=30) %	Total (N=203) %
A	7	39	27	26
B	42	76	100	58
C	27	67	50	44
D	9	50	-	19
E	15	60	30	46

It might be possible to explain the differences in involvement of whanau in different areas with reference to the four factors just mentioned – offence seriousness, source of referral, previous offence history and ethnicity – and indeed a regression analysis showed that ethnicity and referral source are the main factors of importance, although the seriousness of the offence may also have

---

[40] The Samoan word 'aiga' is very similar in meaning to the Maori word 'whanau'.

played a part. But Table 6.7 shows that area differences are most important for Pakeha families and the effects of area cancel out other factors for them. Thus, the differences in DSW practice between one area and another are likely to result in different experiences for Pakeha families depending on the area in which they live. On the other hand, there are high levels of involvement of Maori families in all areas (Pacific Island families also have a moderately high involvement in all areas), suggesting that cultural factors rather than area differences are affecting practice for Maori and Pacific Island families. However, it should be noted that on occasion whanau were invited by DSW without the knowledge and apparently against the wishes of the immediate family, an issue to which we will return shortly.

Of course, we have no way of knowing whether or not there were whanau or members of the extended family who were not present at the FGC but who could or should have been invited. But we asked both families and YJCs about whether or not the 'right' family members had been present. Generally they felt that the right people had been present, but this was not always so. The involvement of whanau or the extended family (or the lack of it) was presented both positively and negatively by families.

The main reason for families wanting whanau or the extended family to be present was the support they offered and this came through the comments from all ethnic groups:

> *I felt safe because my whanau were with me. I would have felt like stink if I had to face it on my own. My auntie explained it so I understood. It was good that she allowed me to take a role. (Young person)*

And it is clear that on occasions families would have liked more support:

> *I felt a bit lonely ... I would have liked more family there. (Parent)*

> *All our family members weren't present because they felt intimidated by it all. It would have helped if they had been there. (Parent)*

The main criticism expressed about the presence of whanau or the extended family was their lack of knowledge about the young person and his or her offences or about the immediate family's situation:

> *Other family members didn't know the facts but they kept butting in and moralising. There were too many relatives who didn't know the facts. (Young person)*

> *There were too many extended family members involved. It felt uncomfortable. It was like strangers telling you how to deal with your child. (Parent)*

> *Ninety percent of them hadn't met him. I thought this is getting worse and worse as it goes on. (Youth Aid officer)*

Some families did feel that the wrong people were present or that they took the wrong approach:

> *My auntie shouldn't have been there. She talks too much. It should have been my mum that decides what happens. (Young person)*

> *I'd prefer not to have had family there. They were the wrong people and I had no say in choosing them. (Parent)*

> *He needed more people on his side; his aunt was vindictive. There was a large weight of adult numbers lined up against him. He was overpowered. (Carer)*

Some families also expressed shame about involving the wider family:

> *I feel really resentful about it. I didn't want to involve the family and burden them and feel shame. (Mother)*

This mother clearly felt pressured into having whanau present at the FGC. This seems counter-productive. Whether or not whanau or members of the extended family should be invited and who should be invited is an issue that many consider should be determined by the parents but an alternate view is that all those who are concerned for the child or young person should be involved[41]. The above examples demonstrate the potential tension between the objectives of whanau and family group involvement and the encouragement of parental responsibility which is embodied in the legislation. We return to this issue later in this chapter.

Family Support And Siblings

Other support people also attended FGCs. For example, siblings were present in 21% of FGC cases (although in 10 of the 42 cases the siblings were co-offenders and the FGC was a joint one) and family friends, teachers, youth club organisers and the like attended in 19% of cases. This varied from a high of 36% to a low of 3% in different areas. It could be suggested that Pakeha families, because they do not have the same extended family ties as Maori or Pacific Island families, might be more likely than the Maori or Pacific Island families to invite friends and the like rather than members of the extended family to FGCs for support. We did not see evidence of this. Indeed both Maori and Pacific Island FGCs were more likely to include family supporters than Pakeha FGCs (see Table 6.8).

Table 6.8
Presence at FGC of Siblings and Family Support by Ethnicity; Numbers and Percentages of Cases in Each Ethnic Group

	Maori (N=91)		Pakeha (N=80)		Pacific Island (N=30)	
	N	%	N	%	N	%
Siblings present*	22	24	10	13	10	33
Family support present	19	21	11	14	9	30

* Includes 6 cases of Maori co-offenders and 4 cases of Pacific Island co-offenders.

Victims

Providing victims with a voice in determining the appropriate response to the offences committed against them is a key ingredient of the new system. A major way of achieving this is encouraging victims to attend the FGC. Overall, 46% of the FGC cases in our sample where there was a victim were attended by at least one victim; this ranged from around a third in three areas to more than a half in the other two.

a) Some Reasons Why Victims Did Not Attend

Some victims, of course, do not wish to attend FGCs for a variety of reasons: they are too busy, uninterested, afraid, fear a loss of control, feel that they could contribute nothing, see no value in the FGC for them and so on. But it is clear from our interviews that some victims who did not attend the FGC would have liked to and the fact that they did not attend is explained quite simply by their not being invited. This was the reason given by a third of the victims who did not attend the FGC. Another 28% said that the time was not suitable for them while 17% said they were not told soon enough about the FGC to make arrangements to attend.

This indicates the lack of priority given by DSW to ensuring victims' attendance. Failure to invite victims occurred approximately twice as often where the victim was an organisation – for example, a shop or school. It was also these victims who were most likely to report that, when they were invited, the time was not suitable for them. It may be difficult in these cases to identify who it is that should be invited, but the fact that the researchers could sometimes make contact with an individual in these organisations who knew about the offending suggests that insufficient efforts were made by those setting up the FGC. Certainly, almost all the non-attending victims from stores

---

[41] Section 250 states that the YJC should consult with the family, whanau or family group about the persons who should attend the FGC.

and schools said that they would have attempted to attend if they had been told of the FGC, if the time had been suitable or if the notice had been sufficient. However, it was also apparent to us that the police did not always provide adequate information to enable victims to be readily contacted and that the persistence required to obtain the necessary information could understandably diminish when faced with other workload demands. This was particularly so for FGC cases which came from outside the area and which did not involve a request for reparation. In such situations, the police often provided minimal information – for example, the address, but not the name, of the victim of a burglary.

A number of quotes illustrate the most common reasons given by victims for not attending the FGC:

> I didn't know it was on. If I had known I would have tried to get there.

> I wasn't aware of the date until I was rung at the last minute and someone left a message. I couldn't go at that time. I had rung DSW many times and left messages. Eventually I gave up. I found them very difficult to get hold of.

> The DSW handled it badly. They never contacted me personally. They only left a message with my flatmate. When I rang them I couldn't get a reply. DSW let me know at the last minute and that's not good enough. I could have helped.

> I would have liked to attend but they rang on the night of the meeting and asked my views. I would have gone to give my opinions if I'd been given more notice.

> I couldn't attend as it was during working hours.

> I was invited to a meeting but I couldn't get there though I'd have liked to go. I was just told a time and place. I was not consulted.

Victims who did attend told the same story about the lack of notice or inconvenient times:

> He rang at 6.50pm the previous evening. He claimed he'd rung many times but that's not true. It's disgusting that there was only 23 hours' notice.

> It's important that the time is OK for victims. Victims should be looked after. It is difficult if it is held during the day.

> I was very annoyed that the notice for both FGCs was inadequate – 24 hours for one and the other was over before I got the letter.

We gave earlier some information on the times of the FGCs in our sample. There was a definite relationship between victims' attendance and the times of FGCs in cases which involved victims: victims attended fewer than half (42%) of the FGCs held before 4pm, they attended only about a quarter (26%) of the FGCs held between 4pm and 6pm, but they attended nearly three quarters (72%) of those held at or after 6 pm. One interpretation of this finding is that victims do not wish to take much time off work and they especially do not wish to give up their time at the end of the day, around 4-6 p.m. Another interpretation is that, where victims indicated that they wanted to attend, the FGC was arranged in the evening. Our data do not explain which interpretation is to be preferred.

In our discussions with professionals in different parts of the country, we were often told that one reason for victims' non-attendance was the place in which the FGC was to be held – in particular, concerns were expressed about holding them on marae or in the offender's home. But concerns about the venue were rarely cited by non-attending victims and there is little evidence that victims were less likely to attend FGCs held at the offender's home than those held on DSW premises. The proportions of FGCs held in DSW and held in the offender's home which were not attended by a victim were very similar (54% and 60% respectively). The number of FGCs held on marae was too small for reliable analysis on this point.

From our interviews, it is also clear that the manner in which victims are invited to attend FGCs is crucial in determining whether or not they decide to attend. In one case, for example, in which a car had been stolen and written off, the victim was told by the YJC that she could 'front' up to the offenders. She thought this would be on a one to one basis and felt threatened by this type of situation. She was afraid that the offenders might get angry at the meeting and burgle her house, as her address had been in the stolen car. This victim felt that if she had fully understood the setting of the FGC she would have attended. In another case, the victim said: The YJC indicated that the FGC was going to be just a bit of talk, and so the victim did not feel it necessary to be there. Another reported being told that it was not really important for him to attend in this type of case (receiving). This importance of the manner of approach was supported by victims who did attend:

> *On the phone, I got the impression that I was going to be the only one [victim] there. I thought it was deliberate intimidation. He referred to THE victim. I nearly didn't go as a result.*

b) Some Reasons Why Victims Attended

Victims expressed a range of reasons for deciding that they would attend the FGC. Some reflect victims' concern to protect their own interests – a desire to obtain reparation, to ensure the process was correctly followed or to confront the young person – but others indicate a willingness to attempt to help or support the young person. Other reasons given include a belief that victims should attend such meetings, a sense of duty and curiosity:

Victim's Interests

> *To try and get reparation ... I thought it would help my case if I attended.*

> *Because I was a victim and wanted to ensure that things were done properly.*

> *Because I could confront them with what they had done.*

> *I like to be heard. I want to have my say. If I didn't, I'd always harbour a grudge.*

> *I hoped my presence emphasised the severity of her actions.*

Offender's Interests

> *To see if we can help to do something about straightening the offenders out ... to see how offenders react to meeting victims.*

> *If the process is going to be of benefit, victims should go.*

> *To see if he was learning anything from it.*

> *I felt it was important that victim and offender make contact.*

> *I wanted him to see what he did was wrong ... personally I believe that he had good in him.*

Other Reasons

> *I went out of curiosity ... and I wanted to see how it all works.*

> *Sense of duty ... out of interest.*

> *Being a Maori myself, I felt it important to support it.*

> *I felt it was my duty to go – it was the right thing to do.*

Enforcement Officers

In the main, representatives of the enforcement agencies attended FGCs. For the police this was usually a Youth Aid officer and, for the MOT, it was usually an MOT prosecutor. Only 6% of FGCs took place without the presence of a police or MOT officer. There was some regional difference here ranging from none in one area to 12% in another. Work commitments or shortage of staff were the most common reasons for non-attendance by enforcement officers. Where the enforcement agency did not attend the FGC, it is not surprising that difficulties tended to arise in obtaining its agreement; this was particularly so with respect to court-referred cases where the police were more inclined to want higher tariff penalties. In one area, the police prosecutor in at least one instance advised the Youth Aid officer not to attend an FGC in a case where he believed that nothing short of a court order would be a satisfactory outcome. Another difficulty that arose with the cases in this area was that, although the FGC might have been attended by a Youth Aid officer who agreed to the decision, a right of veto was retained by the prosecutor who sometimes indicated disagreement as late as the morning on which the court hearing had been arranged and thus allowed no further time for negotiation.

FGCs are mostly, but not necessarily always, attended by the Youth Aid officer[42]. In a few of the very serious cases in the study, the detective involved in investigating the offence attended the FGC. There were a few other examples during the research when the front-line police officer involved in reporting the offence attended the FGC. There seemed to be no set pattern as to when the reporting or investigating officer would attend; for example, in one offence involving three offenders the investigating detective attended two of the FGCs and the Youth Aid officer attended the third. The reason mentioned for the detective's attendance for this offence was to provide continuity of support to the victims but in practice such a concern was balanced against considerations of when the FGC was to be held and other competing demands on the time of the officer.

The attendance of investigating or reporting officers could be a disadvantage when they had little previous experience of FGCs and were uncertain about how to contribute to the process. On the other hand, their attendance made some discussion of the summary of facts possible and could make the process more realistic for the young person. Certainly some of the young people would have preferred the officer who they had dealt with previously to be present:

> *I would have preferred the male cop, the one I'd already dealt with.*
>
> *It would have been better if the actual officer had been there. He [the Youth Aid officer[didn't know much about the case.*
>
> *I wondered why the MOT officer who picked me up wasn't there.*

And in certain cases it was felt that the person with the power to agree to the decisions should have been there. As one parent put it: *the prosecutor should be there if he's the one to decide*.

While it may be unrealistic given the work pressures on police personnel to expect other police or MOT officers to attend FGCs routinely in addition to specialist Youth Aid officers, it was noted that where the reporting officer was the 'victim', as in cases involving assault, he or she was never present at any FGC during the research. This is more difficult to gloss over, given that the police feel that victims generally should be encouraged to attend FGCs.

Youth Advocates

In cases referred from the Youth Court for an FGC we would also expect that court-appointed youth advocates would attend the FGC. This was not always the case. Youth advocates attended in less than two thirds (59%) of court-referred FGC cases. The numbers involved, however, were too small for reliable conclusions to be made about regional variations.

The reasons given by youth advocates for their non-attendance include complaints about a lack of adequate notice for the FGC and inconvenient scheduling of FGCs (by this they meant meetings in the evening and during court time), but there seems also to be an issue of the priorities of youth advocates here and a lack of awareness of their responsibilities. For example, a youth advocate who could not attend a court hearing would normally ensure that a colleague was adequately briefed to represent the client. This did not happen with respect to FGCs. And yet the FGC is a crucial stage in determining the eventual outcome of the case at the Youth Court and if the youth advocate has not been present at the FGC he or she cannot adequately represent the way in which the recommendation was reached, the reasons for it and so on.

Social Workers

Social workers are only entitled to be present at FGCs in certain clearly defined situations and not as of right. These are when the young person has been placed in the custody of the Director-General of Social Welfare, where the Director-General is the guardian of the child or young person or where the young person is under the supervision of the Director-General. The underlying rationale for this is that the new system reflects a philosophical shift in emphasis from the offenders' welfare to their accountability. However, in practice, social workers attended in many cases where there was

---

[42] We can not provide an exact number as this detail was not necessarily recorded on every file but it is unlikely that a detective or front-line officer attended in more than 5% of cases.

no statutory justification for their presence and the reasons given for their attendance bear little relationship to the legislation.

Over all the research areas, social workers were present for 62% of the FGC cases. However, this ranged from 84% to 26% in different areas (see Table 6.9). Such marked variations can only really be explained by variation in DSW policy in the different districts about the appropriateness or otherwise of social workers attending FGCs. Whether or not there was a specialist youth justice team in the district did not satisfactorily explain the differences. Nor were they explained by whether or not social workers rather than the co-ordinators set up the FGC, as in both of the areas at the extremes of the range the FGCs were usually arranged by social workers.

Table 6.9
Presence of Social Workers by Area; Percentages

	A %	B %	C %	D %	E %	Total %
Present	30	84	80	26	79	62

In the 10 DSW areas we visited, only three reported that social workers rarely attended FGCs. A wide range of rationales was offered for social workers' attendance at FGCs. In some cases, the social workers had contacted the victims to invite them to attend or to ascertain their views and so attended the FGC themselves in order to represent the victim's views. In other cases which we observed, social workers seemed to have taken on a case management, interventionist role and acted very much as traditional social workers. That is, they introduced background information on the young person or the family where they were known to DSW, suggested particular programmes and hence tended to influence outcomes. Many other reasons were given to us for social workers' attendance including ones reflecting Departmental interests: *to represent the Department's interests, to indicate their ability to support the family's plan and to provide particular programmes, to provide information on options open to the family, because the social worker may have to write a report, prepare a plan for the Youth Court, or provide follow-up support for the young person or the family, and because there may be care and protection issues in the case.* Sometimes the reasons referred to the needs of the family: *to provide support for the family and to help them express their views, to act as an advocate for the offender.* Even personal professional reasons were cited: *job enrichment.* The need for general supervision was expressed in one comment: *to prevent 'unrealistic' decisions.*

Many of these reasons are clearly **not** in tune with the philosophic shifts intended by the new legislation and, in particular, the shift toward family control over decision-making. It is clear from the Act that it was only intended that social workers would attend the FGC when the Department already occupied a guardianship responsibility or a custodial role in the life of the young person. The argument that the social worker, having been involved in setting up the FGC, could thereby provide support for the family appears plausible but comments from families to the effect that such support was appreciated were rarely noted. Furthermore, if the justification for the social worker's presence is to provide family support, then it might be appropriate to ask the family their views on the matter but, from our observations, families were not normally asked whether or not they would like the social worker to attend. Also, many of the above reasons for social workers attending FGCs could be as well served by contact with the family and young person before or after the FGC or at an FGC adjourned for a particular purpose – for example, to formulate a plan.

Furthermore, we noted that, in some of the FGCs we observed, the social worker, though present, tended to play a minimal role; indeed, we observed some FGCs at which the social worker was silent throughout. One senior social worker was heard to say at the team meeting: *I don't know why we're there. I feel redundant.* This suggests that some social workers had a sense that they were expected to abandon their previous role, but were unsure what their new role should be. They did not yet see it as primarily ensuring that FGCs were well set up and as providing follow-up after the FGC when DSW had a continuing involvement.

Co-offenders
Co-offenders are also not entitled to attend each others' FGCs, but where co-offenders were siblings or where siblings were the subject of FGCs at around the same time, it was usual to arrange a joint FGC for obvious reasons. This occurred five times in the sample period involving 10 FGC cases. However, it was rare to hold joint FGCs when co-offenders were unrelated. This occurred on only four occasions. For the vast majority of cases involving co-offenders, separate FGCs were held. Yet this must have inconvenienced the victims who wished to attend the FGC – that is to say, they would have had to attend additional FGCs – and 11 victims[43] attended the FGC for one or more of the co-offenders but not for others whose FGCs were held subsequently.

There are other justifications based on notions of justice, accountability and equity for dealing with co-offenders together. There is the possibility of differential outcomes for co-offenders, something which young people seem to feel very strongly about, when they are dealt with separately; it is also difficult if not impossible to determine the respective roles of co-offenders and hence decide on differences in culpability when the FGCs are held separately. Counter-arguments are that there might be practical difficulties in finding a suitable venue or in getting everyone together at the right time. But we did attend some very large FGCs, one of which involved four families and another (outside the research areas) which involved five families and a considerable number of victims. Families might not feel able to raise more personal matters in the presence of other families, but this difficulty could be overcome if each family also spent some time as a separate smaller family group.

The Adequacy Of The Composition Of FGCs
Only 42% of FGCs cases were coded by us as having the 'right' composition of participants; young person, family, enforcement officer, youth advocate and, where relevant, the victim. This picture does not look quite as bad when we add those cases where the only missing person was the victim. It should be recognised that victims have the right not to attend FGCs and we were not always able to determine, because of our methodology for contacting victims[44], whether victims had chosen not to attend, whether they had not been invited to attend or whether they had found the time unsuitable. While regarding FGCs where no victim was present as having the 'right' composition is without doubt over-generous, the proportion of FGCs that can be regarded as having an 'adequate' composition, except for the victim, rises to over eight out of ten (83%). However, again there was some regional variation here. The most marked discrepancy was that a third of FGC cases in one area were coded as not having an adequate composition. This is almost entirely explained by the large number of court-referred FGC cases which proceeded there without the presence of youth advocates.

A question also arises about who monitors whether or not the FGC has been adequately constituted; judicial review of this, for example, is rare. There was at least one case in the sample in which we doubt that an FGC, properly or legally speaking, took place at all. This was a situation in which the court had ordered an FGC for an 18 year old whose offence had been committed just before his 17th birthday. On the day before the court hearing, the YJC went to the youth's address and was told by a brother that he was at the periodic detention centre. As the YJC left to go there, he rang the Youth Aid officer to inform them of the FGC in 10 minutes' time. The Youth Aid officer was unable to attend at this notice. When the youth arrived at the periodic detention office, the YJC discussed the offence with him. The bulk of the discussion focused on the youth's belief that he had already been dealt with for this offence and this was accepted by the YJC and subsequently put to the Youth Court. At the Youth Court hearing, the youth's legal representative who was acting on behalf of the youth's appointed youth advocate opened by saying that according to both the youth advocate and the youth an FGC had not been held. The judge's response was to refer to the document submitted to him (842) containing the FGC outcome. This document clearly stated that

---

[43] There are more victims than cases involving co-offenders because there were multiple victims in several of these cases. The 11 victims represent 9% of the total sample of 123 victims interviewed.

[44] To remind the reader, we attempted to interview all those victims who attended FGCs and at least one victim who could potentially have been involved in the FGC but who did not attend. This means we interviewed a relatively higher proportion of victims who attended than victims who did not attend.

only the youth, the YJC and the researcher had been present and yet no inquiries were made as to whether or not the parents had been informed or whether or not Youth Aid and the youth advocate had been given adequate notice (both were noted as having apologised for their absence, though it is clear from the legal representative's opening remarks that the youth advocate had not been aware of the FGC).

Briefing The Participants

The success of an FGC depends to a large extent on the way in which the various parties, in particular the families and victims, have been briefed. Neither party is likely to have had any or very much prior experience of such a meeting and is unlikely to know what to expect. Hence the best outcomes are likely to result if all parties are carefully prepared with information on both the process and procedures to be followed and on possible outcomes. Generally, both the families and the victims need information in advance of the meeting to assist them to identify their principal objectives at the FGC and ways of meeting them.

Parents

Although the introduction of FGCs was to some extent premised on families having the ability and resources to determine appropriate sanctions for their children's offending, it is quite clear from our interviews with families that many families did not know where to start. They were unfamiliar with what options there were for both sanctions and services and, in particular, what resources, programmes or facilities were available to them locally. The following quotations from parents demonstrate this lack of briefing. It was a recurrent theme:

> *There was not as much information as I wanted. I needed more information on the options available.*

> *We were flung into the meeting without much information.*

> *They should have explained more. We were a bit confused.*

> *We found it hard to make decisions – because we didn't know what was available in the community.*

> *The YJC sent a list of outcomes but no appropriate ones were highlighted. This contributed to our fear.*

> *DSW should provide a list of community venues for work. It's hard finding things to do.*

It was not uncommon for us to observe requests from parents for information during the FGC itself. In one case, for example, when the YJC suggested that the non family members now withdraw so that the family could discuss the appropriate penalty in private, the father interrupted and asked but what are the options? The YJC then repeated what he had said previously about likely penalties if the case had been referred to the District Court – a fine plus costs. He also raised further possibilities: a letter of apology, reparation, community work or a donation to charity. The professionals then withdrew and the family subsequently suggested a letter of apology and reparation (though the sum was slightly greater than the actual loss to the victim) which was later accepted by those present at the FGC. This example clearly demonstrates a lack of adequate briefing prior to the FGC about possible outcomes. Where the parents and young person have had little opportunity in advance of the FGC to consider what might be the most appropriate outcome from their point of view, the suggestions of the professionals are very likely to be those which are adopted.

There is a careful line to be drawn here. We are not suggesting what has been called a 'rehearsal with a script', where in effect professionals shape the eventual decision by providing families only with information of a particular kind. Rather we are pointing to the fact that a lack of information will inevitably mean that families have to turn to the professionals whose views are then likely to determine the outcomes. Knowledge is power and if families are denied or given limited knowledge then they are denied or given limited empowerment.

Victims

Our interview data indicate the need for better briefing not just of families, but of victims. Victims need to know what to expect not just in terms of their immediate role in the FGC, but also what it might be like to meet the offender in person. They should not be encouraged to enter the meeting with unrealistic expectations. In one area outside the sample, there was a very high level of attendance by victims at FGCs. In part, if not principally, this was due to the fact that in this area there was a victim advocate who contacted all victims and in doing so told them that their chances of reparation would be higher if they attended the FGC. In reality, the vast majority of the families we talked with had limited financial resources and, if victims were led to believe that their attendance would be more likely to secure reparation, then they would be likely to be greatly disappointed (and indeed we understand that, in the area just referred to, many victims found their hopes of reparation were disappointed). Victims expressed their concerns about briefing prior to the FGC to us as follows:

> *[The FGC] took a long time so I left before it finished – about two and a half hours. I expected only an hour. It would be good to tell people how long to expect.*
>
> *It would be better to explain the procedure fully before you get there.*
>
> *There wasn't adequate preparation for meeting the offender – the psychological preparation for meeting offenders needs more thought.*

Young People

On the other hand, young people appeared to have been reasonably well briefed before the FGC. They generally had a good understanding of why they had been referred to an FGC and their comments reflected well the legislative objectives – reparation and reconciliation, individual accountability and family responsibility:

> *To find out a way I could be made to pay for what I'd done.*
>
> *To talk about what I'd done and how to make things right.*
>
> *To decide what I would do to pay everyone back.*
>
> *To get offenders together with victims, discuss what we did, why we did it and work out the punishment.*
>
> *So the different sides wouldn't keep fighting with each other. We were to talk together about things and try to solve the problem.*
>
> *To let the family have a say.*

The FGC Process

Facilitating FGCs

Table 6.10 presents data from the Department of Social Welfare quarterly returns on the extent to which FGCs were 'facilitated' (conducted) by YJCs. Overall, 84% of FGCs were facilitated by the YJC but it is apparent from this table that there was considerable regional variation in who facilitated the FGCs. In some areas, the YJC facilitated all or almost all the FGCs. In other areas, the facilitation was delegated to others, as in Wellington where the YJC only facilitated 35% of the FGCs in the period examined. In Wellington, social workers facilitated many of the FGCs in the early part of the year, although this pattern changed in the latter half of 1990. Thus patterns not only differed between areas but also changed over time. In Henderson, to give another example, the YJC was the facilitator in 13% of the FGCs in one quarter, 61% in the next and 33% in the next.

Table 6.10
Number of FGCs and Proportion Facilitated by YJCs for 1990 in Selected DSW Offices

Area	FGCs N	Facilitated by YJC %
Auckland	336	95
Christchurch	99	89
Henderson	172	53
Lower Hutt	238	100
Masterton	136	83
Kapiti-Mana	136	93
Wellington	150	35
New Zealand	5,851	84

Source: Unpublished Department of Social Welfare quarterly returns.

Table 6.11 presents similar information on facilitation for the research period.

Table 6.11
Number of FGCs and Proportion Facilitated by YJCs During the Sample Period of Three Months

Area	FGCs N	Facilitated by YJC %
Christchurch	32	94
Henderson	43	51
Lower Hutt	72	94
Masterton	136	83
Kapiti-Mana	136	93
Wellington	150	35
New Zealand	5,851	84

The proportion of FGCs facilitated by YJCs during the sample period closely corresponds in all areas to the proportions recorded in the annual statistics for those areas.

Procedure

It should not really be possible to describe the procedures adopted at a 'typical' FGC, for the intention of the legislation was to allow families to adopt whatever procedures they wished[45]. However, this rarely happened. Co-ordinators, in the main, have developed routine procedures which suit them and which are followed in almost all cases. Thus a common pattern can be described.

The most usual beginning for FGCs was for everyone to introduce themselves, although in some areas this may have been preceded by prayers or a karakia (a blessing) and a welcome in Maori. The co-ordinator then explained the procedure to be followed, invited the Youth Aid or MOT officer to read the summary of facts and then asked the young person whether or not these were accurate. Although the detail was questioned in a considerable number of the FGCs we observed and this was seen as important by families and young people, denials were in fact rare. Where the young person

---

[45] Section 250 states that the YJC should consult with the family, whanau or family group about the procedure to be adopted at the FGC.

admitted one offence and denied another, the FGC usually proceeded to determine an outcome for the offence admitted, a practice which contrasts with the courts' usual practice of adjourning matters until guilt in the denied matter has been determined. Denials occurred in only 1% of the non-court referred FGC cases in our sample, although if we include those cases where there was both a denial and an admission this would increase to 2%.

Once an admission was made, the co-ordinator usually then asked any attending victim to speak or reported any views from victims who were not present (in some areas this was done by a social worker). Being asked to speak at this point was not always welcomed by victims and this may have reflected their inadequate briefing on what would happen at the FGC:

> *I felt put on a judge's seat – a lot of pressure – a bit intimidated.*
>
> *I was put on the spot by having to speak first. He could have got away with saying nothing.*

Well prepared or well briefed victims, on the other hand, could play a very positive part in the proceedings. YJCs, in particular, remarked on this:

> *She had a clear agenda and put her position well in emotional terms. She clearly indicated what she thought was a reasonable outcome.*
>
> *The victim was very important ... contributed a lot to the meeting.*
>
> *They played a particularly significant role and in most cases it was satisfying for them.*

The primary focus in FGCs is intended to be on the offence and the young person's accountability for it. Our observations confirmed that the offence and finding an appropriate response to it were the main focus of discussion at FGCs. This does not mean that the discussions never focused on attempts to understand the reasons underlying the offence or the surrounding circumstances. And, as we will see later, outcomes could involve responses to such perceived problems – for example, a requirement that the young person undertake drug or alcohol assessment, join a youth club or sporting facility or receive counselling. But an exploration of the factors leading up to the offending was either rare or made in a random and haphazard fashion. Alcohol or drug use, for example, was raised and discussed for only some of the young people whose pattern of offending seemed to involve substance abuse.

Following a general discussion of possible outcomes, families may withdraw to discuss these suggestions in private. We comment on the frequency with which this actually occurred and the possible consequences of failure to do so in a later section. What happened next was the formulation of a 'plan', 'response' or 'outcome', which in theory was shaped by the family. There may have been some further discussion or negotiation at this point with the non-family members. Then agreement was sought by the co-ordinators from the enforcement agency and, again in theory, from the victims who were present. We will comment on practice here at a later point. The agreed plan is then recorded by the co-ordinator and the meeting was closed, sometimes with a prayer.

Length of FGCs

The FGC process which we have just outlined differs enormously from usual courtroom procedures and takes much longer than the few moments of the average court appearance. Just under a third of the FGC cases in the sample took less than an hour, almost a third took between an hour and an hour and a half and more than a quarter took between one and a half and two hours. Around 10% took more than two hours.

There were no clear area differences, although in one area almost 20% of FGC cases took more than two hours. Youth justice FGCs are, on the whole, considerably shorter than care and protection FGCs, of which 93% took more than two hours with an average time of just under 3.5 hours (Paterson and Harvey, 1991). Such a difference may reflect the greater complexity of issues in care and protection cases. On the other hand, the relatively short time taken in youth justice FGCs may in part be due to a determination to focus on issues relating to accountability rather than allowing discussions of welfare issues to predominate.

FGCs also differ from the court process in being more commonly resolved in one session. Remands in court are usual (we discuss this in Chapter 8); 86% of the FGC cases, on the other hand, were resolved in one meeting. This figure of 86% is very similar to the figure of 84% for care and protection FGCs resolved in one meeting as reported by Paterson and Harvey (1991). There was some area variation here (see Table 6.12), with almost all cases being resolved in one meeting in two areas, but only 60% being resolved in one meeting in another area. In the latter area, 28% of cases required two meetings and 12% required three or four meetings.

Table 6.12
Numbers of FGC Meetings Needed to Resolve Matters by Area; Percentages

Area	1 FGC %	2 FGCs %	3 or more FGCs %
A	93	5	2
B	97	3	0
C	60	28	12
D	87	10	3
E	83	15	2
Total	86	11	3

Additional FGC meetings were required for a variety of reasons including: the absence of the family or young person, the need for more time to involve victims, a desire to involve more family members and the need to allow the family more time to canvass the available options.

Holding more than two FGC meetings before an outcome was reached was uncommon in most areas, although one case required six meetings. The family were most concerned about the delay in the resolution of this case which seemed at least in part due to the failure of the professionals to prepare adequately for the FGC and to ensure that the necessary reports were available on time. The reasons for delay in the sequence of FGC meetings in this case were as follows:

- 'decisions delayed (for four days) because of possible further charges

- 'decisions delayed (for six and a half weeks) because one offence was denied and the court wished to keep all matters together (although in the interim the FGC recommended that the boy be disqualified from driving for six months and undergo anger management counselling)

- 'decisions delayed (for two and a half weeks) for the same reason as above

- 'decisions delayed (for one week) because the family did not attend

- 'decisions delayed (for one month) because reports had not been prepared.

At this fifth meeting, the co-ordinator said he thought that vital people were missing – a teacher and a social worker – and that they needed an alcohol assessment. The mother's response was: *this is all a bit slack*. The father added: *we are going through a fair bit of pressure because of this*. The youth advocate said that there was no choice but to meet again: *We must have proper professional reports; we could be making decisions that are wrong*. The final outcome was 200 hours' community work, reparation, disqualification from driving, an apology to the victims and counselling about alcohol abuse.

The Youth Justice Co-ordinators' Role

Of the 48 co-ordinators employed as of 1 September 1990, 26 identified themselves as Maori, 13 as Pakeha, three as of Pacific Island origin and two as part Maori and part Pacific Island in origin (Renouf et al, 1990). The co-ordinators in the research areas reflected this balance. Although, in all, 18 individuals (either co-ordinators or social workers) acted as facilitators for the FGCs in the research sample, the bulk of them were facilitated by ten co-ordinators (holding either permanent or acting appointments) of whom seven identified themselves as Maori, three as Pakeha and none as being of Pacific Island origin. This meant that about a third (32%) of FGC cases were facilitated by Pakeha co-ordinators (excluding those facilitated by social workers) and more than two thirds (68%) by Maori co-ordinators. There appears to have been little attempt in the areas we studied to match the ethnicity of the co-ordinator with that of the young person. Although two thirds of Maori young people had Maori co-ordinators, one third had Pakeha co-ordinators. On the other hand, less than a quarter (21%) of Pakeha offenders had a Pakeha co-ordinator and more than three quarters (79%) had a Maori co-ordinator.

YJCs have a complex role to play. Their overall responsibility is to ensure that the Act's objectives and principles are being met. In a sense, the YJC is the guardian of these. With respect to the FGC process, the objectives and principles are ensuring that the young offender is held accountable for his or her actions, that families are empowered by handing over decision-making to them, that least restrictive alternatives are used while maximising the well-being of the young person and that the rights of young people are protected. In the FGC itself, the YJC's role is to provide further information if it is required, to facilitate the conference and to mediate between the family and the enforcement agency or between the family and the victim. This was certainly how co-ordinators most commonly described their role at the FGC to us:

> *Trying to keep the process honest and keep people focused on the task at hand. Providing support for the young people and their parents.*
>
> *I don't try to predict or guess what the family might decide. I have no preconceived ideas – that would be inappropriate vis-a-vis the co-ordinator's role. I want a resolution, but not a particular outcome.*
>
> *More mediation really in the interests of getting a compromise which the father and son could live with, hopefully.*
>
> *To facilitate and to ensure that the victim could present her views. The family could state their response to the offending and come up with an agreed recommendation.*
>
> *Giving information, ensuring views were heard and supporting the family's decision.*
>
> *Making sure something happened to enable the judge to make a decision on a level as low key as possible.*

However, there are conflicts inherent in the objectives of the new system (we referred to these in Chapter 1, pages 10-11) and these emerge as conflicts in the roles co-ordinators play in FGCs. At a rather basic level, co-ordinators, for example, may try to emphasise the need for reconciliation at one point in the proceedings and the need for punishment at another. We observed examples of uncomfortable shifts between these two emphases which could only have been confusing for the young person concerned, if not for all the participants.

Families, on the whole, were appreciative of how the co-ordinators handled matters, but there were three areas in which some negative comments were made: their lack of cultural knowledge or sensitivity, their lack of familiarity with the details of the case and their role in determining the outcome.

Cultural Insensitivity
The clearest example of cultural insensitivity was the failure to organise an interpreter to brief the family and attend the FGC or to ensure that the interpreter's English was adequate. Even where the YJC had arranged for an interpreter to be present at the FGC, it was often apparent that the interpreter had not been involved in providing the family with information prior to the FGC and hence the families came to the FGC not knowing what to expect and unaware of what was expected of them.

One FGC involved a Tongan family whose son had committed a very serious offence and the researcher commented that, until the FGC met, the family had not fully realised all that had happened. The family's English was not good and an interpreter was present at the FGC. However, both the interpreter and a friend of the family said that, although the parents were a bit confused, they were not given a break or an opportunity to discuss things: *They were pushed into a decision. Put on the spot instead of being given a chance to go away and talk about it.* In retrospect, because of the language difficulties and the family's lack of prior awareness of the gravity of the offence, it might have been preferable to adjourn the FGC to allow the family to consider the matter more carefully.

Some co-ordinators developed a stylised response to cultural difference by providing a multi-lingual greeting and a prayer at the start of all FGCs. This seemed at times to the researchers to be inappropriate, especially for families from smaller ethnic minorities and it generally appeared to be accepted with tolerance rather than appreciated as meeting the specific cultural and family needs which were more diverse than these formats allowed. Such openings with a prayer and a few Maori or Pacific Island words (not always in the right language for some of the Pacific Island people), were generally seen as a token gesture rather than a truly culturally sensitive way of doing things.

YJC's Lack of Knowledge of the Case
In not all cases did the YJC ensure that he or she was adequately briefed before the FGC. Such a lack of knowledge tended to be most obvious when an FGC was reconvened or a second FGC was held for the same person. The following case history is an example of this:

> *In S's case, the FGC decided, amongst other things, that S should make reparation to the victim and undergo drug and alcohol assessment. Some weeks later S committed further offences and was again sent for an FGC. These discussions took place without any referral to the earlier FGC outcome or to whether or not S was paying reparation (he was not). The drug and alcohol assessment was on the DSW file at this stage and again no reference was made either to it or its recommendations. S was continuing to abuse drugs and alcohol.*

One parent summed up this concern:

> *I felt the YJC was incompetent. He didn't run it fairly or efficiently. He didn't appear to be conversant with the case.*

Determining outcomes
In some cases the YJC clearly played a major role in determining outcomes. One such example is provided by the case of M:

> *In M's case, it was apparent from both the researcher's notes of what happened at the FGC and the interview with the mother that the recommendation (supervision with residence) was not one promoted by the family. At the FGC, for example, in reply to a question from the mother of what the options were, the YJC replied that some kind of supervision was a must: "maybe a section 311 is the only option". The YJC then asked the mother whether the youth could be sent to whanau in another area. Her response was "not really". The YJC then continued: "for the time being then the suggestion is that supervision with residence for three months be considered followed by a three month period of supervision". There was no withdrawal by the professionals to allow the family to deliberate privately at any point during the FGC, and the youth advocate's role seems to have been limited to agreeing that the court was unlikely to contemplate anything other than a section 311. The researcher's field notes indicate that the mother and the youth participated little in the discussion, that discussion was dominated by the YJC and that it was, in essence, he and the other professionals present who made the decision.*

Professionals' Withdrawal From The FGC

We came across many examples of failure on the part of the professionals to withdraw during the FGC and to give the families some time to consider the decision on their own. Table 6.13 provides information on this for each area.

Table 6.13
Withdrawal of Professionals; Percentage of Cases Where this Did Not Occur, by Area; N=177*

	A %	B %	C %	D %	E %	Total %
Did not withdraw	58	19	5	63	49	42

* Don't knows were excluded and there were missing data on this variable as not all FGCs were attended by the researchers.

Overall, the professionals did not withdraw in well over a third (42%) of FGC cases. The regional differences in this case were considerable. In one area, the professionals did not withdraw in only one case (5%) and this was where the young person's parent was not present. In two other areas, on the other hand, the professionals failed to withdraw in more than half of the FGC cases we observed and this reflected the way matters were managed by the YJC who either did not make an offer to withdraw or made the offer in such a way that it was not taken up. This failure to withdraw was commented on by some parents:

> It would have been better to let the parents have some time by themselves. This didn't happen.

> It was all a bit much at once – we needed time to think about it now we knew what had happened.

We explore in the next chapter the possible effects of this failure to withdraw on families' involvement in the FGC process and on their satisfaction with FGC outcomes.

FGC Outcomes

The primary emphasis in the new system is intended to be on young people's accountability either through the young person accepting responsibility for their actions, by them making good the damage that was done or by accepting a penalty. In practice in the FGC this is most likely to mean that the young person apologises, pays reparation or makes a donation to a charity, undertakes some type of work (in some cases for the victim) or accepts some form of restriction on their liberty such as a curfew, grounding or agreement not to drive. In some cases, warnings are given or there may be an agreement about the consequences of any further offending: outcomes which do not necessarily imply that the young person was held accountable, although in some of these cases the young person may have given an undertaking not to reoffend. If, as a result of the FGC, some form of accountability which is acceptable to all the parties is unable to be arranged (in non-court cases) or recommended (in court referred cases), then the matter is likely to be laid before the Youth Court where orders for transfer to the District or High Court, supervision with residence, supervision with activity, community work, supervision, disqualification, reparation, fines and orders to come before the court if called upon within 12 months are set down in the Act as a rank ordered set of tariffs. However, it is recognised that in some cases, particularly those involving younger offenders, the primary issues may be ones of care and protection of the child or young person, in which cases the emphasis in the FGC may be on care and protection arrangements or a referral may be made to the Care and Protection Co-ordinator.

Accountability

The distribution of FGC outcomes confirms that accountability is being achieved. Table 6.14 provides national data on outcomes for 1990 based on nearly 6,000 Family Group Conferences and shows that two thirds of cases involved a recommendation for some type of penalty and that reparation was recommended in nearly a third. Interpretation of the information is complicated by the fact that multiple entries are possible. However, when the figure for prosecutions is added to the penalty figure it seems likely that some type of accountability is occurring in the vast majority of cases.

Table 6.15 sets out in full the range of outcomes agreed to at the FGCs held in the research areas over the period of the study. The classification used here is more detailed and, we believe, more informative than that used by DSW for the national figures. Broadly these data confirm that by far the majority of outcomes reflect responses to young people's offending rather than to their welfare needs.

Table 6.14
Main Results for Those Involved in the Youth Justice Family Group Conferences 1990;*
N=5851

	N	%
Warning	517	9
Caution	167	3
Care and Protection	105	2
Penalties	3,993	68
Reparation	1,728	30
Prosecution	900	15
Other	1,384	24
No further action	401	7

* Data supplied by the Department of Social Welfare. Note multiple entries are possible.

Table 6.15
FGC Outcomes of FGCs by Area; Percentages; N=200*

	A %	B %	C %	D %	E %	Total %
Apology	69	79	71	47	77	70
Work in the community	64	64	50	60	60	58
Reparation						
a) % of total cases	33	21	42	23	28	29
b) % of cases with victims	39	24	45	30	29	32
Work/education programmes	21	21	29	27	26	25
Counselling/support	14	32	8	27	20	21
Change residence	17	5	25	17	14	15
Curfew	7	45	0	13	6	14
Disqualification	10	6	8	37	3	11
Monetary	0	11	4	17	3	6
Supervision with activity	2	0	0	7	6	3
Supervision with residence	0	3	4	3	2	2

* In the remaining three cases, the offence was denied and the case had not been concluded at the end of the research.

Overall, the most common outcomes were apologies (in 70% of cases) and work in the community (in 58% of cases). When work in the community was imposed, the number of hours ranged from 2 to 200 with an average of 65 and a median of 48[46]. Perhaps surprisingly, given the focus on victims in the legislation, little of the work in the community was done directly for the victims. (Less than a quarter (23%) was done directly for victims compared with almost two thirds (65%) for the community more generally. We did not know who the recipient of the work was in 12% of cases. However, when a victim was actually present at the FGC and there was a decision to arrange work in the community, it was arranged that work should be done for the victim in two fifths (42%) of cases.

---

[46] These results contrast with the diversion of adult offenders when community work hours are normally limited to 50, but it is likely that FGCs are dealing with more serious cases, for example, burglary and unlawful taking of a motor vehicle.

Reparation was not widely used overall; approximately a third (29%) of the cases involving victims resulted in reparation. This is very close to the 1990 national figure of 30%. To some extent this indicates the limited financial resources of the families concerned, but it is important to note that in many cases stolen goods were recovered or the offence was not one for which reparation was appropriate. Reparation was slightly more frequently awarded at FGCs where the victim was present but this happened in only 42% of these FGCs which gives little support to the **belief** that the victim's presence at the FGC is **more likely** to ensure reparation. Orders for supervision with residence and supervision with activity were the least common outcomes: 2% and 3% respectively.

Table 6.16 presents an analysis of the frequency with which different types of outcomes resulted after the main outcomes were grouped and given a priority order. The ordering was initially based on the relative severity of penalties as set down in section 283 of the Act. However, we gave more weight to financial methods of accountability compared to work in the community for the reason that, in our observation, plans involving work in the community were usually seen by the FGC as an alternative when the young person and their family were unable to pay reparation. This ranking decision is arguable and contrary to the priority ordering in section 283 but, in practice, this is probably unimportant as it was rare for both types of penalty in the same case. Restrictions on liberty such as curfews, groundings and voluntary restrictions on driving, were ranked as less severe than work in the community or financial payments, in line with the provisions of section 283. Apologies were weighted ahead of reprimands on the grounds that they were more likely to be accompanied by remorse and more meaningful to victims. All the possible forms of accountability including custodial sentences, supervision, financial penalties, work in the community, restrictions on liberty, apologies and warnings were placed ahead of recommendations and plans about welfare matters even though some of the welfare arrangements could be seen as also involving an element of penalty.

Using these general guidelines, we divided outcomes into three main categories. First, where there were clear penalties such as financial payments (that is, monetary donations and reparation), work in the community, specific restrictions (including curfews, groundings, disqualification from driving and non-association with co-offenders), recommendations for court orders of supervision, supervision with activity or a custodial penalty, we have called the category *active penalties*. The second group has been called *apologies and reprimands*. This included apologies, warnings, cautions, and decisions about what should happen if there was further offending. The final group of outcomes could loosely be described as *welfare* outcomes, as they were put in place to reduce the chances of reoffending and/or to promote constructive alternatives for the young person. They included changes of residence, counselling programmes, training programmes, drug assessment and supervised leisure activities. While we have called the first group active penalties in contradistinction to the other two, such a distinction is somewhat arbitrary and does not necessarily reflect the psychological impact of the outcome on the young person. Sometimes verbal reprimands had an immense impact and, similarly, the so-called *welfare* outcomes often had a strong element of penalty in the eyes of the young person – for example, being sent away from home or having to undertake supervised activities.

In analysing the data, the court and non-court cases are shown separately. A priority has been given across the categories and within the categories as follows:

- '*Active penalties:* orders for supervision or custody, financial, work, restrictions
- '*Other:* apologies or reprimands, welfare, no action.

Table 6.16 shows that 83% of the non-court sample received 'active penalties' involving money, work or restrictions and that another 12% received reprimands or made apologies. For only 5% of the sample was there no clear evidence of accountability. Table 6.16 also shows the nature of the 'active penalties' for the non-court group. As multiple penalties were possible we have, as stated above, given priority to any financial penalties followed by work in the community with restrictions being recorded only if no other 'active penalty' was used. Similarly 'other' outcomes are only in the table if the case did not appear under an earlier category. Financial penalties, reparation or monetary donations were used in less than a third of non-court cases while half the non-court group undertook work in the community as the main penalty. Various restrictions were the main outcome for only a small group. In those cases with 'active penalties', further data analysis showed that apologies or reprimands also occurred for 80% of these cases and some 'welfare' arrangements were made for almost half of them (46%). Similarly, about half of the 'apology and reprimand' group also had some welfare outcomes.

Table 6.16
Outcomes Recommended by FGCs Showing Numbers and Percentages

a) Non-court FGCs; N=133

		N	%
Active penalties	Financial	39	29
	Work in the community	66	50
	Restrictions only	5	4
Total		110	83
Other	Apology and reprimand	16	12
	Welfare only	5	3.5
	No action	2	1.5
Total		23	17

b) Court Ordered FGCs; N=66

		N	%
Active penalties	Prison/corrective training	3	5
	Supervision orders	14	21
	Financial	26	39
	Work in the community	16	24
Total		59	89
Other	Apology and reprimand	3	5
	Welfare only	3	5
	No action	1	1
Total		7	11

Further inspection of the *other* group showed that a quarter of these had committed relatively minor offences – that is, offences of minimum or minimum/medium seriousness. 'Other' cases in which the offences were more serious often resulted in quite major life changes – a third of the group experienced a change of residence, sometimes to another country. Some of the cases involving 'welfare' responses only were those where the young person had offended with an older brother on whom the FGC had focused. The two non-court cases where no action was recorded included one case which was referred to the Care and Protection Co-ordinator and another case where the primary offender was seen as the young person's older brother.

Thus real and sometimes quite heavy penalties were being agreed to for almost all the FGCs which did not go to court. This is not to say that every single young person was adequately held accountable for his or her offence, but it does demonstrate far more satisfactorily than the national data do that some form of accountability occurred in the vast majority of cases.

When cases were referred for an FGC by the court, the offences were generally more serious and this was reflected in the recommendations from the FGC about outcomes. In 89% of these cases 'active penalties' were recommended and in 5% the penalties anticipated a prison sentence or a sentence of corrective training. Supervision orders were recommended in a further fifth. In only seven of the court cases were there no 'active penalties' although 'apologies or reprimands' were recommended in three of these. In three more cases, which are discussed in more detail later, involved 'welfare' outcomes only. The remaining case in which no action was recommended was one where a number of charges were already being processed in the District Court.

These outcomes can be collectively viewed as offence and accountability oriented, a view which is reinforced by the fact that there was a relationship between the severity of FGC outcomes and the seriousness of the offence committed, the number of offences committed, and prior offending history. Indeed, if we try to explain the severity of FGC outcomes (we describe how we coded these in Appendix 2), these three offence-related factors have a substantial influence. However, when offender characteristics are also included in the regression analysis, age replaces previous history as the third independent predictor variable. Seriousness of the offence by itself, for example, accounts for 18% of the variance in outcomes. When the number of offences are added to this, these two factors explain 26% of the variance and when age is added the multiple correlation is 0.53 and 29% of the variance is explained. The effect of these characteristics as predictors is not as strong in the FGC cases as it is in the Youth Court cases (we discuss this in the Chapter 8), but nevertheless they have a significant effect on FGC outcomes. Significant area differences in severity of FGC outcomes were not observed in the regression analysis, although area differences were noted in the analyses that attempted to predict police and court decision-making.

We also examined severity of outcome by sex, ethnicity and age. Although Table 6.17 shows that a greater proportion of girls than boys were given either no sanction or a sanction in one of the three **least** severe categories (71% compared to 61%), this was not statistically significant; nor was the apparent finding that a greater proportion of Pacific Island than Maori or Pakeha young people were given one of the **most** severe sanctions (ie rated 4 or above); the figures are 52%, 32% and 39%. However there was a significant relationship between age and severity of sanction. A very small proportion of those aged under 14 (6%) were given a sanction rated 4 or above for severity. On the other hand, the proportion of 14, 15 and 16 year olds given sanctions rated 4 or above for severity were not dissimilar: 38%, 43% and 44% respectively. Some of the most severe sanctions are, of course only possible for those over 14 as anyone under 14 cannot be charged in court. But the FGC can still make recommendations for severe sanctions for younger offenders. Some of the age difference is likely to be explained by differences in the gravity of offending and prior offence history but both regression analysis and an examination of individual cases showed that there was also a real and significant tendency for younger offenders to receive lesser penalties.

Table 6.17
Severity of FGC Outcomes by Sex, Ethnicity and Age Ranked from 0=Least Severe to 9=Most Severe; Percentages; N=199

Rating of Outcome	Sex		Ethnic group			Age			
	Boys %	Girls %	Maori %	Pakeha %	Pacific Islander %	>14 %	14 %	15 %	16 %
0	6	0	2	5	14	13	0	11	1
1 or 2	24	32	33	23	6	29	30	18	25
3	31	39	33	33	28	50	31	27	29
4	14	6	9	15	21	3	19	13	14
5	13	13	10	12	21	3	8	20	14
6 to 9	13	9	13	12	10	0	11	10	16
N	168	31	90	78	29	32	36	45	85

The overall focus on offending and accountability is in accordance with legislative intentions. There were a few cases, however, where the outcome seemed, to the researchers at least, to outweigh the gravity of the offence. The following case histories are examples of this:

> *W is a 13 year old who shoplifted items to the value of $65. This was a first offence and the property was recovered. Because of her "surly attitude" and the fact that her mother said she*

could not do anything with her, the police officer involved recommended a prosecution. Instead an FGC was held at which it was decided that she would:

- *write a letter of apology*
- *undertake 16 hours' work at the hospital*
- *be placed on a curfew from 6pm to 7am for 5 weeks*
- *undertake 6 hours' correspondence school each day*
- *attend counselling.*

D and D are 14 and 13 year olds who committed three shoplifting offences, taking a video game, a soldering iron and a pair of sneakers, to the value of little over $100, all of which were recovered. Both had previously offended though they had been dealt with only by a warning or informal police action. At the FGC it was decided that they would:

- *carry out tasks for the victim for one morning*
- *keep to a curfew from 5.30pm to 7am for one month*
- *be barred from all business premises without permission*
- *make a written apology*
- *attend counselling.*

The fact that the three key variables mentioned above – seriousness of offence, number of offences and prior offending history – and demographic effects including age did not completely explain the variance in FGC outcomes means that other factors influenced outcomes too and it is clear that the welfare needs of young people were not entirely ignored. Overall, about a quarter of outcomes addressed the work, educational or skills needs of the young people and a fifth advocated some measure of support and counselling (see Table 6.15).

Welfare

There were a few cases, as already noted, in which the young offender's accountability was ignored and the FGC only addressed welfare concerns. We coded 4% of all FGC outcomes in this way. This tended to occur in particular with respect to those aged under 14, but it also occurred for a few quite serious and persistent offenders. The following case histories provide an idea of the types of situations in which this happened:

G, aged 15 and having committed previous offences, was referred to an FGC for the cultivation of three cannabis plants and a minor theft from his school. His mother was described as lacking in parenting skills and his father had died a few years earlier. Two days after the offence, the boy moved to live with his grandparents. This change of residence was recommended as the sole outcome of the subsequent FGC.

H, aged 13 and with no history of offending, was referred to an FGC for one offence of burglary and one of unlawful interference with a car. Neither offence was particularly serious and both involved other boys as well. Before the FGC, this boy was sent to his uncle's farm and it was arranged for him to attend a boarding school. The FGC did no more than endorse this.

B, aged 15, had committed previous offences and had been the subject of an earlier care and protection FGC. He was referred to an FGC after writing off a car which he was driving after taking it unlawfully. The loss to the victim was $10,000. This boy was not actually present at the FGC, the outcome of which was that the boy would live outside the area with relatives for 12 months.

W, aged 16 and intellectually handicapped, had previously sexually assaulted a four year old boy but was dealt with for this under care and protection proceedings, in part because of the youth's own sexual victimisation. After further offending, it was resolved initially that all matters relating to youth justice would be handled by the youth justice team and that all matters relating to care and protection would be handled by the care and protection team. However, a short time later, the care and protection social workers argued that the boy's difficulties and the reason for his involvement with social welfare related directly to his offending and that their *involvement disguised the **true nature** of the boy's problem which was his history of serious violent sexual offences. Because of the nature and degree of his offending and the danger which it posed to others in the community, they argued that the boy's case clearly belonged in the sphere of youth justice. A youth justice FGC was held and the family proposed a supervision with residence order – the Youth Court order at the top end of the tariff. The youth justice social worker in a subsequent report to the Youth Court, however, wrote as follows: "I am loathe to recommend transfer to the District Court given the uncertainty of how he would cope but the reality is that there are simply no resources available that can accommodate a person with the behavioural complexities that he is presenting. Consideration to the victims ... must also be taken into account when sentencing is made." He felt there was no alternative to a sentence of imprisonment. After a large number of adjournments and meetings between various professionals and the judiciary, the Youth Court made an order 'to come up for sentence if called for' within 12 months, in effect, a conditional discharge for two serious sex offences. This was made in the knowledge that the Family Court had placed the boy in a DSW residence.*

This case shows the difficulty that can arise in attempting to separate out issues of care and protection and youth justice. Certainly this boy was not held accountable for his actions.

At the same time, there were examples of FGC cases in which care and protection issues were apparent but seem to have been ignored. The case history below is a particularly puzzling one as schoolteachers, DSW staff and police alike agreed that the boys were totally out of control and it was suspected they were being physically mistreated by their family. We can only speculate that the Department's failure to act reflects the internal problems that can occur in making care and protection referrals in cases that involve offending.

At the end of 1990 four boys, two sets of brothers, aged between 9 and 11, were referred for an FGC. They had been involved in a burglary and had already come to the notice of the authorities several times for offending, truanting and disruptive and unruly behaviour. DSW had been involved with the family K on the basis of care and protection issues a year previously and during the first 6 months of 1990 they had been clients of the family preservation service. The C boys first came to notice for offending in 1987, although it was not until 1989 that they were referred to DSW on care issues (it was noted that the younger boy was in a detrimental environment). DSW then became involved in providing support for the school holidays and the older boy received counselling and supervision. As a result of the previous problems the four had been separated and sent to different schools.

At the FGC held in December, arrangements were made for the boys to do community work over the Christmas vacation at the school they had burgled and their parents agreed to organise the boys' time over the holidays. Despite their ages, the extensive and wide ranging nature of their problems, and their previous involvement with DSW, care and protection issues were not addressed at the FGC, even though the professionals attending the FGC believed that parental supervision had not been effective for some time. It was thought that severe punishment was being used and there was no adequate supervision of whether or not they went to school and what they did after school.

Within a fortnight the boys had been reported for offending again – this time breaking windows at the school where they were doing community work and shoplifting in two different stores. A complaint was laid by the headmaster of the school they had damaged and burgled about the failure to take action over the boys. By the time of the next FGC in January there was also a potential charge of offensive use of a telephone. Both families were unable to reach decisions, with the C father saying his boys were out of control and could not be trusted. It was agreed that there would be an application for a declaration under the care and protection provisions but nothing appears to have been done to follow up on this agreement. A third FGC was convened for the C boys in February to discuss the same offences plus a burglary. At this FGC the C family arranged for the boys to be supervised after school and on Saturday morning at a local marae, counselling by a psychologist was arranged for the older boy and it was stated that the younger boy should also have arrangements made for counselling. Similarly a new FGC was convened in March for the K boys where they were required to write apologies and undertake 50 hours' work in the community but there was no mention of any actions to address the care and protection issues.

Another example of a case where care and protection needs were ignored was as follows:

D, aged 15, initially came to the notice of DSW when he complained of being severely beaten by his father. No action occurred on that complaint but shortly afterward D appeared in the Youth Court on a charge of breaking and entering his father's house to steal the car keys and unlawful taking of his father's car. Other offences occurred over a period of several months, yet there was no successful resolution of the issues relating to where the young person would live and nor has the complaint about beatings been investigated.

Parents can also have expectations of the FGC which are at odds with the official philosophy underlying FGCs. For example, in S's case, the offence and the appropriate response to this were the primary focus in phase one of the meeting. After the family had discussed in private what an appropriate outcome would be and returned to the meeting to suggest an apology and reparation, the mother then brought up the fact that S did not contribute to his board and brought lots of friends home. Two additions were then made to the report outlining the FGCs recommendations:

  a) S will pay his mother $40 per week
  b) S has agreed not to have more than one friend at home at one time.

What if, after the Youth Court's approval of the recommendations, the boy refused to pay the board money and had lots of friends at home? Would these essentially intra-familial arrangements be grounds for a return to court for a breach of the recommendations? Neither of them is offence focused and their status is unclear.

Area Variations

As can be seen from Table 6.15 above, area variations in outcomes were considerable. Curfews, for example, were never used in one area but were imposed in close to a half of the cases in another. Drug assessment was recommended in a significant minority of cases in two areas and hardly ever in two others. There were also clear area variations in the severity of outcomes. Table 6.18 presents this information.

Table 6.18
Severity of FGC Outcome by Area; Percentages; N=199

Severity	A %	B %	C %	D %	E %	Total %
0	5	3	7	6	4	5
1-2	21	37	20	24	21	25
3	14	45	33	39	25	32
4	14	5	17	12	21	13
5	33	5	3	8	12	13
6-9	12	5	20	11	17	12

If we look at the three least severe codes for outcomes, the overall proportion was 30% but was much higher in one area: 40%. Around a third of outcomes fell into the next most severe category but this ranged from almost half (45%) to only 14% depending on the area. At the other end of the spectrum, 12% of outcomes overall fell into the most severe categories, but this varied from 5% to 20% depending on area.

To some extent, variations in both type and severity of outcome can be explained by differences in the FGC cases in each area – for example, the differing levels of disqualification from driving as a penalty in the five research areas is explained by the much higher proportion of MOT referrals in one area. Differences in the use of alcohol and drug assessment may reflect differences in the lifestyles of the young people in the different areas. One of the areas that rarely made referrals for drug and alcohol assessment was an area where offending tended to be less serious than elsewhere and a higher proportion of offenders there had no previous history of offending. Similarly, in one of the areas where drug and alcohol assessments were more likely to be arranged, offences tended to be more serious than elsewhere and a greater proportion of offenders had previously had an FGC.

But other differences in outcomes must reflect the different approaches of the **professionals** in the various areas in either the type of information they provided to the families or the way in which that information was presented. It seems unlikely, for example, that nearly all the parents in one area would spontaneously think of curfews as an appropriate outcome while parents in another would not. This difference suggests to us rather that parents in the first area were sometimes presented with the idea of a curfew as a possible penalty in a fairly routine way by the other participants in the FGC. In this way, parents' 'decisions' can be constructed through professionals' management of information.

There was also a significant difference in the five areas in the number of outcomes which involved a recommendation for some measure of support or counselling. The overall figure was 21%, but this varied from very few to almost a third. This again seems likely to reflect the way in which possibilities were presented to families and the way in which professionals view the purpose of the FGC rather than differences in the needs of the young people concerned. This would also seem to explain the low proportion of 'active penalties' in the area with the highest proportion of support or counselling outcomes.

Constructing Decisions

We have discussed previously the possibility of professionals 'constructing' families' decisions by the selection of information used for briefing prior to the FGC, but this can occur also during the FGC itself. In one case, for example, where the whanau were unsure about reaching a penalty, the YJC explained that the FGC was taking the place of the court and that the decisions that the family had to make were in place of a judge. The YJC then asked the social worker to explain how to reach a decision and to suggest what she felt was best. The following case history also demonstrates this point:

> *In E's case, although reparation had been raised during the FGC by both Youth Aid and the YJC, the parents, after speaking privately for a short time, felt that the young person should, in addition, do some work in the community to make her realise that what she had done was wrong. They felt also that she should receive a police warning. The Youth Aid officer asked them what kind of community work they had in mind and suggested that she could check elderly people's homes or go to the hospital. He then continued:*
>
>> *"But maybe community work is too harsh. A formal caution is really a counselling one carried out by an inspector. However, community work is up to the parents to impose if they desire or deem it necessary. You've probably already imposed your own penalties at home as well so perhaps community work is not appropriate. We must be fair to E."*
>
> *The YJC then summed up the FGC's recommendations and included reparation and a police caution but made no reference to community work. When asked by the researcher who really decided the outcome of the FGC, both the young person and her parents identified the Youth Aid officer and the Youth Justice Co-ordinator though they did feel that they had been consulted. The YJC, on the other hand, identified the parents and the young person as the people who had decided the outcome.*

Further illustrations of how families' decisions can be constructed by professionals are provided by the following transcripts of FGC discussions:

From T's case

> YJC: *We need now to discuss penalties.*
>
> MOT: *I'd like to hear whether he has an income or savings.*

> YJC: You can either make a donation to a community group or carry out community work.

The MOT can give an indication of this. The law allows FGCs to impose between 200 and 300 hours' community work.

> MOT: I'd be happy for him to be restricted to driving for employment. He could also do community work for X or Y.
>
> Father: He could do community work for Z.
>
> YJC: We just need to determine the number of hours. I suggest 100 and see what people think.
>
> MOT: I was going to suggest 120 hours but we must take into account that he has paid $300 and also that the victim was partially responsible.
>
> YP: 90 hours?
>
> YJC: So the FGC recommendation would be for 90 hours.

From G's case

> *After some general and unfocused discussion, the YJC said: We should adjourn now. Did you get a list of tariffs?*
>
> Father: Yes.
>
> Youth Aid: Do you understand 'suspended sentence'?
>
> Father: Not really.
>
> *The Youth Aid officer then explained this and the YJC added "It's a good behaviour bond". The family withdrew. Three minutes later they rejoined the meeting. The father began to talk about irrelevant issues, and the YJC interrupted: "We thought of a three month suspended sentence."*
>
> Youth Aid: What do you think of that?
>
> Father: Yes.
>
> Youth Aid: Seems good lads.

From F's case:

> YJC: We can break and have a private consultation. I may break with Youth Aid and you can talk about what is appropriate.
>
> Youth Aid: A suspended sentence is also possible.
>
> *After a five minute break the family returned and were asked what they thought.*
>
> Mother: Suspended sentence and an apology.
>
> YJC: That's very similar to what we decided.

However, there was also evidence of the opposite extreme: both a lack of information and a reluctance to provide it. We observed a YJC ask the family now to consider the penalty and he suggested that the professionals should leave the room. The father at that point asked what penalty would be suitable for an offence such as the young person's. The YJC replied that what should be done was up to the family and that he could not influence the decision at all.

The intention in the new legislation was to encourage families to come up with their own solutions to their child's offending. However, we came across few outcomes which could be described as 'imaginative'; most were fairly conventional. This is hardly surprising given that the more experienced professionals also fail to come up with creative responses to offending and that families seem heavily dependent on professionals. Families are also working within a financial framework imposed on them by others. DSW will only fund community services which have received their approval and it will only provide funds for supports of any sort, when the plans are the agreed outcomes of an FGC. At the same time, the economic climate is increasingly depriving families of personal financial resources and leading to the closure of programmes.

Removal from the Area

During the research we observed a number of cases where the matter was resolved by sending the young person to distant family, including sending the young person to a country of which he or she had little personal knowledge. In five cases the decision was made to send the young person to the Pacific Islands. In all of these cases, both the parents and the young person had some reservations, but the professionals encouraged a resolution that solved the problem from their perspective. This is inconsistent with the principles of the Act which require the agreement of the family and young person to the FGC outcome and which prefer solutions that allow young people to remain in their own communities. One mother put it this way:

> *I am now thinking about the decisions made – that they are wrong. I wasn't prepared for the meeting and whatever that was said – I had to agree with it. I want my son here in New Zealand not in Samoa. He was born in New Zealand and he's got to be fixed here in New Zealand – not in a different world. I miss my boy.*

Our interview data therefore indicate that some families were prepared to comply with what others thought was best, despite private reservations.

What Happens after the FGC

We refer in this section to three measures taken after the FGC which could, to some extent, indicate the success or otherwise of FGCs: completing FGC tasks, reconvening FGCs and reoffending. In the following chapter we refer to other possible criteria of success: participants' satisfaction with the FGC process and with the FGC outcomes.

Completing FGC Tasks

One measure of the success or otherwise of FGCs is the extent to which the young people satisfactorily completed the tasks they agreed to perform. The information on task completion has been recorded in one of three categories: 'completed', 'partly completed' and 'not completed'. 'Completed' refers to the cases where all the tasks were done. 'Not completed' includes cases where the bulk of tasks had not been undertaken. 'Partly completed' refers to cases where most of the tasks were done: for instance, cases where 80 of the 100 hours work in the community had been completed or cases where reparation had been made but only some of the counselling sessions had been attended.

Overall, where we were able to obtain information[47], tasks were completed within three to four months in over half of the cases (59%) and partly completed within this time in more than a further quarter of the cases (28%). Thus in only 13% of cases did the tasks remain largely uncompleted after four months. There was no significant regional variation in the level of task completion. For the most part, where young people reoffended they tended not to carry through the plan agreed at the FGC.

Reconvening FGCs

Another potential indicator of the success of the FGC is whether or not the FGC needed to be reconvened. There were a number of situations in which this could occur: for example, non-completion of the tasks agreed at the FGC or further offending by the young person, but in some cases the reconvening was arranged in advance in order to provide a method of monitoring progress. Overall, within 3-4 months of the FGC, only 18% were reconvened (see Table 6.19).

---

[47] Information was available for 184 of the 188 cases where tasks had been agreed at the FGC.

Table 6.19
FGCs Reconvened within Approximately 3-4 Months of the Original FGC by Area; Percentages; N=203

	A	B	C	D	E	Total	
	%	%	%	%	%	N	%
Reconvened	23	0	23	17	32	37	18

Again some regional variation is apparent. This occurred in almost a third of the cases in one area and never in another. This could of course be linked to the rate of non-completion of FGC tasks indicated above. But these differences might also be partly explained by different levels of monitoring of the progress or otherwise of cases and different levels of reoffending by the young people concerned. Where young people reoffended, FGCs were usually reconvened and there were clear differences between the areas with respect to reoffending.

Reoffending

Reoffending is not a particularly good indicator of the success or otherwise of FGCs (or any other criminal justice process for that matter; see Rutter and Giller, 1983 for a review). One of the difficulties is that reoffending rates are vulnerable to changes in practice such as changes in levels and patterns of policing. Increases in serious adult crime, for instance, could divert police attention away from juveniles. Changes in the availability of effective services and programmes to which FGCs can refer young people could also affect reoffending rates. Aggregate reoffending rates are also insensitive to the relative seriousness of the reoffending – yet the public may not be so concerned where offenders subsequently commit only minor offences. Furthermore, research demonstrates that many factors other than the way in which the criminal justice system intervenes impact on reoffence rates: in particular, economic difficulties, unemployment, mental disorder and disturbed personal relationships. Finally it must be noted that reoffending rates are of little value unless there is a base-line measure on a similar group with which comparisons can be made.

Nevertheless, we provide information on reoffending because it is often perceived to be relevant. Overall, less than half (48%) of those referred for an FGC in the sample period had reoffended within six months. There was some regional variation in reoffending rates, ranging from 33% to 66%, but the differences were only borderline in statistical significance.

Evaluating this finding, that approximately half of those referred to FGCs reoffended within six months, presents some problems. There is no baseline against which to make any effective comparison. Some may contend that the figure is too high. On the other hand, those referred for an FGC made up less than a third of all offenders and included those who had committed the most serious offences, those who had committed multiple offences and those who had a previous history of offending. Thus the fact that over half did not re-offend can perhaps be viewed as a positive result.

Cultural Issues

In general, there were relatively few differences between cases including Maori, Pakeha and Pacific Island families in the way the FGC process was managed. Below we summarise and comment on those differences that did emerge. We also comment on the extent to which there is a case for more difference than at present exists if the needs of different cultural groups are to be truly met.

Maori researchers were concerned about the number of Maori FGCs that were held in DSW offices. Yet, as we noted earlier, more Maori than Pakeha FGCs were held in the homes of families or on marae (40% compared to 20%). The researchers asked how an FGC held in DSW offices or facilities could be culturally appropriate for Maori and how Maori families could be empowered by such a foreign environment for their people. The Maori researchers noted a considerable contrast in how the family responded when the FGC was held on a marae, or even in the family's home if it was held in accordance with Maori kaupapa (customs). Two examples of this are provided below:

Case Study 1

This FGC took place in the home of the young person's auntie. Although it was not held on a marae, formal Maori protocol was observed. This was made possible by the presence of two kaumatua, both men of standing in the local community, and by the presence of various aunties, uncles and cousins from the young person's family. The actual chairing of the FGC was carried out by the more senior of the kaumatua and responsibility for this was passed over by the two co-ordinators present.

Although the FGC included two social workers, two co-ordinators and a Youth Aid officer, these professionals did not dominate proceedings. There were 18 family members present and kaupapa Maori (Maori process and spirit) prevailed. That is, the meeting was controlled by the people rather than the professionals, whose role became that of advisers.

Whaikorero (speeches of welcome), waiata (songs) and karakia (prayers) opened the FGC, the YJC made a short speech of acceptance of the kaumatua as facilitator and outlined the requirements of the FGC, the Youth Aid officer read and checked the charges and then the family began to speak. First, concern was registered for the victims and about why they were not present. One of the YJCs said work commitments precluded their attendance (this was a day time meeting) but that she had their concerns and suggestions on paper. She proceeded to present these. The family then discussed for a while the victims' position, reparation issues, the ability of the young person's immediate family to care for him and also the need for him to realise the consequences of his actions. At appropriate times DSW people added suggestions or information about the resources and services that could be available. At all times, the professionals remained respectful and acted in a way conducive to the process taking place as the whanau wished.

At what may have been a turning point in the korero (discussion), the kaumatua asked the professionals to leave for a time. In a very short time after this, around 12 minutes, the family decided on a series of recommendations which they put forward to the professionals. These were well thought out and took into consideration the wishes of the victims, the well being of the young person, the fragility of his immediate family and the resources available within the wider hapu. In the light of this, both the police and DSW agreed to the plan and undertook to convey it back to the judge at the Youth Court.

It was interesting to note that at first the young person did not agree with some of the recommendations and so the family negotiated a compromise with him. It seems unlikely that the young person would have been so outspoken in an institutional setting. Follow up for this case showed that this young man fulfilled all the FGC requirements.

Case Study 2

This case took place in the home of the young person's parents. Although it was not run according to formal protocol in all details, it was a situation where all those present, including the victim, the young person and his family operated in a Maori hui (meeting) type environment. That is, everyone seemed to feel supported enough to be able to speak as openly and as frankly as they wished. It was facilitated by an acting YJC who was at pains to be sensitive to the Maori environment of the family home. She actively encouraged people to speak and was respectful and tolerant to all parties.

The FGC started with a karakia from the young person's uncle after which the YJC advised the meeting of the requirements of the Act. The Youth Aid officer read and checked the charges with the young person and then the YJC stood back to let the young person's family discuss the offence and reparation with the victim and his mother. The victim was present with both his mother and sister. The young person had his parents, two aunties and an uncle present.

> *Crucial to the conciliatory atmosphere of the FGC was the young person's family taking responsibility for his actions and then offering sympathy and understanding to the victim. If the FGC had taken place in an institutional setting the family may not have felt secure enough to be supportive to the victim and his family. The focus of all the discussion was reparation, accountability and development of the young person. The YJC offered to withdraw with the Youth Aid officer but this was not seen as necessary by the family.*

The Maori researchers also commented on the extent of whanau participation and the conflicts and tensions that could flow from this. We have already noted that extended family or whanau participation was higher for Maori (58%) than for Pakeha (20%) and to some extent this is probably a reflection of the acceptance by co-ordinators that whanau participation is important for Maori people as well as the fact that Maori more often retain strong links to their wider family. Although the researchers commented that many families felt whakamaa (a deep sense of shame) at sharing their problems with their whanau, they also pointed to some Maori families which only reluctantly allowed whanau to be invited but who were later grateful for the support provided because it enabled solutions to be found that would not have been within the power of the household. Earlier we reported cases where families resented the fact that whanau had been invited without their knowledge (page 78) but we also recorded cases where bitterness arose about the exclusion of one side of the family. There is clearly a tension between the rights of the immediate family and the whanau. Our Maori researchers held the view that a return to Maori cultural practices through the participation of the whanau, hapu and even iwi was the preferred course both culturally and in terms of potential effectiveness. On the other hand, the wishes of parents and young people also deserve consideration. In practice we suggest that the co-ordinators should discuss with the immediate family the matter of who should be available to help the child or young person. Nevertheless, there will undoubtedly be a few difficult cases which are not readily resolved by negotiation. In these, we suggest that when the young person agrees with the whanau's wish to be present, the wider whanau should be represented even if the caregivers are opposed to this. Our reasoning is that the young person has the right to have all those concerned about his or her welfare present when decisions are being made about his or her future. On the other hand, if parents and young people both agree that they do not accept the right of wider whanau to be present, it is our tentative view that their wishes should prevail, at least on the first occasion on which an FGC is held. However, we recognise that Maori may have a different view and that, in some cases, the presence of wider whanau may allow for a more effective resolution.

Whanau participation is, by itself, however, insufficient to guarantee positive outcomes. In some cases, whanau were not necessarily as effective as they might have been because they were unaware of the role that was expected of them, because the management of the process remained in the control of DSW and because they had not had time to consider the options. The case history of the young person described earlier in this chapter (page 74) provides a dramatic example of the fact that it was both necessary for whanau to participate and for them to have knowledge of what was needed to produce an effective solution. The earlier details demonstrate how important the setting and kaupapa were. The additional details below show that knowledge of the requirements was also an important element:

> *O and his whanau had three separate FGCs as well as a number of informal meetings. The charge was very serious and the police were arguing for a transfer of the case to the District Court in order to ensure a custodial sentence.*
>
> *The family wanted to keep O out of institutions and were worried about the consequences for him of a sentence to prison or to corrective training. The problem lay in understanding and developing a proposal for an effective alternative. A large number of whanau who were both willing and capable became involved. Nevertheless, they did not understand how to formulate a plan that could be acceptable until the arrival of an aunt who worked for the Department of Social Welfare in another city. She explained to the family what was needed by way of a plan. Thus the final FGC for O was one where the Act operated as intended – with a knowledgeable and empowered group of family members who drew up a plan that was accepted by both the police and the Youth Court. However, achieving family empowerment had been a long and*

slow process where the family needed both to absorb a lot of new information and also to change their attitude to how they could play a role in being responsible for O and providing for his needs.

We have noted that most Maori young people had a Maori co-ordinator, which resulted from the fact that more of the co-ordinators were Maori in the areas we studied. In practice, always matching the ethnicity of the co-ordinator with that of the family is unrealistic given existing staffing levels. While matching the ethnicity of the co-ordinator and the family is of value, it is even more important that the co-ordinator has access to quality advice on cultural issues from members of the Maori community, both tangata whenua (local people) and tauiwi (people from another tribal area). This is true whether the co-ordinator is Pakeha or Maori, as it is important that the co-ordinator has the appropriate links to be able to find family and tribal connections for those who have become separated from their origins.

Similarly, in terms of process it is important to go beyond the tokenism of including greetings and prayers in a different language. Cultural appropriateness cannot be achieved without handing the management of the process over to those who fully understand the culture. In Maori terms, this means running the entire FGC according to the Maori kaupapa (the word refers to both format and values) appropriate for that iwi, as exemplified by the two case studies presented earlier in this section.

This is not to suggest that we believe that every Maori FGC should necessarily become a tribal matter involving kaumatua (tribal elders) and full whanau participation. It is recognised that, in more minor cases, satisfactory solutions may be able to be achieved in meetings involving only the immediate family. However, where the offending is persistent or serious and where immediate family resources seem insufficient, the importance of careful preparation, the involvement of whanau, hapu and iwi and the adoption of a Maori approach to the process needs to be recognised.

Finally, it is important to comment on the cultural appropriateness of sending young people back to the extended family in other areas. The idea of reintegration of the young person with his or her culture can be appealing to the police and DSW, not only because of its potential value to the young person, but also, perhaps, because it means that the young person will no longer be a problem to them locally. However, the reality of such solutions needs to be considered carefully. There can, indeed, be real advantages in allowing Maori urban youngsters the opportunity to live in a community with their tribal elders which retains many aspects of traditional Maori life and where they can learn about their origins and gain a pride in their Maoriness; that is, *to allow them to stand tall in their own culture*. Another rationale for this comes from the practice of whangai (Maori adoption) which, by demonstrating that children or young people are wanted by more than just the immediate whanau, can be very positive and can add to their resources (Cairns, 1991) as well as enrich their knowledge of their background. When, however, the immediate whanau agree under pressure to approach extended whanau, hapu or iwi to find alternative care for the young person, the outcome may be rather different. The new caregivers may have accepted the young person only reluctantly and may not have been fully informed of the extent and nature of his or her problems. In one case in the sample, the new caregiver agreed on the understanding that the young person was simply coming for a brief period. There the outcome was far from satisfactory:

The FGC itself was unusual because the young person (W) was not present (he had temporarily run away). The only member of the family present was W's father. After some discussion the police, the social worker and the co-ordinator all decided that the young person should leave the area because of his repeated offending, because his father could not control him and because it was likely that he would have to be placed in care if he continued to offend.

This put W's father in an embarrassing position. In the past W had been sent to relatives who had returned him to Wellington in disgrace because of unacceptable behaviour. The professionals continued to pressure the father and interpreted his reluctance as a lack of interest in W, failing to understand the real sense of whakamaa (shame) which was affecting him.

Eventually the father contacted his relatives but only asked if W could go to stay for a holiday. The professionals were confused about this outcome but accepted it. Thus when W was finally located and sent to his relatives, it was some time before the relatives realised that W had not come for a holiday but to live.

Finally another FGC was called to inform the relatives of all that had happened and the reason that W was there with them. The relatives were very supportive despite the fact that they were short of space and had had to place their grandson outside in a tent unless it was raining. They asked for help from DSW with housing. DSW offered to write a letter supporting an application to Housing Corporation for finance to extend the home.

W's stay with his relatives lasted about three months before he returned to Wellington.

The above considerations apply equally to the practice of sending young Pacific Islanders back to their island of origin. This practice can create even greater problems. The distance involved means that there has usually been no prior contact between the young person and the people with whom he or she was to live. As the way of life is so very different from that in New Zealand, the young person may experience considerable culture shock. Continuing communication between the young person and his or her New Zealand family is also more difficult.

An appraisal of the FGC process from the perspective of Pacific Island families and young people was made difficult by the variety of different Pacific Island groups involved, by the fact that we only had one Pacific Island researcher, and by the relatively small number of cases involving Pacific Island young people. However, the researchers who attended Pacific Island FGCs were concerned not only about the communication problems generated by the lack of adequate arrangements for an interpreter, but also by the general bewilderment of the Pacific Island families. Difficulties due to cultural misunderstandings and differences seemed even greater among Pacific Island families than among Maori families who have had a longer experience of living alongside Pakeha New Zealand society. It is our view that, in general, the cultural issues for Pacific Island families are similar to those experienced by Maori families but the problems in relating to Pakeha processes not in keeping with their own cultural practices are almost certainly magnified.

Conclusions

We have shown that considerable regional variation exists in almost every aspect of FGC process and practice: differences in the characteristics of the juveniles dealt with at FGCs, differences in the arranging and setting up of FGCs, differences in the composition of FGCs and differences in the outcomes reached. Explanations for these variations are not straightforward, but one factor which cannot be dismissed is that much depends on the quality and style of the professionals who take part in the system. We develop this theme further in the following chapter.

We have also pointed briefly to some potential indicators of the success or otherwise of FGCs. Overall, more than three quarters of the young people in the sample took some or all the steps necessary to complete the tasks agreed to at the FGC. Relatively few FGCs were re-convened and half the young people who had been dealt with at the FGC did not reoffend within six months. We are not able to compare these results with data collected prior to the implementation of the Act.

However, despite the optimism for the future shared by all researchers on the project, there still appears to be some way to go before the FGC process is implemented as intended. That there has been considerable agreement between Maori, Samoan and Pakeha researchers working on this project about deficiencies in the practice of FGCs demonstrates that these deficiencies were readily apparent from a variety of cultural perspectives.

Our research has clearly indicated that Maori, Pakeha and Pacific Island families alike became distressed when FGCs were not adequately set up or managed. It may be that it is inevitable that, given their workloads and pressures, the needs and interests of professionals will take precedence over the needs and interests of families in relation to such matters as the timing, venue, and the procedures of FGCs. This means that if the needs and interests of families are to be given the importance intended by the legislation we must put specific systems in place in order to achieve this. We return to this in Chapter 9.

However, it must be said in conclusion that families from all ethnic groups at times expressed appreciation of the informality of FGCs, the facility for all to express their opinions, the possibility of having the FGC in their own home and the opportunity to have family support available. Many families found the FGC far preferable to court as a method of reaching decisions and involving them. We elaborate on these issues in the following chapters.

Chapter 7

PARTICIPANTS' VIEWS OF FGCS

Introduction

An important aspect of the philosophy underlying the new system, which we discussed in Chapter 1, is the empowerment of parents, young people and victims. One way of exploring whether or not FGCs have been successful in achieving this is to describe how the various participants felt about the FGC. We asked questions about both process and outcome (though admittedly it is difficult in practice to disentangle the two). We deal first with two key measurements of the empowerment of parents and young people: their involvement in the decisions made at the FGC and their satisfaction with the outcomes of the FGC. We then refer to their views of the extent to which another objective of the new system is met: reconciliation between families and victims. The views of victims on these same objectives are outlined and then the views of two key professional groups, co-ordinators and enforcement agencies, are presented. Finally, the views of parents and young people on cultural issues are described.

Parents' and Young People's Views of the Process of Decision-making at FGCs

We asked parents and young people how involved they felt they had been in the decision making process and who they felt had made the decision. The interviewers were given some basic questions and a series of prompts to use as necessary (see Appendix 2). They were also trained to ask additional questions to ensure that the views of the person being interviewed were fully explored. The replies were coded in order to provide quantitative data and, in addition, we used the richer information from the full interviews to assist in interpreting the findings.

Key questions were: "Did you feel that you made the decisions?", "How involved were you in reaching the decisions?" and "In your view, who really decided?" We regarded responses which indicated that the respondent was involved, that the decision was made by everyone present or that it was made by the family and then agreed to by the other participants, as ones which were in keeping with legislative intention.

Although a number of parents (10%) and young people (10%) expressed no opinion, two thirds (67%) of the families and a third (34%) of the young people who were interviewed felt that they had been involved in the process. If we include responses which indicated that interviewees felt 'partly' involved, the figures do not change much for parents but increase to nearly half of young people (see Table 7.1). We coded the responses to this question in a fairly generous way so that statements such as 'they decided but I agreed to it', 'I wasn't involved – I just agreed to it', 'I just agreed with what they thought best' or 'they decided but I was consulted' were viewed by us as indicating that the young person had, at least to some extent, not felt completely excluded by the process.

Table 7.1
Involvement in FGC Decisions Reported by Parents and Young People; Percentages[48]

	Parents (N=168) %	Young People (N=152) %
Yes, involved	67	34
Partly involved	3	11
No, not involved	20	45
No opinion expressed	10	10

Typical responses by the young people who said that they were involved in the process of making a decision are as follows:

> *It was quite open and quite good ... you get to talk openly. It's not as if there's any pressure on you.*

> *It seemed pretty fair with people sitting around talking about things.*

> *The FGC was really good. I was able to say what I wanted.*

Similar sentiments were expressed by parents:

> *It was very open for free speech. We had the opportunity to say everything.*

> *I had the chance to say what I wanted to say.*

> *It gave us a chance to sort things out ... that was important. It made us feel respected.*

> *We got more out of this one than any of the ones previously ... more discussion and involvement. We weren't left out so often.*

> *I felt quite good about the whole thing. Certainly I didn't feel threatened in any way.*

> *Everything that should have been talked about was talked about ... we shared what we had to say ... excellent.*

On the other hand, nearly a half (45%) of the young people interviewed (though only a fifth of parents) felt that they had not been involved in the process. The responses of these young people are perhaps best summarised by the boy who said: *I didn't know why I had to be there.* Other young people answered questions about their involvement in the process in a way which indicated that they were either excluded by the adults present (literally by the adults ignoring them almost entirely or by the way in which adults asked questions) or that they did not feel able to participate through feelings of shame, embarrassment or simply not knowing what to say:

> *I never said anything ... everyone was too busy arguing. Every time I tried ... [they] would butt in.*

> *I never got the chance to say what I wanted or thought.*

> *I didn't want to say much ... just get it over with.*

> *I wasn't too anxious to talk.*

> *I didn't really know what was going on – left it to my parents and the lawyer.*

The silence and lack of participation of many of the young people in FGCs are borne out by our observations. It was common for the researchers to note that the young person contributed little, sat passively by and spoke only when asked specific questions. This does not sit well with notions

---

[48] The ratings of involvement were based in part on responses to a direct question and in part on a judgement by the researcher's reading of the interview transcript. They were not based on observations during the FGC. Any measure based on observations during the FGC would have probably estimated less involvement on the part of the young person and their family.

of accountability, for accountability requires public acknowledgement of wrongdoing and an attempt to make amends. Some victims certainly felt that young people should have been made to contribute more:

> *The person at fault has to be made to speak. Needs to face it ... all very anodyne ... whereas I was put through the mill.*

> *He should have been questioned more about why he did it ... it's up to the officials to do that, not me. Nobody had anything to say; it was all put on me.*

> *I wanted answers, but he just shakes his head ... he didn't even open his mouth.*

And in one of the FGCs we observed, towards the end of the proceedings, the victim said *We haven't heard from [the young person] yet. What about him?*

The difference between the parent's and young people's responses is interesting and probably reflects the fact that many parents (and, indeed, adults) do not feel it appropriate for young people to have a voice which is counter to theirs:

> *The family decided for the best for my son, but he didn't accept it so it was his decision. ... Everyone in the FGC should agree with me.* (Parent)

> *Do you think these young people should have a say in what happens to them? He needs to be taught he can't do these things. I don't think he has any choice. If he's given a choice, it becomes a joke, a playground.* (Carer)

The ethnicity of parents and young people[49] and the age and sex of young people did not have a significant effect on parents' or young people's levels of involvement. However, the area variation in perceived involvement was significant: for example, three quarters (76%) of the parents in one area said they had felt involved compared with only just over a third (37%) in another; and just over a third (38%) of young people in one area said they had felt involved compared with less than a fifth (18%) in another. There is a range of possible explanations for these differences – the 'climate' created by the co-ordinators, the way in which information on options was conveyed to parents, the adequacy of prior briefing, the personalities of the individuals involved in the FGC and the role the various professionals played in the FGC itself. Thus it may be relevant that professionals were more likely to withdraw from the meeting to allow the family to deliberate privately in one area where parents perceived their level of involvement to be relatively high whereas they were less likely to withdraw in another where parents perceived their level of involvement to be relatively low.

The numbers are too small to allow an analysis of the relationship between the level of parental involvement and professionals' withdrawal by area, but there was a significant relationship between these two factors over the whole sample. Thus almost two thirds of the parents who said they felt involved had taken part in FGCs where the professionals had withdrawn from the meeting at some point; on the other hand, almost two thirds of the parents who said they did not feel involved had taken part in FGCs where the professionals had not withdrawn from the meeting at any point. On the other hand, there is no relationship between young people's level of involvement and professionals' withdrawal. Nor did parental involvement go hand-in-hand with the involvement of the young people. Given their lower level of involvement overall, this is not entirely surprising.

Parents' and Young People's Views on 'Who Decided'

When interviewing parents and young people we asked them for their views on who decided on the recommendations of the FGC. We also asked the researchers to state their opinion on who made the decision on the basis of their observations in the FGC. The results are presented in Table 7.2.

---

[49] In fact a slightly higher percentage of Maori than Pakeha parents and young people reported that they had been involved but this difference was not significant.

Table 7.2
Who Decided the Outcome: Views of Parents, Young People and the Researcher; Percentages

	Young Person (N=149) %	Parents (N=165) %	Researcher (N=174) %
Young person	9	5	3
Family	32	46	20
Professionals	15	19	10
Family & professionals	8	6	20
Victim	2	2	1
Professionals & victim	2	3	2
All	7	10	11
All except YP	2	0	0
Professionals & YP	0	2	2
Family & victim	0	0	3
Other	0	1	0
Don't know	22	6	28

The answers generated a large number of different combinations of participants because of the number of different people who were present at the FGCs. We have, therefore, simplified the combinations in the table according to whether the people nominated were professionals, family members, victims, or the young person. We discuss these results separately in terms of their meaning for young people and for their parents.

Young People

Not all respondents gave answers to questions about who decided the outcome; indeed, nearly a quarter of the young people who were interviewed said they did not know (see Table 7.2). The most frequent response by young people, however, was that their family had decided (32%), while approximately another quarter identified the professionals or both the family and the professionals as having made the decision. Only a few identified themselves or everybody as making the decision. Thus, overall no more than 16% of the young people who were interviewed said that they themselves had specifically been involved in making the decision.

The fact that not all young people were interviewed and that some of those who were interviewed gave no clear response to these questions means that we have a relatively high rate of missing information here (generally 40% but in two areas around a half) and so we have to be cautious over area variations. But what emerges from the comparison between areas is a pattern of large differences. For example, the family was identified by the young people as having decided in half of the cases in one area compared with 12% in another. Similarly, the young people identified themselves as having made the decision in 28% of cases in one area compared with none in another. The following responses from young people about their role in the decision are typical of those which indicated that they had been involved:

Really me, I suppose. I said what I was going to do.

Dad and me did it together.

However, as the above table shows, young people mainly indicated that they had not been a party to the decision. As with the responses to the question on involvement in the process, young people generally indicated either that adults had not allowed them to be involved in the decision or that they themselves did not feel it appropriate for them to be involved in the decision. Typical replies were as follows:

My dad decided, but I feel OK about it.

> *The person who decided was OK. I didn't have much choice. [This boy's parents identified the YJC as the person who decided the outcome.]*
>
> *I felt that they had decided on what I had to do before I got the chance to talk. I wasn't really involved. The MOT decided. I didn't like it. I didn't like the decisions made, but there's nothing I can do about it.*
>
> *It wasn't up to me.*
>
> *I wasn't involved in the decision at all.*
>
> *I felt snowed under – like I had to do it or else.*
>
> *The decision was made for me – they didn't listen to me.*
>
> *I offended so I had to take whatever was coming to me.*
>
> *I was talked about but had no say in the matter.*

The FGC process, therefore, can not generally be said to be empowering young people.

Parents

With respect to parent's responses to the question about their involvement in the decision, again we have some missing information (6%) though less than from the young people. Parents were more likely than the young people had been to identify themselves as the ones who decided. Overall, this response was given by almost half the parents we interviewed. If we add to this those responses which indicated that the decision was made by both the family and the professionals or by 'everyone' we find that nearly two thirds (62%) of the parents who were interviewed identified the family as having been involved in the decision, at least in part. This view of the way the decision was made emerges clearly from the comments made by parents:

> *We decided as a family.*
>
> *Everybody. I think we all did.*
>
> *They made us think about possibilities and strive for them instead of sitting back and letting the professionals come to decisions.*
>
> *I decided for my son and he agreed when I told him he couldn't get off scot free.*

Of course, some parents were not entirely happy about being asked to make such decisions. One mother felt that she had made the decision with some help from the lawyer. But she went on: *how can a mother decide on a punishment for her own kids?*

Perhaps the more disturbing feature here is that the professionals alone were identified by the parents as the decision makers in 19% of the responses. The police or the MOT, in particular among the professionals, were identified as being either the sole decision-maker or among those who determined the decision in 60% of these cases. In the total sample, the influence of the police was specifically mentioned by a quarter of the families. Some of the quotes below demonstrate the impact on decisions of professionals generally and of the police specifically:

> *The family [decided] but it was a decision we thought we should reach because of the views of the victim and MOT.*
>
> *I had to agree with the decisions. I felt that I got pushed to the decisions but that's not what I wanted.*
>
> *Not the family. It was the others – they did all the talking.*
>
> *Social Welfare [decided]. I was pissed off because we weren't allowed to make a decision – they had too much to say – they should have shut up – they weren't listening to what the family wanted for [the young person]. Any plan involving him leaving the area won't work.*
>
> *I told the people who were there about the boys and what I wanted to do but they just ignored me. They wanted to do what they think, but never listen to the parent.*

> *I felt the YJC acted as judge and made the final decree. He had the final say by either agreeing or disagreeing with what was wanted.*
>
> *The police viewpoint carried too much weight. I would prefer no police presence. They take over. It's hard to disagree with them.*
>
> *The police [decided]. The family decision ended up being based on what the police were insisting on after the previous decision was thrown back at us by the court. The judge wasn't supporting the family at all. We thought $1000 reparation was a reasonable penalty for two burglaries. It destroyed our faith in being able to make decisions. The family were left with nowhere to go by the police and the judge's attitude.*
>
> *The police [decided]. There didn't seem to be any other option.*
>
> *The YJC and MOT seemed to have already made up their minds.*
>
> *It seemed they had decided before we got there – the YJC told me that.*

Again, large differences are evident across the five areas. For example, the proportion who identified the family as involved in the decision ranged from 74% to 30% in different areas and the professionals were seen as being involved by between 31% and 9% of parents depending on area.

Researchers

We asked the researchers who had attended the FGCs to record who they felt to be the key decision makers. This was not always done and in one area we have no information for almost half the cases. We also can not be confident that the researchers made the same kinds of judgements since the judgement was, in essence, a subjective one. It is possible, therefore, that differences in the researchers' perspectives led to professionals being identified as the decision makers more frequently in some areas than in others. But what does emerge from this exercise is the frequency with which the researchers identified the **family** as playing some part in the decision. Their figure of 54% is not too dissimilar to the figure of 62% of families who felt they had been involved, at least in part, in the decision. However, in all areas except one, a greater proportion of families than researchers identified the professionals as having been involved in the decision.

Whether or not the professionals had withdrawn at some point in the FGC was not significantly related to who was identified by researchers or families as having decided the outcome, but as we suggested earlier it is likely that the professionals' influence on the decision operated in more subtle ways. Professionals may have shaped the information given to families in a way which 'constructed' that decision and which in effect gave the families little real choice or voice. That is, parents may have been operating within a pre-defined framework. Davis (1985) refers to this as a kind of 'theft' of decision-making. At the same time, families may have felt, despite this intervention by the professionals, that they did actually make the decision. The two suggestions are not necessarily inconsistent.

One further point should be made before this section is concluded. The victim was rarely identified by either the parents, young people or researchers as having made the decision although, of course, it is impossible to quantify the effect their presence or words might have had on the families in coming to their decision. And one parent expressed some doubt about whether the victim's views **should** be taken into account:

> *We were surprised to hear that we were talking about a unanimous decision. The final decision should be made by the parents and Social Welfare. We were surprised that others, such as the victims, seemed to have so much of a say.*

We comment later on the role that victims themselves felt they had in determining the outcome.

Parents do seem to be empowered in the FGCs in a way that previous research indicated they were not by the courts. We expand on this in the next section. Nevertheless, there are still question marks over the degree of intervention by some professionals in both shaping and determining outcomes. We commented earlier that there was a range of possible explanations for differences in parents' perceived level of involvement – the 'climate' created by the co-ordinators, the way in which information on options was conveyed to parents, the adequacy of prior briefing, the personalities of the individuals involved in the FGC and the role the various professionals played in the FGC itself. The same factors seem likely to explain differences in participants' perceptions of who were the key decision makers.

Parents' and Young People's Satisfaction with Outcomes

Overall, despite occasional concerns about the **process** of decision-making, levels of satisfaction with **outcomes** were high. Table 7.3 sets out the responses to the question which asked how satisfied parents and young people were with the outcomes.

Table 7.3
Parents' and Young People's Satisfaction with FGC Outcomes; Percentages

Satisfaction	Young people (N=152) %	Parents (N=169) %
Yes	84	85
Partly satisfied	2	3
No	9	11
Don't know	4	2

Overall, 84% of the young people in the five research areas (the range was between 74% and 94%) and 85% of parents (the range was between 79% and 89%) said that they were satisfied with the outcome of the FGC. Typical responses were as follows:

> *Yes, fair. I quite like community work. (Young person)*
>
> *Fine. I expected a lot worse. (Young person)*
>
> *It's good to have him pay back for his wrongdoings. (Parent)*
>
> *I am impressed with how well things went and the quality of the punishment. The punishment was fitting. (Parent)*
>
> *It was a good decision. It put the responsibility back on the kids. (Parent)*

Only a few parents (11%) and young people (9%) actually expressed dissatisfaction with the outcome. For parents, the issue seems to have been either that the young person 'got off too lightly' or, more commonly, that some kind of help or treatment they thought necessary was not offered:

> *The offences he's done. He's not being accountable for them. He should be punished for the offences. If he's old enough to offend, he's old enough to be punished.*
>
> *She needs more counselling, counselling for drug and alcohol use.*
>
> *All a waste of time. He needs counselling. He needs treatment for his drinking. I'm worried. I wanted something done about it.*

For the young people, the issue was almost invariably how their outcome compared with that of co-offenders or, more generally, with their notion of appropriate penalties. This is consistent with earlier research on the juvenile court in other jurisdictions (Morris and Giller, 1977; Parker et al, 1981) and with earlier research in New Zealand (Morris and Young, 1987):

> *I had to pay my own $20. He [a co-offender] got to wash ambulances. That wasn't fair.*
>
> *They seem to have got away with it. I'm taking the blame.*
>
> *The other guy didn't get punishment.*

> *I felt it was a bit unfair to get the same punishment as the worst offender.*
>
> *Not really fair. I got the same treatment as the rest, but they did more.*
>
> *It was too tough. Quite a lot was unfair. Others have got away with it. They're pushing me too much.*
>
> *It's not fair. I know a Maori guy who's committing more serious offences and he got off with it.*

The levels of satisfaction were high regardless of whether the case came as a referral from the Youth Court or directly from Youth Aid or the MOT, but there was a difference: in 87% of the cases that came directly to the FGC both parents and young people said they were satisfied with the outcome, whereas, when the Youth Court was the source of the referral, satisfaction dropped to 80% for young people and to 78% for parents. This greater expression of dissatisfaction with court referred cases may be linked to dissatisfaction with the Youth Court rather than with the FGC process and outcome per se.

We have referred throughout these discussions to the fact that the professionals sometimes failed to withdraw from the FGC. In fairness, we should stress that neither parents' nor young people's satisfaction with the outcome is significantly related to whether or not the professionals withdrew. But this is not surprising. Researchers have uniformly failed to identify what it actually means when parents and young people say that they are 'satisfied'[50] and we raised elsewhere (Morris and Young, 1987) the possibility that this means nothing more than relief that 'nothing worse' happened. There is some support for this suggestion. Young people who received the most severe penalties were almost three times as likely to express dissatisfaction as those who received less severe penalties and the parents of those receiving the most severe penalties were twice as likely to express dissatisfaction as the parents of the young people who received less severe penalties.

Table 7.4 sets out the percentages of parents and young people who said they were satisfied with the FGC outcome classified by the severity of the outcome. Interestingly, it shows not only that there was less satisfaction with the most severe penalties than with moderate penalties but that even less satisfaction was reported where there was no effective penalty at all, although the numbers involved here are small.[51]

Table 7.4
Satisfaction with FGC Outcomes and Severity of Penalties for Young People and Parents; Percentages Expressing Satisfaction

Severity of Outcome	Young people (N=151) %	Parents (N=169) %
0	50	63
1	82	89
2	91	86
3	96	91
4	83	74
5	74	95
6-9	70	74

---

[50] This is not to suggest that 'satisfaction' is not a useful measure. Indeed, in some senses it is, by definition, the most important measure of how clients view processes in which they participate. The failure to deconstruct 'satisfaction' almost certainly reflects the fact that people vary both in their level of expectation and in the types of outcomes that they view as appropriate and, hence, their 'satisfaction' cannot be predicted from examining outcomes alone.

[51] The apparent anomaly of 95% of parents expressing satisfaction with outcomes of severity 5 is simply a random fluctuation as the number of cases declines with increasing severity.

Families' Views on Meeting Victims

The presence of victims was mainly accepted by the parents and young people. This was felt to be important, not only as part of a process of reconciliation and healing, but also as a means of teaching the young people to accept responsibility and to be accountable for what they had done. The following quotes from parents sum this up:

> *I really enjoyed being in the meeting as a father. It's great to have the victims as well, and that makes me feel better. I listened to their concerns and everything they said. I felt for them and the pain and hurt they have got. The input that they had ... taught me a lot ... I won't forget it.*

> *I'm glad they [the victim's parents] were there. We can share, tell them we know how you feel because we've been there.*

> *It was really good to meet the victim, it brings it home to him, it brings home reality. They don't like to face victims.*

Young people also referred to the impact and value of the victims' presence:

> *I didn't want to see the victims but it did have an impact, especially seeing [the elderly victim].*

> *Really good. I got to see the victim. I could apologise and help her with money.*

And one family was very unhappy that the victim was not present:

> *It's not possible to get to the bottom of things when there is no face to face meeting between the victim and the offenders. There could be no reconciliation. It is unfinished for the victim if they do not meet.*

In some cases, however, the victim's presence was not seen as a positive influence; rather it inhibited discussions. Indeed, on a few occasions, it was felt to be counter-productive:

> *My family felt that they should not have been there, the victims that is, because it made it difficult to suggest a proper penalty for myself.*

> *It was not a bad idea for us to meet them [the victims] and for [the young person] to meet them but they shouldn't be there for the discussions. It had to be done but not with the part where we're forming the plan.*

> *The only bad thing was the victims – us against them – it made everyone edgy.*

> *I didn't like the first meeting with the victims. I felt very defensive. They wanted to send my son to prison and that made me feel protective.*

> *The victim was not helpful. He was very aggressive.*

> *I felt wild with that lady – so I just let it go in one ear and out the other.*

These comments reinforce a point we have made repeatedly: the need for good preparation of families before meeting victims. They also indicate the need for co-ordinators to be given training in how to handle these meetings better. The meetings are often emotional occasions, but these emotions can be used constructively if the co-ordinator possesses the right skills. These points apply equally to preparing victims for the FGC.

Victims' Satisfaction with the FGC Process

The theory underlying the bringing together of the victims, the young offenders and their families is to effect a reconciliation between the parties. The offender should accept responsibility for the wrongdoing done to the victim and should offer to make amends to the victim. In particular, it is intended that attendance at the FGC should in part be a healing experience for victims. Our questions explored victims' feelings about the FGC and their involvement in it; in particular we asked if "attending was something that made you feel better or worse about what had happened?"

and "Do you think the right decisions were taken?" We analysed the replies to these and to the other questions (see Appendix 2 for fuller details) to determine whether attendance at the FGC made victims feel worse or better and to determine whether they felt, on the whole, satisfied with the decisions of the FGC. Overall, a victim was identifiable in 177 FGC cases, ie 87% of the sample, and we interviewed at least one victim in 146 of the FGC cases. In just over half these cases (51%), the victim had attended the FGC.

Because the same victims attended more than one FGC and sometimes there was more than one victim at the same FGC, there are two ways of analysing the data. We have chosen to present data based on each FGC but when difference are large, we have also presented data for each victim interviewed. If multiple victims present at the same FGC had different views, we have counted the more negative view of the FGC in data analyses based on FGCs. However, the views of both victims are represented in data based on individual victims and the most negative of a particular individual victim who attended more than one FGC. But before presenting the results of the quantitative analysis it is useful to explore the variety of responses that we received.

There is no doubt that some victims found the experience of attending the FGC and, more importantly, actively participating in the FGC helpful, positive and rewarding. Overall, for over a third of the FGCs attended by victims (39%) who were interviewed by us, the views were positive. If we look at the total number of victims rather than FGCs, the figure rises to 59%. The following quotes present some positive views:

> *I was impressed with it. It was a very useful exercise – very positive.*
>
> *A bit strange at first, but in general jolly good.*

Generally, it seems that these positive feelings were linked to careful briefing prior to the FGC about the victim's role in the FGC and what to expect there, the victim's satisfaction with the outcomes reached, and the victims' reasons for attending the FGC in the first instance[52].

The victims who felt better as a result of the FGC said that they had been involved in, rather than excluded from, the process. They understood better what had happened and why:

> *To know what is happening is to be involved.*
>
> *I was involved in the whole process.*
>
> *It helped me to understand what had happened.*
>
> *I had a better understanding of the situation. I felt alarm at first, then sympathetic.*

In some ways also the meeting with the offender was seen as a cathartic experience; negative feelings about the offence and the offender could be released:

> *I got the ill feelings out of my system.*
>
> *It was very good; to be able to air my feelings.*
>
> *It made me feel better; that I got my message across.*

Victims also commented on two other specific 'benefits' for them: providing them with a voice in determining appropriate outcomes; and meeting the offender and the offender's family face-to-face so that they could weigh up their attitude, understand more why the offence occurred and assess the likelihood of its recurring:

> *Have been an advocate of this type of thing for years – that is, for the victim to have a say.*
>
> *It worked with [the young person] – he's a first offender. He's remorseful, he's doing something, the family are sorry and trying to make up.*
>
> *I was very pleased about the family's concern.*

---

[52] This finding is confirmed by an analysis of victim's satisfaction with and feelings about the outcome which showed that 81% of those who felt better after the FGC were satisfied with the outcome while 72% of those who felt worse were dissatisfied.

> *I felt able to understand the girl and her problems – she was receptive.*

> *You get some say in reparation and the chance, perhaps, to get some insight into the young person's background – how they come to offend.*

Not all victims, however, were as enthusiastic. Some victims clearly felt worse after attending the FGC. Overall, over a third (38%) of FGCs attended by victims who were interviewed, resulted in the victim saying they felt worse. If we look at the total number of victims rather than FGCs, however, the proportion dissatisfied drops to a quarter (25%). Negative feelings were linked to dissatisfaction with outcomes and the victims' reasons for attending the FGC in the first instance. They were not related to the seriousness of the offence, as we found that for minor, medium and the most serious offences, victims were equally as likely to feel better as to feel worse after the FGC. The victims who said they felt worse after the FGC expressed feelings of depression, fear, distress and unresolved anger:

> *After the meeting I felt very depressed as if it was my fault and I was causing the bother.*

> *It made me feel worse. He's only 15 but he's big and strong and so I was more fearful and when I heard he had stabbed someone, I wondered what would have happened if I had woken up.*

> *I'm still very angry. There was nothing in the meeting – it was silly – he's just laughing at you.*

> *I didn't sleep for three nights after for fear. I felt vulnerable. They could look up my address and set fire to it.*

> *I felt worse – very, very angry. I was shaking. She didn't seem to care what she had done.*

Specific reference was made by some victims to the lack of support they had in the FGC, in contrast to how they perceived the offender's situation to be:

> *He had a free lawyer. We had no help.*

> *I felt unsupported and it was of no benefit to me.*

This point was raised in particular when there were a large number of whanau present at the FGC:

> *The first family had up to twelve and there was just me – it was very unbalanced.*

> *It was an intimidating and large group.*

> *Too much weighted for the offender's family. There should have been less people there.*

Some victims, as a result of their experience, doubted the value of FGCs generally:

> *They may be fine for theft but not for something more serious.*

> *I don't approve of FGCs for such a serious offence. It was not a child's crime.*

> *If they commit adult crimes they should be punished as adults.*

> *It is not fair if he is tried in the Children's Court. He acts like an adult, treat him like an adult. I can't believe that he will end up with only 3 months' punishment. It's not enough.*

But others felt that the system might generally be appropriate for young people and voiced criticisms only of the FGC they had attended:

> *They are good in principle but, in these cases, pretty damaging.*

> *In general they are a good idea but it was badly stage-managed. It never touched the heart of the issue.*

> *Nothing was accomplished – comic opera. It was well-intentioned but ...*

> *It was unprofessional, disorganised and there were hidden agendas.*

> *They might be OK for some – but this one? What a waste of time. There were more there for the offender than the victim. The victim's point of view was lost.*

Other victims felt unable to say what they wanted to at the FGC for a range of reasons:

> *I didn't want to upset the grandparents. I didn't want to hurt the family and so in effect I was silenced by the process.*
>
> *I had to tailor down what I wanted to say. I had to be more polite. I felt on show and couldn't show my real anger.*
>
> *I didn't say everything I wanted for fear of being thought racist.*
>
> *We couldn't say what we felt in front of them. We were fearful of revenge if I said what I felt about the penalty.*

To assume that victims and offenders can simply be brought together and reconciled without careful briefing of the parties first and without considerable training of co-ordinators to manage such emotional and, by their nature, unpredictable meetings is a mistake but one which is remediable. We return to this in the concluding chapters.

Victims' Satisfaction with Outcomes

Those least satisfied with the outcomes of FGCs, perhaps predictably, were the victims. Overall, only about half (49%) of the FGCs resulted in victims expressing some satisfaction with the outcome and for nearly a third of FGCs, the victim expressed dissatisfaction. However, if we look at the total number of victims rather than FGCs, the figure rises to 53%. These percentages changed slightly when a distinction was drawn between non-court and court referred cases, with satisfaction increasing to 53% for the non-court referrals and dropping to 41% for court cases. It is possible that this was because court cases took time to resolve and hence tasks were not necessarily completed when we interviewed victims.

It is also important to note that many of the victims who had not attended the FGC had not been fully informed of what had happened to the young person at the FGC. For nearly a third of the FGCs where victims did not attend, the victims, therefore, were unable to have an opinion about the appropriateness or otherwise of the outcome. Table 7.5 shows how satisfaction varied according to attendance at the FGC.

Table 7.5
Victim Satisfaction with FGC Outcome as a Function of Attendance at the FGC; Percentages Sum in Rows; N=141 FGCs*

Satisfied Attended	Yes %	Partly %	Don't Know %	No %	Total %	Total N
Yes	51	4	5	40	100	73
No	47	0	31	22	100	68
Total	49	2	18	31	100	141

* Three cases where victim supporters were present have been omitted from this table.

Where the FGC was attended by a victim, they were obviously more likely to have an opinion about the outcome and they expressed dissatisfaction in about 40% of cases. For almost a quarter (22%) of FGCs not attended by victims, dissatisfaction was expressed with the outcome. This figure would probably have been higher had they known more about the outcome. Examples of what was said by some non-attending victims who were dissatisfied with the outcome are as follows:

> *It's a token gesture. How sincere is it? $20 is peanuts.*
>
> *It's a bit light. I'd like to give him a kick up the bum.*
>
> *Bullshit. It's an insult to write it down.*

> *He got off scot free. He should have got community work and paid some of the reparation.*
>
> *Young people are just laughing at FGCs. They know that nothing much is going to happen to them. There has to be something better put in place.*
>
> *The $10 they had to pay only covered the cost of dry cleaning the jacket that got dirty. Nothing was really taken away from them.*

One non-attending victim (the offence involved a series of obscene phone calls) contacted DSW to complain about the FGC decision which involved a letter of apology, $50 reparation, 10 hours' community work and the removal of a telephone extension. She wrote:

> *I feel that a harsher punishment should apply. Big deal, 10 hours mowing lawns isn't much of a punishment. That would be forgotten pretty easy.*

Since for a significant number (40%) of FGCs attended by victims, there were strong reservations expressed about the FGC outcome, this raises questions about the extent to which they were fully informed that, when they were present at an FGC, their agreement was necessary for the outcome to be accepted. That is to say, victims may not have realised that, in a sense, they could veto any proposal put forward by the family. From our observations, it was relatively common that there was a failure to ascertain whether or not the victims agreed. We do not mean by this that victims frequently did disagree with the outcome at the FGC meeting; rather we mean that their agreement was often not specifically sought in the way that, for example, the agreement of the enforcement agency was sought. In one case we observed, the victim was asked how she felt about a proposal for the boy to perform 150 hours' community work. She replied:

> *It's disgraceful – not punitive. Even 200 hours' community work to compensate for $4,000 worth is like $20 an hour payment. I get paid $12 an hour. It's a let off, an easy option.*

Yet, despite this remark, there was no further discussion of the penalty and the victim's disagreement was not mentioned in the official record of the FGC's recommendations produced for the Youth Court.

Thus, although 95% of the FGC cases in our sample are recorded as having had an 'agreed' outcome, this does not sit well with the high levels of dissatisfaction expressed by victims. The following comments illustrate the views of victims who were dissatisfied with the FGC outcome:

> *It is a soft option. He needs jail. It was very serious. I could have been killed.*
>
> *The crime stinks, but the punishment stinks more. Disgusting – he's being allowed to get away with it.*
>
> *It's lenient. He's only paying $20 a week. I had to pay out cash and lose interest. It's me that suffers – it's not good enough. I'd shoot the bastards.*
>
> *It stinks. He's not going to do $4,000 worth of work. It really stinks.*
>
> *It's all a farce. He doesn't give a shit. None of the options were the punishment he deserves. Community work through the church is a cop out. It's too sheltered.*
>
> *It's not a punishment. The effect he's had on other people's lives – all damaged in one way or another. I'd have liked him in a road gang, hard work and aching bones. He doesn't need treatment; he needs a good kicking.*
>
> *In retrospect I think I could have been tougher and insisted on more community work. He knows he got off lightly.*
>
> *Jail for the older one definitely. The younger one should have got more than supervision. He should get corrective training.*
>
> *The laws aren't tough enough. Next time, he [the victim] has decided to defend himself. He has got a baton now hanging in the back room. (Comment from victim's spouse)*

This failure on the part of FGCs to satisfy victims may reflect the point we made earlier about the lack of adequate briefing. If victims attend FGCs with false or unrealistic expectations, it is not surprising that they often remain dissatisfied. Alternatively, maybe it is unrealistic to expect many of the victims to have recovered from their outrage and hurt about the offence by the time of the

FGC. Similarly, it may be unrealistic to expect them to appreciate an outcome which takes into account the needs of the young person and his or her family. It is also the case that some members of the public hold views which are not in tune with the current laws on dealing with crime. At any rate, it seems clear that the goal of reconciliation between offenders and victims was not always met in the FGCs we observed.

Professionals' Views of the FGC Process and Outcomes

Youth Justice Co-ordinators

Since in most areas the co-ordinators do not set up the FGC, we asked them whether or not they had been satisfied with the way this had been done. Generally, the co-ordinators expressed satisfaction; for two thirds (68%) of the cases there was an unqualified yes. Clear dissatisfaction was expressed in only a few cases in two areas and in about a quarter of cases or slightly more in the other three areas.

Reasons for dissatisfaction with the setting up of FGCs included the absence of a Youth Aid officer, parent or young person at the FGC. Co-ordinators can always adjourn in such situations but they may feel some pressure to continue when others, particularly victims, are present and would be further inconvenienced by an adjournment.

Given the large proportion of FGCs in some areas which proceeded without a victim being present, these levels of satisfaction may indicate a rather uncritical approach to the question. But interpreting the nature of particular responses is not always as straightforward as it might seem. It is not clear, for example, whether such responses to this question as 'yes, but I'd have preferred the victim there' mean the same as 'no, I'd have preferred the victim there'. 'Yes but ...' responses were common (the caveats frequently referred to the abuse of particular people such as the other parent where only one was present, additional whanau, additional victims and an interpreter). Thus 'Yes but ...' responses compared to 'No' responses may simply reflect differences in language (and critical style) between co-ordinators.

Co-ordinators in the main felt that a satisfactory outcome had been reached. More than four fifths (86%) of the outcomes in the FGC cases met with the approval of the YJCs:

> *This is a copy book outcome. What happened is exactly what the Act wants. Both families are taking responsibility.*

> *They were good decisions.*

> *It was a learning experience. It reinforced their determination not to make the same mistake again.*

> *Until then, he probably felt he could do these things and get away with them. Hopefully the FGC changed all that.*

The main exception was when they viewed the young person as 'having got off too lightly'. Other areas of concern included a lack of consideration for the victim's interests:

> *It wasn't enough. I felt the issue of reparation was overlooked. He got away with the offending.*

> *It was a good decision for [the young person] but did not address the victim's needs.*

> *The victim got ignored at the FGC in October and I was unable to get any concept of consideration from the family for the victim in this one.*

Concerns were also expressed about the failure to address the longer term, usually welfare, needs of the young person:

> *It was appropriate for the incident but left issues unresolved ... I would like to have seen a family decision addressing more long term issues of his behaviour.*

> *It's like working in a box and the only thing being dealt with was that particular incident. Next week we could have another little box. We only dealt with that incident. We could have looked at attitudes, behaviour and potential for further offending.*

> *OK as a penalty but it won't deal with the problems he faces. There are other matters which will have to be dealt with some time, somehow.*

This highlights the tensions which can exist in some cases between care and protection and youth justice issues. It was very rare for Care and Protection Co-ordinators to be present at youth justice FGCs or for referrals to be made to the Care and Protection Co-ordinator after the youth justice FGC.

Enforcement Agencies

The vast majority (91%) of enforcement officers said that they agreed with the FGC outcome. This is hardly surprising, as their agreement is necessary for the acceptance of the FGC recommendation, but it does show that one of the objectives of FGCs – reaching decisions by agreement – is being met, at least with respect to families and enforcement agencies:

> *Relatively happy given the set up. There was no reparation but that's a fact of life. It's not worth talking about.*

> *Amazing that they came to that outcome and agreed on restitution. A commendable decision.*

> *Satisfied. He seemed pretty affected by the outcome.*

Those few cases where enforcement officers did not agree with the outcome tended to be cases where a representative of the enforcement agency had not been present at the FGC, where a different officer had attended the FGC in place of the Youth Aid officer dealing with the case or where the family seemed unaware at the time that their proposal had not met with the enforcement agency's approval. On occasions, the enforcement officer present at the FGC would have preferred an outcome which was not in fact legally possible – for example, corrective training for a thirteen year old!

The generally favourable views of Youth Aid and MOT officers who attend FGCs are at odds with the views of many front-line police officers. We referred to these in the chapter on police actions. This seems to indicate a need for better liaison and feedback between the two groups. Front-line officers' concerns seem generalised rather than related to specific cases. If they were informed of the actual FGC outcomes then their attitudes might well change.

Families' and Victims' Satisfaction with FGC Follow Up

Monitoring of FGC outcomes was generally poor. Although it was common to see in the record of the FGC that particular outcomes would be completed by a particular date, our experience was that little attention was paid to monitoring whether or not this occurred. Often when we asked social workers and/or co-ordinators as part of the research project whether or not the young person had completed the tasks agreed on at the FGC, we encountered a lack of awareness and a promise to 'check up on it'. This may be due to the fact that, in some areas, there was no particular senior social worker who had responsibility for youth justice work, but the failure to ensure that tasks were carried out seemed more prevalent than that. Overall, 16% of families reported such problems and the figure was 14% for those who were otherwise satisfied with the outcome. Thus, even amongst those who said that they were satisfied with the outcome at the time of the FGC, substantial concerns were being voiced both about subsequent follow-through of the promises made by the young person and their family (for example, with respect to reparation) and subsequent support from DSW.

With respect to victims (including those who had not attended the FGC), we also found that few had been informed of the eventual success or otherwise of the outcome[53]. This was a source of considerable anger for them and absence of this type of information made victims who did attend

---

[53] Figures are not available as this question was not routinely asked of victims. Indeed, we only became aware of it as a problem because many victims asked us what had happened after the FGC and thus alerted us to the fact that they had never been told.

re-evaluate the experience. Thus the FGC per se should not be viewed as the climax of the incident for victims; they desire, and are, in our view, entitled to further feedback. It is worth noting in passing here that in managing diversion programmes for adult offenders, the police routinely inform victims of the completion of the tasks required as a condition of diversion (Young and Cameron, 1991). The following quote provides an example of the type of concern victims expressed about events after the FGC:

> *It seemed to solve the problems at the time but we have had difficulty getting the decision upheld. It is too light and flimsy, especially in enforcing the decisions.*

The concerns of parents were almost always that something promised at the FGC never materialised:

> *Not one of the people at the FGC ... have kept to their offers ... or done anything to help.*

> *I'm still waiting to hear about the appointment for the assessment. I think that's bad. I'm waiting for help for my son. Social Welfare have not followed through.*

> *If it had all happened it would have been good – but input has been zero after the meeting.*

> *Two weeks after the FGC, nothing's happened.*

> *The women from the community work came. [The young person] said he wasn't feeling well on the Saturday. He didn't turn up the next two times. We've heard nothing more but [the young person] hasn't done anything.*

Our observations confirm that promises were on occasions made by DSW staff and then not followed through. In one case, for example, the FGC was adjourned for 10 days for the social worker to assist the boy in his efforts to find some work or training. This never happened. In others, FGC plans remained unacted upon for, quite literally, months. It was agreed at one FGC held in December, for example, that the boy should be enrolled in anger management counselling. His first session was in late March. In another case the social worker disagreed with the family's choice of counsellor, but many weeks later he had failed to make arrangements for an alternative. Eventually the family went to their original choice of counsellor, but because of the social worker's inaction the case was unable to be dealt with by the Youth Court and was delayed for several months. The most obvious examples of these failures to monitor progress or follow-through on agreed actions were where subsequent FGCs were held and no attention was paid to whether or not decisions reached at the earlier FGC had been acted upon.

It is clear, too, that idealised notions of family 'empowerment' can mean putting responsibilities on families which they are not able to cope with. Some of the families we met during the research could not be said to be functioning well. Such families cannot be expected to suggest ways of dealing with their child's offending when they have reached the end of their own resources and probably their tether. DSW staff on occasions did not offer support or advice in situations in which families would have welcomed it and were plainly asking for it:

> *[The FGC was] a waste of time. They did nothing except make him our responsibility. They just said: "you sort it out".*

> *It's hard for parents to police community [work] hours. [The researcher's notes accompanying this interview state that this mother was very worried about this responsibility. The boy was not doing the community work although she tried to get him to do it. This boy did not actually live with his parents and, in the researcher's opinion, the mother was not functioning well and was already under stress.]*

> *I'd have liked support afterwards, I felt left on my own. I had to find community work on my own.*

> *Cost cutting in DSW means that problems are put back on families when they are asking for help.*

> *A bit too much was left up to us as parents. He needs stricter supervision – he needs more help – perhaps medical help.*

> *It's difficult to cope with [the young person] at the moment – quite beyond me. I could do with some support. I've contacted Toughlove.*
>
> *You need help and support and you ask DSW about it but nothing happens.*
>
> *I can't get hold of DSW. They don't do anything for their clients. I've needed them to give him a talking to but they're not bloody interested.*

It was clear from the interview with one mother that she wanted more support:

> *I need a break from S, from the things he does. I feel as though I've had enough.*

She continued:

> *I'd prefer time away [for him] for a short time. I thought that they might have helped by taking S somewhere, to a foster home, to give me a break.*

Subsequently, this youth committed a further offence and, at a meeting with the youth's social worker (almost one month after the first FGC), the mother requested a further FGC to consider placing the youth in a family home. At this new FGC (convened because of the further offending), this request was never raised. A new social worker had been allocated to the boy.

The following interchange at an FGC which was reconvened because of reoffending also illustrates the failure by DSW to act as far as the parents were concerned:

> Mother: *I contacted the social worker. He was going to help get a placement but he hasn't written or phoned. There has been no contact at all. I have gone to see him and phoned him but I was not able to get him.*
>
> Priest: *I got in touch with the social worker. He said DSW can't help. He's exhausted all possibilities.*
>
> Stepfather: *The social worker hasn't done anything. How can he have exhausted all possibilities?*

Failure on the part of DSW to follow through was also felt by some parents to detract from the FGC's supposed emphasis on the young person's accountability for his or her actions:

> *I'm disappointed with the follow-up. [The young person] could have the impression he's getting away with it.* (Parent)
>
> *It needed closer monitoring - a quicker response when things went wrong. I was concerned that DSW did not help sooner. It seemed that the stipulated consequence – the threat of going to court – didn't happen.* (Parent)

Cultural Issues

Three questions were designed to probe people's awareness of whether or not their ethnicity made a difference to the FGC process:

- Did being Maori/Samoan/etc make a difference?
- Was the FGC run in a Maori/Samoan/etc way?
- Was it all right for you?

In the earlier chapter on the methods used in the study we commented that, with hindsight, these were not the best questions. The fact that most families did not describe the effect of their ethnicity on their experience probably reflects, in part, the reality of a uniformly Pakeha world of official procedures, in part, a lack of awareness that the procedures could have been modified in accordance with the family's own culture and, in part, the fact that people only had their own experience to comment on and could not, therefore, evaluate it in comparison with that of others of different ethnicity. Because of these difficulties we have not attempted to analyse the answers quantitatively.

Nevertheless, the flavour of the answers we received are worth reporting. Most can be divided into two different types of response depending on whether the respondents perceived the process as Pakeha or whether they perceived elements in the process that gave it a cultural emphasis.

The Pakeha Way

Some saw the process in Pakeha, rather than Maori or Pacific Island, terms but felt that this was not necessarily bad:

> *It seemed to be done in a Pakeha way ... we expect the Pakeha system ... we like it as it is.*
>
> *It was a Pakeha scene ... it's OK.*
>
> *It could have been more culturally appropriate in terms of process ... the whole system ... but it was sensitively done given the constraints of the system.*

This type of response was summed up by a Cook Island young person and endorsed by his father:

> *It made no difference. They should all be the same.*

Other respondents felt differently and more negatively about the process remaining in Pakeha hands:

> *It was Pakeha kaupapa (procedure) ... if done in a Maori way, it would take longer; it would involve understanding everyone present and their roles.*
>
> *It gives power to the whanau, but the ultimate power is still in Pakeha hands.*

For these young people and their families, a different process would have been preferable.

The Cultural Way

For other families, the presence of whanau, the opportunity to explore wider issues and the fact that they were able to have the FGC in their own home or on a marae was seen as part of what it meant to do things their **own** way. These aspects of the FGC were appreciated:

> *The setting is important – at home is good; it gives us back some power.*
>
> *It was great. The boys felt shame. We had a kaumatua there, there was a powhiri (Maori welcoming ritual), karakia (prayer), and kai (food). All could speak.*
>
> *He (the offender) hadn't known Maori culture and now he will.*
>
> *I don't understand Maori too well, but it was good for my family that we had prayers. I know they were praying for me.*

There were a number of FGCs in which the Maori observer commented that it had been a 'model' Maori FGC. The two case histories at the end of Chapter 6 provide examples of FGCs which strengthened families and began a process of renewal for the young person.

Only a few Maori explicitly disassociated themselves from attempts to create a Maori process:

> *I don't like this Maorified way of doing things – waste of time ... don't need all those relatives there.*
>
> *Too much shit about the Maori way ... waste of time deep down.*

And there were three occasions when parents and children differed as to whether there should have been more or less cultural input. In one case, for example, the young person said: *I would have preferred more Maori input.* But his parents did not agree with this: *We have lived all our life in a Pakeha world.*

Overall, our assessment from both observation and interviews is that, although the FGC can be adapted to different cultural processes, this did not often occur. However, for those families who did manage the process in accordance with their own customs, the experience was very positive.

It is clear that much more opportunity should be given to families to consider the procedures they wish to adopt at the FGC, including the venue and the possibility of using the marae.

Real difficulties can arise, however, when offenders are of one ethnic group and victims are of another. Pakeha victims on occasions claimed not only that they felt intimidated by the presence of a large number of whanau but also that they resented discussions in Maori and felt alienated in a Maori environment. And in at least one case in the research the family would clearly have preferred to hold the FGC on their own marae but did not do so out of deference to and concern for the victim. In some cases, the dilemma over whether to use the setting that best meets the needs of the young person and his or her family or one which will be more comfortable for the victim can be resolved by negotiation between the family and the victim. In other cases, it might be preferable for the process to have two distinct stages: a first stage where the victim, young person and family members meet on the victim's territory and a second stage where the family and young person meet in their own setting to decide on their recommendations, taking into account the victim's views. In one case we observed something akin to this where the Youth Justice Co-ordinator effectively acted as a go-between to negotiate an agreed settlement between the two groups who did not wish to meet one another. But, while the resolution of cultural differences may be possible in some cases, there is also the wider issue that certain processes may empower one group – for example, the family – but disempower another – for example, the victim.

From our observations, we saw examples of both cultural process in action – Pacific Island families making apologies in the traditional manner – and cultural conflict in action – for example, in one case involving a Samoan family, the professionals endorsed a solution in line with the wishes of the young person but which was directly in conflict with the wishes of his father. The Samoan social worker and researcher both saw this as contravening cultural norms. There were also occasions in which interpreters should have been arranged for the FGC and were not. The absence of interpreters was in some cases a real barrier to effective communication.

In addition, we observed instances of what we believe to be breaches of protocol – for example, co-ordinators welcoming families when the FGC was held in the family's own home in the same manner as they did when the FGC was held in DSW; and not using kaumatua who were present to facilitate the FGC. Cultural advisers were rarely used and the appropriate whanau were not always notified when one of their young people was involved in serious offending.

In the view of the Maori researchers, most of the FGCs they attended were instances in which the interpretation of the Act or neglect of the intent of the Act resulted in culturally inappropriate processes taking place. They felt that families had not been able to be strengthened because, often, the processes were not culturally appropriate, and that the objective of making available services and facilities which were appropriate to the needs, values and beliefs of Maori families had not been attained. As Maori researchers, they saw this situation as arising from ignorance of the Act, a dearth of resources and mismanagement of the processes rather than from any inherent faults in the legislation itself.

Conclusions

As is clear from the interview data already cited, there is no doubt that the reported level of involvement of families and young people in the youth justice process is far greater now than in the former system where many of them would have been part of the court process. In previous research (Morris and Young, 1987), families and young people saw the court as alien, remote and frustrating, described their participation as rare and their communication as routine and felt that they had wasted their time. Now most parents and at least some young people describe their involvement in FGCs in positive terms: they felt able to say what they wanted. Parents, in particular, also identified themselves as having been involved in the decision at the FGC in a significant proportion of cases. This is very different from the previous system and from systems of juvenile justice elsewhere, where decision making by either courts or welfare panels provides for little effective participation from parents (Martin *et al*, 1981; Asquith, 1983).

However, the fact remains that the majority of young people felt that they had not been involved in the FGC process or in the decision about the outcome. This gives the lie to the notion of a Family Group Conference as a forum that involves the whole family in the making of decisions and we are reminded of the comment made in the report on the previous juvenile justice system in New Zealand (Morris and Young, 1987) that, because of children's limited participation in the former Children's Boards, one of the researchers re-named them 'Parents' Boards'. The stress on accountability in the new system demands an increased involvement of young people in the process, since otherwise they will not only continue to fail to understand fully the consequences of their actions but they will also fail to take responsibility for what they have done.

The empowerment of young people depends not just on the actions of the professionals but also on the active collaboration of the family. The extent to which this is possible may be affected by beliefs about the part which young people should play in decision making about their own lives in a family context. Some have suggested that the active involvement of the young person is not part of a Maori (or Pacific Island) cultural pattern. Indeed in Maori cultural terms, it has been suggested that even the families themselves and whanau may have a limited decision making role and that it is kaumatua who should decide what happens to young people. However, other Maori to whom we have spoken see no conflict between the participation of the young person and whanau decision-making.

Thus the role which adults allow young people to play in the decision-making is not self-evident, uncontentious or culturally uniform. The effective participation of young people, therefore, can not be taken for granted simply because it is stated as being important in the legislation. It must be actively encouraged by those arranging youth justice processes. Furthermore, the notion that young people who have offended should legitimately play a role in the decisions about how they should be held accountable may be one with which the community must become familiar before it can be effectively accepted in practice. We suggest that the achievement of the participation of young people is not purely a private or family issue. It is an issue which warrants full and public discussion in order to increase public understanding of the rationale underlying the legislative attempt to encourage young people to be accountable for their actions.

On the other hand, levels of satisfaction with outcomes amongst both parents and their children were generally high. But they were high among respondents in the research on the previous system too (Morris and Young, 1987) and they tend to be high in jurisdictions with very different philosophic bases (see, for example, Martin et al, 1981 and Morris and Giller, 1977). This again raises questions about what such statements really mean. The fact that satisfaction was lower when the outcome was a more severe penalty may indicate that parents and young people who express satisfaction might simply be relieved that nothing worse (more severe) happened, and that parents and young persons will always be satisfied with a light penalty. However, our data contradict such a conclusion. It certainly cannot be said that the penalties that resulted from FGCs were uniformly light. Many seemed in excess of what would have been ordered under the previous system by the Children and Young Persons Court where, in 1988 (the last full statistical year before the new Act), 38% were given nominal dispositions (that is, they were either discharged, dismissed, admonished and discharged, or given a suspended sentence) and another 19% were fined. Comparisons can also be made with dispositions elsewhere. In England and Wales, for example, in 1989, 29% of male young people were discharged and 20% were fined (the comparable figures for girls were 51% and 18% respectively) and the discharge figures for children (10-13 year olds) were even higher: 50% for boys and 64% for girls (Home Office, 1990).

A key determinant of the success or otherwise of the new system is whether parents and young people are satisfied with both the process and outcomes of FGCs. The emphasis on empowerment of families surely demands it. Moreover, Matza (1964) has shown that for young people, a feeling of a sense of justice is crucial in inhibiting a further drift into delinquency. Although Matza's discussion arose in a very different context (a critique of juvenile justice in the United States in the 1960s), his words remain potent. Whenever a sense of injustice prevails, he argues, the moral bind of the law is loosened. A sense of involvement in the process, a role in determining the appropriate outcome and a belief that the outcome was fair are likely to be components which prevent the development of a sense of injustice.

Victims also play a greater role now than previously. However, attendance rates at FGCs are not yet as high as they might be and victims' levels of satisfaction remain low. This contrasts with overseas research on Victim/Offender Reconciliation Programmes (VORPs). Coates and Gehm (1989), for example, report that almost two thirds of victims were satisfied with their experience of such programmes and that only 11% of victims expressed dissatisfaction. Those victims who were most satisfied identified as contributing to this the opportunity to meet with the offender and thereby obtain a better understanding of the offender's situation, as well as the opportunity to receive reparation, the expression of remorse by the offender and the concern of the mediator. Those victims who were least satisfied were usually unhappy about the lack of follow-up to ensure that the offender fulfilled what he or she had agreed to. This latter factor must play at least some part in the lower levels of satisfaction expressed by the victims in our study. We certainly became aware during our interviews that the timing of the interview could be crucial. There was a tendency for those who were interviewed shortly after the FGC to express some satisfaction with the outcome. Where the interview was delayed, and hence where the time for the performance of certain tasks had elapsed, we were more likely to find expressions of dissatisfaction.

A further factor which is likely to explain the difference between our findings and those of overseas studies is that mediation programmes in other countries tend to focus on reparation and where this is obtained we would expect victims to be satisfied. Reparation was agreed on in 29% of FGCs in our study (the national figure was about 30%). If victims attend FGCs in the hope that reparation will be provided, then it is not surprising that many remain dissatisfied. Another difference between FGCs and overseas programmes is that the latter are selective and the selection is based as much if not more on victims' interests and needs than on offenders'. The intention in FGCs is to involve victims of all types of offences.

It could also be argued that many victims remain dissatisfied with the process and outcomes in their cases because victims 'naturally' want heavy penalties to punish the offender for what he or she has done. While undoubtedly that happened in some of the cases in this study, it did not occur universally. Overseas studies support such a conclusion. Hough and Mayhew (1983), for example, on the basis of data drawn from the first British Crime Survey, argue that people are much less punitive towards offenders than is commonly imagined. Data from the second survey (Hough and Mayhew, 1985) also indicate that there is support among victims for the idea of reparation, either for victims directly or for the community. Furthermore, almost half of the victims of crime identified in that survey said that they would be willing to meet the person who had offended against them. It must, however, be kept in mind that in our study a third of victims said they felt worse as a result of the process. We have already identified some of the factors which seem likely to have caused this – the failure to keep victims informed, a lack of reparation and inadequate monitoring of outcomes. Other factors which also seem to be important are the choice of venue for the FGC, the number of people attending the FGC and the amount of support at FGCs for victims. We touch on these in the final chapter.

One of the reasons for encouraging victims' participation in FGCs is that it might effect some reconciliation between the victim and the offender. Although objective measurement of the extent of reconciliation was not possible, this clearly occurred in some of the FGCs we observed. At one, after tearful apologies had been made by both the youth and his family, there seemed to be a reluctance amongst the parties to leave the meeting. There were handshakes and embraces all round and finally a suggestion by one of the victims that the offender and his family join him for a meal at a later date. In another, the victim became very sympathetic towards the youth and, after the break, moved to sit by him in a sort of symbolic alliance. In yet another, victims who were initially very angry with the young person became supportive after spending half an hour with her on their own and subsequently offered to attend court with her. The researcher's field notes ended: *I feel privileged to have been at such a touching and effective FGC.*

We end this chapter with some quotes from those who took part in the FGCs which, we feel, capture the spirit and potential of the new system:

> *A great idea – we were really involved. It is an excellent idea to sort it out in the home and to involve families. (Parent)*

I'm really pleased that it doesn't go straight to court like the old days. The kids are given a chance now. (Parent)

Really good. I got to see the victim, apologise and help her with money. The victim also got a chance to say things. (Young person)

I like the idea of the victim getting reparation. It is good to meet the victim, good to involve the parents. (Parent)

It was a good idea to meet the offender and his parents and understand how people got to be like this. I was angry at first but later I was sympathetic. I feel we decided the right thing. I preferred this system to the court. At the FGC you get to know what happened and to be involved. (Victim)

Chapter 8

THE YOUTH COURT

Introduction

The principles set down in the Act predicate changes in the nature of Youth Court proceedings that affect young people. These changes are designed to emphasize a justice rather than a welfare model; to involve families and young people in the process and decisions; to achieve time frames that are suitable for young people; to protect the rights of young people and ensure due process; and to make sure that the procedures do not increase the chances of criminalising offenders. Many of these changes can be seen as addressing the issues described in our earlier report (Morris and Young, 1987) which noted that: a welfare orientation led to disparate outcomes; the formality of the court led to difficulties for young people and families in understanding proceedings, there was a perceived remoteness and a lack of participation in the process by families and young people; there was variability in whether or not the young person was represented; court proceedings were often protracted; and waiting rooms were inadequate and crowded due to the lack of an appointment system.

A Justice Model Rather than a Welfare Model

Under the previous legislation it was possible to use sentences which placed children or young people in the care of the Director General of Social Welfare whenever it seemed appropriate for their welfare. The result was that some young people remained wards of State, living in institutions for the remainder of their minority. Under the new legislation any matters relating to care and protection that are sufficiently serious to warrant the removal of the child or young person from his or her family are not normally dealt with under youth justice proceedings. Rather the youth justice provisions have the goal of ensuring that a penalty appropriate to the offence is arrived at. Custodial sentences are limited to relatively serious offences and, within the Youth Court jurisdiction, do not exceed three months' supervision with residence. There are very limited grounds for remands in police custody or in secure care. Normally, if a custodial remand is considered necessary, DSW is charged with the responsibility of attempting to place the child or young person with his or her family except in the most serious cases where public protection is an issue. Efforts are made to ensure that, wherever possible, the young person is kept within the community and that accountability is achieved through reparation and penalties that are meaningful and related to the magnitude of the offending. Hence the range of penalties and the jurisdictional limits already described in Chapter 1.

Involving Families and Young People in the Processes and Decisions

The Act specifies that young people and their families should be involved not only in the FGC process but in the proceedings of the Youth Court itself. Section 288 says that an order shall not be made unless the parent or guardian has been informed of the proposal to make that order and been given an opportunity to make representations to the court. Sections 329-330 set out the entitlement of the young person, parent or guardian and advocates to be present and to make representations to the court. Section 278 enables the Youth Court to summons a parent or guardian to a hearing. Section 279 requires the Youth Court to consider the recommendations and plans of the FGC before hearing the information relating to the offence and section 281 requires the Youth Court not to make orders unless an FGC has been held.

As well as setting out extensive provisions to ensure family involvement, the Act makes clear that the Youth Court is required to explain its procedures and actions fully to young people and their families. Section 10 requires that both the court **and** counsel, when a young person or a parent or other caregiver appears before the Youth Court, shall explain the nature of the proceedings in a manner and language that can be understood by the young person. Furthermore, the youth advocate, or alternatively the court if no advocate is present, shall satisfy themselves that the young person understands the proceedings and explain any order made by the court in a language and manner that can be understood by the young person or caregiver including the nature and requirements of the order, any provisions for variation and the existence of appeal rights. Section 437 requires that the court give notice of any proceedings or application (for example an application for a warrant to arrest) to any parent, guardian or other person caring for the child. The information supplied should give sufficient detail and be in a suitable form to enable the parent or guardian to understand both the nature and the implications of the application or proceedings; and it should include information on their rights to appear or to be represented. They should also receive a copy of any order explained in sufficient detail for them to understand its nature and implications and should be informed of their rights to appeal. Section 340 requires that a written statement of the terms of any orders be given to the young person and that this should include appeal rights. The requirement to ensure that the young person is represented also provides a mechanism for increasing the young person's understanding of the charges, procedures and outcomes.

Time Frame

A number of sections of the Act attempt to give effect to the principle that actions should occur within a time frame that makes those actions meaningful to the child or young person. Section 322 allows a Youth Court judge to dismiss any information if the judge is satisfied that the time that has elapsed between the commission of the offence and the hearing has been unduly protracted. Section 281 requires that any FGC ordered by the court shall be convened within 14 days. Section 332 says that, as far as is practicable, proceedings in the Youth Court shall be arranged in a manner that keeps to a minimum the time for the proceedings to be heard.

Representation and Protection of the Rights of Young People

The court is required to appoint a barrister or solicitor to represent any child or young person not already represented (sections 322-325). Provision also exists for the appointment of a lay advocate (sections 333-339) to ensure that the court is made aware of all relevant cultural matters and to represent the interests of the child's or young person's whanau, hapu or iwi (or their equivalents, if any, in the culture of the child or young person) to the extent that those interests are not otherwise represented in the proceedings. These provisions give a mechanism both for ensuring due process in cases that appear before the court and for redressing some of the criticisms that have been made, in recent years, of the criminal justice system in dealing with Maori people (Te Whainga i Te Tika, 1986; Jackson, 1988).

Minimising Criminalisation

Requirements that limit the publication of proceedings (section 438) and the congregation of offenders are specifically included. Section 331 effectively requires separate waiting rooms or appearance times from other court proceedings to avoid contact between young offenders and offenders in other jurisdictions and subsection (b) states that the extent to which children and young people are able to associate with other offenders while awaiting their hearing is to be reduced to a minimum. These provisions are clearly intended to change earlier practice when court waiting rooms provided an opportunity for young offenders to meet one another and had allowed them ample time to become acquainted over a period of weeks while their cases were being heard.

In this chapter, we first review national statistics on cases appearing in the Youth Court since the Act came into effect, making comparisons, where possible, with previous data. We then present data from our study that can be compared with the national statistics, describe the hearing process in the Youth Court and provide an evaluation of the extent to which the parts of the Act relating to the Youth Court have been successful in achieving their objectives.

National Statistics on the Youth Court

Information from the Courts Division, Department of Justice

One indicator which informs us about changes in the use of the Youth Court is the number of informations laid at court since the 1989 Act came into force. Table 8.1 compares these data for the period January to September 1989 and January to September 1990. It shows that the number of informations being laid in the first nine months of 1990 was barely a third of those which were laid for a similar period in the year before the Act. It also shows that there are very marked district variations in the amount of change that has occurred since the Act. Because some offenders were charged with a large number of offences, comparisons over a relatively short time frame like the one used here may be unrepresentative. Nevertheless, it appears that reductions in the number of informations laid have been much more marked in the Masterton, Christchurch and Henderson Youth Courts than in the Porirua Youth Court.

Table 8.1
Number of Informations Laid in Selected Youth Courts; National Data Comparing Pre- and Post-Act periods

	Jan-Sept 1989	Jan-Sept 1990	1990 as % of 1989
Auckland Central	1,424	623	44
Christchurch	1,482	339	23
Henderson	656	138	21
Lower Hutt	498	213	43
Masterton	317	45	14
Porirua	476	263	55
Wellington	689	278	40
New Zealand Total	18,473	7,009	38

Source: Unpublished Department of Justice statistics

Each juvenile who appeared in court, however, might have been the subject of more than one information. As fewer cases now come to court, it seems likely that those which do will include a larger proportion than previously of persistent offenders facing multiple charges. Thus the figures for the number of informations laid are likely to under-estimate the level of reduction in the number of juveniles appearing in court.

Information from the Department of Statistics

Two alternative sources of data based on figures entered in the Wanganui computer provide information on distinct cases appearing before the Youth Court. They come from the Department of Justice and from the publication on Justice Statistics prepared by the Department of Statistics. One problem that arises is that the number of cases reported are very discrepant. The Department of Justice reports that 1,952 cases appeared in 1990 while the Department of Statistics reports 2,587 cases for the same period. Much of this difference occurs because the Department of Justice did not include offenders over the age of 16 who appeared in the Youth Court to answer for offences committed while they were still under the age of 17. Thus for the most part we have preferred the Department of Statistics data as the source for the following analyses. This has the additional advantage of allowing comparisons with similar analyses of data prior to the Act.

Figure 8.1
Youth Court or Children and Young Persons Court 1980-1990; Distinct Cases Involving Young Offenders

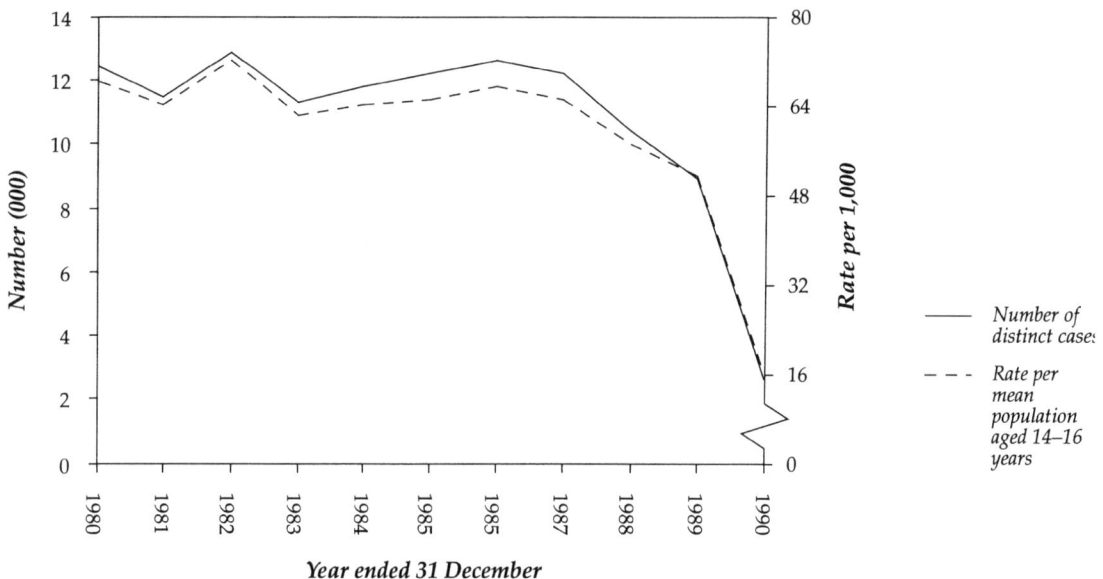

Source: Department of Statistics, 1991.

The Department of Statistics data show that there has been a marked decline in the number of juveniles appearing in the Youth Court since the Act came into effect. In the eight years prior to the introduction of the 1989 Act, distinct cases varied between 10,300 and nearly 13,000 (see Figure 8.1). In the first full year since the Act (1990), there were only 2,587 distinct cases recorded. In terms of population rates, this represents a drop from rates of between 57-72 court appearances per 1,000 young people aged 14-16 to a rate of only 16 per 1,000, a drop to nearly a quarter, on average, of the pre-Act figures.

Department of Statistics data also show that the change in Youth Court appearances is not simply one of numbers. The type of offences on which young people appear in the Youth Court has changed with an increase in the proportion of offences against the person. The offenders are also slightly more likely to be male, older and Maori. The details are as follows:

- The proportion of male offenders has tended to increase. Males made up 82% of the cases appearing in the Youth Court in the three years leading up to the Act. In 1990, they made up 85%.

- The proportion of older offenders appearing in the Youth Court has tended to increase. Sixteen year olds made up 53% of the cases in the three years leading up to the Act. In 1990, they made up 56%.

- Maori made up 47% of the cases appearing in the Youth Court in the three years leading up to the Act. In 1990, they made up 51%.

- Offences against property made up 63% of the cases appearing in the Youth Court in the three years leading up to the Act. In 1990, they made up 56%.

- Offences against the person made up 11% of the cases appearing in the Youth Court in the three years leading up to the Act. In 1990, they made up 21%.

The pattern of disposal of cases has also changed dramatically according to the Department of Statistics information[54].

- In the three years leading up to the Act, 39% of cases were dismissed, withdrawn or discharged. In 1990, half the cases recorded were dismissed, withdrawn or discharged.[55]

- In the three years leading up to the Act, on average 374 cases per year, which represents 3% of all cases, resulted in sentences of imprisonment or corrective training in the Children and Young Persons Court. In 1990, 4% of cases resulted in sentences of imprisonment or corrective training in the Youth Court, but this represents only 112 cases, less than a third the average number for the preceding three years.

- In the three years leading up to the Act, on average 9% of cases were transferred to the District or High Court for sentence.[56] In 1990, only 4% of cases were transferred to the District or High Court for sentence.

Thus, not only are there fewer cases appearing in the Youth Court, but also an even smaller proportion of these cases are resulting in an order than in the past. Half the Youth Court cases are being either dismissed or dealt with informally through the recommendations of the FGC. Furthermore, the reduction in the number of custodial and other adult court-based sentences points to a very different pattern of disposition of cases.

Information from Department of Social Welfare

Additional information on the type of orders being made by the Youth Court comes from a study by Levine and Wyn (1991) which examined data collected from DSW districts over the period November 1989 to December 1990. Their work focused only on the five highest tariffs available to the Youth Court and these did not include orders for disqualification from driving, forfeiture, restitution, reparation, costs, fines, deferred sentences, admonitions and discharges under section 283(a). Table 8.2 below sets out the use of these orders. It shows that 73 cases were transferred to the District or High Court, which represents a very small number compared to the total of nearly 5,700 FGCs that were held in the same period. Similarly small numbers of cases resulted in orders for the other four high tariff penalties and altogether these orders accounted for only 6% of the cases in which Family Group Conferences were held.

Table 8.2
Youth Court Orders, National Data for November 1989 to December 1990, on the Five Highest Tariffs; N=357

	N	% of Total FGCs (N=5675)
Supervision	98	1.7
Community Work	72	1.3
Supervision with Activity	49	.9
Supervision with Residence	65	1.1
Transfer to District or High Court	73	1.3
Total	357	6.3

Source: Levine and Wyn (1991)

---

[54] Unfortunately the information available on the disposal of Youth Court cases is very limited. Apart from a special study carried out by the Department of Social Welfare, the only information is that stored on the Wanganui Computer and the categories used on the database make no reference to the types of dispositions normally made by the Youth Court. Thus the data presented here have been inferred from the Department of Statistics' presentation of the Wanganui categories and may not be entirely accurate.

[55] These figures include a small number of defended cases where the case was not proved.

[56] Cases transferred to the District or High Court for sentence become eligible for the full range of penalties available for adult offenders. In practice, most juveniles transferred to an adult court receive a custodial sentence of corrective training or imprisonment.

Inferences from All Sources

Information on the use of the Youth Court can also be inferred by combining the data previously described on the outcome of police non-arrest cases with the data on the incidence of police arrests. Hassall and Maxwell (1990), using official police figures, calculated that 74% of all detected juveniles were being dealt with by 'police diversion', 20% were being referred for FGCs without a prior Youth Court appearance, and only the 6% arrested necessarily appeared before a Youth Court judge. However, given the finding reported in Chapter 3 that police records underestimate arrests, these calculations must be reassessed. The data from the present study, which probably provide the most accurate information on which to base estimates of the ways in which cases have been dealt with since the Act, suggest that arrests make up 10% rather than 6% of cases involving young people. Thus 'police diversion' probably involves about 70% of cases rather than the 74% estimated by Hassall and Maxwell.

It should be noted that it is possible for an FGC to refer a case onward to the Youth Court even when the case was not referred through the Youth Court in the first place. But not many FGCs resolve to forward the case to the Youth Court. The police data quoted earlier suggest that this occurs for one in five cases where charges were laid, which represents 4% of all cases referred for an FGC by the police from non-arrest sources. Including arrest cases, a reasonable estimate is that, in total, 14% of detected juvenile offenders now make an appearance in the Youth Court.

It is also possible for cases that go to the Youth Court initially to be eventually resolved by an FGC and for the charges to be withdrawn or dismissed. Data from the Department of Statistics and the Department of Justice provide an indication of the frequency with which this occurs and support the view expressed by judges and Youth Justice Co-ordinators that, nationally, the recommendations of the FGC are adopted in at least half of all the cases that appear in the Youth Court. Thus the total number of court cases, including both arrests and summons cases, which were eventually resolved through the use of Youth Court orders is likely to make up about 7% of the total number of detected juvenile offenders.

These results show a marked contrast with data from before the 1989 Act. Morgan's 1984 study showed that only 55% of juvenile cases were handled by 'police diversion', while the remaining 45% were referred to the Children and Young Persons Court by way of arrest, summons, or complaint. This figure of 45% can be compared with the estimate above that only 14% of cases now appear at some stage in the Youth Court. In the old days, too, most of the offenders who appeared in court would have received a court order (other than admonition and discharge) compared with the present estimate of about half of those appearing in the Youth Court since the Act.

Data from the Research Study

Description of Clients by Type, District and Decision

A total of 69 individual offenders appeared before the Youth Court as a result of offences committed during the sample period. In several cases, the same individual was charged more than once during the sample period and in all but one of these cases, matters were brought together for disposal by the court. The data in this section are based on 70 distinct cases that came to notice and were disposed of independently.

Most (80%) referrals to the Youth Court came as a result of police arrests; only 10% came as a result of police summons, 6% came as a result of MOT arrests or summonses and the remainder involved charges laid by both the MOT and the police. These figures accord well with the analysis by the Justice Department of the total cases for 1990, where 88% of cases dealt with in the Youth Court were police prosecutions and 10% were prosecutions by the MOT.

As well as complications arising from multiple offending by the same individual within the sample period, some of our cases are complicated by the fact that they were already before the court on earlier matters when an offence arose in the sample period. In other cases, offending committed after the sample period delayed the resolution of matters in the sample period. A further factor that complicated disposal was when there was a denial of the charge and a defended hearing needed to be arranged. Because of these complications we have chosen to make a distinction between 'simple' and 'complicated' cases. A case can be defined as beginning when a charge is laid and as ending when a **final** decision is made on any charges laid since the case began. A **simple** case is defined as one where charges were laid only on a single occasion and none of these charges were denied; thus in these cases there were no special complications due to the actions of the offender which could have caused delays. 'Complicated' cases are defined as those where there was reoffending, where the police later laid additional charges or where at least one of the charges was denied, so that additional remands often occurred. 'Simple' and 'complicated' cases together make up **total** cases.

Thirty-four distinct cases were 'simple' cases and 36 were 'complicated' ones. In other words, about half the cases that came to court became complicated with other matters before they could be finalised (25 cases) or else involved denials (11 cases). This contrasts with the cases resolved by FGCs which rarely became complicated in these ways. The difference, as we will see, reflects not only the relative seriousness of the court cases, but also the delays accompanying the resolution of matters before the court.

Description of the Sample

Data on the characteristics of the sample of young people who appeared before the Youth Court are presented in Table 8.3. Ninety percent of those appearing in court were boys. As already noted in Chapters 2 and 3, Maori youth were more likely to appear in court than would be expected from the rate at which they were detected for offending. The reasons are more fully dealt with elsewhere but, to recapitulate, they lie partly in the fact that Maori youth were more likely to be involved in moderately serious offending but also in the fact that Maori youth seemed more likely to be arrested than Pakeha youth for similarly serious offences.

Sixty percent of the court cases involved 16 year olds and another quarter involved 15 year olds, leaving only a few cases involving those aged 14. One case involved an 18 year old who, at the time he was arrested for other offences as an adult, was found to have committed an offence as a juvenile for which there was an outstanding warrant.

Eighty-six percent of court cases involved young people who had a previous offence history. The ten cases involving first offenders were examined in greater detail. Two were rated as minimum/medium in seriousness, six were rated medium, one was rated medium/maximum and one was rated maximum. All but one of these cases, the most serious, were eventually withdrawn or discharged.

Table 8.3
Description of the Court Sample; Distinct Cases; Percentages; N=70

OFFENDER CHARACTERISTICS	N	%
Sex		
Boys	63	90
Girls	7	10
Ethnicity		
Pakeha	27	39
Maori	35	50
Pacific Island	8	11
Age		
14 years	9	13
15 years	18	26
16 years	42	60
18 years	1	1
Previous Offending		
Yes	60	86
No	10	14

OFFENCE CHARACTERISTICS	N	%
Rated seriousness of offence		
Minimum or medium/minimum	10	14
Medium	44	63
Medium/maximum or maximum	16	23
Co-offenders		
No	41	59
Yes	29	41
*Type of offences**		
Theft, Fraud, Receiving	20	29
Burglary	25	36
Unlawful vehicle offences	21	30
Assault, robbery, sex or arson	21	30
Drugs, damage, other	19	27
No of offences		
1	21	30
2	18	26
3-5	23	33
6 or more	8	11
Denial		
No	59	84
Yes	11	16

* Note that some offenders committed more than one type of offence so the figures sum to more than 100%.

These findings further reinforce the suggestion that some relatively non-serious cases involving first offenders are being brought to the court when in fact matters could have been, and indeed eventually were, resolved through the use of an FGC to the satisfaction of the parents and law enforcement agencies alike. This issue is discussed further in the next chapter. Two examples of these cases are given below:

A young lad, T, was caught with his brother-in-law one night after they had just stolen and butchered a sheep valued at $50 [rated seriousness = minimum/medium]. He had not previously offended. At the FGC he expressed considerable remorse and paid his share of the cost to the farmer who accepted the apology and reparation. He then went on a vocational programme and later returned to family in another area. He has not reoffended.

Four young people stole a car which was wrecked after a chase [rated seriousness = medium]. The ringleader was an older boy with a previous history of offending, who appeared in the District Court. The three younger boys, two of whom had no previous offending history, had FGCs where they expressed remorse, paid some reparation and agreed to do community work which was successfully completed. The court discharged them and congratulated them. None has reoffended.

Fourteen percent of the offences were rated minimum or minimum/medium in seriousness. It is perhaps surprising that these more trivial cases led to a charge in the Youth Court, even though they involved offenders with prior records who satisfied the arrest criteria[57]. Nearly two thirds of the offences were rated medium in seriousness, with less than a quarter being rated medium/maximum or maximum in seriousness. Less serious cases were more likely to be brought before the court in some areas. Data on the severity of outcomes appear to confirm our view that not all these cases were sufficient to merit court attention, as nearly half (48%) of them resulted in withdrawal or discharge after an acceptance by the court of the recommendations of the FGC.

Nearly half the offences were committed in the company of others. Court cases involved proportionately fewer simple dishonesty offences than did cases involving an FGC or 'police diversion'. Those appearing in court were most likely to have committed a burglary, to have been involved in unlawfully interfering with or taking motor vehicles, or to have been involved in offences of violence (including sexual offending and arson). In 84% of the cases the offence was not denied.

Court process

Denied cases

The first issue to be determined at both an FGC and a Youth Court hearing is whether or not the matters are denied. When there is a denial, then the 'denied' matter is remanded by the court for a defended hearing. In all, 11 cases or 16% of the Youth Court sample (including one case which was initially referred directly for an FGC) involved the denial of at least one charge. Ten of these were dealt with in the Youth Court; the eleventh case was transferred to the District Court.

Resolution of 'denied' matters proved to be a lengthy process. One relatively minor matter was **decided** two weeks after being first called but this was the exception. In other cases, reaching the **decision** about guilt involved delays of 6, 10, 13, 13 and 17 weeks, with five cases, including the four most serious, still awaiting determination eight months after the first Youth Court appearance. Although the length of these delays exceeded the period that might normally be expected in the District Court, it was difficult to determine the reasons for them. In the four most serious cases, little attempt seemed to be made to determine a hearing date over the first six weeks. Reasons that were given for the delay included the need for more time for the Crown to prepare for the preliminary hearing, difficulties in setting a preliminary hearing date, difficulties in fixing a trial date, the need for a different trial judge from the one who had been involved with the preliminary hearing, and the need to wait for a date when the young person's advocate would be available.

Even when guilt was determined, finalising matters usually added further to the time that elapsed between the first and final hearing. The shortest time taken to **finalise** (as opposed to determine guilt) any of these defended cases was 3-4 months after the first appearance while five took at least eight months (although in three cases the time to finalise the case included time to complete tasks). Not only were there substantial delays in deciding matters, but the young people and their families

---

[57] Additional information on some of these cases has already been presented in Chapter 3 which discusses reasons for arrest.

were called many times to court, often for no effective reason as the matter was simply remanded to another date.[58] These 'denied' cases (other than the minor matter which was resolved in two weeks) involved only three appearances in one instance where the plea was changed, but involved five, six, eight or nine appearances in all the other cases, with more to come in the three cases which were not finalised at the end of the study period.

Whatever the reasons for these delays, there is clearly a conflict between our findings and the principles of the Act, which require a speedy resolution of cases so that penalties will have the maximum meaning and impact on the young people who can then proceed with their lives. Furthermore, delays and repeated appearances effectively imposed additional 'penalties' on those young people who took advantage of their right to have matters heard before the court. The effects of these delays were also felt by members of the family who often had to take time off work to support the young person during the court appearances.

Only one of the finalised denied cases was successfully defended. Here the matter was dismissed because the judge held the arrest to have been wrongful. Where the offence was proven, two offenders received a discharge; two were referred to the District Court where the youths were given a sentence of corrective training; and two others, where there was a change of plea before the defended matter was concluded, resulted in sentences of corrective training and supervision with activity after other more serious matters were taken into account.

The denied cases where the matter was proven but the offender was discharged are worth further inspection. The two examples below include one which was completed after the eight month cut-off point for the collection of quantitative data:

> *E was found guilty of being associated with an attempted unlawful taking in an incident when the owner came out to find two young men pushing his car across the road. The owner chased the offenders down the road before the police and a dog handler arrived. In this case the young person received dog bites as he did not respond to a police call to come out of the bushes where he was found. The case was of concern to the family for many months until it was eventually discharged after the eight month cut-off point for data collection.*

> *D was found guilty of assaulting a police officer in an incident to which the police were called one evening. D had lived with his grandparents and, at the time, his grandfather had just died and D was caring for his sick grandmother who also subsequently died. The incident occurred when D overheard slighting remarks in the pub about his grandfather. He visited those involved who told him to leave their property and called the police. D, who was intoxicated at the time and later had little memory of the incident, resisted arrest. He was eventually brought under control by two fairly severe blows from a constable and he was sat on while being brought into the station where he was arrested. His lawyer argued in mitigation that D had been through a bad patch with the illness and subsequent death of both his caregivers. D had now settled down and was no longer drinking. Furthermore the circumstances of the arrest and the time D had spent in the cells constituted an adequate punishment. The case was discharged just before the eight month cut-off.*

In both these cases there were costs from the repeated delays in the court process both to the court and to the young people and their families, even though the court outcome was slight. The existence of such costs can increase the pressure not to deny the offence (compare Wundersitz *et al*, 1991).

Procedure when there Is No Denial

In this section, we discuss the procedure for those 59 cases where matters were not denied.

Four cases were dealt with on the first court appearance. This rather unusual occurrence came about because in some of the cases an FGC had already been held about other matters and had

---

[58] There were occasions where the case was called and the young person was excused appearance or failed to attend but, despite the routine nature of the matters being dealt with, being excused attendance happened no more than once or twice in these cases.

covered the new charges or because, in a rare instance, the co-ordinator anticipated the matter laid in court at an FGC relating to a non-court referral.

But normally, in all the areas in our sample, on the first occasion on which the young person appeared in the Youth Court, even when he or she was accompanied by family members who may have taken time off work, the advocate would simply indicate that the charge was not denied and ask for the case to be remanded for an FGC.

Admittedly, custody was an issue in some cases; in 11 of the 55 cases involving more than one appearance there was an immediate remand to the care of the DSW[59]. However, the offender was usually remanded on bail. In 34 cases, bail conditions were set and another 10 were remanded at large. The details of bail conditions are given in Table 8.4.

Table 8.4
Bail Conditions; Percentages; N=34

	N	%
Residence	29	85
Curfew	24	71
Non association	9	26
Other	4	11

The most common bail conditions were a residential condition (ie a requirement to reside at a stated address) and/or a curfew which was usually imposed after a discussion between the judge and the parents as to whether or not the parents would be able to supervise the conditions. The use of non-association conditions did not always seem to be a realistic requirement as the co-offender, who was usually the person with whom the young person was not to associate, was often waiting outside the courtroom at the time. In some instances co-offenders actually waited together for their bail notices to be drawn up. Occasionally, other conditions were set such as being supervised, not drinking or driving, reporting to the police station (in a case where the offender had previously gone missing) and attending the FGC.

There seemed to be an odd mix of motives in the practice of setting bail. The decision to remand on bail rather than at large appeared to depend on the practice of the local judge and prosecutor rather than on the need to impose special conditions. The use of a residence requirement to ensure adequate supervision of the young person to prevent reoffending would seem appropriate when there has been a history of offending or evidence of a spate of recent offending. But the police seemed to believe that a residence requirement would also be an appropriate measure to ensure the welfare of the young person. It would seem similarly sensible to set curfews when there has been a history of night time offending. But curfews were set more regularly than this and sometimes seemed to be being used, and were certainly perceived by young people, as an interim punishment.

Time Frames
When there is no denial it should be possible to deal with a case fairly rapidly provided the FGC can be held within the statutory 14 days. However, few cases proceeded smoothly and rapidly to a conclusion. In part, this was because the courts, after approving the FGC tasks, usually remanded cases to a later date in order to ensure that the FGC tasks were carried out. There has been debate about whether or not remands until tasks are done are in the spirit of the Act. Judicial practice varied. About 60% of the cases were not remanded for tasks to be completed. When there was such a remand, cases required on average an extra 14 weeks from the time the FGC recommendations were approved to the time that the case was **finalised**. The range was from 2 to 36 weeks.

---

[59] In an additional 7 cases, young people were later remanded to the care of the DSW. This means that a total of a third of the cases where the charges were not denied involved a remand into custody at some stage during the hearing of the case. One case subsequently involved a remand to prison and another involved a remand to police custody.

But a more serious concern is the fact that even reaching a **decision** was not a rapid process in most cases. As shown in Table 8.5, only a quarter of the cases were able to be **decided** within a fortnight. It took up to eight weeks to get a decision in three quarters of the cases and it was at least 20 weeks before three quarters of the young people were able to put the episode entirely behind them.

Table 8.5
Times to Decide and Finalise Youth Court Cases where there has been No Denial; N=59

	Time to decide		Time to finish	
	%	Cum. %	%	Cum. %
Same day	7	7	7	7
1-2 weeks	17	24	8	16
3-4 weeks	25	50	14	30
5-6 weeks	12	62	8	38
7-8 weeks	15	77	10	48
9-12 weeks	8	85	10	58
13-16 weeks	3	88	8	67
17-20 weeks	7	95	8	75
21-25 weeks	5	100	8	84
26-33 weeks			11	95
34+ weeks			5	100

It might be expected that the time to decide and to complete cases would be extended by the complexity of the cases and that the Youth Court would be able to deal with 'simple' cases without the lengthy delays that characterise the 'complex' cases. But although there was a slight tendency for this to be true, overall the Youth Court seemed unable to process even the relatively uncomplicated cases quickly; it took up to eight weeks to get decisions for three quarters of both the 'simple' and 'complex' cases and, equally, it took 20 weeks to finalise three quarters of both types of case.

Times Called
Problems with time frames reflected the number of appearances that were required to resolve matters. On average, each case was **called** (that is, came before the court) just over four times and each young person **appeared** (that is, was present when the case was called) over three times. Table 8.6 below shows that over a third of the cases involved four, five or six appearances and 20% involved seven, eight or nine appearances. Even allowing for the fact that there was multiple offending in some of these cases, it seems likely that the number of times young people are required to appear before the court could be reduced. By looking at the reasons for delays, it is possible to examine this issue further.

Table 8.6
Number of Times Called and Times Appeared; Percentages for Not-Denied Cases; N=59

No of times	Times called		Times appeared	
	%	Cum.%	%	Cum %
3 or less	46	46	46	46
4	28	74	16	62
5	0	74	0	62
6	9	83	19	81
7	2	85	14	95
8	12	97	3	98
9	3	100	2	100

Reasons for Delays

The case of Q provides an illustration of how delays can accumulate. A remand over the Christmas period extended the total time by around 3 to 4 weeks and this also occurred for many other young people in our sample.

The Case of Q

> Q was 16 years of age. He first appeared before the court on charges relating to offences committed a few months after his 14th birthday. Initially his offences were burglaries related to his solvent abuse habits, but his illegal activities later extended to other types of offences, although none in themselves could be regarded as very serious. The FGC held not long before his 15th birthday considered 15 different offences. A reconvened conference 4 months later considered another 9 matters. At this point some of the offences fell into our sample and we began to follow Q's court appearances.
>
> A chronology below shows that proceedings on the original charges in our sample were held up on his second appearance by new matters, again on his 4th appearance by new matters and on his 6th appearance by his failing to appear. A supervision with activity order was made on his eighth appearance, 23 weeks after entering the sample, which sent him out of the area. However, he was arrested and appeared again a month later charged with a new offence: the theft of a car in which to return to his home. He was held in custody over the following six and a half weeks that it took before the decision was taken to revoke the previous order and make an order for supervision with residence. In all, the penalty was finally put in place 35 weeks after his original appearance and over 6 weeks after his last offence.

Box 8.1
A Chronology of Q's Court Appearances and Remands

No.	Week from start	Reason for reman or outcome if final
1	1	Remanded for an FGC
2	5	New charges; remanded for an FGC
3	9	Remanded for a social work report and plan
4	11	New charges; remanded for an FGC
5	17	Remanded for more time for an FGC and a report
6	19	No appearance; a warrant issued for arrest
7	20	Appeared in District Court and remanded in DSW custody
8	23	Excused appearance; sentenced to supervision with activity
9	28	Appeared in District Court on a new charge; remanded in police custody for next Youth Court date
10	29	Remanded for an FGC and DSW report in DSW custody (secure care)
11	31	Remanded in custody for DSW report and plan
12	35	Sentenced to supervision with residence to be followed by supervision.

Q's case could almost certainly have been handled more expeditiously. Although matters were undoubtedly delayed by reoffending and absconding, they were also delayed by the number of remands and the length of remand periods required to arrange FGCs, complete plans and obtain reports. Furthermore, one remand, for a Youth Court hearing, involved Q in being held in police custody for ten days.

While Q's case is an extreme one, similar types of delays occurred in other cases. In fact, in only 24% of the cases finalised during the sample period were the remands held to the minimum number needed to arrange the FGC, to arrange a hearing if there was a denial and to await completion of tasks before finalising matters. In another 26% of cases, the delays could be attributed to the young person, as they resulted from absconding, reoffending, or a failure to complete tasks. In 50% of cases, at least some of the delays resulted from system failures in making such arrangements as obtaining a plea before the appearance, arranging a hearing date, arranging an FGC, arranging subsequent FGCs, negotiating agreements with the police, ensuring crucial participants were present in court, obtaining further information or arranging a sitting of the Youth Court.

It is worth examining these factors in greater detail to determine how such delays could be reduced through improved practice. Thus we amplify our description of practice with respect to most of these factors in this chapter and, in Chapter 9, make suggestions for changes in practice.

Absconding
At first sight, there would appear to be little chance of reducing delays caused when an offender can not be located for an FGC or for a court appearance. However, in the eight such cases (12%) in our sample this was not necessarily true because there had also been delays by the police in preparing reports or by DSW after the case had been referred for an FGC. Thus more rapid processing could have led to matters being concluded before the young person went missing. Furthermore, the young person, in all cases in our sample, returned home after a period. Thus matters could have proceeded in these cases if those making the arrangements had kept in touch with the family; but often there was no action for weeks or even months after the young person had returned home because of a failure to continue to check on the young person's whereabouts.

Further Offences
Some of the most unsatisfactory cases we observed were those where the offender continued to offend while decisions were being taken; this factor led to additional remands in 8% of the cases in our sample. New charges usually led to delays in sentencing, so that an offender who offended every four to six weeks could find that he or she was repeatedly appearing on each court day but that no sentence was ever passed and no accountability occurred even approximately close to the time of the original offence. But it is important to remember that such cases represented only a small proportion of the sample; two thirds of young people were only charged once before matters were finalised, a quarter were charged twice and only four (6%) were charged more often than this.

One example of a case involving repeated offending has already been cited; the case of Q. Another example is given below:

> *In the case of N, who committed an offence in August 1990 which was not denied, a solution was only reached in March 1991, seven months later. In the time between each FGC and the next court hearing, further offences occurred and each time the judge asked for the FGC to be reconvened so that all matters could be considered.*

To some extent the delays that occur when there is repeated offending are created by a practice which was designed to be in the best interests of the offender: that of trying to ensure that all matters are brought together in a single hearing for sentencing. It is the opinion of judges, and we are sure the belief is well grounded, that when matters are dealt with separately, the combination of tariffs is likely to be more severe than a single tariff on all charges. Perhaps it would be possible for judges to review their sentencing practice both to enable a rapid response to specific offences and at the same time to avoid unduly severe penalties when offences committed over a similar period of time are dealt with separately. Furthermore, it could be argued that subsequent offending might not have occurred had the offender been dealt with promptly at the time of the first charges.

Tasks Not Completed
In 13% of cases in the sample, the failure to complete tasks in the time originally allocated led to additional remands.

Obtaining a Plea
Normally on a first appearance the youth advocate appears with the young person and his or her family to state whether or not the charge is denied. However, in many cases in our sample the youth advocate had not consulted the young person prior to the appearance. In some cases matters were stood down to give time for consultation that day but 5% of cases were remanded to the next court date.

This problem arises because the youth advocate can not always arrange a meeting with the young person before the first Youth Court hearing. Most Youth Courts are prompt in sending out notices of appointment but where the young person is not on the phone, the lawyer has to rely on a letter asking the young person to make contact. Many lawyers, because of the lack of success of past attempts to contact young people before the first hearing, rely on seeing them in the waiting room beforehand or asking for a stand down after the case has been called.

Some courts overcome the problem by instructing police, DSW and youth advocates that they do not normally expect cases to appear until after the FGC has been held except in cases where issues relating to interim custody need to be decided. This was not the practice in the courts we observed, although in 14% of the cases in our sample the FGC was held before the case was first called, generally because the FGC had been arranged to deal with other matters already before the court. Only one FGC was held in anticipation of the court's request and this practice was actively discouraged in three of our sample areas. We consider that this is a matter deserving further debate. The advantage in hastening a decision can be balanced against the relatively low risk that an FGC will be convened only to find that the charges are denied.

Arranging Hearings
As well as the delays in obtaining a hearing date which were experienced by those who denied a charge (see above, pages 139-140), some of the 'not denied' cases in our sample encountered similar delays when the appropriate judge was not available or when there was a transfer to the District or High Court. A total of 12% of the cases in our sample experienced delays arising from difficulties in obtaining a hearing date.

Arranging FGCs
Delays in arranging FGCs occurred in 11% of cases, in part because of difficulties in locating people, but also because of work pressures within the local DSW office. At times the numbers of FGCs to be arranged were so great that YJCs were unable to meet statutory deadlines without delegating cases to social workers or spending less time in preparing for the FGC and locating extended family. At other times the failure of the police to provide information on victims and on the costs of damage to property delayed arrangements for FGCs.

Delays also resulted in some districts outside our sample because of requirements set by police, social workers or youth advocates for a limit on the times at which FGCs could be held (eg between 8am and 4pm) or for advance notice (eg three days if in work time or one week if out of working hours).

Obtaining family co-operation was a further factor that caused delays in another 3% of cases, but this often depended on the quality of the professional's contact with the family. Some of the families who had not attended FGCs had only been contacted by phone or letter. One family's reason for non-attendance was that, on a previous occasion when they had arrived, they found that the DSW office doors were locked and that they could not get in[60]. Another family had made arrangements to hold the FGC at their home early in the morning. Whanau had arrived and food was prepared. Then a call was received saying that the police had refused to allow the young person, who was in their custody, to attend an FGC in the family home and it was held in DSW without the attendance of all family members.

---

[60] This occurred because of an emergency staff meeting about restructuring.

In other cases, as already discussed in Chapter 6, the non-appearance of a crucial participant such as the youth advocate or the police representative led to the need to reschedule an FGC.

Multiple FGCs

The reasons for multiple FGC meetings in our sample were varied and some examples are given below:

> *Resolution of the case of F required three meetings. At the first meeting the family did not at first accept the views of the victim and the professionals about the seriousness of the offence and the extent of its impact. They argued that the offending was not part of a pattern but something that had occurred during a particularly difficult time for the young person and that circumstances had now changed. The victim and the police took a different view in the light of both the circumstances of the offence and the prior offence history of the young person. A very emotional meeting was adjourned after several hours. When it was reconvened the victim did not attend because the previous meeting had caused her such distress. At this meeting an agreement was reached between the police and the family but a sufficiently detailed proposal for an extended period of family supervision was not able to be completed in the time available so that a third meeting was required to complete the plan.*

> *The case of H: The first meeting lasted for an entire morning and continued over the lunch period because of a disagreement about the acceptability of a proposal for supervision with residence. Staff at the residence opposed this option which was acceptable to all the other participants. Agreement was reached after a second meeting.*

> *The case of T: After discussion about what had been happening at home it was recognised that the mother had a real problem in managing the young person. Thus it was decided that, as plans for the care of the young person needed to be developed, the meeting should be reconvened with the involvement of additional family members.*

These examples indicate some of the main reasons for multiple FGC meetings. Families do sometimes need time to come to terms with what has happened and to reach suitable arrangements. Both emotional acceptance of the offence and appropriate responses to it can not always be arrived at in a short space of time. Details of complex plans can not always be resolved in single meetings. However, in other cases, it was clear that better planning and simpler procedures for obtaining approval of financial support could have hastened the process.

Negotiation of Agreements

For Youth Court cases the agreement of the enforcement agency is usually the critical factor in determining whether or not the FGC recommendations will be accepted by the court. In cases where the family, enforcement agency and victims are unable to agree, the court decides the outcome. Thus there is strong pressure on families who want to avoid a court solution to reach agreement. In such cases (for example, the cases of F and T described above) this can lead to lengthy negotiations and, hence, prolong a resolution by requiring further remands.

Thus it is not surprising that the police agreed with the FGC recommendations in 88% of the cases that came before the Youth Court compared with 98% for the non-court FGC cases. The lower rate of agreement in the former category principally resulted from the fact that, where there was disagreement, this was most likely to be signified after the FGC had been held and the officer who had been present had reported back to a senior officer. In 7% of Youth Court cases, the police prosecutor indicated after the FGC had been held that the recommendations were unacceptable to the police:

> *On his first appearance A did not deny the charge and was remanded for an FGC. The Youth Aid officer was present at the FGC at which a social worker read a letter from the victim. The FGC participants agreed that A would apologise and undertake community work. At the next Youth Court appearance, the police prosecutor refused to accept the FGC proposal on the grounds that no counselling was included. He said that counselling had been requested in the letter from the non-attending victim and was viewed as necessary by the police. A second FGC*

was held which approved counselling, but several remands occurred before the arrangements were made. In the end, it was only after several months' counselling had been completed and a report had been made which was satisfactory to the police that they agreed to withdraw the charges.

W's case required four remands in the Youth Court before an FGC plan was presented. The delays resulted from the desire to get extended family to attend the FGC because of W's prior history of offending and to prepare a detailed plan. Finally, after two months, a detailed plan was prepared for a placement on a farm programme with relatives in a rural area for 3-6 months and this plan was brought by the youth advocate to the Youth Court with a recommendation that it be carried out under an order for supervision with activity. The judge, on hearing the proposal, said he would be very happy to accept. The prosecutor objected that he did not know about the plan, did not agree with the recommendations and wanted the case to be referred to the District Court. He also raised the issue of other offences that had not been laid in the Youth Court. The youth advocate responded that the FGC had considered all matters including those referred to by the prosecutor and that the programme had been tightly constructed because of W's prior offence history. Furthermore, the Youth Aid officer had participated in the development of the proposals at the first two FGCs, although he was not at the third one where the details of the plans were finalised. The social worker and the young person both spoke and the judge made the order for supervision with activity rather than referring the matter to the District Court, but he commented that the plans should have been made available to the police prior to the Youth Court hearing.

These two cases had different outcomes. In the latter the judge, after listening to the submissions of both the prosecution and the youth advocate, accepted the plan of the family. In the former, a further FGC was needed and the resolution of the case was delayed. Whether or not such problems could be resolved by better procedures for consultation between the police and the family before the FGC plans are presented to the court is an issue we will return to later.

Absence of Crucial Participants in Court
In 5% of cases remands were necessary because of the absence of a crucial participant at the Youth Court hearing. In a number of cases it was the youth advocate who failed to attend, usually because of other court appointments, which led to a remand or alternatively to the appearance of another lawyer who was not necessarily well briefed. At other times the social worker who had been required to prepare the court report was absent and the judge was unable to obtain the necessary information to make a sentencing decision.

Remands to Obtain Information
In 27% of cases remands were made to allow time for reports to be prepared, usually social work reports. In 10% of cases there were at least two such remands. In all cases where the judge considers an order involving supervision, community work or transfer to a higher court, a social work report is required under section 334. It might therefore be expected that DSW would anticipate the need for the provision of a report where sufficient time was available between the FGC and the next court appearance. In our sample, however, the need for a DSW report was rarely anticipated. Furthermore, in a few cases, the report, when it was eventually provided, proved inadequate and a further report was requested. In addition, there were occasions when the judge remanded the case to seek additional information from a specialist before making a final decision.

In another 3% of cases remands were needed because of a lack of accurate information about the cost of damage or the impact of the offence on the victim or to a lack of detail in the plan provided by the social worker.

Frequency of Sitting
The frequency with which the Youth Courts met varied. The courts we visited were most likely to meet fortnightly, although four of the 15 met monthly, another four met weekly and the largest

court met twice weekly. Weekly sittings, wherever possible, might hasten the conclusion of cases. However, even when the Youth Court did meet weekly, remands for a fortnight were still often used to allow time to hold an FGC or to ensure continuity of judges.

Number of Judges

Because of the number of appearances that can occur, several judges can be involved in a particular case which, as we will see from the comments below (see page 154), can lead to dissatisfaction on the part of the young people and their families. Only 15% of cases involved the same judge throughout, about half (48%) involved two judges, a third involved three judges and a tiny minority (3%) involved four or five judges. 'Complex' cases were more likely to involve several judges but, even allowing for this, few of the 'simple' cases involved only one judge and a quarter involved three or more judges.

In general, it was the view of judges that continuity in a particular case was desirable and, in some cases, a remand occurred to ensure that a judge previously involved in the case could also conclude it. While there are arguments for rotating judges, it appears that this practice can lead to delays in the Youth Court.

Remands in Custody

Somewhat less than a third (29%) of all the court cases involved a remand by the Youth Court in the custody of the Director-General of Social Welfare at some point during the proceedings. The grounds for the Youth Court order for custody are very similar to the grounds for arrest (see sections 238 and 239); namely, to prevent absconding, further offending or interference with witnesses or evidence. The Director-General can exercise discretion about where these young people will be held and the current policy is to attempt to find a family placement or a community placement wherever possible rather than placing a young person in a residence. However, the likelihood of reoffending or absconding are factors which are considered in making the placement.

There has been some controversy about DSW policy; in particular, the police have expressed concern about the fact that sometimes placements are insufficiently secure for young offenders whom they consider require restraint. Thus we examined the data from the study to determine whether or not problems were occurring as a result of DSW placement policy.

Seventeen percent of those appearing in the Youth Court were remanded in the custody of the Director-General of Social Welfare on their first appearance because of a previous history of offending (often still unresolved by the Youth Court), absconding and non-appearance or the lack of a suitable alternative placement. In all these cases the initial placement was in a residence. In one case, the parents would not have the young person home. He was then placed in a residence and later placed with a foster family. In another case involving a serious first offence, the young person was initially placed in custody and remained there because of a lack of suitable alternatives.

Another 12% of cases were placed in the custody of the Director-General of Social Welfare on a later appearance due to a breach of bail conditions, further offending or absconding. All but one of these cases were remanded to a residence. In the exceptional case, the young person was placed by DSW in a family home, but because the family home could not assure adequate supervision, he was later moved to a residence.

Thus in our data almost all of the 20 cases involving a remand in DSW custody resulted in an immediate residential placement. We found no examples of cases where young people were remanded in custody and placed by DSW in the community and then became involved in further offending or non-appearance, although some of those placed in a residence absconded and were subsequently placed in secure care.

The Youth Court from the Perspective of Parents and Young People

In court you are on edge. (Parent)

The ride down the slide begins. (Young person)

The Atmosphere of the Youth Court

The psychological impact of the court on the young offender and his or her family is seen as an important part of the Western criminal justice tradition; the rituals, the courtroom's arrangement, the dress and the language are all part of a process by which added meaning is conveyed underlining society's view of the offence, the validity of the sanctions and the need for the offender to repay his or her debt to society.

But questions need to be raised about whether or not the Youth Court is actually assisting the process of accountability. To the extent that the courtroom is incomprehensible in its rituals and language, to the extent that it spends time on discussion of legal and practice issues rather than focusing on the offence and the offender, and to the extent that it alienates young people and their families, it is unlikely to be effective as a means of creating the conditions that make remorse possible and accountability a psychological reality. We have already referred to these issues in Chapter 1 and contrasted the reality of the Australian court as described by O'Connor and Sweetapple (1988) with the goals set out for an informal, humane and comprehensible Youth Court in New Zealand.

How does reality match the rhetoric? We have come to the conclusion that the Youth Court has, in most areas, failed to create the kind of environment anticipated by the Act. While for lawyers, judges and court staff it is noticeably more relaxed and informal than other criminal courts, to us as outsiders it was undoubtedly a very formal and alien setting and one which seemed little different in atmosphere from the Children and Young Persons Court which operated before the Act. If the courtroom seemed formidable to us after the familiarity of many weeks of observation, it must surely appear even more so to the young people who appeared before it and their families.

The formidable nature of the courtroom derives both from the physical lay-out and from court etiquette. The physical setting itself was, for half of the areas we visited, a standard District Court room in which the judge sat at an elevated bench with lawyers facing, the public at the rear and the young person in the dock. The only standard modification in these courts (see Example Y in Figure 8.2) was that the family usually sat on the chairs in the area normally occupied by the witness box to the right of the judge. In the other courts, smaller Family Court rooms were used but families still tended to be placed near the back as if they were visitors while the professionals occupied the front rows[61]. People stood to greet the judge's entrances and exits, stood to address the court using a formal language, and required permission to speak. The order was controlled by the judge and, excepting formal addresses by lawyers, it rapidly became apparent that the role of participants was to answer questions. While much of the formal etiquette is undoubtedly functional in allowing for an orderly process, it also contributed to the fact that, when asked a question, most young people or family members did so with a mumbled 'yes' or 'no'.

Another factor that affected families was the number of people present. Few Youth Courts required lawyers to wait outside with their clients and we observed as many as five lawyers inside the courtroom at once. DSW and the police also each had as many as five representatives in the courtroom. Up to three court attendants were present as well as the court clerk and the judge. During the study, we added to the problem as one or two researchers also attended.

But in contrast, we noted that some Youth Courts had made major changes in their procedures and physical layout. The most informal arrangements involved the use of a small Family Court room, excluded all people from the proceedings except those actually needed for the particular case and did not use a dock, although people still normally stood to address the judge.

---

[61] In the 16 courtrooms we visited, there were two notable exceptions where the family and young person were placed amongst the professionals in the body of a small courtroom.

Figure 8.2
Sketch Plan of Two Contrasting Youth Court Rooms

Example X

Example Y

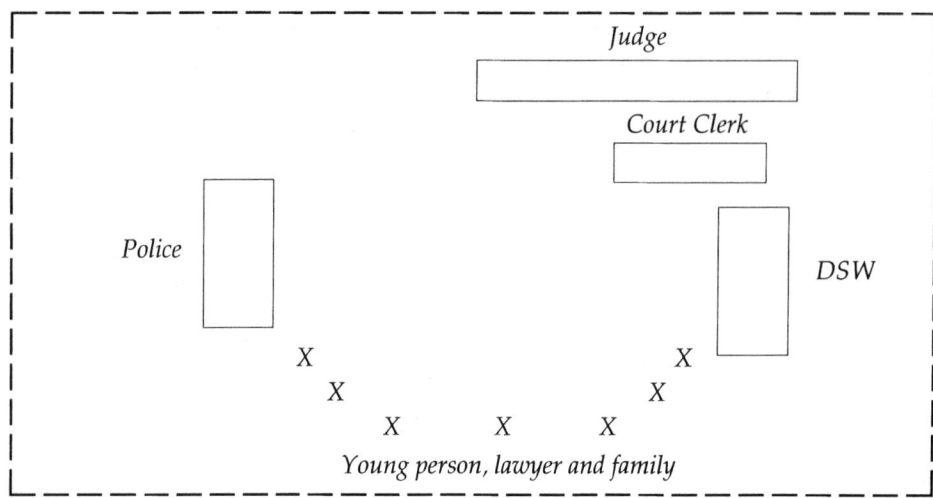

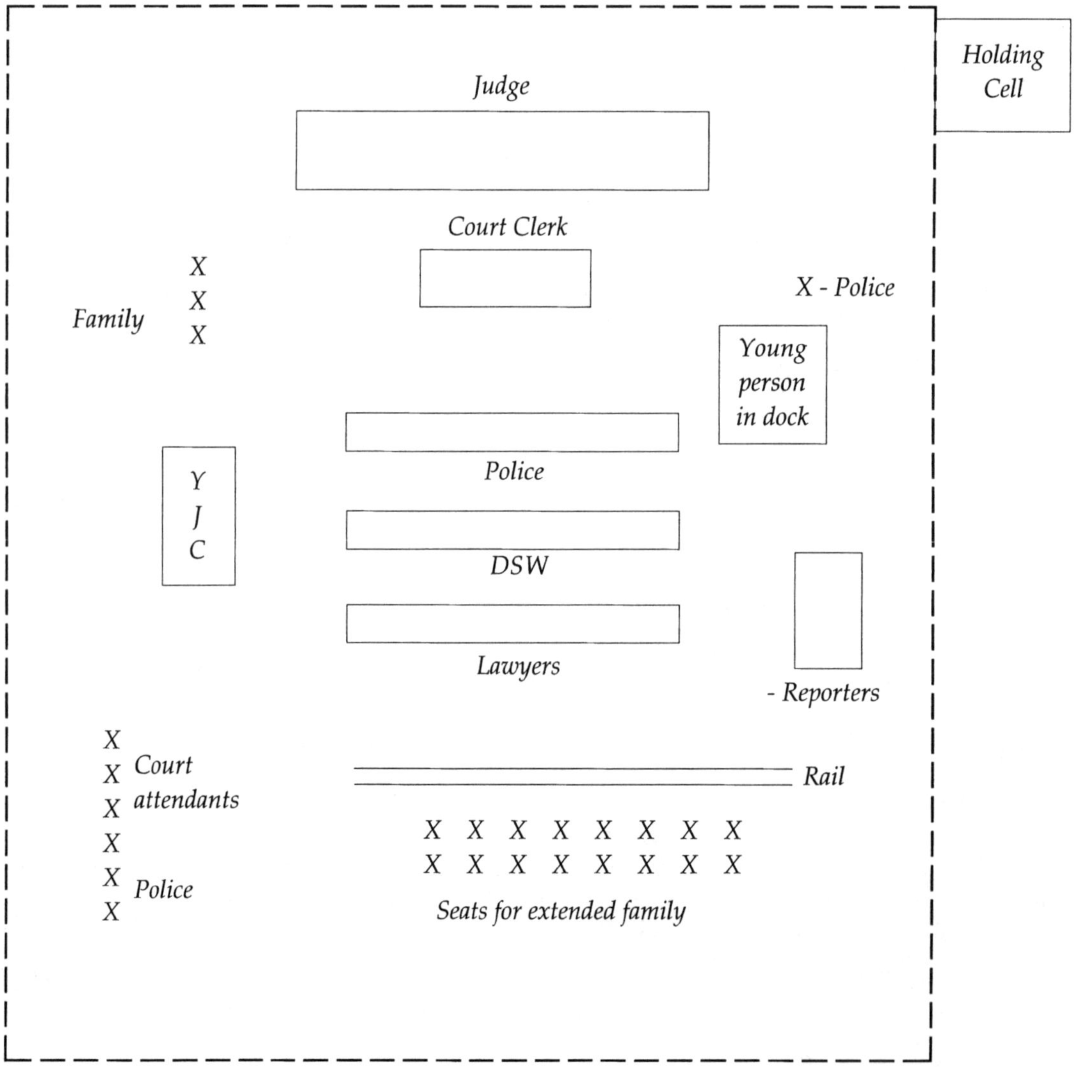

We detail two contrasting courtroom examples on the previous page (Figure 8.2). Example X represents a very informal court and Example Y represents the opposite extreme.

In example X there were usually only seven people present in the courtroom at one time excluding the family and young person. Excepting the court clerk and the judge, each one of these people had already met and been involved with the young person who was appearing before the court. The youth advocate came into the courtroom with the young person and his or her family, introduced them, sat with them and left with them. The judge sat at a table on a slightly raised dais but off to the side of the room with the court clerk beside him or her.

By contrast, in example Y it was usual to find as many as 12-17 people present at any one time in the court, in addition to the family who would normally have previously met only two of these people (the youth advocate and the YJC unless the family's social worker was also present). The additional numbers of people and the relative unfamiliarity of most of them resulted from the practice of most lawyers of remaining in the courtroom throughout all cases, the presence of two DSW clerks to record information, the attendance of police prosecutors rather than Youth Aid officers, the presence of escorting constables and the presence of two court attendants.

Participants' Views

Most of the comments by parents and young people reflected their relative disengagement from and helplessness in the Youth Court. The comments ranged from an acceptance of all that happened and a perception that the system was fair to expressions of despair at their helplessness:

> *Yeah it was fair, I understood things, I was asked my views and listened to, I had support. The lawyer was helpful. It was OK.*

> *All I can say is, once the police have a grip of you, it's all the way to the top of the slide. Once you hit the courtroom, the ride down the slide begins. Beat the system – a challenge I impose to anyone. [This young person is now serving a prison term.]*

The first question we asked young people about the Youth Court was 'what happened?' This produced an interesting variety of responses which highlight some of the salient features of the perceptions of the young people who appeared:

> *We went to court and the charges were read and the judge said we had to have an FGC.*

> *Not much – I just stood in the dock.*

> *Well, I stood in the box while the lawyer and the police were telling the judge what I had done.*

> *It was very quick.*

> *It is hard to remember clearly what happened.*

> *I had a long wait the first time. I was nervous.*

> *Got boring after a while. All the remands – getting put in holding cells etc.*

Many young people and family members said they understood what was happening:

> *I understood everything. (Young person)*

> *I understood it, but was too nervous to talk properly. (Young person)*

> *[Did you understand?] Yes. The judge went to pains to explain and did a good job. (Father)*

> *I understood most and was asked my views. (Mother)*

Others were clearly confused by the process and the language:

> *[Did you understand?] No, I didn't know what was going on. My lawyer didn't tell me what to expect – who the people were. (Young person)*

> *[Did you understand?] No, not really – bits and pieces of it. I'm not sure who everyone was. (Mother)*

> *It got held over. I didn't want to return home at first. I wish they didn't use such big words. I couldn't understand it all. (Young person)*

When sitting at the back of the courtroom behind all the other participants, parents could not always hear properly:

> *The lawyer wasn't loud enough and I couldn't hear – so I didn't understand. (Parent)*

As noted earlier, sections 10 and 11 of the Act require both the Youth Court and the youth advocates to explain fully the proceedings and to encourage and assist the young person to participate in them. We were not privy to discussions between young people, their families and the youth advocates but we were able to observe and record the extent to which explanations were given in the Youth Court. The data collected on 46 cases appearing in three Youth Courts served by a group of five judges were examined to determine judicial practice in relation to explanations. Almost always the judge explained bail conditions, orders and plans carefully and clearly to the young person and the family. On the other hand, only two of the five judges routinely explained the proceedings to the families and young people. At no time did we observe a case where the judge pointed out to the young person or the family their right to participate and when they would be able to do so. Nor did we ever see the judge introduce the people in the courtroom to the young person and their family, although the youth advocate was normally required to introduce all the family members and supporters to the judge.

When asked whether or not they had felt involved in the proceedings in the Youth Court, half the parents we interviewed said 'yes'. Another 41% said 'no', 2% were absent from the proceedings and the remainder said 'don't know' or 'partly'. Although the Act (sections 288 and 329-330) clearly sets out the entitlement of parents and young people to have their views heard, our observations showed that it was rare for parents and young people to participate actively in the Youth Court proceedings.

The reasons for this lie partly in the nature of the court atmosphere and the effect this has on young people and their parents, and partly in the practice of the judiciary. Participation by young people and their parents usually depended upon the judge deciding to ask a question and questions were usually restricted to a specific issue. One parent commented that the atmosphere was *like going back to school*. Indeed, on more than one occasion a parent wishing to say something was observed to raise a hand. The court was, as another parent put it, a *very intimidating place*. This meant that some people were too upset or confused to contribute effectively even when they were given the opportunity. Occasionally, the lawyer requested permission for the parents or young person to speak and this was usually granted. However, overall, most of the court sessions we observed involved little or no participation by young people and their families. There were exceptions depending on who the judge was; three of the 11 judges we observed had the ability to involve young people and families in effective discussions and this involvement was almost always appreciated. The other notable exception was when whanau requested the opportunity to make submissions and descriptions of some of these occasions are presented later in this chapter. The preparation of submissions which are presented by the family offers an alternative model which could be used to enable Pakeha as well as Maori to play an active role in the court room.

We have chosen a large number of comments to illustrate the variety of the experiences of parents and young people in the court and the effect it had on them. The following comments illustrate the experiences of those who felt that they had been involved in the proceedings and that their views had been considered:

> *[What happened?] The judge went over the case and said another FGC was needed. We understood, our views were asked and he thanked us. (Parents)*

> *The family spokesperson, my cousin, spoke. In the long run the family views made a difference. (Parent)*

> *All my whanau came to court with me. The judge set a time aside for us because my whanau wanted to speak. I was able to speak to the judge. (Young person)*

> *I knew all my family were sitting behind me. (Young person)*

In contrast, the following comments emphasise the observer status that other parents and young people felt they had in the court and the shyness and loneliness that this often provoked:

> *I didn't say much – just shook my head. (Young person)*
>
> *I was not asked my views and felt alone. (Young person)*
>
> *There was a defended hearing. Others were allowed to object to what I was saying, but I was not allowed to question others on the stand. I felt all by myself. (Young person)*
>
> *At court the youth advocate spoke for me, I wasn't asked my views. (Young person)*
>
> *I understood everything, but no-one asked me my views. The judge just asked if everything was OK at home. (Young person)*
>
> *Everyone was there but I didn't listen much – I was just dead. (Young person)*
>
> *I can't remember what happened – I wasn't listening. They were going to send me to the District Court. They didn't ask my views. The judge hates me. I didn't have a lawyer as far as I know. (Young person)*
>
> *[Were you asked for your views?] No – they just told me off. (Young person)*
>
> *[Were you asked for your views?] Not really – I was asked questions once or twice – they were more procedural than anything. (Parent)*
>
> *I get a bit shy to stand up and speak. If asked my opinion, I am too shy to speak. (Mother)*
>
> *We weren't asked if we wanted to say anything and didn't know we were allowed to. (Parents)*
>
> *I wasn't asked my views and I felt alone. (Mother)*
>
> *It would help if the parent could talk to the judge. I could have said a few things without the solicitor saying it. (Father)*

In most cases the Youth Court decisions were expected and were accepted as being fair. The involvement of the police in court was rarely remarked on adversely, although in some cases they were seen as being out for blood:

> *The police tried to put me in [prison] [during the three-day period between sentence and being sent on the corrective training programme] but my lawyer rang the judge who stopped it. The cops were just pissed off – they wanted me to go away for 14 years.*

The youth advocates were often seen as doing a fine job keeping families informed, involving them in decision-making as much as possible, making the Youth Court comprehensible, enabling parents and young people to participate, being effective advocates for their clients and being concerned for them. Below are some quotes from young people:

> *[Was your lawyer helpful] – Yeah, yeah, yeah; far out, man.*
>
> *My lawyer explained it all to me, what was going to happen and who would be there.*
>
> *I didn't want to say anything, but my lawyer said I should – it would be good for my case. I was very nervous.*
>
> *My lawyer worked very hard for me.*

And the mother of the young person last quoted above commented:

> *The lawyer was very helpful, became personally involved, shed a few tears.*

In other cases, the lawyers were not seen as having been helpful, either because of their failure to consult with the family, because they asked others to stand in for them or because they failed to advocate on behalf of the family or young person:

> *I was asked my views about [a drug and alcohol programme] and was listened to, but the lawyer added things like: "I'm not sure this is good for him". (Young person)*

We didn't understand – we had a different lawyer every time and they didn't know the case. It would have been better if it had been less formal so we knew what was happening – and had more lawyer support. (Mother)

My lawyer seemed nervous and not wanting to say things that might look bad for him. It would have been better to have a fairer judge and to have someone in court to support me. I was upset about the outcome, I expected to get off. (Young person)

At court the youth advocate spoke for me, I wasn't asked my views. [Was your lawyer helpful?] No. I wasn't expecting to lose my licence. The court was more formal than the FGC and in the court the lawyer spoke 'funny'. Why did my lawyer suggest I lost my licence? Just cos my co-offender did. (Young person)

The lawyer wasn't helpful, he brought up prison – it was not his place to tell the judge that – he always brought up the negatives. (Father)

The lawyer was not helpful – not on my side, didn't give a damn. (Young person)

The mother of the young person last quoted endorsed his view:

The lawyer was hopeless – not on my son's side.

Another young person said:

It is hard to remember clearly what happened. The youth advocate suggested the Rs care for me but had not previously consulted them. They were pleased to have me. [Were you asked your views?] No. I had the support of the Rs and my mother. The major problem was I had two youth advocates for two appearances and no one for the other and they didn't have the full story. The youth advocate should have understood the situation better.

And his caregiver said:

The lawyer wasn't helpful at all really – didn't even talk to us. He didn't bring up the issue of C's mistreatment by the police. They didn't discuss hardly anything. The police read the charge, the lawyer said C should stay with us and the judge said an FGC should happen. Police mistreatment should have been raised. The lawyer should have consulted us. We felt intimidated by the court environment.

In one case the issue of confidentiality was raised:

Within three hours of the court case three lawyers in town mentioned it to me. Confidentiality doesn't exist in the court. (Father)

Finally, there were adverse comments from young people about the amount of waiting, the number of remands, the court environment and changes in judges:

The first time there was a shocking wait – 2 hours [we arrived quarter of an hour early]. Getting restless added to the worry.

I have had many appearances over the past 6 months, most for only a very short hearing. We often wait hours for a two minute hearing.

There's a lot of mucking round with the court and all the meetings. Why can't they just get to the point? They kept remanding me and going backward and forwards.

The judges vary in the way they handle the case. Why can't we have the same one?

We had four different judges.

Parents agreed:

The waiting room was disgusting, the police looked half asleep. We felt humiliated by the surroundings [at Youth Court]. The language and atmosphere was disgusting – the kids had no respect.

Some of these comments suggest that the pattern of the 'bad old days' (see Morris and Young, 1987), when the waiting rooms were full all day and provided a meeting ground for young people, still exists in some courts, at least some of the time. This was certainly the impression of the researchers. In some courts, the appointments system worked well; in others it had been abandoned and in others it had mixed success as the timetabling was poorly managed or families were informed by lawyers or the police to get there at 10 am (the usual start time). As in the past, the comments of families and young people show that many felt excluded from the process and unable to participate effectively.

Comparing the FGC Process and Courts

Although most families and young people accepted the verdict of the court as fair, there is little doubt that, overall, parents and young people preferred the process of the FGC. The comments highlight the participatory nature of the FGC process, the greater degree of support available at the FGC and the stress that accompanies a court appearance:

> *It is good if you can have your say – that doesn't happen at court. (Young person)*
>
> *I found the FGC much easier to handle. I would recommend it to the court option any day. (Young person)*
>
> *The court was more nerve-racking than the FGC. (Young person)*
>
> *FGCs are much better than going to court – more relaxing. (Young person)*
>
> *The FGCs are better – more caring and not so formal. (Mother)*
>
> *FGCs are a good idea; they are more easy going. You can say more. In court, you're on edge. (Parent)*

One or two parents expressed the feeling that the court might have more impact and one young person felt that, compared to the FGC where the wider family was present, the court protected his privacy:

> *I preferred court because there was only me and my family there. (Young person)*

However, for the most part parents and young people not only felt more comfortable at the FGC, but they also understood more of what happened and believed that it provided a more realistic forum for decision-making:

> *They could have been tougher, moving H. I think it was the wrong decision from the judge [he should have been moved] before he got involved with more things. An FGC with the right people is best because of the involvement of all concerned. (Parent)*
>
> *The FGC is better – it is a good idea for the young person to know what is going on. I was quite happy with the family meeting. (Mother)*
>
> *The FGC is superior in the sense of better for all participants. Everything is open. (Parent)*

Decisions

Although court processes appear to have changed little since the introduction of the Act, there have been major changes in the types of decisions arrived at by the Youth Court.

Jurisdiction

The vast majority of finalised cases were dealt with in the Youth Court, but 13% were transferred to a higher court. Thus six cases were transferred to the District Court and three to the High Court. These figures represent a considerably higher proportion than the 4% recorded as having been transferred to a higher court nationally in 1990 and probably reflect the more serious offending that occurred in our sample areas. In addition, 3% of cases in our sample were transferred to the Family Court, as it was considered that the most urgent issues related to care and protection.

Outcomes

In almost half of the cases that were finalised, the charges were withdrawn or dismissed (see Table 8.7), and this figure agrees closely with the 50% recorded nationally in 1990.

Table 8.7
Decisions of the Court; N=66

	N	%
Withdrawn or discharged without record	29	44
Convicted and discharged	4	6
Supervision, disqualification, reparation under $100 or community work under 100hrs	7	11
Community work 100-200hrs or reparation $100-1000	3	5
Supervision with activity	9	14
Supervision with residence	4	6
Corrective Training	6	9
Prison	2	3
Other*	2	3

* In one case where a young person was sent to the Pacific Islands, a warrant was issued for his arrest in order to prevent his return from the Islands to New Zealand. Another involved an order to come before the court if called upon within 12 months.

The less severe court orders (such as admonishment, an order to come before the court if called within 12 months, fine, costs, reparation and forfeiture) were rarely used. However, these types of penalties were often reflected in the FGC decisions. Community work orders and supervision orders were virtually the only two of the minor orders used in our sample, accounting for 16% of cases. The two high tariff sanctions available to the Youth Court were used in almost a fifth (20%) of cases, with supervision with activity being used twice as often as supervision with residence. Twelve percent of the cases were transferred to a higher jurisdiction for sentence, where most received a custodial sentence: six were sent to corrective training and two went to prison.

This pattern of outcomes appears to be consistent with the principles of the Act which favour avoiding the use of court orders wherever possible and, where court orders are used, minimising sanctions. These decisions are also consistent with the recommendations of the FGC (see Table 8.8): 81% of the Youth Court decisions followed the recommendations of the FGC and only 17% resulted in heavier penalties than those recommended by the FGC. A more detailed examination of the type of decisions made by the Youth Court is, nevertheless, instructive.

Table 8.8
Comparison of FGC Recommendations and Court Decisions; N=63

	N	%
Endorsed FGC plan	32	51
Made order recommended by FGC	19	30
Made order higher than recommended by family	11	17
Made order lower than recommended by family	1	2

Cases Which Were Withdrawn or Discharged
In three quarters of the 32 cases where charges were withdrawn or discharged, moderate penalties were put in place, involving supervision arrangements within the family or community work. In all but one of the remaining cases, apologies and/or curfews were arranged.

Some judges adopted the practice of discharging these cases without record, others ordered a discharge under section 283(a) which meant that the outcome was recorded, while in other cases the police withdrew the charges.

To us as observers, it was sometimes difficult to be sure which of these actions had been taken and the court records did not always make the matter clear either. In some ways, there is little difference between these three ways of finalising a case as no further action is to be taken. On the other hand, many young people and families wish to avoid a criminal record, especially as such a record may be a barrier to future activities (such as entering the armed services). Thus consistency and clarity in practice would seem to us to be desirable.

Cases Involving Minor Orders

Supervision, small amounts of reparation or community work of less than 100 hours was ordered by the court in seven cases and community work of 100-200 hours or larger amounts of reparation was ordered in another three cases. In most of these cases, the order exactly paralleled the recommendations of the FGC. It could be suggested that where the family was in agreement with these penalties, it would have been more in keeping with the spirit of the Act to give the family the responsibility of ensuring that these tasks were completed and reporting back to the court rather than making a court order.

Cases Where Penalties of the Court Were Heavier than the FGC Recommendations

There were 11 cases where the Youth Court penalties exceeded those recommended by the FGC, all of which involved offences rated as at least medium in seriousness. Four of these cases involved a transfer to a higher court for sentence and resulted in corrective training, although the FGC had recommended supervision with activity or community work and reparation. Two of these cases involved offending classified as maximum in seriousness. The other two cases involved offenders with a previous history of offending appearing on multiple charges (10 and 24 respectively) where the offences were rated as medium in seriousness.

Three of the four cases resulting in orders for supervision with residence were contrary to the FGC recommendations for community work and reparation. All these young people were previous offenders appearing on multiple charges (15, 3 and 5 respectively) and had committed offences rated as medium or medium/maximum in seriousness.

Another three cases resulted in orders for supervision with activity, although the family had recommended lesser penalties. All three involved offences rated as medium/maximum (four and five charges) or maximum in seriousness (two charges).

Generally, the heavier penalties were awarded by the judge after considering the social welfare report. In only two of these 11 cases did the police actually disagree with the FGC recommendations and urge a higher penalty. This finding confirms our observations of the role that the police often play in supporting family recommendations in an FGC. In contrast there were eight cases where the police raised objections to the recommendations of the family after the FGC but where the judge's decision, in general level of severity, agreed with the family recommendations. The remaining case where the police disagreed with the family resulted in a reconvened FGC which accepted the police view that counselling should be arranged.

Predicting the Severity of the Court Decision

In previous chapters we showed that the decision to arrest, the decision to refer for an FGC and the severity of the FGC recommendation were all related to a number of variables, both offence-related and offender-related. When it came to predicting the severity of the court decision[62], we found that the offender-related factors we were able to measure were not significantly related to the decision.

However, if the severity of the FGC recommendation was included in the regression equation, it was found to be the sole independent predictor of the severity of the court decision resulting in a

---

[62] The coding for severity of court decision is presented in Appendix 2.

multiple correlation of 0.59 and accounting for 35% of the variance. On the other hand, if we set aside the FGC recommendations, two offence-related factors emerged as important predictors: the seriousness of the offence and the number of offences being considered. Seriousness of offence correlated 0.45 with the severity of the court decision and accounted for 20% of the variance. The number of offences being considered was the next most important factor; it increased the multiple correlation to 0.54 and, in combination, the two variables accounted for 29% of the variance in the severity of the court decision. Although previous offence history was also correlated with severity of the court decision, it did not contribute any additional effect to the prediction over and above the seriousness of the offence and the number of offences being considered.

We also found that different courts were responding differently: some courts appeared to be making orders only at the top of the tariff range (for example, supervision with activity, supervision with residence or transfer to a higher court) whereas other courts were more likely to formalise the recommendations of the FGC for community work or supervision by making orders. In addition, when the FGC recommendations were accepted, one court customarily used a discharge under section 283(a) which would be recorded on the offender's file, whereas, in other courts, matters were generally withdrawn or discharged under section 282 without a record.

Follow Up

Many of the cases in the study were not concluded in time for us to be able to be certain whether or not tasks were completed. However, for those cases where sufficient time had elapsed, more than two thirds (68%) of the young people had completed their tasks[63]. Twenty percent failed to complete their tasks and the remainder had partly completed their tasks. It should be noted here that these data came from our own follow-up of cases and, as with the FGC cases, there had often been no follow-up by DSW. Thus the police and victims were not always aware of whether or not the tasks had been completed as agreed at the FGC. To our knowledge, no action was ever taken as a result of finding that tasks had not been completed excepting in cases where the young person offended subsequently and the failure to complete previous tasks was taken into account in the subsequent FGC and/or court hearing.

Maori in the Youth Court[64]

Pretty much a Pakeha scene (Young person)

– But one with many Maori actors (Researcher)

At each stage of the process we have shown that Maori young people were more likely to become involved than Pakeha young people. They were more likely to come to the notice of the police, more likely to be referred for an FGC, more likely to be arrested and summonsed and hence more likely to appear in court than Pakeha youngsters. The important issue that we have attempted to answer is why? So far, we have seen that the offences that brought Maori young people to notice tended to be less trivial than the offences that brought many of the Pakeha youngsters to notice and that, once the case went to Youth Aid, the decision about whether to warn or reprimand the young person seemed to be based on the nature of the offence and the previous history of the offender rather than on his or her ethnicity. On the other hand, the decision to arrest might have been made more readily in the case of young Maori offenders, perhaps because of attitudes and behaviour at the time of arrest on the part of both the police and young offenders themselves.

To examine these issues in more depth, we carried out a further analysis of the data on the sample of young people who came before the court to determine whether or not ethnicity played a part in the way the cases were handled and in the way that decisions were made. For the most part, there were very few differences between Maori and Pakeha offenders and what differences there were

---

[63] These data exclude those who received custodial orders.

[64] Much of this section, as well as some of the earlier material in this chapter, was originally prepared by a member of the Maori research team.

lay in the nature of the offence rather than in the way that matters were handled by the court. Table 8.9 presents the few significant results from comparisons of Maori and Pakeha young people together with data on some of the more interesting, although non-significant, differences relating to the characteristics of offenders, the offences they committed and the outcomes of decisions. Because of the small numbers, similar comparisons can not be made for Pacific Island young people, although we believe that these families were likely to experience more difficulties than Maori families, particularly because so many are recent immigrants who are less familiar with either the English language or the New Zealand judicial system than Maori or Pakeha families.

Offenders' characteristics were rarely different when Maori and Pakeha young people were compared. The only statistically significant difference was that Maori offenders were younger; there were seven 14 year old Maori offenders but no 14 year old Pakeha offenders came into our sample of court cases. Previous offending histories were slightly more common among young Maori offenders than among Pakeha (91% compared with 78%), but this difference was not significant as the numbers were fairly small and there were no differences between the two groups in whether or not the young person had previously been dealt with at an FGC.

When it came to offence characteristics, young Maori offenders were rather more likely to be appearing on a charge of burglary than Pakeha offenders (see Table 8.9) and the ratings of the seriousness of the offence also showed a tendency, though not a statistically significant one, for young Maori to be more likely than young Pakeha to have had their offences rated *medium* in seriousness as compared to *minimum* or *minimum/medium* in seriousness. There were no significant differences between Maori and Pakeha offenders with respect to other types of offences, the number of offences committed or whether or not co-offenders were involved.

In terms of court process, there were no differences at all between Maori and Pakeha offenders. Both were equally likely to deny or admit the charges, to be bailed or held in custody, to have similar bail conditions, to come before the court the same number of times on average, to have their parents involved in the process and to have the police agree to the recommendations of their FGC.

The outcomes of court cases appeared slightly more severe for young Maori offenders but this is because they were less likely to be charged with least serious offences. Young Maori offenders were as likely to complete FGC tasks as Pakeha offenders and the tendency for slightly more young Maori than Pakeha to reoffend was not statistically significant.

Thus the conclusion from this analysis, at least on those factors which we were able to measure, is that there appeared to be no difference in the way the court handled Maori and Pakeha young people; neither the court process nor the court outcomes were discernibly different for the two groups.

Table 8.9
Maori-Pakeha Differences in Offender and Offence Characteristics and Outcomes; Distinct Court Cases; Percentages of each Ethnic Group

	Maori (N=35) %	Pakeha (N=27) %
Age		
14	20	0
15	23	37
16 or more	57	63
Previously offended		
Yes	91	78
No	9	22
Seriousness		
Min or min/med	6	26
Medium	74	48
Med/max or max	20	26
Type of Offence		
Burglaries	46	19
Other	54	81
Previously YJ FGC		
Yes	58	44
No	42	56
Severity of FGC Recommendation		
0-3	47	52
4-6	25	32
7-9	28	16
Type of Outcome		
Discharge	41	58
Youth Court order	41	35
Higher Court sentence	18	8
Reoffended		
Yes	65	50
No	35	50

Questions can be raised, however, about the quality of the process and its impact on young people who might have different values and expectations as a consequence of their different cultural background and experience. Furthermore, unlike young Pakeha offenders, young Maori offenders were sometimes supported by whanau, who sometimes came in large numbers and made submissions to the court on their behalf.

Comparison of the comments of Maori, Pakeha and Pacific Island offenders showed that all groups considered the court to be part of an alien world, but a world that was seen by the Maori and Pacific Island young people and their families as, in the words of one young person: *pretty much a Pakeha scene*.

To most of the Maori and Pacific Island families, 'a Pakeha scene' was what they expected and accepted from the court, although there were certainly no suggestions from anyone that the court was biased in its decisions. Comments that contrasted the approach of the court with the approach of the FGC emphasised not only the features discussed earlier (page 155) but also the fact that the FGC was more of a Maori way of doing things:

> *The court was more strict. At the FGC you are with your whanau. (Young person)*
>
> *Whanau had more say at the FGC because it was done in the Maori way. (Mother)*
>
> *Things were not done in a Maori way – there was no support in court. (Parent)*
>
> *The court was frightening – it wasn't done in a Maori way. (Young person)*

Sometimes the court accepted the presence of the whanau and recognised the differences in cultural practices by listening to their submissions and hearing their prayers. Such occasions could be very impressive and moving for all concerned, sometimes leaving few dry eyes in the courtroom. When this happened, it was always appreciated and seen as important by the young people and their families even if the basic formality of the court still had an overriding impact:

> *I don't understand Maori too well, but it was good for my family. The court allowed prayers and I knew they were praying for me. I knew all my family were sitting behind me. The High Court really freaked me out. (Young person)*
>
> *The judge gave the family a chance to speak, even in the High Court, and that was very much appreciated. It was OK, but it was still a formal intimidating institution. (Parent)*
>
> *All my whanau came to court with me. The judge set a time aside for us because my whanau wanted to speak. The court wasn't done in a Maori way, but my whanau were able to speak. (Young person)*
>
> *Being Maori made a difference – it always does. It affects your treatment – your chances are never as good. Things were done the Maori way at the FGC [on the marae] and in the court a bit. We were allowed to speak out. It was the right way. (Mother)*

In contrast, when Maori families who had come together collectively to provide whanau support were not recognised and listened to by the court, there were strong feelings of dissatisfaction:

> *He has a whanau to go to. The FGC was very much in a Maori way. The court, no. The whanau were very unhappy at court. They feel the judge did not listen to the support that will be available by the whanau and maatua whangai [an officially recognised support group for Maori offenders]. The whanau wish me to put to you [the researchers] that they feel that the judges should be present at some whanau-based FGCs so they can understand what goes on and get an appreciation of the cultural setting and support. My feeling is the judge is not at all impressed with cultural alternatives for dealing with problems such as this. (Aunt)*

And in this case the interviewer commented:

> *The judge did not accept the FGC recommendations as [the judge] believed there would be no backup if P got into trouble, but the judge was not told that the aunt was maatua whangai. (Maori court support group)*

When whanau members wanted to make submissions it was apparent that this posed a dilemma for a number of judges as the following case histories illustrate.

In the case of W, the whanau, which included some elderly people and some very young children and a baby, waited from early morning to mid afternoon before the case was heard. For most of that time they did not know whether or not they could go away and return. Some whanau members were only able to remain after rescheduling flights back to other parts of the country. Meanwhile in the courtroom the judge commented:

> *It is a pity no one knew [they were coming]. I would have arranged a special hearing. This courtroom isn't big enough. I have all these cases scheduled.*

The Youth Justice Co-ordinator was indignant on behalf of the family:

> *They have been abused by the court – keeping them waiting. I felt like crying. It was difficult telling them out there, especially the great grandmother and the children and the baby.*

Differences can arise between the family and the court in the perception of who is whanau. In one case, the whanau group which came to court included not only kin but also five classmates (including a co-offender) and a tutor[65]. The judge queried the presence of those who were not kin and the following dialogue ensued:

Judge: Is there any necessity for you to be here?

Supporters: We would like to give support.

Judge: Would you please wait outside.

Supporter: We would like to see what happens to her.

Tutor: I would like to stay.

Judge: There is an overkill in the representation. Do you really need to be here? This seems a remote connection. Are we getting carried away with the numbers who are here?

At this point the tutor and classmates left.

A problem with the issue of whanau submissions in court is that little information is usually given to whanau about what they can expect. According to our observations of practice, families are usually informed that making submissions to the court is unusual and will require special permission from the judge. No information on the outcome of the request to the judge is usually available before the hearing, so that whanau need to arrange to attend in the hope that they will be able to participate. The very fact of their attendance may then lead to delays in hearing the case.

Summarising this section, we can say that there is no evidence, either from an analysis of the factors we measured or from the comments of those we interviewed, that the court was influenced in its judgment by the ethnicity of the young offenders and their families. There is evidence that, at times, the courts responded to the desire of whanau to be present, to offer prayers and to make submissions on behalf of their young people. When the court accepted the presence of whanau and heard their submissions, there was considerable satisfaction with the process on the part of young people and their families. But the court was not always responsive to requests for changes in its normal procedures and, when whanau felt that they had not been heard and listened to, the process drew considerable criticism. Problems were compounded by the fact that whanau had to rely on the goodwill of the judge if they were to be heard and were not able to plan ahead for what would happen.

Conclusions

How, then, does the Youth Court measure up to the objectives of the Act? The results reported in this chapter show that there are elements of both success and failure. The move towards a justice rather than a welfare model of offending has been achieved. Most young people who have offended are held accountable for their offences, and at the same time the State is no longer using indeterminate institutional placements on the grounds of welfare needs. Furthermore, parents and young people seemed satisfied with the outcomes and generally felt that the decisions of the court were fair.

There were, however, some issues about the extent and effectiveness of accountability in the new system. Sanctions recommended by families were often quite severe compared with the type of penalties that would normally be awarded by the court. On the other hand, tasks agreed to at the FGC were not always completed and the lack of follow up by the system means that the extent of this was not known. We return to these issues in the concluding chapter.

Other goals of the Act relate to court procedures. These include efforts to reduce time frames; to enhance due process; to avoid labelling, stigmatisation and the congregation of offenders; to

---

[65] Although whanau originally meant kin, for many Maori today it means those who provide you with the close emotional and social support that one might expect from close family members. Thus many Maori will see all the immediate members of their social network as part of their whanau.

improve the atmosphere of the court; and to involve families in the decision-making process. In these areas, there has been less success in achieving change. Court cases are still protracted with many hearings that make slow progress. The time taken to reach a decision far exceeded that achieved in FGC cases that did not come to court and the reasons did not necessarily lie in the complexity of the case but rather in the nature of the court process itself. These problems were exacerbated by the multiplicity of different judges involved in many cases, the failure of the appointments system and the seeming pointlessness for young people and their families of the many brief appearances that occurred. Considerable improvement could be achieved in many of these areas.

The potentially serious consequences of multiple remands was highlighted in cases involving repeat offenders. The problems caused by delays in the process combined to make it difficult for the Youth Court either to ensure that the young person was held accountable for his or her offences or to ensure that his or her welfare needs were met. In many cases, there was a failure to reach a decision before further offences were committed. When this occurred, matters already in hand became further delayed, so that no effective measures were put in place to make these young people accountable or to provide needed support to them or their families for many weeks or even months. In such cases, there was a tendency to blame the young person or the Act. Unfortunate phrases such as 'the Act does not deal with the hardened offender' were heard from the very professionals who had the responsibility for the management of the processes. The key, in our view, lies in changing the procedures so that the principles and objectives of the Act, especially in regard to time frames, are made more meaningful and effective.

The universal representation of young people by a youth advocate is a considerable advance on the situation before the Act (Morris and Young, 1987) but, at the same time, this representation was not always effective in ensuring the protection of young people's rights. In part this was because the quality of representation was uneven but, in part, too, it was because of the pressures on young people to plead guilty. Research in South Australia (Gale *et al*, 1989) drew attention to a number of features of the South Australian system which created a pressure to plead guilty: the promise of shorter time frames; the possibility of resolution through relatively informal means; the securing of police agreement to outcomes; and the more subtle pressures that arose through the effective complicity of the permanent actors on the courtroom stage arising from the shared culture of the courtroom. These factors would also appear to affect the Youth Court in New Zealand today. Indeed, perhaps because of the possibility of rapid solutions through an FGC, the pressures not to deny charges are greater in New Zealand since the Act came into effect. Thus, while the Act emphasises due process, in the reality of courtroom practice this is not always assured. Whether or not this is a good or bad feature is debatable. Perhaps it would be possible to emphasise aspects of due process at the FGC (for example, by ensuring that the summary of facts is agreed to, and, if not, by providing clear procedures for action) so that the advantages of family empowerment and a more informal method of resolution of cases are not gained at the expense of due process.

To the extent that stigmatisation and labelling are a consequence of court appearances then a decline in the number of young people appearing before the court reduces the chances of this occurring. Moreover, a large number of those who do appear in court leave the courtroom without a formal record of conviction. On the other hand, the visibility of the young person to many unknown participants in the courtroom and the rituals of standing in the dock and being escorted by the police remain unchanged in most of the courtrooms. And while there has been some improvement in the crowded waiting room scenes of old (Morris and Young, 1987), there is still plenty of opportunity for young people to meet old friends and make new ones, both in the waiting room and while awaiting bail notices. Effective appointments systems have rarely been achieved.

The atmosphere of the court still seemed to young people and their parents to be intimidating rather than informal. Matters were still often impossible for a lay person to understand and real participation by young people and their families was rare. Attempts by whanau to use the provisions of the Act to participate in proceedings were usually greeted with courtesy and accommodated, but at times the way arrangements were organised, made it very clear that their participation was an inconvenience. Hence, a supplicant family often had doubts as to the effect of their presence on the outcome for the young person, despite the fact that whanau submissions seemed to us to be almost universally beneficial to the young person. There was also no comparison between the court and the FGC processes in the minds of participants. Thus, in the area of effective participation of young people and their families, the performance of the Youth Court has been poor.

Issues of cultural appropriateness were rightly raised by the Maori researchers, but equally the court was uncomfortable for Pakeha young people and their families. A real and meaningful revision of the outdated rituals, seating arrangements and procedures seems to us long overdue if the Youth Court is to play an effective and meaningful role in assisting young people and their families to understand the consequences of their offending and to participate in the process of reparation in the widest sense. To be responsive to different cultural groups, the court would need to change even more and such changes should be seriously considered if the process is to become effective and meaningful for Maori and Pacific Island families.

It is unfortunate that, while so many aspects of policing and DSW practice have changed dramatically, so little change has occurred in the courtroom. In the next chapter, we outline proposals for change that would need to be implemented if the Youth Court is genuinely to achieve the role set down for it in the Act and if it is to meet the principles and objectives laid down as the basis for the new system of youth justice.

Chapter 9

YOUTH JUSTICE IN NEW ZEALAND: AN EVALUATION

Introduction

We identified in the introductory chapter the key principles and objectives which underlie the Children, Young Persons and their Families Act; and much of what has gone before has dealt with how these principles have been translated into practice. In this chapter, we review how well the Act has performed in meeting its objectives, but also look more critically at the underlying principles, many of which are reflected in current approaches overseas. We use the New Zealand experience to comment on the ways in which the new system avoids or demonstrates the deficiencies identified in the literature as problematic in these approaches. We also consider the extent to which the New Zealand system is able to reconcile apparently contradictory principles and objectives. Underlying this is a discussion of the ways in which principles and objectives translate into practice and practice meets principles and objectives.

Models of Juvenile Justice

In the Western tradition, a number of philosophies of juvenile justice have emerged which contrast with the indigenous New Zealand approach that we outlined in Chapter 1. Principal amongst these Western models is a concern for 'welfare' or alternatively 'justice'. These two models replaced an earlier emphasis on 'crime control', although this has never fully disappeared and is currently the object of renewed interest. More recently there has been a focus on 'diversion and decarceration' and 'mediation'. Before elaborating on these alternative rationales, a word of caution. For ease of presentation we have identified these as 'models'. As such they have been idealised and stereotyped. They rarely exist in such a pure form and, in truth, most systems of juvenile justice are an amalgam of these diverse approaches. Certainly traces of each are apparent in most jurisdictions though at different times one may be more 'popular' or 'visible' than another.

It is usual for commentators to assess the practice of current juvenile justice systems through two critical dimensions: welfare and justice. Thus Klein (1984, 13) refers to the 'seemingly inevitable tug of war' between the two (see also Farrington, 1984; Faust and Brantingham, 1974).

Principles of a Welfare Approach

The main principles of this approach are as follows:

- the offence is regarded as a symptom of an underlying disorder
- lack of responsibility of the offender for his or her behaviour is implicit
- responses should be individualised in terms of the 'best interests' or 'needs' of the young person
- the influence of background, particularly family factors, is emphasised
- treatment and rehabilitation are emphasised
- responses to offending require a broad discretion
- early and long term intervention (often indeterminate) is predicated
- procedural safeguards are seen as secondary to welfare
- solutions are arrived at by informal procedures or tribunals.

The origins of this model lie in 19th century beliefs that crime had many causes which did not necessarily lie within the individual's control but which were, in the main, remediable. This is usually referred to within criminology as positivism. In this view, every event was caused; human freedom was illusory (Matza, 1964). In time, the emphasis in the search for factors to explain criminal behaviour shifted from socio-economic and hereditary factors to the psychology of the individual offender. Criminals and the law-abiding were viewed as differing in certain characteristics, but the characteristics assigned at any one time depended on the theory in fashion. The maxim was 'punishment should fit the offender, not the offence'.

Thus a 'welfare' approach assumes that something has gone 'wrong' when a juvenile commits an offence (or truants, sleeps around or the like) and that to a large extent the behaviour is due to deficiencies in the individual, family, school, neighbourhood or some other aspect of the situation. The focus is on finding out what went wrong and putting it right. The behaviour itself is no longer the primary focus but rather the 'needs' or 'best interests' of the child. Any information may be 'relevant' in determining these needs and best interests and legal rights are an unnecessary hindrance to providing the right 'help'. Tariff considerations are also regarded as inappropriate and so early and extensive intervention in the juvenile's life may be justified on the basis that it is beneficial and 'treatments' may be changed as conditions warrant. Medical analogies are not uncommon in the literature on this approach at least in its original forms.

Examples of a welfare approach in practice are the early juvenile courts in the United States (for a description see Platt, 1969), the welfare boards of the Scandinavian countries (for a description see Stang Dahl, 1974) and the children's hearings, at least in their idealised form, introduced into Scotland in 1971 (for a description see Morris and McIsaac, 1978).

Concerns about a welfare approach are well rehearsed (see Morris and McIsaac, 1978; Morris et al, 1980) and in summary are:

- the offence is ignored
- subjective, and possibly discriminatory, decision-making leads to disparities
- the net of social control is expanded
- it is empirically unsound: causes are unknown and the treatments are ineffective
- intervention is itself harmful
- due process is ignored.

Generally these reflect the disillusionment in the 1960s among academics with positivism and among practitioners with 'the rehabilitative ideal'. Optimism gave way to scepticism, best summed up in Martinson's (1974) often quoted and exaggerated claim that 'nothing works'. In brief, critics argue that the approach over-simplified our understanding of the causes of crime. They pointed to the fact that research findings were inconclusive and demonstrated that the rhetoric of 'welfare' concealed a range of abuses. Research also showed that certain groups (primarily black and working class juveniles) were being differentially treated and that so called 'treatments' could be potentially harmful. In New Zealand, for example, research showed that State wards (that is, children removed from their parents' care in order to provide for their welfare) were more likely to offend as adults than children reared in their own homes (Lovell and Norris, 1990). However, few jurisdictions have been prepared to abandon considerations of welfare entirely, particularly with respect to juveniles. And these principles are reflected in the New Zealand legislation in terms of the requirements to consider the wellbeing of the child or young person, to enhance their development and to provide services to meet their needs. Later we consider how well these objectives have been met in practice and, in as far as our data allow, the extent to which the current youth justice system in New Zealand avoids the criticisms outlined above.

Principles of a Justice Approach

The main principles of this approach are:

- the offender is responsible for his or her behaviour and should be accountable for it

- the offence is important and is the focus of decision-making
- dispositions should be equated with the gravity of the offence
- dispositions should be determinate
- the least restrictive sanction should be chosen
- treatment is secondary or optional
- there should be an emphasis on rights, due process and procedural safeguards
- procedures should be formal.

This approach was responsive to criticisms about 'welfare' and to some extent its principles are mirror images of those underlying a welfare approach: an emphasis on the gravity of the offence and not the juvenile's underlying needs; on responsibility and free will and not determinism; on equality of sanction and not individualised treatment; on determinacy of sanctions and not on indeterminacy of treatment and so on. Proponents (Morris *et al*, 1980; Taylor *et al*, 1980) viewed themselves in essence as protecting juveniles from the excesses of welfare.

Examples of a fully implemented justice approach in the youth justice context are more difficult to find than welfare-oriented systems, but attempts have been made to introduce such an approach in a number of American states, for example, Iowa, Delaware and Washington. Elements of a justice approach are, however, apparent in many juvenile justice systems where legal representation is common, where penalties are determinate and where restrictions are placed on the use of custody in an attempt to encourage the use of 'least restrictive alternatives' (as in England and Wales since 1982 and in most American states). In New Zealand, the appointment of youth advocates for juveniles appearing in the Youth Court, the determinacy of dispositions, the stress on accountability, limits on the use of arrest and custody for juveniles and the restriction on using the youth justice provisions of the Act to meet welfare needs all reflect the endorsement of justice principles.

A justice approach is also not without its critics (Clarke, 1985; Hudson, 1987) and their main criticisms are as follows:

- it ignores the underlying causes of crime and, in particular, the reality of social disadvantage
- equality of penalties leads to injustice
- it can be co-opted by the right wing 'law and order' lobby
- increased legal representation is not necessarily effective in preserving due process
- discretionary decision-making moves to other arenas.

The most important of these is that the stress on formal or procedural aspects of justice has led to a failure to address adequately issues of substantive justice and hence leaves issues of social deprivation untouched. We commented in previous chapters and comment again later in this chapter on the extent to which this can happen in New Zealand by stressing accountability (rightly in our view) while at the same time not responding adequately to obvious needs (wrongly in our view). Later we will also discuss whether or not the system in New Zealand provides 'justice for juveniles'.

In trying to understand current trends in juvenile justice and the shape of the particular youth justice system in New Zealand, it is clear that other philosophies are also operating and so we turn now to a description of alternative approaches.

Principles of a Crime Control Approach

In most jurisdictions there has been a revival of traditional criminal justice concerns, concerns which stem from the need to protect victims from offenders irrespective of their age. This approach can be categorised as crime control. Its main characteristics are as follows:

- the law breaker chooses to offend and must be held responsible for his or her actions
- there is a bifurcation between the 'acceptable' (minor) and the 'unacceptable' (serious and/or persistent) offender
- punishment, deterrence, public protection and incapacitation are emphasised
- strong penalties, especially custody, are preferred
- the interests of society are stressed.

The re-affirmation of this approach is primarily a response to perceived high levels of crime, to perceived increases in the seriousness of crime, particularly among juveniles, and to growing concerns about both individual and neighbourhood safety (especially in the light of the emergence of neighbourhoods where a diversity of values and culture can seem threatening). These 'fears' were especially apparent in the electoral campaigns of the Conservative party in England in the 1970s[66], where it presented itself as the party which would and could take a strong stand against crime in contrast to the Labour party which was presented as excusing crime and as sympathetic to offenders. Advocates of a crime control approach often stressed, too, making parents responsible for the offences of their children by making them pay, quite literally. This has always been possible in England and Wales in certain circumstances, but since the Criminal Justice Act 1982 the juvenile court has had a *duty* to impose financial penalties (fines, compensation orders and so on) on the parent or guardian rather than the child or young person.

An extreme example of a crime control approach is the fact that in some American states juveniles as well as adults can be sentenced to death, but other examples include transfer from the juvenile court to higher courts where the juvenile has committed certain serious offences and long-term detention in certain circumstances. In New Zealand, the provisions for transfer of jurisdiction from the Youth Court to the District Court and to the High Court and the availability then of 'adult' penalties for juveniles reflect these principles.

The principal concerns about a crime control approach are as follows:

- it ignores social disadvantage
- it results in a large number of offenders in custody and high re-offending rates
- it may actually result in an increase in crime
- due process may be disregarded
- it has a high cost, both financially and in human terms.

The most important of these criticisms is that this approach too ignores the social deprivation that is so often part of the background of juvenile offending. Because of this failure to address the factors underlying offending behaviour and because of the preference in this approach for custodial penalties even for first and minor offenders, a crime control approach may have a paradoxical consequence: increased offending. The reason for this is that a crime control approach is **not** constrained by notions of a tariff or by proportionality. Thus, in England and Wales in the 1970s, there was a massive increase in the number of juveniles in custody. An analysis of this by the DHSS (1981) showed that this was not due to increases or changes in juvenile crime but rather to changes in sentencing practice. Quite simply, the magistrates had become more punitive. Later we discuss the way in which the youth justice system in New Zealand has resisted pressures to adopt a crime control approach with its associated problems.

Principles of a Diversion/Decarceration Approach

At the same time that there has been a return in certain jurisdictions to aspects of crime control, there have been some quite contradictory trends: in particular, the emphasis on diversion (keeping

---

[66] Similar themes and issues emerged prior to the 1987 election in New Zealand (Pratt, 1987).

juveniles out of court) and decarceration (keeping juveniles out of institutions). These are not strictly speaking models in their own right, as they can sit comfortably alongside each of the models described so far, but it makes sense here to describe briefly their main features:

- they reduce stigma and contamination
- they protect from the adverse effects of 'treatment', court processes and institutionalisation
- they can be a gateway to earlier and better treatment.

Diversion and decarceration are probably the most dominant trends in juvenile justice (and they are now beginning to have an impact in the criminal justice system more generally). Few of us can honestly say that we have never committed a criminal offence, especially as juveniles, but few of us have experienced the full sanctions of the juvenile justice system. If we were caught, we were probably dealt with informally by parents, neighbours, schools – perhaps even by the police. And most offending by juveniles is minor and transient. It is a phase which many of us – boys and girls, black and white, middle class and working class – both go and grow through. Yet most of us apparently become reasonably law abiding citizens. These simple truths underlie the common sense appeal of diversion and decarceration, particularly for juveniles. Their intellectual roots lie in labelling theory (see, for example, Lemert, 1971) and differential association theory (Sutherland and Cressey, 1974).

In essence, the expansion of diversion and decarceration practices – primarily taking the form of police warnings and community programmes – is based on the view that the juvenile court experience and institutionalisation are potentially negative and harmful and should, therefore, be reserved for the more serious and persistent offenders. In New Zealand these views have been promulgated by Doolan (1988). Thus, it is argued that the juvenile court and institutions should be used as a last resort after other less formal strategies have been tried and failed. Diversion here is a protection from the consequences of a juvenile court appearance; decarceration is a protection from the consequences of institutions.

However, there is another major rationale for diversion and decarceration which is, in a sense, the precise opposite of this. They provide an earlier and better opportunity of working with juveniles than would otherwise be possible which, in turn, provides hope that such work will be more successful. Diversion and decarceration, therefore, in this context are a gateway to resources. This view is obviously favoured by those who still prefer a more welfare-oriented role for the juvenile court and it is apparent in the development of a wide range of diversion and community based programmes in the United States (for a description see Klein, 1979) and of intermediate treatment in England (for a description see Bottoms *et al*, 1990).

Diversion and decarceration are obviously primary foci in the New Zealand system, not only through the encouragement of police warnings but also, arguably at least, through the introduction of FGCs instead of courts for the vast majority of juvenile offenders. The closure of most of the residential institutions for juveniles and an emphasis on keeping juveniles in their community and on using the least restrictive alternative reflect this trend too. The destruction of all records of juvenile offending when offenders reach the age of 20, the possibility in the Youth Court of withdrawing or discharging a case without a record, the suppression of offenders' names and the limitations imposed on the publication of details of the proceedings in the Youth Court, and the attempt to introduce an appointments' system for the Youth Court are all further examples of minimising the potentially harmful effects of formal interventions. However, with respect to both diversion and de-institutionalisation there has also been a well sustained critique (see, for example, Polk, 1987; Morris, 1978).

In summary, the main points of criticism are:

- the concepts are ambiguous
- there is a tendency to 'net-widen' and to expand social control
- there is potential for discriminatory decision-making

- too little emphasis is placed on due process protections
- deterrence is minimised
- the approach is ineffective.

The present study adds nothing to the debate on the theoretical soundness of diversion or decarceration, nor does it provide empirical evidence of their effectiveness, but our data address some of the above criticisms. We review these criticisms in greater detail now and discuss the relevant data later.

Net Widening

Probably the best documented and most discussed feature of diversion is the tendency to bring more juveniles into the juvenile justice system than would otherwise have been the case: the so called net-widening phenomenon. In England and Wales, for example, it was acknowledged early in the 1970s that a paradox had developed: an increase in the use of a measure intended to divert juvenile offenders from the juvenile courts – police warnings – was not, in fact, having the effect of reducing the number of juveniles entering that system (Ditchfield, 1976; Farrington and Bennett,1981). This was a feature well documented at the time in the United States: for a review, see Morris (1978). Rather than operating as real diversion, the cautioning procedure was said to be 'widening the net' of available labelled delinquents[67].

'Net widening' can, however, also occur in three other senses: the development of an informal system of police warnings which deals with juveniles by means of words of advice or warning; the possibility that 'voluntary' involvement in a diversion or decarceration programme as a result of police or social service intervention will be for longer and will be more intrusive than the outcome which the juvenile would have received if referred to the juvenile court; and the risk that failure of the juvenile during or after participation in a diversion or decarceration programme will lead to greater intervention by the juvenile court on a subsequent appearance.

Discriminatory Decision-making

A second danger with diversion or decarceration is that those operating the system – in particular, but not solely, the police – may employ discriminatory selection criteria over which there is little scrutiny or control. There may be pre-judicial/prejudicial decision-making. Gravity of the offence and prior offending history are widely accepted decision-making criteria. However, research overseas indicates that decisions whether or not to refer young offenders to court have also been influenced by more subjective, less acceptable, criteria too. Landau (1981) and Landau and Nathan (1983), for example, found that the type of offence and previous record were of primary importance in the decision whether or not to prosecute a juvenile. But superimposed on these were the age, family background and race of the offender. Other researchers have pointed to the relevance of class and parental attitudes (Farrington and Bennett, 1981; Fisher and Mawby, 1982).

A different form of discrimination is through what has been called 'justice by geography': variation in police and court practice in different geographical areas. Some geographical variation will occur because of differential crime patterns (for example, the proportion of minor offences in an area) and differential offender populations (for example, the proportion of first offenders in an area). Some may be due to differential police and court policy and practice.

Due Process

A third area of concern, with respect to diversion, is what can broadly be called the lack of due process protections. In essence, diversion schemes are often decision-making behind closed doors and this raises issues of the accountability of decision-makers for their decisions and scrutiny of these decisions by external authority. Juveniles also usually have no right to legal advice before making the admissions on which the diversion decision is premised. There can be, at the very least,

---

[67] The evidence in England and Wales now indicates that this is no longer so (Bottoms et al., 1990).

implicit pressure on the offender to accept the proposed outcome if the perceived alternative is a court appearance, the possibility of stronger sanctions and a criminal record.

Principles of Victim Mediation, Reparation and Reconciliation

A final model, if indeed we can call it that, has only recently been used in a criminal justice context and indeed in some ways it is an alternative to it: it stresses reparation and reconciliation through mediation involving victims. A major criticism that can be made of all the models identified so far is that they have ignored victims' interests. A key component of mediation is that it addresses these. The main principles are as follows:

- it results in increased involvement of both offenders and victims
- decisions are by 'agreement'
- reparation, redress and reconciliation can be achieved
- there can be improved understanding between the victim and the offender
- it may avoid a court appearance, a criminal record and custody.

As we noted in Chapter 1, this model was first used to resolve disputes between landlords and tenants, employers and employees and the like, but its underlying principles are apparent in ideas of restitution, reparation and compensation for victims of offences. A range of schemes are now in existence both pre-and post-court (see Marshall and Merry (1990) for a review of practice in England and Wales and Wright and Galaway (1989) for a review of practice there and elsewhere). The role given to victims at FGCs and the emphasis given to reparation and work in the community as 'appropriate' penalties make clear the impact of this approach in the New Zealand youth justice system.

The principles of modern mediation programmes can be compared with the traditional Maori justice system described in Chapter 1. In Maoridom, the shame felt by offenders who were confronted with the effects of their offending led to remorse, followed by reintegration into the whanau which took responsibility for any actions necessary to redress the social imbalance, both towards victims and offenders. Very similar theoretical ideas are advanced by Braithwaite (1988) who uses the term 'reintegrative shaming'. Braithwaite distinguishes non-integrative shaming, which is associated with traditional court procedures and their resultant stigmatisation of the offender (encapsulated in Garfinkel's (1956) notion of status degradation), and reintegrative shaming, which seeks to combine shaming with reconciliation between the offender and the victim and reaffirmation of the offender's status in the community rather than his or her exclusion from or rejection by the community. Reparation (actual or symbolic) may affect reintegration (actual or symbolic). He argues that the process is more likely to be effective when it involves *relatives, friends or a personally relevant collectivity* (1989, 69).

But such trends are not without their critics (see, for example, Merry 1989). The main criticisms of the model are as follows:

- it can result in the infringement of the rights of the weaker party
- it is open to manipulation by mediators (or professionals)
- subtle forms of coercion can be applied to encourage 'agreement'
- it can be incorporated within traditional institutions rather than exist as an alternative to them
- subjectivity can affect outcomes
- there is the potential to further victimise the victim
- there is a lack of due process
- it may lead to increased intervention and 'up-tariffing'

- it may be subsumed by other priorities (for example, diversion)
- it is unclear whose interests are being served.

In theory, mediation is a meeting of equals. In practice, in the criminal justice system and in schemes involving adults (either as professionals or victims) and juveniles (as offenders) it is not a meeting of equals, by definition. An examination of practice in New Zealand youth justice system illuminates this concern and some of the others which have been listed above.

The New Zealand Approach

It should be apparent from this brief review that all of these models have had an influence on the particular form of the youth justice system in New Zealand. For example, Doolan (1991), whose earlier work (1988) influenced the development of the legislation, argues that 'welfare' and 'justice', though often represented as at opposite ends of a continuum, are, in reality, not true opposites and that both are important parts of the New Zealand system. He describes the system as moving towards the principles underlying the justice model 'without embracing its more doctrinaire aspects' and as moving away from the principles underlying the welfare model without 'a loss of interest in achieving positive outcomes for young persons' (1991, 2). Thus the importance of reinforcing accountability through penalties has been emphasised alongside the objectives of enhancing the wellbeing of young people and strengthening their families.

The legislation also emphasises the importance of diversion and decarceration but retains some aspects of a crime control model by allowing certain offenders to be transferred to a higher court for custodial sentences and requiring judges to take previous history into account when sentencing. Concerns for due process have been emphasised in both police and courtroom procedures.

There are innovatory features too; we described these in detail in Chapter 1. For example, the notion of reaching a consensus between the State, the family, the young person and the victim has been given a central place in the system although the balance to be struck is not entirely clear. The rationale for a participatory system comes in part from research on human behaviour which demonstrates that people respond more effectively when they have control over their own lives and the decisions that affect them (Rappaport, 1977). This research has led to a new approach to the provision of social and psychological services which emphasises the empowerment of people by their involvement in decisions rather than consultation with an expert whose advice is then followed. In the area of social policy, the same philosophy emphasises partnership and joint participation between the State and communities (Fulcher, 1991) and this philosophy has considerable attraction at a time when governments are attempting to reduce the extent of State responsibility for social services (Cody, 1990).

In contrast to the emphasis placed by most YJCs on the participation and empowerment of families and young people, the Principal Youth Court Judge has emphasised that the victim is at the heart of the process (Brown, personal communication, 1992). The FGC is a mechanism for achieving reconciliation between the victim and the offender and, as in the traditional Maori model, achieving social balance by reintegrating the young person in their family and determining an appropriate means of redress for the victim. Rapid solutions appropriate to the age of the offender have also been set down as legislative objectives. And finally there is an attempt to develop a system of justice which allows different ethnic groups to resolve matters in customary settings using customary procedures and which provides access to culturally appropriate services.

The principal features of the New Zealand youth justice system are summarised in Box 9.1.

Box 9.1
The Goals of Youth Justice in New Zealand:

- **diversion** – keeping young people out of courts and preventing the use of labels that make it difficult for young people to put early offending behind them

- **enhancing wellbeing and strengthening families** – making available services that will assist the young person and his or her family

- **accountability** – emphasising the importance of young people paying an appropriate penalty for their crime and making good the wrong they have done to others

- **reducing time frames** – making time frames realistic given the age of the child or young person

- **due process** – emphasising the protection of young people's rights

- **family participation** – involving families and young people in making the decisions for themselves and taking charge of their lives

- **victim involvement** – involving victims in the decisions about what will happen

- **consensus decision making** – arriving at decisions which are agreed to by the family, the young person, police and victims

- **cultural appropriateness** – providing for different ways of resolving matters and obtaining help depending on the culture of the young person and his or her family.

Inevitably, diverse objectives conflict and combining models may solve none of the potential problems; it may even create new problems. And, furthermore, practice may fail to meet stated objectives. We now summarise the extent to which these principles and objectives have been realised in practice and whether or not the criticisms identified previously have been met; we then return to the issue of inherent contradictions.

Meeting Objectives

Diversion and Decarceration

Diversion and decarceration have a range of meanings. In the New Zealand context, we use these terms to describe practice with respect to limiting the appearance of young people in court and restricting the use of residential or penal establishments for young people. To determine the extent to which diversion and decarceration have been achieved in the new system we, therefore, examine:

- the use of arrest
- the laying of charges after an arrest
- the use of 'police diversion' and FGCs
- the use of remands in custody
- the recommendation by FGCs of Youth Court orders
- the number of court appearances
- the use of Youth Court orders
- the use of supervision with residence

- the use of penal custody.

Each of these is discussed in turn.

The Use of Arrest
The Act redefined the situations in which a young person could be arrested in order to avoid both the unnecessary detention of young people and the use of the Youth Court. The clear preference was to deal with young people less formally. The results of the research show that since the Act there has been a considerable reduction in the arrest rate: from approximately a third to 10% of those coming to attention. This at first sight seems to confirm that practice has changed in line with the new provisions. However, our data also suggest that, despite the changes in the law and the reduction in the number being arrested, the reasons for arrest are, in practice, not dissimilar from those that emerged from the study conducted prior to the Act (Morris and Young, 1987). The most common grounds for arrest were to prevent the young person's reoffending or to ensure the appearance of the young person in court, but it is apparent that these were being interpreted very broadly (and interpreted differently in different areas). Central to this is the very real problem of predicting what offenders will do in the future. Inevitably, the subjective nature of these assessments that need to be made by the police officers makes it possible that decisions will be made on the basis of general judgements of the young person's character or even the response he or she makes to the assertion of police authority. While factors such as previous recent offending and the number of offences admitted to on this particular occasion are, arguably, useful indicators of the probability of reoffending, factors such as association with known offenders, coming from a family containing known offenders and general attitude at the time of the apprehension are more dubious. Similarly, judgments about whether or not an arrest is necessary 'to ensure appearance' could be reasonably based on knowledge of a history of absconding, but factors such as behaviour at the time of apprehension and the offender's home circumstances are more problematic.

In addition, other motives emerged for making an arrest. In some instances, concerns about the home background of the young person were undoubtedly very influential and this conflicts with the principle that criminal proceedings should not be brought to advance welfare outcomes. Views on the desirability of ensuring a high tariff sentence and on the inadequacy of FGCs in resolving the outcome satisfactorily and rapidly were also expressed by some officers. Yet, except in serious cases, arrest is not likely to achieve a different result from a referral for an FGC, as the decisions of the court were in our research rarely very different from those recommended by the FGC. Further, by referring the young person for an FGC the police do not abandon their control over the case.

Finally we note that a regression analysis showed that to some extent the decision to arrest could be predicted from information about the seriousness of the offence, the time of the offence, and the age and ethnicity of the offender. The importance of ethnicity is a matter of some concern, especially as there is no evidence of differences in practice for different ethnic groups in Youth Aid decisions or in the sentencing practice of the Youth Court. The evidence is insufficient to determine whether or not this arose from prejudice; but it is obviously one possibility. Certainly, some parents and young people believed that some front-line police officers discriminated against them on the grounds of race.[68] If this is true, it could be linked to negative perceptions of Maori families by some police officers.[69]

The Laying of Charges
Section 208(a) of the Act states that, unless the public interest requires otherwise, criminal proceedings should not be instituted against a child or young person if there is an alternative means

---

[68] A recent draft article (Fergusson, Horwood and Lynskey, 1992) presents an analysis of self reported offending compared with police contact for Maori and Pakeha young people. It also suggests that a higher proportion of self admitted young Maori than Pakeha offenders came to the attention of the police.

[69] We understand that recruit training involves at least 12 hours on cultural issues and, in addition, all recruits spend three days on a marae. Post recruit training programmes are currently being revised and new modules on cultural issues are being planned.

of dealing with the matter. Even when an arrest has been made, the police are still able to release the young person without charge. However, in our study, out of a total of 75 police arrests, only five cases involved release without a charge and the remaining 70 cases proceeded to a Youth Court appearance. The eventual outcome in approximately half of these cases was that the charges were withdrawn or the case was discharged after the Youth Court had received the recommendations agreed to at the FGC. Thus the practice of almost automatically laying a charge upon arrest is questionable. It is possible that recent changes to police instructions which emphasise the need to review matters before making a charge after an arrest[70] will further reduce the number of court appearances without affecting the likely outcome.

The Use of 'Police Diversion' and FGCs

On the face of it, police practice is definitely more diversionary than in the past. Official statistics (Department of Statistics, 1991) record a court appearance rate for 1990 of 16 per 1,000 young people aged 14-16; this can be compared with an average rate of 63 in the three calendar years prior to the introduction of the Act. Only 10% of the cases in our sample resulted in court appearances. The remaining 90% were dealt with by the Youth Aid section of the police through a series of diversionary strategies: warning, warning plus some form of informal sanction or referral for an FGC.

But there are other questions to consider. Firstly, are FGCs being used to deal with some young people who would previously have been warned rather than those who would previously have gone to court? Secondly, to what extent is diversion by referral to an FGC 'real' in the sense that sanctions have indeed been minimised compared to those that might have been expected had the sanctions been made by the court?

In examining these issues, we are handicapped by the fact that there is relatively little reliable data on past practice. However, in our sample the combined group of those who appeared in court and those referred for an FGC is approximately equivalent to the court appearance rate reported in the years prior to the Act[71]. This seems to indicate that it is the young people who would previously have gone to court that are now dealt with by FGCs.

On the other hand, in the past, only about three out of five[72] of those who appeared in court received any formal penalty. In our sample, about 95% of those who attended FGCs or who appeared in court were made accountable for their offence either by receiving a penalty or making an apology. In addition, 11% of the total sample had some form of informal sanction arranged through the Youth Aid section. Thus the total number who now receive some form of penalty is almost certainly greater than in the past – in other words, the net appears to have widened.

To say this ignores the possibility that merely appearing in the court or being bailed involved some 'penalty', at least in the eyes of the young person concerned. It also presupposes that no sanction is preferable to some. It is our view that, although more minor offenders are now receiving some kind of sanction, nevertheless the overall consequences may be less deleterious than the previous system, where large numbers were processed through a court system which stigmatised young people, introduced young offenders to one another and acted in other potentially destructive ways.

A further issue with respect to whether or not FGCs can properly be described as diversionary is the relative severity of the penalties which are now imposed. Using as a benchmark penalties rated as equivalent in severity to at least 100 hours' community work, we found that less than a fifth of

---

[70] The October 1991 amendments to the Police General Instructions, section Y63 (3) states that where the arrest action achieves its immediate objective, ie to prevent further reoffending, the member in charge of the station shall consider whether it is necessary to charge the offender or release the offender (234(a)) and deal with the matter by way of a warning or reporting the matter to Youth Aid for consideration.

[71] In our sample, 10% appeared in court and 28% were referred for an FGC. The combined of 38% is nearly 4 times the court appearance percentage and so was the average court appearance rate of 63 per 1,000 14-16 year olds in the population for 1986-1988 compared with the rate of 16 in 1990.

[72] On average in 1986, 1987 and 1988, 39% of charges were not proved or were discharged, possibly after admonition (Department of Statistics 1991).

FGC cases that did not go to court resulted in such penalties although about half the court cases did. Thus FGC penalties are, for the most part, less severe than the type of penalties now imposed by the court, although it is probable that most of these cases are ones that would have been discharged in the past. Comparisons between past and present severity of penalties are difficult because of the changes in the tariffs, but the use of custodial penalties has certainly been vastly reduced, with less than half the number receiving such penalties in 1990 compared to 1988.

What then can we say about the frequency and severity of penalties in the past compared to now? The answer would appear to be that, although fewer young people are now being sent to court and although fewer young people now receive custodial penalties, more young people are receiving moderate penalties through the FGC and 'police diversion' processes.

The Use of Remands in Custody
Issues surrounding the use of remands were custody are discussed in Chapter 8 (pages 141 and 148). The data showed that, of the cases in which full information was available and where there was no denial, one in five involved a remand in custody. Without comparable data on practice prior to the Act or, alternatively, a clear set of criteria for deciding when custody should be ordered, it is difficult to determine the extent to which these figures are in line with the objectives of the Act, although we noted variation in court practice across districts.

An order for police custody was made in only one case in our sample suggesting that the courts regard this as an option to be used rarely. On the other hand, the use of Social Welfare custody has given rise to concern, particularly among the police, but much of this concern is unfounded.

When the court remanded a young person to be detained in the care of the Director-General of Social Welfare in the past, it was usual to place the young person in one of the many DSW residences or family homes in a locality as close as possible to the home of the young person. The closure of residential institutions has changed this practice in several ways. In particular, not only are there fewer residential places available now but there is also less likely to be a residence in the local community and the residences that remain have become places of containment for the most difficult young offenders. Thus, in line with the principles of keeping young people in their families, in their communities and separate from other offenders, DSW policy is, whenever possible, to return the child or young person to his or her family or to place a young person in the community (for example, a foster home) rather than in a residence.

There are two issues here. The first is an issue of principle about who should make a decision to remand in custody. It could be argued that when the Youth Court orders that a young person be remanded in custody, a family or community placement is not appropriate and that such discretionary power should not lie with DSW. This is not an empirical question. The second issue is one of practice: what are the consequences of such a policy? This is an empirical question. All of the young people detained in DSW custody on an order from the Youth Court during our research – 20 in total – were in fact placed in a residence, although one was not placed there immediately and another was later placed in a family home. The problems of absconding and reoffending so often referred to in the media or by the police were not attributable to this group; rather these problems lay with those young people placed on bail.

The Recommendation by FGCs of Court Orders
In none of the cases in our sample where there was a direct referral for an FGC and in only just over a quarter of the court-ordered FGCs did the FGC recommend that matters be resolved by an order from the court. Thus FGCs are responding to offending in a way that obviates the need for a court order.

The Number of Court Appearances
We commented earlier on the fact that there were a number of cases where matters could have been resolved without the laying of charges in court. The research data also showed that there were frequently several appearances in the Youth Court before an FGC was held; and, even after an FGC had been held, families and young people often appeared only to have their case remanded because

of the need for further information. Not all of these appearances seemed necessary and practice elsewhere suggests that the number could be reduced. For example, one judge from outside our research areas normally dispensed with a Youth Court appearance before the young person had attended an FGC and so the issue of bail rarely arose. He also encouraged the use of a little used (and apparently little known) provision in Schedule 1 of the Act which allows a Youth Justice Co-ordinator to excuse the young person's appearance at the Youth Court when an FGC has not been able to be concluded or the necessary reports are not assembled.

Another reason for more court appearances than may be strictly necessary is the assumed need to consider the question of bail. In our sample, almost two thirds (62%) of young people were released on bail. However, in the district just mentioned bail was rarely an issue as both the judge and the police agreed to attempt to minimise the use of bail in order to meet the objectives and principles of the Act. There is, as far as we know, no evidence that this caused difficulties in this area.

The Use of Youth Court Orders
The Youth Court itself is more successful than the old Children and Young Persons Court was in avoiding the use of court orders. As stated earlier (page 175), national data for 1990 showed that, despite the fact that a relatively smaller proportion of cases are now prosecuted in the Youth Court, half the cases were dismissed, withdrawn or discharged compared with only 39% in the three years leading up to the Act. Evidence on the extent to which the Youth Court endorsed the recommendations of FGCs is described in Chapter 8 (pages 155-158). The data there showed that the FGC plans were endorsed in half the cases while, in almost another third, the orders made were consistent with the FGC recommendations.

The Use of Supervision with Residence
Nationally there has been a decline in the absolute numbers of young people receiving custodial orders in the Youth Court compared with what happened previously in the Children and Young Persons Court. The number of cases resulting in sentences of supervision with residence in 1990 was less than half the average number for the previous three years (see Chapter 8, pages 134-135).

The goal of reducing residential placements has been achieved both through a reduction in the use of 'supervision with residence' orders by the court and through changes in practice in DSW. DSW has given residential staff the role of 'gatekeeper' to ensure that admissions occur only when:

- there has been a supervision with residence order by the court; or

- the young person has been remanded by the court to the custody of the Director-General of Social Welfare and there is no other suitable placement option or

- there is a need for an emergency temporary placement after an arrest and prior to a court hearing in order to provide protection for the public or young person and there is no other suitable placement option.

There have, not surprisingly, been difficulties in limiting admissions to residences, given the expectations that were built up over the years when they were a commonly used option for young people who had offended, been neglected, been abused or were just difficult to manage. The gatekeeping role of residential staff in this regard has been effective in restricting their use.

More problematic is the issue of whether or not the residential staff should have a gatekeeping role at the point where an FGC is considering the possibility of supervision with residence. Residential social workers may be present at FGCs when they are needed to provide information to the family about what has been happening to a young person who has been in the residence on remand; when they are needed to inform the family about what would happen if a supervision with residence order were made; and when they are needed to help draw up a plan for such an order. However, in some of the cases we observed, the residential social workers seemed to enter the negotiations in order to encourage the family to choose an alternative to placement in a residence. In one such case, the FGC lasted over 5 hours and then had to be adjourned and continued at a later time. During much of the FGC, the debate centred on alternative views among the professionals about the legitimacy of a residential placement. The family left bewildered and exhausted and certainly not strengthened or empowered.

Ultimately, it is the Youth Court judge who will decide whether or not to make an order for supervision with activity or supervision with residence and it is the **judge's** responsibility to ensure that such orders are not used inappropriately. For any of the professionals to have a prior gatekeeping role within the FGC, therefore, not only undermines the autonomy of the FGC but also usurps the role of the Youth Court judge.

The Use of Penal Custody

National data show that in 1990 the number of cases being transferred to higher courts was reduced both in proportion and numerically compared with the previous three years. The number of cases of young people who were sent to prison or corrective training in 1990 was less than half the number pre-Act: it decreased from 262 cases in 1988 to 112 in 1990. These offenders had either committed very serious offences (for example, aggravated robbery, rape or arson causing major destruction), had committed a large number of offences (one youth was finally sentenced on 117 charges) or had an extensive history of previous offences. Thus there is no evidence that an escalation in custody has occurred in New Zealand: quite the reverse is the case. However, there are currently indications of a 'moral panic' about youth crime which is being orchestrated in part by some sections of the police and in part by the media. This is reminiscent of events in England and Wales which preceded the increased use of custody in the 1970s. The police (and magistrates) there claimed that they were powerless to deal with juvenile crime and that juvenile offenders were running amok. Neither was true; nor are many of the claims now being made in New Zealand. However, they may create a climate of public opinion which makes it increasingly difficult to resist pressures for change in a more punitive direction.

Observations from the research raise an additional issue about the custodial placement of young people who have been sentenced to prison in the District or High Court[73]. There are two opposing arguments with respect to the custodial provisions for these children and young people. On the one hand, holding them in prison undoubtedly puts them at risk of abuse by older prisoners or, alternatively, requires that they be segregated and confined in relatively unsuitable and isolated conditions. On the other hand, detention in DSW institutions often poses management problems that adversely affect the operation of the institution for staff and other residents. Only a few such cases came within our sample but they exemplify the tensions and problems of both responses.

In each of three High Court cases which we monitored[74], the judge recommended that the young person, as provided under section 142A of the Criminal Justice Act, should be held in a DSW institution until the age of 17 years and that programmes should be provided to ensure that, on release, the young person's chances of reoffending would be minimised. In two cases, the young person was immediately placed in prison and has remained there ever since, despite, in one case, appeals by his youth advocate. The mother of one of these young people also became seriously concerned over the deteriorating mental condition of her son during his prison term and about his prospects on release. She enquired of us why the treatment spoken of by the judge had not been provided. She had expected that, in endorsing the prison sentence for her son, something would be done for him at last.

In the third case, involving a 13 year-old convicted of murder, a placement was made in secure care in a residence and extra staff were employed to provide full surveillance of the boy to ensure that he remained secure and separate from other residents. When we visited this residence, staff were very concerned about the impact on the institution of holding dangerous young people who were very difficult to manage. Their training as residential social workers involved the general care of young people but did not give them any special skills to care for those who were borderline

---

[73] The law provides that, in such cases, the Director-General of Social Welfare and the Secretary for Justice, by virtue of the discretion vested in them under section 142A of the Criminal Justice Act 1985, may hold the young person in a DSW institution until the age of 17 years.

[74] Only two were strictly speaking in the sample.

psychiatric cases or who needed intensive custodial management. They said that the impact on both the staff and other residents was damaging.

There seem to be two issues of concern here in terms of the development of a coherent policy regarding the custody of young people. The first is how the decision to place the young person in a DSW residence or in a prison is taken and whether or not it is possible for the youth advocate to ask for a judicial review of such a decision. There seem to be no clear guidelines on this. The second relates to ensuring that an appropriate placement is possible for all young people in terms of providing public protection, protecting the young person from further harm and providing for a programme that is likely to enhance the young person's wellbeing, or at least respond to any treatment or educational needs. Both DSW residences and prison appear to be unsuitable in some cases.

Enhancing Wellbeing

The starting point in the New Zealand system is to separate out youth justice and care and protection issues: separate co-ordinators, separate procedures and separate courts. Young people's needs and behaviour are not so easily separable, however, and an emphasis on one can mean neglect of the other. It is perhaps self evident, therefore, that if outcomes stress accountability they can only enhance young people's development in an indirect sense (by encouraging them to accept responsibility for their actions). The legislation precludes referral into the youth justice system on welfare grounds, yet seems to expect or encourage discussion **within** the FGC of welfare issues at the same time as it expects or encourages resolutions which emphasise the accountability of young people for their offending. Thus two distinct and, at times, contradictory expectations exist side by side. In our experience welfare issues were, not surprisingly, a secondary consideration. Certainly, we observed cases in which the needs of families and young people were ignored at FGCs and where no 'welfare' type follow-up was provided. We gave examples of this in Chapter 6 (pages 97-99).

In cases where there was a history of abuse, where the family were not prepared to take responsibility for the young person, where the family were unable to control the young person or where the family had a history of being unable to provide adequately for the care of the young person, it would have been appropriate to make a referral for consideration under the care and protection provisions. Yet, such action rarely occurred in our sample.

The legislation also aimed to encourage the strengthening and support of families. If what was envisaged was the provision of resources to families in need by social services and programmes, this has not occurred. We have commented previously on cases in which families were clearly asking for but did not receive help. A particular area of need was support for the family in managing their teenage children and programmes that would provide assistance with parenting skills. Many parents who had been unable to control rebellious teenagers in the past found that life after the FGC was unchanged. In several cases, a referral was made to an overloaded counselling service which was not able to provide any support for some months. In other cases, young people had long waits for vocational and anger management programmes.

Since the inception of the Act, the DSW has abandoned its earlier role of being a social service provider itself in favour of a role as referral agency and funder. The DSW has also moved away from funding many of the earlier programmes which dealt with young people in groups or in situations outside their families and communities. The districts in which the study was based did not have an adequate range of suitable, approved services to which families and their children could be referred. The new emphasis on culturally appropriate services did not appear to be matched by resources for the setting-up and development of iwi and marae programmes. In addition, those operating some of the programmes we visited regarded the complexities of DSW requirements for applications for funds as a barrier to obtaining access to funding. Youth Justice Co-ordinators often relied on Access and Maccess training programmes[75] but, shortly after the

---

[75] Government funded job skills training programmes.

conclusion of our data collection, these were cut by a third in some of the districts in which we were working. One consequence of the paucity of programmes is that those that did exist tended to receive a number of referrals of young offenders and thus to create, yet again, some of the conditions necessary for 'a school for crime'.

At one level, the problem can be said to reside with the failure to develop community-based services. At another level, it can be seen as the result of a lack of legislative emphasis on service provision. In England and Wales, the Children Act 1989 vests local authorities with responsibility for providing a specified range of services. Such an emphasis can be contrasted with the DSW's monitoring role in ensuring the quality of community based services. The failure to empower and fund iwi authorities to provide culturally appropriate services has also created problems in meeting the objectives of the Act.

There is one further point to note here: the tendency for some youngsters to be sent to relatives or programmes some distance from their community and, indeed, on occasions to the Pacific Islands. There seem to be two main reasons for this: pressure by the professionals on families to agree to this (sometimes presented by the police as the 'bottom line') and the lack of good local programmes.

We did observe, however, situations in which families were strengthened and supported by the presence of their whanau or extended family. It is worth noting that in almost all cases families came to the FGC and supported their young people when they appeared in the Youth Court. And on occasions services were provided within iwi for Maori families, although they did so in the main without adequate state funding. Overall, in our view, the provision of adequate and accessible services to the young people in our sample was poor.

Accountability

Most juveniles referred to FGCs or to the Youth Court agreed to perform tasks which were intended to make them accountable for their actions. What we have called 'active penalties' were agreed to by 83% of those involved in non-court referred FGCs and by 89% of those involved in court referred FGCs. If we add 'apologies' to this, the figures become 95% and 94% respectively. Thus nominal dispositions were rare, as were solely welfare-oriented outcomes. More importantly, the vast majority of FGC plans were either either completed fully (58%) or in part (29%).

However, on a few occasions, we observed FGCs in which young people were not held to account for their actions. We provided examples of this in Chapter 6. Particularly with respect to those aged under 14 and possibly with respect to some girls, minor offenders and first offenders, there seemed to be some evidence that the commission of an offence was being used as an excuse to intervene in a perceived 'welfare' or 'parenting' problem. In other words, unlike the situation described in the previous section where needed services were not made available for young offenders, in these instances, young people who had committed first or minor offences were being referred to FGCs in order to secure services. We also provided examples in Chapter 8 of such long delays in the Youth Court before cases were finalised that any accountability must have had a fairly remote connection with the original act.

Time Frames

Most FGCs, while not always occurring within the time limits set down in the Act, were being held and resolved within time frames that made the process meaningful. Undoubtedly, improved checking systems in DSW could eliminate some of the delays but we also recognise the importance allowing sufficient time to ensure that the right people are present and to adequately prepare all the participants. However, we do not think that it is desirable to increase the flexibility in the definition of the time limits by interpreting 'convened' to mean 'setting a time, date and place and notifying those entitled to attend' as opposed to actually holding the FGC. Such an interpretation could potentially license even more extensive delays than we observed and would be, in our view, contrary to the spirit of the Act.

Delays were also created by the fact that, in some cases in the research, the police representative did not object to the recommendations at the time of the FGC but later consideration led the police to disagree. Disagreements may arise for a number of reasons, including the fact that the victims or the police believed that the penalties were inappropriately light.

The Youth Court often performed very poorly with respect to operating within meaningful time frames. The worst delays occurred in cases where the charges were denied. One case in the sample was heard 11 months after the offence and another, nearly a year after the offence, had still not been heard. The reasons for such delays were similar to those which affect the adult courts: delays in gathering evidence, briefing lawyers, arranging appropriate hearing dates for all parties, arranging a hearing before a judge not previously involved and so on. However, the relative rarity of Youth Court fixtures and the small number of judges exacerbate matters. Nor does there appear to be any policy within the court system which gives priority to cases involving juveniles.

The Youth Courts we observed adopted the practice of waiting until all matters could be brought together before determining an outcome. This practice may offer an advantage to the young person in terms of the eventual penalty, but it often resulted in lengthy delays during which nothing was arranged to make the young person accountable for his or her offences. The result was that penalties were imposed many months after the offence.

Finally, the infrequency of sittings of the Youth Court can create problems. In some areas, sittings only occur every four weeks with the result that every remand is for four weeks and every minor hitch automatically extends matters for four weeks.

Protecting Rights

Some of the most hotly debated aspects of the Act have been sections 214 to 232 dealing with rights relating to arrest and questioning. Two main issues have emerged from this debate. The first is the use of the detailed caution which informs young people of their right not to accompany the police officer to the station and their right not to make a statement. The second concerns the requirements for the police to notify the parents about their child's involvement with the police, to allow the young person to consult with a parent or nominated adult prior to questioning, to ensure a nominated adult is present when the young person is questioned and a statement is taken, and to inform the young person of his or her rights to consult a barrister or solicitor and to have a barrister or solicitor present while being questioned.

Police have complained that reciting all the details of the caution set down under section 215 results in refusals by young people to accompany them for questioning and encourages young offenders to treat officers with derision. During the research we found no examples of such behaviour. All the young people in the sample collaborated with the police officer or were arrested. And most police officers in our sample appeared able to operate successfully within this framework although, as the data show (Chapter 3), many did not comply with the provisions on the mistaken understanding that the caution was only necessary when a statement was to be taken.

A major complaint with respect to the caution about making a statement was that it prevented officers from obtaining a confession. Some officers were of the view that having to inform young people of their right to remain silent was inappropriate when a crime had been committed because it could prevent the officer from solving the case by questioning the alleged offender. In effect, this criticism is directed not merely at the Children, Young Persons and Their Families Act 1989 but at a right which has been traditionally been regarded as at the core of common law jurisdictions[76]. The right to silence is mandated by New Zealand's commitment to Article 40 of the UN Convention on

---

[76] For example, the Judges' Rules about the questioning of adult suspects require that a police officer who has made up his or her mind to charge a person with a crime should first caution the person before asking any further questions (Rule 2) and that a person in custody should not be questioned before the usual caution has been first administered (Rule 3). The caution includes the words you are not obliged to say anything unless you wish to do so. Section 20 of the Evidence Act 1908 also confirms the right to silence by placing limits on the admissibility of confessions obtained by violence, threats or other inducements.

the Rights of the Child and is also encompassed in the New Zealand Bill of Rights Act 1990 (section 25(d)).

However, the provisions of the Children, Young Person and Their Families Act 1989 with respect to the cautioning of young people do go further than in the case of adults; in particular, the principle in section 208(h) emphasises the vulnerability of children and young people and their rights *to special protection during any investigation relating to the commission or possible commission of an offence.* Undoubtedly, it is hard to appreciate this vulnerability when faced with a disrespectful child or young person. However, except in one or two very exceptional cases, we do not share the view that the young people we interviewed were hardened criminals, well informed about their rights and determined to make a mockery of the law. Rather we concur with those who drafted the legislation: these young people were generally unaware of their rights and very vulnerable to pressure from authority.

In general, the police attempted to notify the families of the young people who were taken to the police station, but in a number of cases there appeared to be considerable delay before this occurred and questioning proceeded meanwhile. Some police officers appeared to hold the view that it was only necessary to notify families and ensure the presence of an adult when a statement was to be taken for use in evidence and that this was not necessary, therefore, during general preliminary questioning about the young person's involvement in the offence. This is clearly a view at variance with the wording of the statute.

Complaints were frequently made by police officers about the time wasted in attending to these requirements and the difficulty of obtaining an adult's presence. Nevertheless, most officers who attempted to do so were able to obtain a suitable adult within a reasonable time. There were no cases in our sample in which either the arresting officer or the young person informed us that a barrister or solicitor had been present during the interview. Quite the converse: a few young people said that they had asked for a lawyer to be present and that this request was treated dismissively. This again raises the question of the extent to which young people are being systematically informed of their rights.

It could be contended that the police did not report to us the specific difficulties they had experienced with cases in the sample, but we believe this to be unlikely as many were concerned to bring difficulties with the Act to our attention. It could also be contended that, had the police followed the procedures exactly in all cases, there would have been some additional difficulties. We cannot know this, but it seemed to us that almost all the cases were very straightforward, with the young person admitting to the offence almost immediately. The fact that there were only a few cases in the study where charges were denied suggests that the requirement to inform young people of their rights was not a substantial impediment to resolving the issue of guilt (although it is of course possible that problems were avoided by non-compliance with the provisions). At worst, the police suffered inconvenience in spending time contacting parents or finding an adult to be present while a statement was taken. Although we heard many stories, we saw no direct evidence that the police were unable to apprehend young people because of the requirement to advise them of their rights[77].

On the other hand, we are concerned about the extent to which the police are following the procedures set down in the Act and the extent to which there is adequate monitoring of police practice. Cases are rarely tested in court, but there have been several occasions when this has occurred and statements have been ruled inadmissible because of a wrongful arrest or failure by

---

[77] This is not to deny the reality of police difficulties in some instances. It is indeed frustrating to be unable to gather sufficient evidence to resolve a case, especially when the police officer is reasonably certain of the identity of the offenders. Groups of young people can be very difficult. They are prone to run away on the approach of the police and often delight in cop-baiting. Many police officers were seriously concerned for the wellbeing of youngsters who seemed to be unsupervised and to be becoming involved in substance abuse. Not unnaturally, they were concerned when parents did not appear to behave responsibly. Nevertheless, we doubt that any legislation is going to solve these difficulties.

the police to follow appropriate procedures when questioning and taking a statement[78]. This occurred in one case in the study. More generally, there are few procedures which provide for monitoring these sections of the Act and these are not always effective. Not all the arrest cases during the period of the study were reported to the Commissioner of Police. Although the police have developed a checklist for use in juvenile cases, its use is optional. We found that these checklists were rarely completed and placed on the young person's file.

In most cases, however, the young people in our sample were dealt with by means of a warning (with or without informal sanctions) or referred to an FGC and, in these settings, there was no opportunity to check whether or not the police had adhered to the required procedures in explaining rights, questioning and taking statements. Nor did there seem to us to be sufficient safeguards against police misconduct and behaviour which can humiliate and degrade.

To some extent, police officers' failure to comply with the requirements of the Act could be due to a lack of training and experience. But, at times, it seemed too that a lack of commitment to the principles and objectives of the Act on the part of some officers led them to interpret their responsibilities in a manner which was at variance with the Act. Also, at the time of writing strong pressure is being exerted, principally by the police, to moderate the provisions for due process (including those prescribed by the Bill of Rights Act 1990), and legislative amendments about the point at which a caution should be given are under consideration. While statutory clarity could improve practice we have a general concern about the current failure of police to follow statutory procedures and think it possible that any apparent liberalisation of the provisions could lead to increased non-compliance with them.

Young people's rights are also protected through the provision of legal representation. However, most young people in our sample were dealt with without legal advice or representation (because they were dealt with by police warning or direct referral to FGCs). Discretionary decision-making does take place at these points, but these young people miss out on appropriate due process protections. In our research there were no examples of youth advocates becoming involved in non-court cases. For example, there was no opportunity for young people attending non-court referred FGCs to have legal advice about whether or not to admit the charge and the consequences of such an admission. Nor did the young people have access to legal advice in the FGC when they wished to question details in the summary of facts.

Even in those cases where the court ordered the FGC, only 59% of FGCs were attended by youth advocates although, in all cases where charges were laid in court, a youth advocate was appointed. Many of the youth advocates we observed served their clients' interests well. In other cases, however, clients received only a token service from the youth advocate with little effective consultation and representation. Some youth advocates were not well-versed in the Act. Others appeared unaware of the details and background of the case. Others again appeared to be arguing in the interests of justice in general or on behalf of the victim rather than on their client's behalf.

Another important component of due process protections is adherence to rules of procedure at the FGC. This should include obtaining admissions before proceeding (we observed FGCs at which this was done at a fairly late stage of the proceedings), not holding FGCs when the young person is not present, ensuring that only entitled persons are present at the FGC and giving warnings about breaches of confidentiality (a number of parents expressed concerns about this to us).

Participation

As is clear from the information in Chapter 7, one of the major weaknesses of the new system must be its failure to engage young people in the decision-making process. Only a third felt involved

---

[78] For example, *R v Toko*, Sinclair J, 9 April 1991, High Court Auckland T.1/91; *R v Irwin*, Fisher J, 3 Dec 1991, High Court Hamilton T32/91; *Police v Edge*, Young DJ, 29 Dec 1991, District Court Oamaru CRN 1245003903; *Ratten v Edge* (on appeal), Holland J, 10 June 1992, High Court. Another case is worthy of note because, in this instance, the judge held that, although all procedures had not been followed, there had been reasonable compliance: *Crime Appeal* 311/91, Cook P, 19 Sept 1991, Court of Appeal.

in the process (although another 11% said they felt 'partly' involved) and less than a fifth (16%) felt that they had been a party to the decision of the FGC. The level of perceived involvement in the court proceedings was even lower. We made the point earlier (Chapter 7) that this casts doubt on the extent to which the FGC can be regarded as truly successful and speculated on reasons for this continued lack of involvement by young people. It may be that both the family and the professionals do not allow young people to become involved; or it may be that the young people themselves do not feel able to become involved. Many jurisdictions throughout the world have tried in different ways to increase the involvement of young people in the decision-making process and all that we can record here is that these have been no more successful than attempts in New Zealand. Indeed it could be argued that even these relatively low figures for young people's involvement reflect some progress. It may be that we have to accept that many young people have very little to say about their offending and what response would be appropriate, at least in the presence of adults who are unknown to them, and that, therefore, we cannot expect them to participate more actively whatever the forum. The problem may lie not in the system's response to young people, but in our unrealistic expectations of them. Alternatively, as we suggested in Chapter 7, more fundamental changes may need to occur in adults' and professionals' attitudes towards accepting that young people **should** have a voice in what should happen to them.

The involvement of parents in FGCs, on the other hand, was considerable. In contrast to young people, two thirds of the parents said that they felt involved in the decision-making process and nearly two thirds (62%) felt that they had been a party to the decision. Thus the notion of 'holding parents responsible for their children's offending', which has often resulted in penalising or blaming parents in overseas jurisdictions, has been given a new and constructive (in both senses) meaning. These results contradict the pessimism often expressed prior to the Act about the impossibility of effectively and meaningfully involving dysfunctional families in FGCs. We certainly observed some families which had not been functioning very effectively, but almost always extended family or community members who could provide support were able to be found. There were certainly examples of successful outcomes in situations where the families could initially have easily been dismissed as dysfunctional.

On the other hand, a third of the families and most of the young people remained, in their own eyes, uninvolved. The formality of the Youth Court, in particular its size, the number of strangers present, the formal seating arrangements, the use of a dock and the strict procedural rules, all inhibited the participation of families and young people in the court process and made it difficult for them to comprehend what was happening. Families or young people only participated in the proceedings when permission was granted after a request by the youth advocate or, at times, at the invitation of the judge. While a few judges made the proceedings as informal as possible and involved the family in discussion, such practice was unusual and was not facilitated by the atmosphere and physical lay-out of most of the courtrooms. As well as these barriers to involvement, legalistic communications from the court, ineffective appointment systems, long delays between hearings, changes in the youth advocate and routine appearances which did little to take the case forward all helped to distance families and young people from the court process.

Information and understanding are a precondition of effective participation. Many families were unprepared for what would happen and puzzlement over both the FGC and the court process reflected the absence of adequate information about and preparation for what would happen during the proceedings. The way in which the FGC and court processes are managed also plays an important part in determining whether or not families and young people are effectively involved. And effective participation does not automatically lead to effective involvement in decisions. Changes in practice with respect to both FGCs and the Youth Court would contribute to improvements in both participation in the proceedings and involvement in the decisions.

Victims' Involvement

Victims simply by their presence participate more in this system than they have done traditionally. However, only about half of the FGCs in our sample had victims or victims' representatives present.

We commented in Chapter 6 on potential reasons for this: in particular, the failure to notify victims about the FGC or to arrange the FGC at a time which was suitable for them. For many victims, the results of FGCs were positive; they received apologies and/or reparation for damage and felt better about the matter as a result of participating in the FGC. But we also commented in Chapter 7 on the relatively high proportion of victims (about a third) who said that they felt worse as a result of attending the FGC. Sometimes this was because they felt unable to express themselves adequately. At other times, they felt that families sided with young offenders and excused their behaviour. A few expressed a fear of reprisals and consequently were constrained in what they were prepared to say. One case of serious injury was dealt with in a large marae-based FGC in which most of the proceedings were conducted in Maori. The Pakeha relatives of the seriously injured victim felt very alienated and hurt by the process which seemed to them to exclude them. They were also distressed to find that most of the time was spent considering the young person and his family rather than their needs.

We have also commented previously (Chapter 7) on the relatively low level of satisfaction victims expressed about outcomes. In part, these views were due to inadequate preparation of victims (and the other participants) about what to expect at the FGC and unrealistic expectations about outcomes, especially with respect to reparation. Arguably these concerns could be remedied by improved practice. But they also raise more fundamental issues about victims' involvement.

Victims' involvement in FGCs needs to be approached with considerable care. Victims require time to think through the possible consequences of meeting the offender and his or her family and in serious cases (such as rape, serious physical injury and arson) to explore (with the help of the YJC or a social worker) the best way they can contribute to the process and what type of contribution they might wish to make. Some victims prefer not to be part of the decision-making but are prepared to explain to the offender the impact the offence has had on their life (although their views can change during a meeting). Others prefer not to meet the offender but would still like to have their views represented.

Victim supporters, in most of the cases in which we attended FGCs, were family members or friends who saw their role as principally supportive rather than involving advocacy. However, the development of Victim Support groups has started to change this in some areas. Although the results were often positive in providing victims with support and advice, there are dangers when the Victim Support person encourages the victim to adopt an adversarial posture in the FGC or acts as the victim's representative to ensure that the victim's rights are dealt with and that reparation is made. When this occurs, other processes, such as the efforts of the family and the young person to develop a new method of working together to prevent reoffending, can be pushed into the background. There is also a danger that publicity from Victim Support can encourage victims to have unrealistic expectations about the likelihood of receiving reparation. When this happens victims may be subsequently disappointed by the FGC outcome in their particular case and hence may feel a further sense of grievance. Thus the role of Victim Support groups and the involvement in FGCs of victims' representatives as opposed to victims' supporters needs, considerable thought. We are of the view that it is appropriate for the victim to have someone at the FGC to act as a supporter, but that representation of victim interests is already provided for through the presence of the police officer.

Victims' satisfaction with the FGC not only depends on the way the FGC is managed, but also, in part, on the general social climate, the amount and kind of information which the police supply to them and the support services available in the community for them. Public outrage over supposedly rising and uncontrollable violence, widespread reports of 'so-called' increasing juvenile crime and a presentation in the media of youngsters who are out of control and who can not be dealt with by the police are not helpful in achieving effective mediation between victims and young people and their families. Well informed and well supported victims are more likely to respond positively to FGC processes. The police, community-based social services and DSW all have a responsibility in this area.

Consensus Decision-making

Agreed outcomes should satisfy participants more than enforced outcomes and most FGC outcomes are 'agreed' outcomes: 95% in our sample and 94% nationally (Maxwell and Robertson, 1991). Thus in these terms, participants at FGCs should be highly satisfied. That this was not always so raises two main points. First, victims were the least satisfied with the outcome: satisfaction was reported by just over half of all victims who attended an FGC (53%). And yet those victims who attended the FGC were supposedly parties to an 'agreed' outcome. In some senses, then, it appears that victims' agreement is being coerced. Secondly, a high proportion of police, YJCs, parents and young people expressed satisfaction: 91%, 86%, 85% and 84% respectively. As we commented above, however, it is difficult to know whether families and young people 'truly' agreed with the decisions or felt 'truly' satisfied with the outcomes. The qualitative data from the research suggest that, on many occasions, they did, but that on other occasions they felt coerced to 'agree' to decisions which in essence had been made by the professionals.

Cultural Appropriateness

As we outlined in Chapter 1, the Act attempts to create a youth justice system which is culturally appropriate. A key issue here is the extent to which Western systems of criminal justice can accommodate elements of an indigenous approach. To be effectively responsive to indigenous needs, there probably has to be a different process, a different type of spirit and underlying philosophy and, potentially, different outcomes from those traditionally available in criminal justice contexts. In each of these respects, practice showed both limitations and successes.

The FGC is an attempt to provide the opportunity for alternative cultural practices, in particular a Maori approach, to decision-making about justice issues. But, as we have seen, it has often failed to respond to the spirit of Maori or to enable outcomes to be reached which are in accordance with Maori philosophies and values. At times, FGCs can and do transcend tokenism and embody a Maori kaupapa, but not often. Furthermore, money has not yet been allocated to iwi authorities in sufficient amounts to allow them to develop a full range of appropriate services and, hence, for a truly cultural approach to be taken.

The Youth Court in particular found it difficult to accommodate Maori process and etiquette. We pointed previously to a number of situations where whanau wanted to be involved in the resolution of cases affecting their kin and yet setting aside time for receiving their submissions and, more importantly, giving real weight to them seemed problematic to the court.

The courtroom rituals that are likely to have the most impact on young people will be those that are most meaningful in terms of the cultural background of the offender. Thus, for Maori families, a court process which blends Maori and Western traditions would seem not only consistent with the objectives of the Act but also more likely to be effective in reinforcing the message of the court than a traditional Western approach. This is especially true given the existence of a Maori protocol, widely understood within Maoridom, for dealing with disputes which involves the expression of remorse, encompasses issues of reparation and allows decisions to be reached that settle the dispute. This protocol includes the participation of the principal parties to the dispute in the proceedings.

An acceptance of the greater costs of the court process in these cases could be justified on the grounds that the outcomes are likely to be better. But there is another issue here: the right of indigenous people to be dealt with in terms of their own cultural traditions and values. And there has been only limited acceptance of the idea that outcomes should stress the restoration of social imbalance by the reintegration of offenders into the social group which can then collectively address the issue of reparation to the victim. Nor has there been any discussion at all in this context of how paying one's penalty might be given a cultural meaning and significance.

In short, our view, and that of many of the Maori and Pacific Island participants in this study, is that the process (and hence its spirit and outcomes) remained largely Pakeha and unresponsive to cultural differences. One particular point to note is that only one lay advocate was appointed to the Youth Court cases we observed during the whole of the research period and only nine lay advocates were appointed throughout the whole of New Zealand during 1991.[79]

However, it is also our view, and that of many of the Maori and Pacific Island participants in the study, that there is at least the **potential** for FGCs to be more able to cope with cultural diversity than other types of tribunals. This is best summed up in the words of the Maori researchers involved in the project:

> *We feel that the Act for the most part is an excellent piece of legislation which promises exciting possibilities for the future. When the processes outlined in the Act were observed, Maori families were indeed empowered and able to take an active part in decisions concerning their young people. It is not difficult to see the beneficial influences that the Act may eventually exert on wider Maori, Polynesian and Pakeha society. Maori society could gain immensely from legislation that acknowledges and strengthens the hapu and tribal structures and their place in decisions regarding the wellbeing of young people and that provides them with an opportunity to contribute to any reparation and to support those offended against. The same scenario would apply to Pacific Island peoples. Pakeha society would also benefit from a process which acknowledges the family and gives redress to victims.*

Practice Difficulties in FGCs in Meeting Objectives

The material in Chapters 6 and 7 shows that there have been many difficulties in developing effective practice in arranging and following-up FGCs and many of these difficulties inevitably impinge on the adequacy of the preparation of participants and their motivation and ability to participate.

Some of these difficulties stem from anomalies relating to the position of the YJC. While there may be advantages for the YJC in having limited managerial responsibility there are disadvantages too. For example, although the YJC has statutory responsibility for managing the procedures relating to youth justice, he or she has no powers with respect to staff, including the social workers who may have made the specific arrangements for an FGC. Nor do they have control over the financial arrangements relating to FGCs; these are the responsiblity of managers whose primary experience may be in other fields and who may not be fully conversant with youth justice principles and practice.

The placement of YJCs in the social service section of DSW (now the Children and Young Persons Service) with its prevailing philosophy of welfare has created further difficulties over expectations. Further, as members of the DSW, it is not easy for them to be perceived as independent intermediaries between social workers, family members and the police. Families often perceived them as part of DSW and did not distinguish them from social workers.

Difficulties have also arisen in offices which operate a generic model of social work requiring all social workers to work on cases of all types. As well as creating problems of lines of responsibility in the youth justice area, there are conflicting priorities, with most offices assigning higher priorities to care and protection cases.

Developing a quality service with well trained and knowledgeable staff in a department which has frequently been restructured over recent years and thus has many recently recruited staff who need training in new operational patterns also creates difficulties. All these factors inhibit effective monitoring of staff and the development of good standard procedures.

Specific problems which were identified with the FGC process included the failure to convene some FGCs, to provide adequate notice of FGCs to participants, to ensure that the right people were present, to arrange a venue at which both families and victims felt comfortable and to prepare

---

[79] Unpublished Justice Department statistics.

participants adequately.[80] The difficulties we noted occurred too often to be disregarded as the inevitable mistakes and inefficiencies of individuals. They can be attributed in part to the structural problems already described and, perhaps, in part to a lack of training. In several districts, differing perspectives among those involved, either within the DSW or between DSW and the enforcement agency, contributed to the difficulties. Moreover, as with the police, a commitment to the principles and objectives of the Act is not shared by all the professionals in DSW who are responsible for its implementation.

Inherent Contradictions

It is apparent from this review that the practice of youth justice in New Zealand replicates many of the concerns already expressed overseas about the models from which it has been derived. It should also be apparent that there are aspects of some of these models which are in conflict with others. Therefore, the New Zealand system can serve as a case study of the ways in which potentially contradictory approaches interact.

Elements of both 'welfare' and 'justice' approaches have been combined in a single system, but in a manner where the potential for conflict remains. For example, the Act specifies that *criminal proceedings should not be instituted ... solely in order ... to advance welfare needs* (section 208); but it also *provides* that the court, in sentencing, shall *have regard to ... the personal history, social circumstances and personal characteristics of the young person* (section 284). While this has been interpreted as being designed to avoid increases in sanctions on the grounds of welfare needs, mitigation of tariffs is seen as possible and, in principle, the Act does not rule out the possibility of movement either upwards or downwards depending on the young person's background. Equally the objectives of achieving accountability and using least restrictive sanctions are **potentially** at odds with the enhancement of the young person's wellbeing. Measures designed to achieve accountability are generally different from those required to meet the young persons' welfare needs. The conflict between 'welfare' and 'justice' is not, therefore, simply a conflict about the **amount** of intervention but also about the **type** of intervention and about the **criteria** on which the intervention should be based.

The New Zealand system has tried to resolve some of these potential conflicts by creating separate systems to deliver 'welfare' and 'justice': a 'care and protection' system and a 'youth justice' system. It was expected that welfare concerns would be primarily met through the 'care and protection' procedures. Thus it is always open for YJCs and police to refer young people who have offended into this jurisdiction. This rarely happened during our research, despite the existence of young people and families who were clearly in need of help and support. Rather there was an expectation that YJCs would ensure that the young person's welfare needs were met by including provision for access to services in FGC plans. But there were insufficient community services available which could respond to the young person's needs either inside or outside of the youth justice context.

Thus, in practice, the way in which the tension between 'welfare' and 'justice' is resolved in the New Zealand youth justice system is primarily to stress accountability at the expense of welfare. By far the majority of FGC and court outcomes reflect responses to the young person's offence(s) rather than to his or her welfare needs. To the extent that this is what the legislation intended to be the **primary** focus, it can be concluded that the system is working well. However, it is not clear from the Act that such a view is justified; there is no explicit or implicit ordering of the objectives of the Act.

The objective of holding young people accountable for their actions is further constrained by the participation of victims, young people and families in a consensus decision-making model.

---

[80] In addition to these problems which may affect participation, we also noted that there were often problems in obtaining the co-operation of other professionals in arranging a suitable time and place, preparing adequate court reports, following up cases where the Department had undertaken to supply services, checking on task completion, dealing adequately and expeditiously with complaints and adequately financing FGC plans. These problems may also affect participation indirectly through their impact on the general image of the Department in the community.

Involvement of both victims and families in consensus decision-making results in individualised outcomes[81], because their varied views on what is appropriate are likely to be at odds with notions of proportionality, equality and frugality[82]. Furthermore, inevitably and almost invariably in practice, some interests are subsumed by others. For example, the primary arena for meeting offenders' needs is the FGC; this aims to achieve both welfare and diversion goals. It is also the primary arena for protecting victims' interests; this reflects the goal of mediation and possibly the goal of crime control. Research overseas (for example, Marshall and Merry, 1990) suggests that when reparation and diversion are sought within the one forum, the victim almost invariably loses out. They argue that whatever aims are subscribed to in practice, in reality diversion becomes the over-riding objective and all other goals become subordinate to it. Thus the offenders' interests are promoted and the victims' interests are neglected. It is our view that this has occurred in the New Zealand system of youth justice too. Tension has been created by expecting diverse interests to be met in a single forum without one or the other being compromised. Even if we enlarged victims' rights to determine process (for example, by allowing victims rather than families to determine the time and venue of the FGC) and victims' rights to determine outcomes (victims' demands may conflict not only with offenders' wellbeing but also with tariff considerations such as proportionality), it would only serve to increase the tensions.

But perhaps the question of greatest concern is 'whose interests are being served?' within the FGC. We have already pointed to tensions between offenders' and victims' interests and we made the point earlier that, at least in theory, FGCs have been set up primarily with offenders in mind, in contrast with many overseas experiments in which victims seem to be the primary focus. Thus it is the offender's family who, at least in theory, determine the place and time of the FGC, who is to be invited to attend the FGC (apart from those who have the right to attend) and the procedures to be used in the FGC. This, of course, is not the reality. Professionals have not yet in most cases handed over these decisions to families and have thus retained control over the process.

There is a deeper point to be made here too. In the end, it is the **State's** interests which are being served. It is a concern about the possibility of increased State control which makes overseas advocates of victim mediation cynical about the real significance of FGCs as a true form of consensus decision-making involving victims (Marshall, 1992, personal communication). It cannot be denied that FGCs are part and parcel of the State's system of social control. Inasmuch as FGCs have increased the number of young people on whom some sanction is imposed, they have expanded the system of social control. And by involving families as well as young people, it could be said that FGCs extend social control to families as well as young people because the sanctions are 'imposed' with their 'agreement'. Families may believe that they have to arrive at a decision which satisfies the victim and the enforcement agency. This may mean that they pitch their 'offer' at a higher level than either the victim or the enforcement agency would have accepted and considerably higher than a court would have imposed, even to the extent of offering more than they can realistically cope with because they fear that 'something worse' will happen if an agreement is not reached. Furthermore, it is difficult to realise family empowerment within a process of mediation in which the State is essentially one of the parties. However, it can be argued that the potentially negative effects of State coercion are **minimised** by participatory decision-making. Social learning theory demonstrates that difficult goals are more likely to be attained when the learner has control over the process and is involved in decisions about goals (Bandura, 1977).

In the same vein, some Maori have suggested that inevitably the Pakeha criminal justice system is oppressive of Maori and that oppression will only end when Maori control their own systems of

---

[81] It is also of interest to note that the Act departs from proportionality, equality and frugality through section 284 which sanctions individualised decision-making by judges by setting out factors for which there should be regard in determining a sentence.

[82] It has been argued that notions of equality and proportionality of outcomes based on an objective scale of tariffs conflict with principles of 'equality' and 'proportionality' of outcomes for different individuals in different circumstances and hence that apparently individualised decisions are more 'equal' because they take into account personal and social factors. But we believe this idea is inherently problematic as it is impossible to imagine how one could arrive at an assessment of the similarity or difference of decisions made about different offenders which take into account personal circumstances.

justice (Jackson, 1991). Alternatively, and this is the position taken by the Maori researchers, the attempt to encourage the use of Maori process in resolving issues can strengthen the position of whanau, hapu and iwi by increasing their involvement in the process.

As we pointed out earlier, aspects of both justice and crime control are incorporated in the New Zealand system, as in other jurisdictions. The offender's previous offence history affects the decision-making of professionals at all points in the system. And in practice, crime control concerns lead to negative attitudes among professionals who blame the Act for failing to deal with serious and persistent offenders because they expect it to stop crime. In fact, the Act works at least as well for serious and persistent offenders as for minor and first offenders in terms of holding them accountable for their offences; in addition, it gives serious and persistent offenders protection through due process and enables their families to participate in decisions, even though those decisions may involve custodial penalties. The new youth justice system has been designed to deal justly with young offenders. It must, therefore, be measured by its success in dealing justly with young offenders rather than by its success in dealing with other agendas: the prevention of reoffending or the rehabilitation of the offender. The fact that the New Zealand system **incorporates** elements intended to prevent reoffending and aid rehabilitation does not mean that it should be judged by these criteria.

One final point before concluding: the very fact that the Act embodies diverse objectives enables practice to vary in different geographical areas. Different objectives can be given different emphases. We referred in earlier chapters to the variation between the research areas in arrest rates, in the characteristics of those referred to FGCs, in the proportion of referrals to FGCs and in Youth Court practices. Though some of this can be explained by the different levels of serious crime in the five areas, this does not explain all the variance. Area was an influential variable in its own right. Thus juvenile offenders living in some areas had a greater chance of being arrested, of being referred to FGCs and of being subject to a court order than juvenile offenders living in other areas even when they had committed similar offences. For example, the arrest rates in this study varied from a low of 6% to highs of 14% and 19% and in all three of these areas there was a relatively equal amount of more serious offending. It was clear that the types of offences which led to an arrest differed widely from one area to another; policies were not operating uniformly. A further example was the marked regional variation in the rates of referral to an FGC in various areas: around half in one area but only 14% in another. Variability was also apparent in some areas, but not others, in the relatively high proportion of offenders in the FGC sample (compared to the total sample of offenders) who were girls, first offenders, minor offenders and those aged under 14. It is not unusual for such offenders to be more likely to be involved in diversion programmes than in court appearances, especially where the referral is on 'welfare' rather than offence considerations (see, for example, Alder, 1984). The greater involvement of these groups in some areas may, therefore, have resulted from the different approaches in these areas to the purpose of FGCs. It also reflects the fact that there were different thresholds in the different areas about what was a 'serious enough' offence to warrant an FGC. The practice of youth justice in New Zealand, therefore, has a distinctly local flavour.

Conclusions

Implicit in these comments about the extent to which practice has met the principles and objectives in the Children, Young Persons and Their Families Act 1989 is an awareness of the power of all old, entrenched and dominant systems to resist fundamental re-shaping by a young, new and emerging system. Resistance by those who actually have to implement new legislation at grass roots level is not unusual. In previous chapters, for example, we referred to front-line police officers using their power to arrest on occasions to ensure that the youth appeared in court and to social workers who found it difficult to give their decision-making power over to families and so continued to make decisions for them. In many respects, practice was uneven and idiosyncratic in different areas; police practices with respect to arrest and referral to FGC varied, DSW practices in arranging and holding FGCs varied, and court practice in the use of court orders, particularly with respect to discharges and withdrawals, varied. Our research also indicated a failure to comply with statutory obligations: for example, on the part of the police with respect to cautioning and awaiting the presence of an adult before questioning a young person; on the part of DSW staff in allowing social workers to be present at most FGCs and in failing to meet statutory time frames for FGCs; and, on the part of the Youth Court in failing to explain proceedings to parents and young people and encouraging their participation. In the long run, whether or not the new system generally, and FGCs in particular, 'work' will depend on the willingness of those in charge of the process to give up their authority and to provide sufficient resources for families and cultural groups to find alternative solutions. To date, there has been little progress in either of these directions.

We have identified much that is positive and novel about the New Zealand system of youth justice. There is no doubt that diversion from court and decarceration were primary aims. Both have been achieved. Only 10% of the juvenile offenders in our sample appeared in the Youth Court and we speculated earlier in this chapter that even this low figure could be reduced further. Overall, only 5% of the juveniles in our sample were subject to court orders and less than 2% were subject to residential or custodial orders. At the same time, young people are being held accountable for their offending through the imposition of sanctions.

Families are participating in the processes of decision-making and are taking responsibility for their young people in most instances. Extended families are also becoming involved in the continuing care of their kin as an alternative to foster care and institutions. Greater acknowledgement is being given to the customs of different cultural groups and in some instances alternative methods of resolution through the use of traditional processes have been adopted. Victims are also involved in the process to a greater extent than previously and than in other jurisdictions.

The new system has not, however, avoided all the difficulties which inevitably arise when attempting to reconcile conflicting objectives and which the researchers would have predicted given experience elsewhere; it was unrealistic to expect otherwise. Nor has the new system fully resolved the issues that surround the attempt to incorporate an indigenous model of justice within a Western system. There are a number of options for dealing with these conflicts: to accept the tensions as an inevitable feature of a system which has multiple objectives; to attempt to achieve greater separation of objectives; to prioritise objectives; or to limit them. These are not necessarily alternatives. For example, it would be possible to increase the separation of welfare and justice, to prioritise offenders' needs over victims' needs (or vice versa) and cultural diversity over standardised procedures, and to accept the inevitability of tensions between empowerment and social control.

Further, there are five areas of practice of considerable concern to us: the tendency for professionals to take over and thereby both distort and undermine the FGC process; the vulnerability of families to this through a lack of information on both the process and the possibilities; inadequate protection of the rights of young people at all stages of the proceedings; the failure to ensure that victims are invited, given adequate notice of meetings and informed about what might happen; and the lack of resources and support services to meet the needs of both families and young people which can undermine FGC decisions. However, it is early days. This research was carried out less than one year after the implementation of the Children, Young Persons and their Families Act. The approach was new and radical. We must wait and see.

REFERENCES

Alder, C (1984). Gender Bias in Juvenile Diversion. *Crime and Delinquency*, 30: 400.

Asquith, S (1983). *Children and Justice.* Edinburgh University Press, Edinburgh.

Auckland District Law Society (1991). Report of the Auckland District Law Society. Unpublished report. Auckland.

Bandura, A (1977). *Social Learning Theory.* Prentice-Hall, Englewood Cliffs, New Jersey.

Bottoms, A (1977). Reflections on the Renaissance of Dangerousness. *Howard Journal*, 16: 70.

Bottoms, A, Brown, P, McWilliams, B, McWilliams, W, Nellis, M in collaboration with Pratt, J (1990). *Intermediate Treatment and Juvenile Justice.* HMSO, London.

Braithwaite, J (1988). *Crime, Stigma and Reintegration.* Cambridge University Press, Cambridge.

Carlen, P (1976). *Magistrates' Justice.* Martin Robertson, London.

Cairns, T (1991). Whangai. In Maxwell, G, Hassall, I and Robertson, J. *Toward a Child and Family Policy for New Zealand.* Office of the Commissioner for Children, Wellington.

Clarke, J (1985). Whose Justice? The Politics of Juvenile Control. *International Journal of the Sociology of Law*, 13: 407.

Coates, R and Gehm, J (1989). An Empirical Assessment. In Wright, M and Galaway, B (eds) *Mediation and Criminal Justice: Victims, Offenders and Community.* Sage, London.

Cody, J (1990). Devolution, Disengagement and Control in the Statutory Social Services. In McKinlay P. (ed) *Redistribution of Power? Devolution in New Zealand.* Victoria University Press, Wellington.

Davis, G, Boncherat, J, Watson, D, and Thatcher, A (1987). *A Preliminary Study of Victim Offender Mediation and Reparation Schemes in England and Wales.* Research and Planning Unit Paper 42. Home Office, London.

Department of Health and Social Services (1981). *Offending by Young People: A Survey of Recent Trends.* DHSS, London.

Department of Social Welfare (1989). *Youth Justice Handbook.* Department of Social Welfare, Wellington.

Department of Statistics (1991). *Justice 1990.* Department of Statistics, Wellington.

Ditchfield, J (1976). *Police Cautioning in England and Wales.* Home Office Research Study No. 37. HMSO, London.

Doolan, M (1988). *From Welfare to Justice: An Overseas Study Tour Report.* Department of Social Welfare, Wellington.

Doolan, M (1991). Youth Justice: Legislation and Practice. Unpublished address to the National Conference of Youth Justice Coordinators.

Ellis, R and Whittington, D (1983). *New Directions in Social Skill Training.* Croom Helm, London.

Ericson, R and Baranek, P (1982). *The Ordering of Justice: A Study of Accused Persons as Dependants in the Criminal Process.* University of Toronto Press, Toronto.

Farrington, D (1984). England and Wales. In Klein M (ed) *Western Systems of Juvenile Justice.* Sage, Beverly Hills, Ca.

Farrington, D and Bennett, T (1981). Police Cautioning of Juveniles in London. *British Journal of Criminology*, 21: 123.

Farrington, D, Ohlin, L, and Wilson, J (1988). *Understanding and Controlling Crime: Toward a New Research Strategy.* Springer-Verlag, London.

Faust, P and Brantingham, P (1974). *Juvenile Justice Philosophy*. West Publishing Co, St Paul, Minnesota.

Fergusson, D. Horwood, L and Lynskey, M (1992). Ethnicity and Bias in Police Contact Statistics. Unpublished manuscript.

Fisher, C and Mawby, R (1982). Juvenile Delinquency and Police Discretion in an Inner City Area. *British Journal of Criminology*, 22: 63.

Fulcher, Leon (1991). The Role of the Support Services in Caring for Children in Families. In Maxwell, Gabrielle M et al (eds) *Toward a Child and Family Policy for New Zealand*. Office of the Commissioner for Children, Wellington.

Gale, F, Bailey-Harris, R and Wundersitz, J (1990). *Aboriginal Youth and the Criminal Justice System: the Injustice of Justice?* Cambridge University Press, Melbourne.

Garfinkel, H (1956). Conditions of Successful Degradation Ceremonies. *American Journal of Sociology*, 61: 420.

Harris, D (1985). Toward Just Welfare. *British Journal of Criminology*, 25: 31.

Hassall, I and Maxwell, G (1990). The Family Group Conference. In Maxwell, G (ed) *An Appraisal of the First Year of the Children, Young Persons and Their Families Act 1989*. Office of the Commissioner for Children, Wellington.

Home Office (1990). *Criminal Statistics, England and Wales, 1989*. HMSO, London.

Home Office (1988). *Report of the Inquiry into Child Abuse in Cleveland 1987*. HMSO, London.

Hough, M and Mayhew, P (1983). *The British Crime Survey*. Home Office Research Study No. 76. HMSO, London.

Hough, M and Mayhew, P (1985). *Taking Account of Crime: Key Findings from the 1984 British Crime Survey*. Home Office Research Study No. 85. HMSO, London.

Hudson, B (1987). *Justice Through Punishment*. Macmillan, London.

Hutton, N and Young, W (1989). The Provision of Assistance for Victims of Crime in New Zealand. Unpublished paper. Institute of Criminology, Victoria University of Wellington, Wellington.

Interdepartmental Committee on Population Policy Guidelines (1990). *The Human Face of New Zealand: A Context for Population Policy into the Twenty-first Century*. Department of Statistics, Wellington.

Jackson, M (1988). *The Maori and the Criminal Justice System, Part II*. Department of Justice, Wellington.

Jackson, M (1991). Criminal Justice for Maori. Unpublished lecture to students. Institute of Criminology, Victoria University of Wellington, Wellington.

Klein, M (1979). Deinstitutionalisation and Diversion of Juvenile Offenders: A Litany of Impediments. In Morris, N and Torry, M (eds) *Crime and Justice: An Annual Review of the Research, V1*. Chicago University Press, Chicago.

Klein, M (1984). *Western Systems of Juvenile Justice*. Sage, Beverly Hills.

Koehler, M (1988). New Initiatives in Sentencing and Corrections: Responding to Victim and Community Interests in the Context of Reparative Justice. Unpublished conference paper, Society for the Reform of the Criminal Law, Ottawa.

Landau, S (1981). Juveniles and the Police. *British Journal of Criminology*, 21: 27.

Landau, S and Nathan, G (1983). Selecting Delinquents for Cautioning in the London Metropolitan Area. *British Journal of Criminology*, 23: 128.

Laycock, G and Tarling, R (1984). *Police Force Cautioning: Policy and Practice in Cautioning by the Police: a Consultative Document*. Home Office, London.

Lemert, E (1971). *Instead of Court: Diversion in Juvenile Justice.* National Institute of Mental Health, Chevy Chase, Maryland.

Lemert, E (1981). Diversion in Juvenile Justice: What Hath Been Wrought. *Journal of Research in Crime and Delinquency*, 18: 34.

Levine, M and Wyn, H (1991). *Orders of the Youth Court and the Work of Youth Justice Co-ordinators.* Department of Social Welfare, Wellington.

Lovell, R and Norris, M (1990). *One in Four: Offending from Age Ten to Twenty-four in a Cohort of New Zealand Males.* Study of Social Adjustment: Research Report, No. 8. Department of Social Welfare, Wellington.

Marshall, T (1985). *Alternatives to Criminal Courts.* Gower, Aldershot.

Marshall, T and Merry, S (1990). *Crime and Accountability: Victim/offender Mediation in Practice.* HMSO, London.

Marshall, T and Walpole, M (1985). *Bringing People Together: Mediation and Reparation Projects in Great Britain.* Research and Planning Unit Paper 33. Home Office, London.

Martin, F, Fox, S and Murray, K (1981). *Children out of Court.* Scottish Academic Press, Edinburgh.

Martinson, R (1974). What works? *Public Interest*, 35: 22.

Matza, D (1964). *Delinquency and Drift.* Wiley, New York.

Maxwell, G (ed) (1991). *An Appraisal of the First Year of the Children, Young Persons and Their Families Act 1989.* Office of the Commissioner for Children, Wellington.

Maxwell, G and Morris, A (1991). Juvenile Crime and the Children, Young Persons and Their Families Act 1989. In Maxwell, G (ed) *An Appraisal of the First Year of the Children, Young Persons and Their Families Act 1989.* Office of the Commissioner for Children, Wellington.

Maxwell, G and Robertson, J (1991). Statistics on the First Year of the Children, Young Persons and their Families Act 1989. In Maxwell, G (ed) *An Appraisal of the First Year of the Children, Young Persons and Their Families Act 1989.* Office of the Commissioner of Children, Wellington.

Merry, S (1989). Myth and Practice in the Mediation Process. In Wright, M & Galaway, B (eds) *Mediation and Criminal Justice: Victims, Offenders and Community.* Sage, London.

Ministerial Advisory Committee on a Maori Perspective for the Department of Social Welfare (1986). *Puao-te-ata-tu: (Daybreak). The Report of the Ministerial Advisory Committee on a Maori Perspective for the Department of Social Welfare.* Department of Social Welfare, Wellington.

Morgan, J (1984). Unpublished internal reports on police files supplied by Inspector D Drummond, Police Headquarters, Wellington.

Morris, A (1978). Diversion of Juvenile Offenders from the Criminal Justice System. In Tutt, N (ed) *Alternative Strategies for Coping with Crime.* Macmillan, London.

Morris, A (1983). Legal Representation and Justice. In Morris, A and Giller, H (eds) *Providing Criminal Justice for Children.* Edward Arnold, London.

Morris, A and Giller, H (1977). The Juvenile Court – the Client's Perspective. *Criminal Law Review*, 198.

Morris, A, Giller, H, Szwed, E & Geach, H (1980). *Justice for Children.* Macmillan, London.

Morris, A and McIsaac, M (1978). *Juvenile Justice?* Heinemann, London.

Morris, A and Maxwell, G (1991). Juvenile Justice in New Zealand: a New Paradigm. *Australian and New Zealand Journal of Criminology* (in press).

Morris, A and Young, W (1987). *Juvenile Justice in New Zealand: Policy and Practice.* Study Series 1. Institute of Criminology, Victoria University of Wellington, Wellington.

Mott, J (1983). Police Decisions for Dealing with Juvenile Offenders. *British Journal of Criminology*, 23: 249.

Naffine, N, Wundersitz, J and Gale, F (1990). Back to Justice for Juveniles: The Rhetoric and Reality of Law Reform. *Australian and New Zealand Journal of Criminology*, 23: 192.

New Zealand Police (1991). *General Instructions*. New Zealand Police, Wellington, New Zealand.

New Zealand Police (1983-1989). *Digest of Statistics*. New Zealand Police, Wellington.

New Zealand Department of Statistics (1976, 1981, 1986). *Census of Population*. Department of Statistics, Wellington.

O'Connor, I and Sweetapple, P (1988). *Children in Justice*. Longman, Cheshire.

Parker, H, Casburn, M and Turnbull, D (1981). *Receiving Juvenile Justice*. Basil Blackwell, Oxford.

Paterson, K and Harvey, M (1991). *Organisation and Operation of Care and Protection Family Group Conferences*. Department of Social Welfare, Wellington.

Pilalis, J, Mamea, T, and Opai, S (1988). *Dangerous Situations: The Report of the Independent Inquiry Team Reporting on the Circumstances of the Death of a Child*. Department of Social Welfare, Wellington.

Police Complaints Authority (1991). Report on Complaint by Mr John Slavich into Circumstances of Discharge of Jason Irwin from Charge of Murder of Steven Slavich. Ref: 91/49 Police Complaints Authority, Wellington.

Polk, K (1987). When Less Means More: an Analysis of Destructuring in Criminal Justice. *Crime and Delinquency*, 33: 358.

Platt, A (1969). *The Child Savers*. University Press, Chicago.

Pratt, John (1987). Law and Order Politics in New Zealand 1986: A Comparison with the United Kingdom 1974-79. *International Journal of the Sociology of Law*, 16: 103.

Pratt, John (1991). Citizenship, Colonisation and Criminal Justice. *International Journal of the Sociology of Law*, 19: 293.

Rappaport, J (1977). *Community Psychology: Values, Research and Action*. Holt, Rinehart and Winston, New York.

Renouf, J, Robb, G and Wells, P (1990). *Children, Young Persons and Their Families Act 1989: Report on its First Year of Operation*. Department of Social Welfare, Wellington.

Robinson, J, Young, W and Haslett, S (1989). *Surveying Crime*. Study Series 5. Institute of Criminology, Victoria University of Wellington, Wellington.

Rock, P (1985). Foreword. In Marshall, T *Alternatives to Criminal Courts*. Gower, Aldershot.

Rutter, M and Giller, H (1983). *Juvenile Delinquency: Trends and Perspectives*. Penguin, Harmondsworth.

Spier, P, Southey, P and Norris, M (1991). *Conviction and Sentencing of Offenders in New Zealand: 1981 to 1990*. Department of Justice, Wellington.

Spier, P, Luketina, F, and Kettles, S (1991). *Changes in the Seriousness of Offending and the Pattern of Sentencing 1979 to 1988*. Department of Justice, Wellington.

Stang Dahl, T (1974). The Emergence of the Norwegian Child Welfare Law. In Christie, N (ed) *Scandinavian Studies in Criminology, Vol 5*. Martin Robertson, London.

Sutherland, D and Cressey, D (1974). *Criminology*. Lippincott, Philadelphia.

Taylor, L, Lacey, P and Bracken, D (1980). *In Whose Best Interests?* Cobden Trust/MIND, London.

Te Whainga i Te Tika: In Search of Justice (1986). (Report of the Advisory Committee on Legal Services). Department of Justice, Wellington.

Wilkinson, C and Evans, R (1990). Police Cautioning of Juveniles: The Impact of Home Office Circular 14/1985. *Criminal Law Review*, 165.

Wright, M and Galaway, B (eds) (1989). *Mediation and Criminal Justice: Victims, Offenders and Community*. Sage, London.

Wundersitz, J, Naffine, N and Gale, F (1991). The Production of Guilt in the Juvenile Justice System: the Pressures to "Plead". *The Howard Journal*, 30 (3): 192.

Young, W and Cameron, N (1991). *Adult Pre-trial Diversion in New Zealand*. Department of Justice, Wellington.

GLOSSARY OF MAORI WORDS

hapu	sub-tribe
hui	gathering
iwi	tribe
kai	food
karakia	prayer, blessing
kaumatua	elder
kaupapa Maori	Maori protocol including language, customs and values; Maori topics and agenda; Maori process; Maori principles and beliefs
korero	to talk
kuia	old woman, grandmother
maatua whangai	recognised support group for Maori in the criminal justice system
mana	dignity, pride, power, identity, prestige, worth and sovereignty
marae	tribal meeting centre, focal point
mokopuna	children, grandchildren, descendants
Pakeha	person of European descent
powhiri	formal welcome
runanga o nga ture	council of law
tangata whenua	the (indigenous) people of the land; also local Maori people
tauahire	incomers as opposed to tangata whenua – the local people
tikanga o nga hara	law of wrongdoing
tohunga o nga ture	experts in law
turangawaewae	standing place, a person's place of origin
waiata	songs
wairua	spirit
whaikorero	speeches, especially those that form an exchange – literally 'chasing talk'.
whakamaa	shame
whanau	family, extended family
whangai	child raised by adoptive parents in the Maori tradition; literally the care of a child; foster child

Note: The meanings given are those that fit in the context of the report.

Appendices

APPENDIX 1

OBJECTIVES AND PRINCIPLES OF THE CHILDREN, YOUNG PERSONS AND THEIR FAMILIES ACT 1989

PART I

GENERAL OBJECTS, PRINCIPLES, AND DUTIES

General Objects

4. Objects—The object of this Act is to promote the well-being of children, young persons, and their families and family groups by—

(a) Establishing and promoting, and assisting in the establishment and promotion, of services and facilities within the community that will advance the well-being of children, young persons, and their families and family groups and that are—

(i) Appropriate having regard to the needs, values, and beliefs of particular cultural and ethnic groups; and

(ii) Accessible to and understood by children and young persons and their families and family groups; and

(iii) Provided by persons and organisations sensitive to the cultural perspectives and aspirations of different racial groups in the community:

(b) Assisting parents, families, whanau, hapu, iwi, and family groups to discharge their responsibilities to prevent their children and young persons suffering harm, ill-treatment, abuse, neglect, or deprivation:

(c) Assisting children and young persons and their parents, family, whanau, hapu, iwi, and family group where the relationship between a child or young person and his or her parents, family, whanau, hapu, iwi, or family group is disrupted:

(d) Assisting children and young persons in order to prevent them from suffering harm, ill-treatment, abuse, neglect, and deprivation:

(e) Providing for the protection of children and young persons from harm, ill-treatment, abuse, neglect, and deprivation:

(f) Ensuring that where children or young persons commit offences,—

(i) They are held accountable, and encouraged to accept responsibility, for their behaviour; and

(ii) They are dealt with in a way that acknowledges their needs and that will give them the opportunity to develop in responsible, beneficial, and socially acceptable ways.

(g) Encouraging and promoting co-operation between organisations engaged in providing services for the benefit of children and young persons and their families and family groups.

Cf. 1974, No. 72, s. 3

General Principles

5. Principles to be applied in exercise of powers conferred by this Act—Subject to section 6 of this Act, any Court which, or person who, exercises any power conferred by or under this Act shall be guided by the following principles:

(a) The principle that, wherever possible, a child's or young person's family, whanau, hapu, iwi, and family group should participate in the making of decisions affecting that child or young person, and accordingly that, wherever possible, regard should be had to the views of that family, whanau, hapu, iwi, and family group:

(b) The principle that, wherever possible, the relationship between a child or young person and his or her family, whanau, hapu, iwi, and family group should be maintained and strengthened:

(c) The principle that consideration must always be given to how a decision affecting a child or young person will affect—

  (i) The welfare of that child or young person; and

  (ii) The stability of that child's or young person's family, whanau, hapu, iwi, and family group:

(d) The principle that consideration should be given to the wishes of the child or young person, so far as those wishes can reasonably be ascertained, and that those wishes should be given such weight as is appropriate in the circumstances, having regard to the age, maturity, and culture of the child or young person:

(e) The principle that endeavours should be made to obtain the support of—

  (i) The parents or guardians or other persons having the care of a child or young person; and

  (ii) The child or young person himself or herself—to the exercise or proposed exercise, in relation to that child or young person, or any power conferred by or under this Act:

(f) The principle that decisions affecting a child or young person should, wherever practicable, be made and implemented within a time-frame appropriate to the child's or young person's sense of time.

Cf. 1974, No. 72, ss.4a-4c; 1983, No. 129, s. 3

6. Welfare and interests of child or young person deciding factor—Where, in the administration or application of this Part or Part II or Part III or Part VI (other than sections 351 to 360) or Part VII or Part VIII of this Act, any conflict of principles or interests arises, the welfare and interests of the child or young person shall be the deciding factor.

Cf. 1974, No. 72, s. 4

PART IV

YOUTH JUSTICE

Principles

208. Principles—Subject to section 5 of this Act, any Court which, or person who, exercises any powers conferred by or under this Part or Part V or sections 351 to 360 of this Act shall be guided by the following principles:

(a) The principle that, unless the public interest requires otherwise, criminal proceedings should not be instituted against a child or young person if there is an alternative means of dealing with the matter:

(b) The principle that criminal proceedings should not be instituted against a child or young person solely in order to provide any assistance or services needed to advance that welfare of the child or young person, or his or her family, whanau, or family group:

(c) The principle that any measures for dealing with offending by children or young persons should be designed—

(i) To strengthen the family, whanau, hapu, iwi, and family group of the child or young person concerned; and

(ii) To foster the ability of families, whanau, hapu, iwi, and family groups to develop their own means of dealing with offending by their children and young persons:

(d) The principle that a child or young person who commits an offence should be kept in the community so far as that is practicable and consonant with the need to ensure the safety of the public:

(e) The principle that a child's or young person's age is a mitigating factor in determining—

(i) Whether or not to impose sanctions in respect of offending by a child or young person; and

(ii) the nature of any such sanctions:

(f) The principle that any sanctions imposed on a child or young person who commits an offence should—

(i) Take the form most likely to maintain and promote the development of the child or young person within his or her family, whanau, hapu, and family group; and

(ii) Take the least restrictive form that is appropriate in the circumstances:

(g) The principle that any measures for dealing with offending by children or young persons should have due regard to the interests of any victims of that offending:

(h) The principle that the vulnerability of children and young persons entitles a child or young person to special protection during any investigation relating to the commission or possible commission of an offence by that child or young person.

APPENDIX 2

Additional Details of Methodology

This appendix contains the most important details of the classification and coding of the data together with the wording of the prompt questions used in interviewing families, young people and victims.

Classification of data and coding definitions

As well as decisions about the number of cases, decisions had to be made about how to code and classify the data. For the most part we describe the classification of the data at the time we report it. In general, where the coding was not immediately self-evident (eg sex) or based directly on the response options presented in an interview, more than one researcher coded the data or else the original interviewer was asked to check the researcher's analysis. In this way we were able to score interviews for items such as: Did the victim feel better or worse; were the family (young person, victim etc) satisfied with the outcome of the FGC, and so on. Sometimes complex categories with small numbers of responses were simplified later by combining them. Finally ratings were made of the seriousness of the offence and the severity of the outcomes by at least two of the researchers in order to assess the qualitative aspects of the data. The categories arrived at are described below with examples.

Seriousness

Although seriousness of the offence was a major factor affecting the decisions of those dealing with offenders, obtaining a good measure of seriousness is very difficult. Many researchers have attempted the problem and some have been able to make very effective ratings of the relative seriousness of different offences but their scales are almost invariably based on aggregated group data for convicted offenders (cf Spier *et al*, 1991). When one has, as we did, full details of the nature and circumstances of the offence it is possible to make much finer distinctions which allowed us to compare both offenders committing similar and offenders committing different offences.

We decided that the best method was for three researchers to make ratings of the seriousness of offences and then determine how well they agreed. Initially we worked independently using a three point scale of *minimum, medium* and *maximum* seriousness. We then worked together examining those cases where we were uncertain or were in disagreement. At this point we added two additional categories for borderline cases: *minimum/medium* and *medium/maximum*. Disagreements and borderline cases were discussed until agreement was reached. Discussion took into account the knowledge we had of the views of the police and our observations of the sentencing practice of judges. Typical examples of the final categorisation of offences are set out in Table A2.1. When more than one offence was involved in a particular case, the seriousness rating of the most serious offence was used.

Table A2.1
Categories Used for Rating the Seriousness of Offences

- *Minimum seriousness* offences included theft and shoplifting of goods valued at under $100, property damage and abuse valued at under $100, burglary where there was no damage or goods taken, and possession of cannabis.

- *Minimum/medium seriousness* offences included burglary with goods taken and/or damage valued at under $100, resisting the police or MOT officers and minor assaults.

- *Medium seriousness* offences included theft of goods valued at $100 to $1,000, burglary involving goods taken and/or damage valued at $100 to $1,000, unlawful taking where damage was valued at less than $1,000, driving with excess breath alcohol, minor assault causing injury, cannabis cultivation, obscene phone calls, possession of a weapon and careless driving.

- *Medium/maximum seriousness* offences included dangerous driving, burglary involving goods taken and/or damage to the value of $1,000 or more, robbery or aggravated robbery with no injury, unlawful taking with damage to the value of $1,000 or more.

- *Maximum seriousness* offences included murder, attempted murder, manslaughter, robbery, aggravated robbery, serious assaults, rape, driving resulting in injury, and arson where the value of the property ran into tens of thousands of dollars.

Severity of Outcomes

A coding system was derived for the severity of FGC outcomes and of court outcomes. The categories were based on the order of the tariffs listed in section 283 of the Act, together with a judgement of the relative severity of financial, community work hours and the lower tariff penalties involving some supervision or restrictions.

1) *FGC outcomes:*
   - 9 Prison or corrective training (CT)
   - 8 Supervision with residence
   - 7 Supervision with activity
   - 6 Community work 150-200 hours
   - 5 Community work 100-150 hours or reparation/monetary penalty $1,000-$1,500
   - 4 Community work 50-100 hours or reparation/monetary penalty $500-$1,000
   - 3 Community work 10-50 hours or reparation/monetary penalty $100-$500
   - 2 Curfews and restrictions, under 10 hours community work, reparation or monetary penalty under $100, voluntary disqualification
   - 1 Apologies, cautions and warnings only
   - 0 Nothing.

2) *Court penalties:*
   - 7 Prison
   - 6 Corrective training
   - 5 Supervision with residence
   - 4 Supervision with activity
   - 3 Community work 100-200 hours or financial/reparation of $1,000 or more
   - 2 Community work under 100 hours, supervision, disqualification, reparation or monetary penalty under $1,000
   - 1 Discharge under section 283(a)
   - 0 No order.

PROMPT QUESTIONS USED IN INTERVIEWING THE YOUNG PERSON AND THEIR FAMILIES

Abbreviated Outline of Interview Record Sheet – Young Person

Basic Questions:
(1) What happened when the Police spoke to you? _____
(2) What happened at the FGC? _____
(3) If Court – what happened there? _____
(4) How does the young person feel about each stage? _____

What happened _____

Before the FGC:
When did the police contact you? _____
Where were you questioned? _____
When were you cautioned? _____
Who was there when you were questioned? _____
How did you feel about it all? _____

FGC:
Why was there an FGC? _____
What happened? _____
Did you understand everything? _____
Were you asked your views? _____
Were you listened to? _____
Did you feel you had support? _____
Were the people there, the right ones or not? _____
Were the things discussed, the right things or not? _____
Was it all fair? _____
How involved were you in reaching the decision? _____
In your view, who really decided? _____
Was the decision OK? _____
Were the contributions of others helpful: (police, facilitator, social worker, victim etc.)? _____
What would have been more helpful? _____

FGC Outcome:
As expected: _____
Right for you _____
If not, preferred outcome _____

If co-offenders, what happened to them and was that fair? _____

Do you foresee any difficulties completing the plans? _____

Overall evaluation and other comments: _____

Youth Court:

What happened? _____

Did you understand everything? _____

Were you asked your views? _____

Were you listened to? _____

Did you feel you had support? _____

Was your lawyer helpful? _____

Was it all fair? _____

What would have been better? _____

Outcome:

As expected: _____

Right for you _____

If not, preferred outcome _____

If co-offenders, what happened to them and was that fair? _____

How do Court and FGC compare? _____

Overall evaluation and other comments _____

If Maori, Pacific Islander etc:

Do you think being a Maori (Samoan etc) made any difference? _____

If so, what and why? _____

Were things done in a Maori way in the FGC; in the court? _____

Was this the right way for you? _____

Abbreviated Outline of Interview Record Sheet – Family Members (Carer)

Basic Questions

(1) What happened at the FGC and how do you feel about it?

(2) Did you feel that you made the decision?

(3) If Court – what happened and how do you feel about it?

What happened? _____

Before the FGC:

How did you learn about the offence? _____

Were you there when your child was questioned? _____

Who told you about the FGC? _____

What were you told would happen at FGC? _____

What were you told about possible results? _____

At the FGC:

Did you have a chance to say everything you wanted? _____

Did you have the information you needed? _____

Were the right people there and the right things discussed? _____

Did you feel you had support? _____

Did you feel you were blamed? _____

In your view, who really decided? _____

How satisfied were you with the decision? _____

Were the contributions of others helpful: (police, facilitator, social worker, victim etc.)? _____

What would have been more helpful? _____

Outcome:

As expected _____

As wanted _____

Right for the young person _____

Preferred outcome _____

Do you foresee any difficulties completing the plans? _____

Overall evaluation _____

Youth Court: (if present)

What happened? _____

Did you understand everything? _____

Were you asked your views? _____

Were you listened to? _____

Did you feel you had support? _____

Was the lawyer helpful? _____

Were the things discussed, the right things or not? _____

Was it all fair? _____

What would have been better? _____

Was outcome as expected? _____

Was it right for the young person? _____

If not, preferred outcome? _____

If co-offenders, what happened to them and was that fair? _____

How do Court and FGC compare? _____

Overall evaluation and other comments _____

If Maori, Pacific Islander etc:

Do you think being a Maori (Samoan etc) made any difference? If so, what and why? _____

_____

Were things done in a Maori (Samoan etc.) way at the FGC? at court? _____

Was this the right way for you? _____

Were there any iwi differences and did they affect things? _____

Abbreviated Outline of Interview Record Sheet – Victims

Basic Questions

(1) What happened at the FGC and how do you feel about it?

(2) Did you feel that you were involved in making the decision?

(3) Where appropriate, why did you not feel able to attend the FGC?

What happened:

Offence type: _____ Where *Home, car, workplace, public place*

What impact did it have on you:

Immediately: *Psychological, physical, loss of property, damage to others* _____

Later: *Change routines, new security measures, fears, other* _____

Rate impact out of 10 _____

What support did you have in coping with what happened? (& from who)

Rate usefulness out of 10 _____

Would you have liked contact with a victim support person (if none)? _____

Reparation

Result preferred for self _____ Desirable in general _____

Role of Police:

Take victim impact statement? *Yes/No* Provide support? _____

What is your view of Family Group Conferences?

In general? _____

Why did you decide (not) to attend? _____

If present:

What did you say? _____

Was there anything else you would have liked to say? _____

What would have made it easier to say everything? _____

Was attending something that made you feel better or worse about what had happened? _____

How did you feel about meeting the young person? _____

All:

Do you think the right decisions were taken? _____

If not, what would you have preferred? _____

Other comments: _____

Background information:

Age group (20s, 30s etc) _____ Gender _____ Ethnicity (iwi) _____

Previously knew/related to young person? _____ Previously victim? *Yes/No* _____

If Yes Opinion of previous involvement as a victim with justice system compared to this time? _____

APPENDIX 3

A Statistical Overview of Juvenile Offending Before and Since the Introduction of the Act

This appendix provides a description of the pattern of juvenile offending in New Zealand over recent years based on police statistics on juvenile crime. The main aim is to determine whether there is any evidence of changes in the numbers and characteristics of offenders, and types of offences, recorded by the police between the period immediately before the Act and the year 1990, which is the first full calendar year after the Act came into operation on 1 November 1989.

More specifically this paper aims:

1) to describe changes over recent years in offending patterns

2) to compare juveniles' and adults' offence rates and patterns

3) to describe the number, gender, ages and ethnicity of juveniles coming to official attention

4) to contrast the juvenile offence rates and patterns for two quarters before the implementation of the 1989 Act and the year 1990.

The information is drawn from police statistics on the detected crime which is attributed to juvenile offenders. While these figures have limitations in describing the amount of crime in the community or even in describing the amount of detected juvenile crime (these problems are discussed in the next section), they do describe the offences and the offenders who are the starting point for the youth justice system. It is these cases that are dealt with by the police and it is these cases that form the basis for the sample chosen in the study. Thus, in presenting this information we provide a backdrop for the detailed research on the effect of the new Act on police practice, on the operation of FGCs, on the operation of the Youth Court, and on the experiences of offenders, families and victims who have become involved in the youth justice system.

Method

The data we have used for comparisons over the years 1978-88 come from the Police Digest which presents annual statistics of all records kept by the police. Whenever an incident is reported to the police and an offender is located, a report is filed giving details of the type of offence, certain offender characteristics and the action taken by the police. Published data were only available up to 1988 but comparable information was obtained for 1989 and 1990 from Police National Headquarters. An additional breakdown of the information on the type of offence and offender characteristics was obtained for each of the four quarters immediately preceding the introduction of the Act and for the five quarters after the Act came into force (ie October-December 1989 and the four quarters of 1990). Thus, we were able to compare data from immediately before the Act with data for the full year 1990, omitting the transitional first quarter immediately after the introduction of the Act.

It is important to stress at this point that police figures do not necessarily present an accurate picture of the amount of crime in the community. We know from research that recorded crime can be a relatively small proportion of all crimes committed. Robinson *et al* (1989) studied two areas of New Zealand and showed that the rate at which offences were reported to the police ranged from just over a quarter to just under a half depending on the type of offence. We know too that legislative changes can influence attitudes and hence reporting rates. It is quite possible that this happened as a result of the new Act but we have no way of measuring this. Furthermore, records of offenders only cover those cases where reported crime has been cleared, ie those cases where offenders have been caught by the police in the act of committing a crime, those cases where an offender has been caught as a result of an investigation, and those cases where an offender confesses to previously unreported crimes. These are the cases which are covered by the police statistics analysed here and which are hereafter referred to as *cleared police offences* or, sometimes more briefly, as *cleared offences*.

Another problem is that the data are based on *distinct* offences and not on *distinct* persons. Thus one offender who has committed several burglaries will be counted in the police statistics as a *distinct* case for each burglary, even though all the offences may come to notice at the same time or be dealt with by the court at the same time. Nor do the data tell us about the number of cases that are eventually proven and dealt with, because police statistics are collected at the time police officers complete their file on the case and before the matter has been dealt with by the court or, in the case of juvenile offenders, by an FGC.

Another complicating factor in interpreting data on cleared offences is that some types of offences are more likely to be **cleared** than others. When making comparisons, for instance between statistics relating to adults and juveniles, it is therefore not possible to draw firm conclusions about the relative proportion of offences actually committed by different groups because the two groups tend to commit different types of offences which have different clearance rates.

However imperfect police statistics are, they provide a starting point for discussions about crime. Comparisons can be made between groups and over time providing the interpretation takes account of the possible distortions that we have described. Furthermore, the data are important, because they provide a description of the types of offences which must be dealt with by the criminal justice system.

Results

Incidents and Offences Cleared by the Police and attributed to Juveniles

Recorded offence rates in New Zealand have gradually increased over the last 20 years. The years 1965 to 1989 saw a trebling in the number of incidents and offences recorded by the police. However, the per capita increase in the number of offences cleared by the police is not nearly so steep, partly because of changes in the proportion of recorded crime for which offenders were detected (clearance rates fluctuated over the period but generally showed a slight decline) and partly because of increases in the total population. Figure A3.1 shows the incidence of cleared crime per 10,000 population from 1978 to 1990.

Figure A3.1
Offence Rates for Cleared Offences attributed to (a) Total Offenders per 10,000 Total Population and (b) Juvenile Offenders per 10,000 Juvenile Population; 1978-1990

Source: Calculated from police statistics on offences cleared and population statistics. The juvenile population was estimated by extrapolation from census findings for non-census years.

The rate of total cleared offences per 10,000 population rose from 374 in 1978 to 525 in 1989, that is less than one and a half times. The rise is consistent with a trend throughout Western countries and is paralleled by an increase in the amount of serious crime (Spier et al, 1991). In 1990 there was a slight drop in the per capita rate of cleared offences, although the actual number of cleared offences continued to rise slightly. It is difficult to know whether this indicates a change in the pattern of rising rates of cleared offences or whether it is simply a chance fluctuation.

Figure A3.1 also shows that the juvenile per capita offence rate rose over this period, although not as much as the total per capita rate. The rate per 10,000 juveniles in 1978 was 332; in 1989 it was 404. The changes in juvenile offending rates paralleled those for the total population until 1985. Since 1985, while total cleared offending has continued to rise slightly, the cleared offences attributed to juveniles have tended to drop, apart from a slight rise from 387 in 1988 to 404 in 1989.

Again interpretation is very difficult. It appears that the rate of cleared juvenile crime up to the time the Act was introduced was generally falling or stable but that a sharper decline occurred in 1990, the first full year since the Act came into force. There are several possible explanations for this change. First, it is possible that the drop is simply a chance fluctuation in the generally downward trend line which has shown similar fluctuations in the past, for instance from 1982 to 1983 and from 1987 to 1988. There are two other alternative explanations: that there has been a drop in juvenile crime or that police practice has changed. The first possibility is that the drop in the rate of juvenile crime may have resulted from a reduction in reoffending because of the effectiveness of the changes in practice under the new Act which keep young people out of institutions and involve families in attempts to prevent reoffending. The second possibility is that, as the amount of serious crime has increased, police may have simply had less time to deal with some of the less serious crime committed by juveniles. A related possibility is that the more time-consuming procedures for processing juvenile offenders may have made the police less inclined to take action when a minor offence has been committed by a juvenile or, even when they have taken some action such as giving a street warning, less inclined to record their action. It is difficult to know which of these explanations is correct, but closer examination of the data provides additional information on the change and we return to this issue later.

Juveniles contribute less than 20% of cleared crime. Those in the 14-16 age group commit the vast majority of known juvenile offences and few are committed by those under the age of ten years. Figure A3.2 presents data over the last 12 years on the numbers of cleared juvenile offences in the three age categories distinguished by law. It shows that, during the years when the number of cleared offences rose, most of the increase appeared to be in the 14-16 year old group. But in recent years, as the per capita rate of cleared offences dropped, this pattern has reversed. From 1987 to 1988 a drop was recorded in 14-16 year old offending and a similar drop was recorded from 1989 to 1990. Thus the decline in cleared juvenile offending seems to have been proportionately greater among older rather than younger offenders.

Figure A3.2
Cleared Offences attributed to Young Offenders showing Ages, 1978-90; Numbers Aged 0-9, 10-13 and 14-16

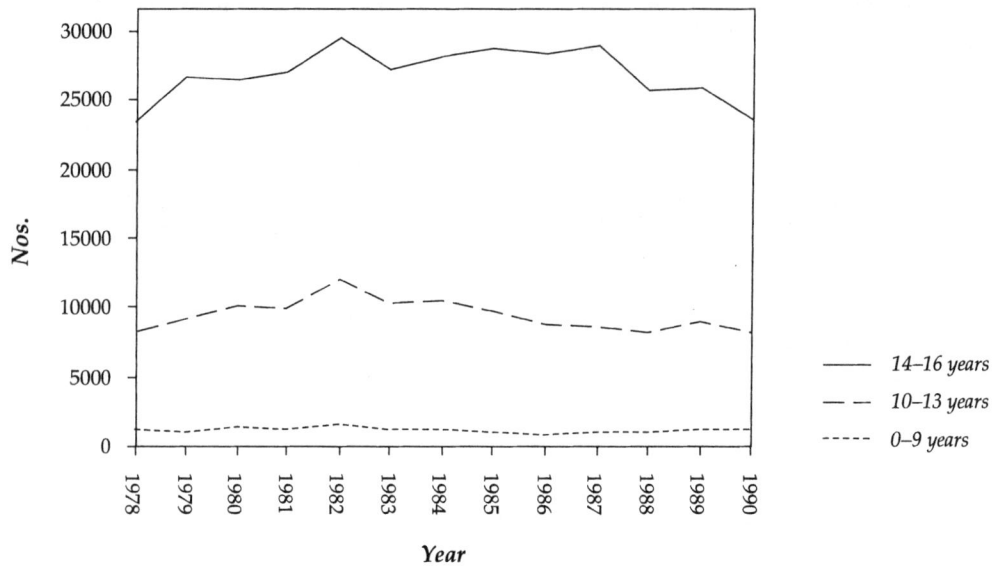

Source: Data from NZ Police Digest of Statistics 1983-89.

Known offenders, adults and juveniles, are predominantly male: 82% of both total offenders and juvenile offenders in 1988 were male. Figure A3.3 shows rates of boys and girls offending over the last 12 years.

Figure A3.3
Rates per 10,000 Population for Cleared Offences attributed to Male and Female Offenders Aged 14-16 Years

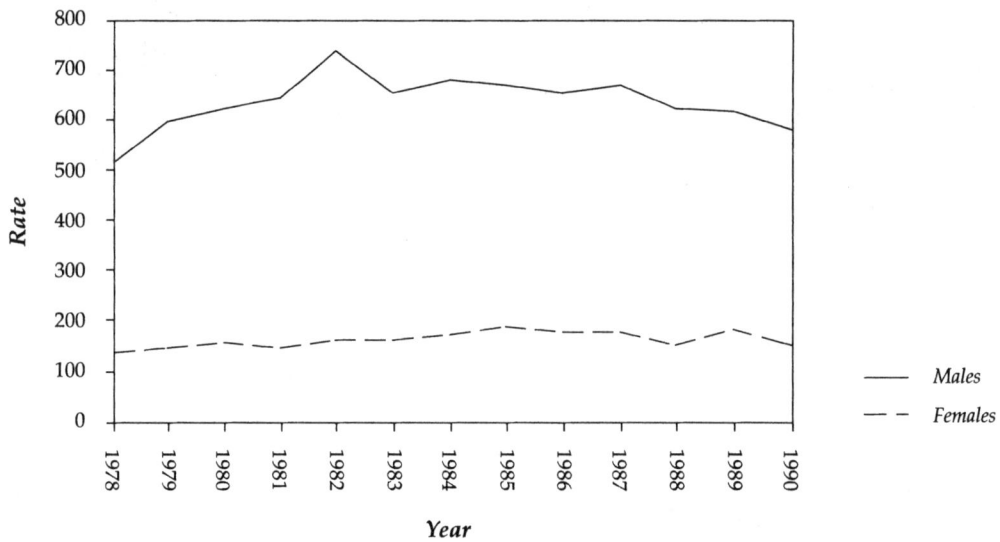

Source: Data from NZ Police Digest of Statistics 1983-89. Rates have been calculated by estimating numbers of males and females from census data.

The proportion of boys to girls rose slightly in the early part of the period, remained relatively constant in the middle years but has dropped more recently, in particular since 1987. Thus, the changes in the per capita rate of cleared juvenile crime seem to have affected not only those who are older more than those who are younger but also boys more than girls.

Maori and Pacific Islanders are also over-represented in known crime data. Police data suggest that, in 1990, Maori committed 37% of all known offending and Pacific Island offenders committed 5%, although these groups only made up 12% and 4%, respectively, of the population recorded in the 1986 census. The comparable figures for known juvenile offenders were 43% and 7%. The slightly higher figures for juveniles are largely explained by the fact that the Maori and Pacific Island populations generally have a younger age structure than the Pakeha population. But, as already noted in Chapter 1, there are problems with the identification of the ethnicity of offenders which may lead to overidentification of offenders as Maori. Thus, rather than presenting offending rates for different ethnic populations we have presented a bar graph giving the relative proportions of juvenile offending attributed to Pakeha, Maori and Pacific Island offenders over the period 1978-90 (Figure A3.4).

Figure A3.4
Ethnicity of Detected Juvenile Offenders 1978-90; Bargraph showing Proportion of Total Offenders in each of the Three Main Ethnic Groups; 1978 to 1990

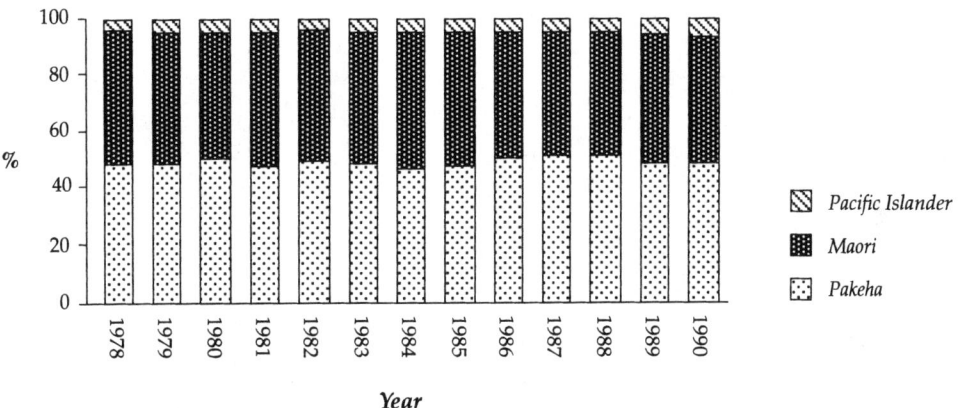

Source: Data from NZ Police Digest of Statistics 1983-89 and Police Headquarters, 1990-91

This figure shows that the proportion of juvenile offending attributed to each major ethnic group has fluctuated relatively little over the twelve year period, except that the increase in the proportion of Pacific Island juvenile offenders parallels the increase in the proportion they make up of the total population.

Table A3.1 presents a comparison of the type of offences committed by juveniles and the type of offences committed by all offenders, based on information on all offences cleared by the police over the 12 month period immediately preceding the introduction of the Act.

In police statistics, offences are classified into eight main categories and, within each main category, into sub-categories. In the analyses presented here, we have combined offences involving property abuse with offences involving property damage. The seven resulting main categories, showing the short titles and police codes, are as follows:

- 'dishonesty' – police code 4000
- 'drugs' including, also, offences against good order – police code 3000
- 'violence' including murders, assaults, and robbery – police code 1000
- 'property' including the abuse of or damage to property – police codes 5000 & 6000
- 'sex' offences – police code 2000
- 'administrative' offences – police code 7000
- 'traffic' offences – police code 8000.

In addition we show separately the three main sub-categories of dishonesty offences which are common among juvenile offenders:

- 'theft' – police code 4300
- 'burglary' – police code 4100
- 'car conversion' – police code 4200.

Table A3.1
Comparison of All Detected Offenders with Detected Juvenile Offenders by Type of Offence; Percentages for Year from 10/88 to 9/89

	All offenders %		Juvenile offenders %	
Dishonesty	32		60	
theft		17		34
burglary		6		14
car conversion		4		9
Drug	25		13	
Traffic	19		7	
Violence	10		6	
Property	11		13	
Administrative	3		1	
Sex	0.8		0.5	

Source: Unpublished police statistics.

Compared with the total group of offenders, juveniles were much more likely to be apprehended for dishonesty offences: 32% of all cleared offences for all offenders were for dishonesty compared to 60% for juveniles. In particular, theft made up 34% of cleared offences by juveniles compared with 17% of all cleared offences; burglary made up 14% of juvenile offences compared with 6% of all cleared offences; and car conversion made up 9% of offences by juveniles compared with 4% of all cleared offences. Traffic, drug, violence and sex offences all accounted for a smaller proportion of juvenile than adult cleared offences.

Tables A3.2 – A3.4 compare the type of offences committed by girls and boys, by younger and older juveniles and by Maori, Pacific Island and Pakeha juveniles. These tables show marked sex, age and ethnic differences in patterns of offending.

Table A3.2 shows that a greater proportion of girls' known offending than boys' involved dishonesty, although there were differences within the general category. Thus theft made up a considerably greater proportion of the known offending of girls than of boys (56% compared with 28%), but burglary and car conversion made up a much smaller proportion of girls' known offending than boys' (6% and 4% compared with 16% and 10%). The proportions of drug and violence offences committed by boys and girls were, on the other hand, not dissimilar.

Table A3.2
Comparison of Girls and Boys by Type of Offence; Percentages for Year from 10/88 to 9/89

	Boys %	Girls %
Dishonesty	57	70
theft	28	56
burglary	16	6
car conversion	10	4
Drug	13	13
Traffic	8	3
Violence	6	5
Property	14	8
Administrative	0.8	0.8
Sex	0.6	0.05

Source: Unpublished police statistics

Table A3.3 shows that a greater proportion of cleared offending by the 10-13 age group than by the 14-16 age group was accounted for by offences of dishonesty (75% compared with 54%). However, again there were clear differences within this category. Theft made up a greater proportion of cleared offending by the younger age group (51% compared with 28%), but car conversion made up a smaller proportion (5% compared with 10%). Perhaps surprisingly, burglary made up a larger proportion of cleared offending by the younger age group (18% compared with 13%). Drug and traffic offences, on the other hand, made up a greater proportion of cleared offences by the older age group (17% and 8% compared with 4% and 2%).

Table A3.3
Comparison of Detected Juvenile Offenders Aged 10-13 with those Aged 14-16 by Type of Offence; Percentages for Year from 10/88 to 9/89

	10-13 yrs %	14-16 yrs %
Dishonesty	75	54
theft	51	28
burglary	18	13
car conversion	5	10
Drug	4	17
Traffic	2	8
Violence	4	7
Property	14	13
Administrative	0.2	1
Sex	0.5	0.5

Source: Unpublished police statistics

Table A3.4 shows that offences of dishonesty made up a greater proportion of the cleared offending by Pacific Island boys than of that by Maori or Pakeha boys; the percentages were 76%, 62% and 50% respectively. Drug and traffic offences, on the other hand, made up a much smaller proportion of Pacific Island boys' offending compared to that of Maori and Pakeha boys (the percentages were 7%, 12% and 15% for drug offences and 1%, 6% and 10% for traffic offences respectively). Maori boys were also apprehended proportionately more often for dishonesty and less often for drug and traffic offences than Pakeha boys. Property offences were more common for Pakeha than for Maori boys and the percentage of Pacific Island Polynesian boys committing these offences was even lower.

Table A3.4

Comparison of Ethnicity of Detected Male Juvenile Offenders by Type of Offence; Percentages for Year from 10/88 to 9/89

	Pakeha %	Maori %	Pacific Island %
Dishonesty	50	62	76
theft	27	26	42
burglary	12	21	19
car conversion	7	12	12
Drug	15	12	7
Traffic	10	6	1
Violence	6	7	6
Property	16	12	9
Administrative	0.6	1	0.9
Sex	0.8	0.8	0.7

Source: Unpublished police statistics

Comparing Recorded Juvenile Offending Before and After the 1989 Act[1]

By examining quarterly police returns which detail the characteristics of offenders in relation to cleared offences from the fourth quarter of 1988 through to the end of 1990, we were able to make a provisional assessment of whether or not there had been any changes in the nature of juveniles' involvement in crime over this period. In particular, we contrasted the year October 1988 to September 1989 with the calendar year 1990, omitting the first quarter of the Act's operation (that is, from October to December 1989). In brief we found that very little change had occurred. Tables A3.5, A3.6 and A3.7 present some selected indices of juvenile offending before and after the introduction of the Act.

Table A3.5

A Selection of Indices showing the Percentage of Juvenile Involvement in Cleared Offending Comparing 10/88 to 9/89 with 1990

	Year before the Act %	1990 post-Act %
Juveniles as % of total offenders	20	19
Girls as % of juvenile offenders	22	20
Under 14 yr olds as % of total offenders	5	5
Under 14 yr olds as % juvenile offenders	28	28
Pakeha boys as % of male juvenile offenders	51	49
Maori boys as % of male juvenile offenders	42	43
Pacific Islander boys as % of male juvenile offenders	6	7
Pakeha girls as % of female juvenile offenders	48	46
Maori girls as % of female juvenile offenders	46	47

Source: Unpublished police statistics

The first point of note has already been alluded to – the juvenile per capita crime rate based on police records of cleared offences shows a decline between 1989 and 1990. There has also been a slight downward trend in total cleared offences. But judging the impact of the Act by comparing 1989

---

[1] The data in this section use unpublished police statistics which provided detailed information for each quarter on sex, ethnicity and age of offender and type of offence. These were used to calculate figures for the four quarters immediately before the Act came into force and for the year 1990, ie the first calendar year post-Act.

to 1990 is slightly problematic as the Act came into force in the last quarter of 1989. The apparent decline in the rate of juvenile crime is actually slightly less marked if the four quarters immediately prior to the Act are compared to the year 1990. In fact, the proportion of juveniles as a percentage of total offenders (see Table A3.5) remained much the same after the Act as before.

In most other respects, juveniles continue to constitute a similar proportion of offenders since the Act was introduced: the sex, age and ethnic profile and the types of offences committed remained relatively unchanged. Some changes since the introduction of the Act are, however, worthy of note. In particular, Table A3.6 shows that the proportion of cleared juvenile offending comprising dishonesty offences and, in particular, burglary and car conversion, has increased (from 60% to 65%), while the proportion comprising drug offences has decreased (from 13% to 10%). However, over the same period the proportion of total cleared dishonesty offences attributable to juveniles has actually decreased (see Table A3.7), suggesting that this change is likely to be part of a general trend for dishonesty offences to make up an increasing proportion of cleared crime rather than a consequence of the Act. But it would be unwise to place too much weight on data over such a short time span and it would be necessary to inspect data over a longer time span before reaching firm conclusions. Apart from the changes in type of offence, the slight variations in the figures before and after the Act can be regarded as random fluctuations rather than showing real differences in the pattern of offending.

Table A3.6

Percentage of Cleared Juvenile Offending by Type of Offence Comparing 10/88 to 9/89 with 1990

	Year prior to Act %		1990 post-Act %
Dishonesty	60		65
theft		34	34
burglary		14	17
car conversion		9	11
Drug	13		10
Traffic	7		6
Violence	6		6
Property	13		12
Administrative	0.9		1
Sex	0.5		0.7

Source: Unpublished police statistics

Table A3.7

Percentage of Cleared Juvenile Offenders Committing Offences of Dishonesty Comparing 10/88 to 9/89 with 1990

	Year prior to Act %	1990 post-Act %
Juveniles as % total dishonesty offences	37	33
Girls' dishonesty offences as % total girls' offences	71	74
Pakeha boys' dishonesty offences as % total Pakeha boys' offences	50	56
Maori boys' dishonesty offences as % total Maori boys' offences	62	68
Pacific Island boys' dishonesty offences as % total PI boys' offences	76	71

Source: Unpublished police statistics.

The information in these tables does, however, enable us to comment on some criticisms which have been made of the Act. The obligation on the police to inform juveniles of their rights before questioning them about their involvement in offences has been alleged to interfere with crime detection and to have resulted in a more sophisticated young offender who 'thumbs his or her nose' at authority. It has been suggested that the police are 'walking away' from juvenile offenders rather than complying with the provisions of the new Act which require the police to protect juveniles' rights by ensuring that an adult, preferably a parent, is present when the child or young person is questioned. Compliance with these provisions, it has been argued, has increased the burden on police officers in processing offenders and has often meant that the arresting officer is tied up for several hours. While it is not possible to draw firm conclusions on the truth of these allegations, the data presented here show no great change in the pattern of detected offending of the sort that would support the view that the police are walking away from juvenile crime to any greater extent than immediately prior to the Act. It is, however, possible that a pattern of giving less attention to less serious crime has been a feature of police practice since at least 1987 and possibly even since 1985, when the drop in the juvenile crime rate first became apparent. The Act could have given this trend a slight impetus.

Nevertheless, much of what has been reported here does not suggest that any major changes in police behaviour have occurred. For example, if the police were ignoring juvenile offenders we might expect the proportion of cleared offences attributed to juveniles to have decreased. But Table A3.6 shows that this proportion has remained almost constant. Similarly, if juveniles aged under 14, who are less likely than those aged 14-16 to commit serious offences, were being increasingly ignored by the police, their representation amongst juvenile offenders would have declined. Again, however, Table A3.6 shows that the proportion of those who are aged under 14 has remained constant both as a proportion of total cleared offenders and as a proportion of cleared juvenile offenders.

On the other hand, it could be argued that the observed changes in the type of offences being attributed to juveniles are an indication of a change in policing. Burglary and car conversions have increased and these are instances where the police respond to complaints from the public, in contrast to offences like drug offences where police action usually initiates detection. Thus it is possible to argue that the changes in the type of offences attributed to juveniles reflect a shift to more reactive as opposed to proactive policing. One way of checking whether or not such a change in police practice has occurred in response to the Children, Young Persons and Their Families Act 1989 is to examine whether or not the changes in the types of offence are peculiar to juveniles or whether or not they also affect adult crime. Table A3.8 sets out comparisons of the proportions of cleared offences of different types that were attributed to juveniles before and after the Act.

Table A3.8
For each Type of Offence, Percentage of Cleared Offenders who are Juveniles Comparing 10/88 to 9/89 with 1990

	Year prior to Act %	*1990 post-Act* %
Dishonesty	37	33
theft	39	37
burglary	47	45
car conversion	39	41
Drug	10	9
Traffic	7	6
Violence	12	11
Property	48	46
Administrative	7	5
Sex	14	13
Total	20	19

Source: Unpublished police statistics

From this, it can clearly be seen that dishonesty offences were less likely to have involved juveniles[2] since the Act came into effect, while the percentage of drug and other types of cleared offences being attributed to juveniles was very much the same before and after the Act. Thus it appears that cleared dishonesty offences have gone up for both adults and juveniles, though rather less for juveniles than for the total known offender population, suggesting that if there is a shift to more reactive rather than proactive policing, it is a shift that has occurred across the board and not simply in relation to juveniles as a response to the Children, Young Persons and Their Families Act.

Conclusions

The main conclusion to emerge from this statistical overview of juvenile offending is that, overall, offending patterns have, to date, probably changed relatively little since the introduction of the 1989 Act.

The general pattern from 1985 to 1988, that is the period immediately prior to the Act, shows no dramatic changes in the per capita rate of cleared offences, either for the total population or for juveniles. The juvenile per capita crime rate was showing a gradual decrease while the total per capita rate of cleared offences generally was stable or showed a slight increase. Since 1988, the fall in the juvenile crime rate may have gained some momentum but the pattern could also be interpreted as being in line with trends already established.

It is against this backdrop of a slightly falling juvenile per capita rate of cleared offences that we examined the number of juveniles coming into contact with the police for the four quarters immediately preceding the Act and the first full year since the Act came into operation. The quarterly numbers showed considerable fluctuation but these fluctuations appeared to be at least in part related to the time of the year. However, juveniles continue to make up much the same proportion of cleared offenders before and after the Act. Similarly, the proportion of cleared juvenile offenders in different age, gender and ethnic groups remained remarkably stable. One exception to this pattern of consistency before and after the Act is that there may have been an overall increase in dishonesty offences since the Act came into force but this increase has affected adults rather more than it has affected juveniles.

Earlier we suggested three possible ways to interpret the changes we have noted here. The first possibility is that the pattern of juvenile offending has remained basically unchanged and that any differences since the Act are simply chance variations on long term trends in juvenile offending. The second possibility is that since the Act the police have continued a pattern of ignoring the less serious juvenile crime when faced with increases in serious crime. The third possibility is that the effect of the Act has been to reduce recidivism among juveniles and hence to add to an already established downward trend in juvenile offence rates. No firm conclusions can be drawn about which of these three possibilities is more likely to be true. All may have some measure of truth. Future statistics will provide further information and may give a clearer answer. It is possible that the Act will have an effect on rates of offending but that any effect will only emerge gradually over time. However, if this is the case it will be difficult to determine whether such effects are indeed attributable to the Act or to other social changes. Thus, on the whole, we are of the belief that the main effects of the Act are not likely to be clearly visible in the police statistics on cleared offenders as these are affected by many other variables beside the ways in which decisions are made about responding to young people. Rather, we believe that the effects of the Act are likely to be most visible in the findings on how young people are being dealt with under the new youth justice system which are documented in the main body of the report.

---

[2] This difference was statistically significant while other differences were not.

APPENDIX 4

Technical Appendix

This appendix is intended to provide additional information on statistical issues. In particular, it contains tables giving the raw numbers corresponding to tables of percentages presented in the text and it provides details of the final output from the regression analyses.

Tables Giving Detailed Numbers

Table A4.1
Detailed Data for Table 3.7: Comparison of Arrest* with Non-arrest Cases on Information Available at Time of Arrest; Based on an Analysis of 462 Distinct Police Cases Aged 14-16, Numbers and Percentages

	Arrest		Non-arrest	
	N	%	N	%
Sex				
Boys	61	88	307	78
Girls	8	12	86	22
Total	69		393	
Ethnicity				
Maori	43	62	150	38
Pakeha	19	28	175	45
Pacific Island Polynesian	7	10	65	17
Total	69		390	
Age				
14	6	9	120	30
15	25	36	136	35
16	38	55	137	35
Total	69		393	
Seriousness				
Minimum	7	10	199	51
Medium/Minimum	14	21	43	11
Medium	35	51	140	36
Medium/Maximum	2	3	8	2
Maximum	10	15	2	1
Total	68		392	
Time of offence				
Daytime (ie before 6pm)	25	42	241	68
Evening (ie 6pm-11pm)	11	18	48	14
Night (ie 11pm-6am)	24	40	63	18
Total	60		352	
Co-offenders				
None	30	46	148	39
With one other	21	32	130	34
With 2 or more others	14	22	103	27
Total	65		381	

Table A4.1 continued

	Arrest		Non-arrest	
	N	%	N	%
Type of Offence				
Assaults/robbery/sex	15	22	41	10
Burglary	20	29	67	17
Car conversion	11	16	53	13
Theft/fraud etc.	11	16	160	41
Social/drugs	3	4	20	5
Other including traffic	8	12	52	14
Total	68		393	

* Includes only those arrest cases where there was a subsequent charge in the Youth Court.

Table A4.2
Detailed Data for Table 3.8: Comparison of Arrest* with Non-Arrest Cases on Information Not Necessarily Available at Time of Arrest; Based on an Analysis of 462 Distinct Police Cases Aged 14-16; Numbers and Percentages

	Arrest		Non-arrest	
	N	%	N	%
Previous history				
Yes	62	90	193	52
No	7	10	177	48
Total	69		370	
Number of Offences Arrested for				
1	39	57	326	83
2	21	31	36	9
3	4	6	9	2
4	2	3	6	2
5 or more	3	4	15	4
Total	69		392	
Live with family				
Yes	45	75	321	92
No	15	25	27	8
Total	60		348	
Unemployed				
Yes	36	52	46	12
No	33	48	334	88
Total	69		380	

* Includes only those arrest cases where there was a subsequent charge in the Youth Court.

Table A4.3
Detailed Data for Table 3.9: Offence and Offender Characteristics by Seriousness of Offending; Percentages of Total Number in Each Seriousness Category Sum to 100% in Each Column

	Minimum		Min/med		Medium or above	
	N	%	N	%	N	%
Sex						
Boys	229	70	66	90	241	90
Girls	98	30	7	10	26	10
Total	327		73		267	
Ethnicity						
Pakeha	156	48	37	51	75	28
Maori	119	37	29	40	137	51
Pacific Island	47	15	7	10	55	21
Total	322		73		267	
Age						
5 to 13	118	36	16	22	70	26
14	69	21	13	18	44	16
15	78	24	19	26	62	23
16	59	18	25	34	91	34
Total	324		73		267	
Time of offence						
Evening or later	50	16	28	39	88	40
Daytime	264	84	44	61	130	60
Total	314		72		218	
Previous History						
Yes	106	35	46	64	182	70
No	195	65	26	36	77	30
Total	301		72		259	
Where Living						
With non-family	12	4	7	11	33	14
With family	271	96	57	89	211	86
Total	283		64		244	
Employment						
At school	295	92	54	74	195	76
Employed	8	3	4	5	13	5
Unemployed	17	5	15	21	49	19
Total	320		73		257	
Area						
A		23		16		35
B		25		10		27
C		12		14		9
D		12		37		11
E		28		23		18

Table A4.4
Detailed Data for Table 5.6: Comparison of 'Police Diversion' (N=415) vs FGC Cases (N=187); Distinct Cases

	'Police Diversion'		Family Group Conference	
	N	%	N	%
Sex				
Boys	314	76	165	88
Girls	101	24	22	12
Total	415		187	
Ethnicity				
Pakeha	194	47	58	31
Maori	146	35	97	52
Pacific Islander	70	17	32	17
Other	5	1	0	0
Total	415		187	
Age				
9 and under	25	6	1	1
10-13	131	32	47	25
14-16	254	62	139	74
Total	410		187	
Seriousness of offence				
Minimum	290	70	30	16
Medium/Minimum	38	9	21	11
Medium	81	20	123	66
Medium/Maximum	2	1	10	5
Maximum	1	0	3	2
Total	412		187	
Time of Offence				
Daytime (ie before 6pm)	323	83	90	59
Evening (ie 6-11pm)	31	8	29	19
Night (ie 11pm-6am)	37	9	34	22
Total	391		153	
Co-offenders				
None	167	41	47	27
With one other	136	34	52	29
With 2 or more others	100	25	79	44
Total	403		178	
Type of Offence				
Assaults/robbery/sexual	17	4	27	14
Dishonesty				
Burglary	52	13	66	35
Conversion	33	8	29	16
Theft/fraud etc	219	53	49	26
Drugs/anti social	26	6	6	3
Property Damage & Abuse	62	15	5	3
Other incl traffic	6	1	5	3
Total	415		187	

Table A4.4 continued

	'Police Diversion'		Family Group Conference	
	N	%	N	%
Previous History				
Yes	119	31	154	83
No	259	69	32	17
Total	378		186	
Number of Offences				
1	379	92	128	68
2	21	5	31	17
3	7	2	9	5
>3	4	1	19	10
Total	411		187	
Live with family				
Yes	343	96	152	86
No	13	4	24	14
Total	356		176	
Unemployed				
Yes	17	4	29	16
No	388	96	149	84
Total	405		178	

Table A4.5
FGC Outcomes; Number of Cases Showing Severity of Outcome for Comparison with Tables 6.16 and 6.17

Severity of Outcome*	N	%
0: No penalties	10	5
1: Apologies, warnings only	22	11
2: >10 hrs work	28	14
3: 10-50 hrs work	64	32
4: 50-100 hrs work	26	13
5: 100-150 hrs work	25	13
6: 150-200 hrs work	10	5
7: Supervision with activity	8	4
8: Supervision with residence	4	2
9: Prison or corrective training	2	1
Total	199	

* Full details of options are given in appendix 2.

Table A4.6
Youth Court Cases Showing Numbers for Maori and Pakeha on a Variety of Variables Corresponding to Table 8.9

Age of Offender in Years

	Maori	Pakeha	Totals
14	7	0	7
15	8	10	18
16	19	17	36
17	0	0	0
18	1	0	1
Totals	35	27	62

Seriousness of the Offence (1=minimum to 5=maximum)

	Maori	Pakeha	Totals
1	0	2	2
2	2	5	7
3	26	13	39
4	2	3	5
5	5	4	9
Totals	35	27	62

Type of Offence: Burglaries versus Others

	Maori	Pakeha	Totals
Burglaries	16	5	21
Other	19	22	41
Totals	35	27	62

Previous History of Offending – Yes or No

	Maori	Pakeha	Totals
Yes	32	21	53
No	3	6	9
Totals	35	27	62

Previously Had a Youth Justice FGC – Yes or No, Care and Protection FGC (C&P), Don't Know (DK)

	Maori	Pakeha	Totals
Yes	19	12	31
No	14	12	26
C&P	0	3	3
DK	2	0	2
Totals	35	27	62

Severity of FGC Recommendation

	Maori	Pakeha	Totals
0-3	15	13	28
4-6	8	8	16
7-9	9	4	13
Totals	32	25	57

Type of Outcome in the Youth Court: Withdrawn or Discharged (Discharge), Youth Court Order (Order) or Transferred to a Higher Court (Higher)

	Maori	Pakeha	Totals
Discharge	14	15	29
Order	14	9	23
Higher	6	2	8
Totals	34	26	60

Reoffending: Yes, No, Don't Know (DK) or Not Applicable as Still in Custody (NA)

	Maori	Pakeha	Totals
Yes	22	13	35
No	12	13	25
DK	0	1	1
NA	1	0	1
Totals	35	27	62

Regressions

The variables used in calculating regressions were either integer (for example, age and number of offences), ordinal (for example, severity of outcomes and seriousness of offence) or binary variables (for example, for comparisons between Maori and Pakeha or between one area and other areas). As a consequence it was necessary to exclude a number of cases that could not readily be categorised. For this reason the numbers are less than the total sample numbers.

In all cases a stepwise regression was calculated first followed by a series of logistic regressions to determine the effects of area and to explore exactly which areas were most distinctive. The results of the stepwise regressions have been the primary source of the interpretation in the text, while the logistic regressions have been used simply to test whether there are also significant area differences. In this appendix we present the summary tables for the main stepwise and logistic regressions, we show the variables not entered and indicate the range restrictions on the data. Tables 1 to 6 above give details of the coding for the variables most commonly used in the regression analyses and Appendix 2 contains additional details.

Table A4.7
Predicting the Arrest Decision; Results of Stepwise Regression; N=363 Cases

Multiple correlation = 0.45; accounting for 20% of the variance.

Variables in the Equation – in order entered:

Parameter	Value	Standard error	Standard value	F to remove
Intercept	-1.036			
Seriousness	.169	.035	.247	23.467
No. of offences	.137	.045	.146	9.136
Time of offence	.127	.046	.138	7.753
Age	.128	.045	.14	8.076
Ethnicity (M vs P)	-.187	.071	-.127	6.875

Variables not in the Equation:

Parameter	Partial Correlation	F to enter
Sex	.033	.397

Range restrictions:

Parameter	Included
Arrest	Arrest and charge only or non-arrest
Ethnicity	Maori and Pakeha
Age	14 to 16 years
Time of offence	Daytime, Evening or Night (exclude weekend)

Table A4.8
Predicting the Arrest Decision; Results of Logistic Regression; N=347 Cases

Association of Predicted probabilities and observed responses:
Concordant = 83.6%; Discordant = 15.4%; Tied = 1.0%

Variables in the Equation – in order entered*:

Parameter	Estimate	Standard error	Wald Chi-Square	Probability
Intercept	17.444			
Seriousness	-.819	.173	22.44	<.001
Time of offence	-1.06	.349	9.222	<.01
Age	-.741	.237	9.763	<.01
Ethnicity (M vs P)	-.979	.365	7.184	<.01
Area A	-1.177	.465	6.422	<.02
Area B	-.793	.402	3.894	<.05

* Note: Number of offences did not emerge as an independent predictor in the logistic regression, presumably because it accounted for variance in the stepwise regression that was accounted for by area in the logistic model.

Table A4.9

Predicting the Youth Aid Decision to Refer for an FGC; Results of Stepwise Regression; N=449 Cases*

Multiple correlation = 0.63; accounting for 40% of the variance.

Variables in the Equation – in order entered:

Parameter	Value	Standard error	Standard value	F to remove
Intercept	1.762			
Previous History	.317	.038	.345	69.849
Seriousness	-.154	.019	-.324	62.656
Unemployed	-.155	.034	-.181	21.013
Time of offence	-.065	.026	-.099	6.059

Variables not in the Equation:

Parameter	Partial Correlation	F to enter
Number of offences	-.082	2.74
Ethnicity	.077	2.437
Age	-.066	1.792
Co-offenders	-.028	.325
Sex	-.026	.295

Range restrictions:

Parameter	Included
Youth Aid case	All cases referred to Youth Aid
Ethnicity	Maori and Pakeha
Time of offence	Daytime, Evening or Night (exclude weekend)

* Note: The greater number of decisions about FGC referral compared to arrest decisions arises because only those aged 14 or over may be arrested while all those aged 10 or more may be referred for an FGC.

Table A4.10

Predicting the Youth Aid Decision; to Refer for an FGC Results of Logistic Regression; N=417 Cases

Association of Predicted probabilities and observed responses:
Concordant = 90.0%; Discordant = 8.3%; Tied = 1.7%

Variables in the Equation – in order entered:*

Parameter	Estimate	Standard error	Wald Chi-Square	Probability
Intercept	4.314			
Previous History	-2.318	.333	48.460	<.001
Seriousness	-.963	.162	35.314	<.001
Area A	1.622	.462	12.341	<.001
Unemployed	1.866	.561	11.075	<.001
Number of offences	-.723	.246	8.656	<.01
Area B	-1.179	.442	7.122	<.01
Time of offence	-.861	.326	6.991	<.01

* Note: In this case number of offences did emerge as an independent predictor in the logistic regression, but not in the stepwise regression although it was close to being significant in the stepwise analysis. Again, the reason is undoubtedly the impact of area.

Table A4.11
Predicting the Severity of the Decision at the FGC; Results of Stepwise Regression; N=168 Cases

Multiple correlation = 0.53; accounting for 29% of the variance.

Variables in the Equation – in order entered:

Parameter	Value	Standard error	Standard value	F to remove
Intercept	-2.18			
Seriousness	.7	.134	.355	27.396
No. of offences	.134	.032	.281	17.244
Age	.215	.095	.15	5.077

Variables not in the Equation:

Parameter	Partial Correlation	F to enter
Previous history	.121	2.44
Sex	-.019	.058
Ethnicity	.00	.00

Range restrictions:

Parameter	Included
FGC cases	Finalised cases
Ethnicity	Maori and Pakeha

Table A4.12
Predicting the Severity of the Decision of the FGC; Results of Logistic Regression; N=165 Cases

Association of Predicted probabilities and observed responses:
Concordant = 67.6%; Discordant = 27.9%; Tied = 4.5%

Variables in the Equation – in order entered:

Parameter	Estimate	Standard error	Wald Chi-Square	Probability
Intercept 1-9	varied			
Seriousness	-.761	.158	23.153	<.001
Number of offences	-.128	.034	11.5	<.001
Age	-.267	.11	5.936	<.02

Table A4.13
Predicting the Severity of the Youth Court Decision; Results of Stepwise Regression; N=62 Cases

Multiple correlation = 0.59; accounting for 35% of the variance.

Variables in the Equation – in order entered*:

Parameter	Value	Standard error	Standard value	F to remove
Intercept	-.316			
Severity of FGC	.574	.108	.589	28.227

Variables not in the Equation:

Parameter	Partial Correlation	F to enter
No of offences	.243	3.263
Previous offences	-.215	2.513
Seriousness	.209	2.383
Ethnicity	-.173	1.607
Sex	-.127	.855
Age	.106	.586

Range restrictions:

Parameter	Included:
Youth Court cases	Finalised cases
Ethnicity	Maori and Pakeha

* When this analysis is run excluding severity of FGC recommendation, the result is that seriousness of offence and number of offences emerge as predictors, as below.

Table A4.14
Predicting the Severity of Youth Court Decision; Results of Logistic Regression both with and without Severity of FGC; N=57 Cases

Association of Predicted probabilities and observed responses:
Concordant = 67.1%; Discordant = 21.4%; Tied = 11.5%

Variables in the Equation – in order entered:

Parameter	Estimate	Standard error	Wald Chi-Square	Probability
Intercepts=7	varied			
Severity of FGC	-.602	.134	20.215	<.001

When severity of FGC was not entered, the result was as follows:

Association of Predicted probabilities and observed responses:
Concordant = 75.2%; Discordant = 20.9%; Tied = 3.8%

Variables in the Equation – in order entered:

Parameter	Estimate	Standard error	Wald Chi-Square	Probability
Intercepts=7	varied			
Seriousness	-1.071	.284	14.17	<.001
No. of offences	-0.124	.047	7.09	<.01
Area A	-1.164	.578	4.059	<.05